CITY OF DUBLIN

The Life and Times of Daniel Murray

Archbishop of Dublin 1823~1852

THOMAS J MORRISSEY SJ

Published by Messenger Publications, 2018

Cover image and facing page:
Portrait of Archbishop Daniel Murray, courtesy Saint Francis Xavier Church, Gardiner Street, Dublin 1.

ISBN 978 1 910248 93 5

Designed by Messenger Publications Design Department
Typeset in Times New Roman
Printed by Nicholson & Bass Ltd

Messenger Publications,
37 Lower Leeson Street, Dublin D02 W938
www.messenger.ie

Daniel Murray

IRISH CATHOLIC ARCHBISHOPS AND BISHOPS REFERRED TO IN 'THE LIFE AND TIMES OF DANIEL MURRAY'

ARMAGH
Richard O'Reilly (1787-1818)
Patrick Curtis (1819-1832)
William Crolly (1835-1849)
Paul Cullen (1850-1852)

ARDAGH
William O'Higgins (1829-1853)

CLOGHER
Charles McNally (1844-1864)

DOWN AND CONNOR
Cornelius Denvir (1835-1865)

DROMORE
Michael Blake (1833-1860)

KILMORE
James Browne (1829-1865)

MEATH
Patrick Joseph Plunkett (1779-1827)
John Cantwell (1830-1866)

RAPHOE
Peter McLaughlin (1802-1819)
Patrick McGettigan (1820-1861)

CASHEL
Thomas Bray (1792-1820)
Patrick Everard (1820-1821)
Robert Laffan (1823-1833)
Michael Slattery (1834-1857)

CLOYNE
William Coppinger (1791-1831)
Bartholomew Crotty (1833-1846)
Timothy Murphy (1849-1856)

CORK
Francis Moylan (1787-1815)
John Murphy (1815-1847)

KILLALOE
James O'Shaughnessy (1807-1828)
Patrick Kennedy (1836-1850)

LIMERICK
Charles Tuohy (1815-1828)
John Ryan (1828-1864)

WATERFORD AND LISMORE
John Power (1804-1816)
Robert Walsh (1817-1821)
Nicholas Foran (1837-1855)

DUBLIN
John Carpenter (1770-1786)
John Thomas Troy OP (1786-1823)
Daniel Murray (1823-1852)
Paul Cullen (1852-1878)

FERNS
Patrick Ryan (1814-1819)
James Keating (1819-1849)

KILDARE AND LEIGHLIN
Daniel Delany (1787-1814)
James Doyle OSA (1819-1834)
Edward Nolan (1834-1837)
Francis Haly (1838-1855)

OSSORY
John Thomas Troy OP (1777-1786)
James Lanigan (1789-1812)
Kyran Marum (1815-1827)
William Kinsella (1829-1845)

TUAM
Oliver Kelly (1815-1834)
John MacHale (1834-1881)

ACHONRY
Patrick McNicholas (1818-1852)

CLONFERT
Thomas Coen (1831-1847)

ELPHIN
George Thomas Plunkett (1815-1827)
Patrick Burke (1827-1843)

GALWAY
George J. P. Browne (1831-1844)

KILLALA
Peter Waldron (1815-1834)
John MacHale (27 May - 8 Aug 1834)

KILMACDUAGH
Edmund Ffrench OP (1825-1852)

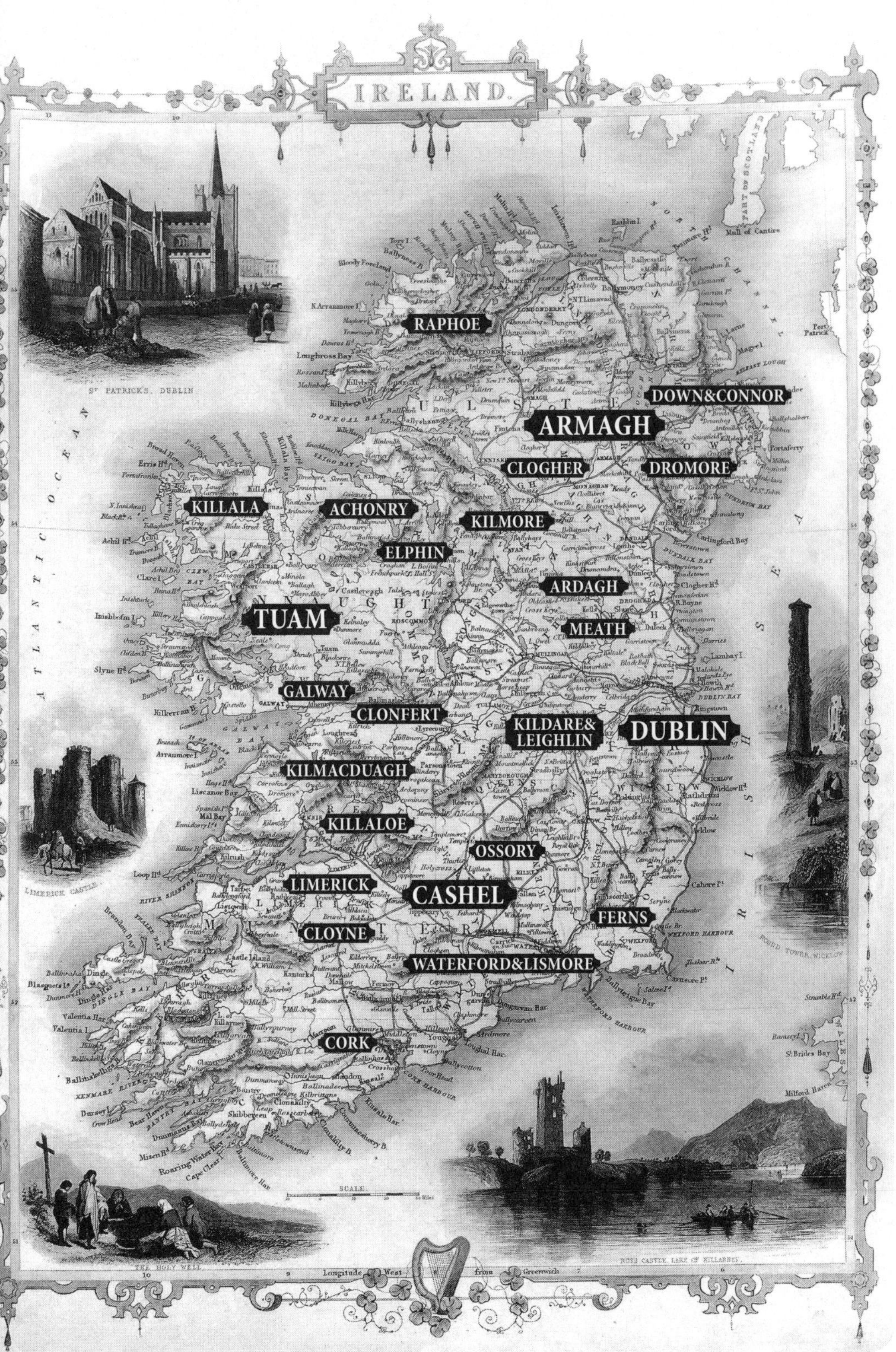

Created by John Tallis, published in Illustrated Atlas, London 1851. ©Shutterstock

St Patrick's College, Maynooth. Engraving. Trousset encyclopedia, 1800s

TABLE OF CONTENTS

TABLE OF CONTENTS

Foreword

A new contextual study of the achievement of Archbishop Daniel Murray during the almost thirty years of his episcopal leadership in Ireland's capital city has been long awaited. The years between 1823 and 1852 witnessed much political, social and ecclesiastical change, not least in the evolving relationship with England and Rome consequent upon the granting of Catholic Emancipation in 1829. The tension generated by conscience and action is as paramount in Dr Morrissey's study of Murray as it was discernible in his earlier biography of Bishop Edward Thomas O'Dwyer of Limerick, albeit the latter was concerned with a later timescale.

The guiding principle of Daniel Murray's public life was a firm belief that progress and development in both social and national identity needed to be governed by a recognition of the value of discussion and a willingness to compromise. As a consequence, there had to exist an ability to accept setbacks, to relate courteously to opponents, and to reserve stamina for renewed or further negotiation as events dictated. It was needful to retain a placid approach to major problems that eschewed the fostering of enmity with opponents and avoided gloating over successful outcomes.

In dealing with issues, however, Murray did not view the necessity for compromise or a painstaking analysis as being antipathetic to retaining a firm approach where innate justice and moral conscience were clearly at risk, or when political attitudes seemed to be leading nowhere. Indeed, he determined early that the willingness to revisit major matters of principle on several occasions was a mark of an inspired reformer. At heart, he was always concerned for pastoral outcomes for the poor and for those misrepresented in their poverty. These characteristics of public policy are amply illustrated in Dr Morrissey's study of the way Murray's efforts were pursued in the field of educational provision.

The schooling of the unprovided classes and their children was the focus of Murray's programme for social advancement. Before becoming archbishop of Dublin, he had encouraged Edmund Rice and his Christian Brothers in their work for the teaching of poor boys, enticing the Brothers to work in Dublin as well as elsewhere in the country. When he was coadjutor archbishop of Dublin he encouraged Mary Aikenhead to establish the Irish Sisters of Charity as a sisterhood intended eventually to work for girls in a way not unlike Rice's mission for boys. Later still, Murray was to support the Sisters of Mercy in related work, just as he was to encourage the Jesuits and Vincentians in their attention to middle-class youths, in the hope of preparing them to take advantage of opportunities opened up by Catholic Emancipation.

As president of Maynooth, Murray realised that many of the ecclesiastical students lacked early preparatory education, and as a consequence were often ill disciplined, if not at times ungovernable. Nearly three-quarters of the youths at Maynooth were children of farmers, but he hoped, with Jesuit help and a more balanced recruitment, to ensure better management of the institution. As archbishop of Dublin, he was to retain his affection for Maynooth and was a strong supporter of increased Government aid for the college when the matter was raised.

In the early approach to emancipation in 1826, Murray gave evidence to committees of both the Houses of Parliament in London. In his analysis of the state of Ireland, he made a lasting impression by his fairness, courtesy, balanced views and accurate knowledge. He gained the reputation of a man to whom committees could relate. Murray, of course, was not averse to the importance of public agitation as a background to parliamentary understanding, but he felt a certain unease at direct clerical involvement in political posturing, especially if it might lead to violence, processes of lasting alienation, or the tendency to confuse the laity about its own role as distinct from that of the clergy. It was a problem he was to face with Daniel O'Connell on the Repeal issue in the 1840s, concerning which he counselled his priests – unavailingly – to avoid direct political interventions.

Education provided a major challenge for Murray because he could see that Government funding and organisation would be of clear benefit to the poor, although presenting a challenge to the propensities of some bishops. In 1826, Murray had been instrumental in setting up an Education Society to support the further establishment of free schools, and in February 1828, on the eve of emancipation, he joined fellow bishops in urging Parliament to improve educational provision. Murray was sympathetic and supportive of the efforts and ideals of Daniel O'Connell, although he was sometimes alienated by the latter's visible rashness of approach and by his unexpected changes of mood and emphases.

On 13 April 1829, the Emancipation Act came into law, and opportunities for professional work were thus ostensibly available to qualified Catholics. In 1831 when the National System of Education in Ireland was proposed in Parliament and an initial grant of £30,000 was awarded, Murray was happy to be one of the two Catholics among the first commissioners appointed to oversee the process, in the knowledge that he could now do something positive to advance the education of the people. Despite his euphoria, he was to find serious opposition to the National System, led by Dr John MacHale who was strident in his opposition to the scheme and, indeed, to all Catholic involvement with it. Murray was soon aware that MacHale adopted political stances without any likelihood of compromise, usually when any government measure from London was concerned. It was an attitude at variance with Murray's own principles, and was to remain a point of opposition throughout the working life of the two men.

Murray fought strongly for the benefits of the National System at home and in Rome. Ultimately, and with much relief, he secured papal approval for the system from the Benedictine, Pope Gregory XVI, who had been elevated to the papacy in the year the National System was born. The refusal of the Anglican Church in Ireland to participate initially in the scheme meant that Catholics were not impeded in their own work with the National System. Murray saw the commission as developing a positively ecumenical approach to the problem of schooling.

The success of the National System formed the basis of Murray's subsequent attitude to university and collegiate education. The concept of 'mixed' education and the lack of Catholic control of the Queen's Colleges incensed Archbishop MacHale and several other bishops influenced by him. The division of views led to polarisation within the hierarchy. Murray and his supporters saw the establishment of the Queen's Colleges as a serious attempt by Government to provide third-level education for Catholic students. Despite the non-denominational nature of the Colleges, Catholics were appointed to the presidency of two of them, Cork and Galway, as a sign of the Government's good will. Murray envisaged no insuperable difficulties in the working of the scheme, especially as Catholics began to be appointed to teaching and managerial positions in the institutions, while Catholic chaplains would keep oversight of Catholic students. MacHale, together with Dr Paul Cullen in Rome, did his utmost to oppose Catholics taking advantage of the education on offer.

Attempting to avoid division among themselves, the bishops held a Synod at Thurles in 1850, which lasted from August to September. In regard to the debate at this synod, Morrissey has shown how Murray's commitment to the Queen's Colleges and his work at the Synod led to an increase of support for him among the bishops, but it was not sufficient to form a majority. The Synod voted against approving the Colleges, and a new Pope, Pius IX, elected in June 1846, was unsympathetic to the minority view. Pius was himself suffering much political unrest, and did not trust English interests in Rome or Ireland. In England, Disraeli saw the decision of the Synod of Thurles as having greater influence on Lord John Russell's anti-Catholic Ecclesiastical Titles Act of 1851 than the restoration by Pius IX of the English Roman Catholic hierarchy in 1850. It seems possible that some of the bishops at the Synod were greatly influenced by political reactions to the widespread Irish famine and the resulting deaths of the 1840s, together with the Government's dilatory ineptitude in dealing with that crisis.

Daniel Murray had himself, of course, been a vocal critic of the Government's ineffectiveness in dealing with the famine in the second half of the 1840s. He was one of the chief organisers of home and foreign charitable relief, assuaging where possible the worst effects of the famine. Aid was sent to him from several countries, from the papacy, and from many English people, in order that Murray could transfer it to the regions most affected by what was to prove the greatest social disaster in Ireland in the nineteenth century. Murray, now an old man, needed an increase of energy to sustain his work for the poor and deprived, and he appointed a special assistant to deal exclusively with the aid he received. Money was transmitted for distribution to parish priests in the areas of most need.

Dr Morrissey's book reawakens an interest in the kind of man Daniel Murray really was. In his development and spirit, he was a bishop essentially for his people, rather than a politician. It is a view of him testified by the immense crowds of priests and laity attending his funeral in 1852, as the cortege wended its slow journey to Dublin's pro-cathedral, the final generous touch of appreciation and affection of his people.

3 January 2018

V. Alan McClelland
Em. Prof. University of Hull

Introduction

Daniel Murray was undoubtedly the outstanding Irish Catholic archbishop of the nineteenth century. He was a man of elegance and charm, ready to listen to others and to find good in them. To the redoubtable Bishop Doyle of Kildare and Leighlin, the Archbishop was 'an angel of a man'. Murray's concern for the education of the poor led to the founding of the Irish Sisters of Charity, and the invitation to Dublin of the Sisters of Mercy and the Irish Christian Brothers. His interest in the education of the middle class was manifested in his involvement with the founding of the Sisters of Loreto, and in his support for the schools of the Jesuits and the Vincentians.

He was also a man of great pastoral energy. He built numerous churches and actively continued the work of his predecessor in restructuring the Irish Church after penal times. He invited the Society of St Vincent de Paul to Dublin, and he readily encouraged lay involvement in the work of the diocese. The Vincentians and the Jesuits were encouraged to develop their parish missions, which became a contributory factor in the later 'devotional revolution'. He was actively involved in assisting the Holy See in the appointment of priests and bishops across the English-speaking world. His efforts to provide aid to the needy during the Great Famine in the 1840s, and the veneration and respect he inspired in his clergy, further contributed to the high esteem in which he was held not only in Rome but throughout the English-speaking world. And yet, he is a virtually forgotten figure in Irish history.

This neglect is related to the stance he took on some issues of the day – his support for certain government initiatives, his opposition to his clergy's involvement in politics and his caution about openly supporting Repeal. With regard to Repeal, his belief was that the government would not yield, and that O'Connell's movement could lead to bloodshed, as had happened in 1798 when he barely escaped death himself. He believed that the best results could be obtained for the Church and for the Irish people, especially the poor, by working with the government rather than being constantly suspicious of, and hostile to, all its proposals. Although seldom mentioned in his lifetime, because of the reverence and affection with which he was held, zealous nationalists posthumously included him among those who supported government policies, and on that account he was deemed to be unpatriotic.

A life of Dr Murray is overdue. Nothing has been written about his overall career, apart from a valuable eulogy by his friend William Meagher, a few insightful articles and two or three pamphlets. Considerably more attention has been given to Murray's role in three public controversies that surfaced during the last dozen years of his long life: the national system of education, the government's Bequests Act to benefit Irish Catholics, and the issue of university education for Irish Catholics by means of the 'Godless colleges'. Murray championed the national education system despite the opposition of the more anti-government members of the hierarchy, who had the support of the Roman curia; he defended the Bequests Act in the face of widespread anti-government feeling and personal attacks; and with similar courage and independence he argued in support of the Queen's Colleges despite opposition from Rome, Daniel O'Connell and the public press. On these three areas valuable research has been done in recent times. Dr Donal A. Kerr, former professor at Maynooth, dealt with all three controversies in the course of books on wider topics. Dr Emmet Larkin, former professor of History at the University of Chicago, published an important article on the bishops and the national education system. Finally, Dr Ambrose Macaulay has also researched and written on the national education system. Sadly, both Drs Kerr and Larkin are no longer with us. This book has availed of the scholarly research of all three.

In the course of my research and reading I have been greatly assisted by librarian June Rooney, and by Ann O'Carroll and Áine Stack at Milltown Park Library; by Noelle Dowling and her staff at the Dublin Diocesan Archives; by Damien Bourke at the Irish Jesuit Archives; by Dr Mary Clarke and staff at Dublin City Library, Pearse Street; and by Dr Ciaran O'Carroll, president of the Irish College Rome, who was most generous in making manuscripts available to me. I also wish to thank Dermot Roantree for his time, expertise and guidance in dealing with computer material, and also Eileen Ellis and Tina Loughrey for their support and assistance. My thanks are due in a special way to the two very generous readers of my manuscript, Maria Mullen for her careful scrutiny of writing and textual failings, and Dr Fergus O'Donoghue SJ for a historian's judgement of the material and how it might be improved. I am both delighted and honoured that Dr V. A. McClelland agreed to write the Foreword. A former Professor of Education at UCC and at the University of Hull, he has made distinguished contributions to Education and Ecclesial History in both Britain and Ireland and, in addition, he is an admirer of Archbishop Murray. In conclusion, it remains to acknowledge that my work has been made possible by the support and encouragement of successive Jesuit provincials and by the forbearance of my Jesuit community.

Thomas J. Morrissey SJ

CHAPTER 1

Years of Change and Development (1768–93)

Daniel Murray was born on 18 April 1768 to Thomas and Judith Murray at their farm in an area known as Sheepwalk, near the town of Arklow, Co. Wicklow. According to the family records, they had held land there for three hundred years. At the time of Murray's birth, the penal laws were still applied to the Catholic population, and their impact, together with the wider historical situation, made a lasting impression on him in his earlier years.

THE PENAL LAWS

Land was the source of wealth and political power. Following King William's victory over the Stuart king, James II, in 1690, the penal laws in Ireland were designed to guarantee the political settlement and to confirm Protestant ownership of landed property. These laws, as they were gradually applied in the early decades of the eighteenth century, fell into two categories: those concerning land and access to public office, and those related to the exercise of religion.

As regards the exercise of religion, in 1697 all Catholic bishops, vicars general, deans and all members of the regular clergy were ordered by parliament to leave the country within a year. Not all the clergy left, of course, but the ruling initiated a period of religious oppression which did not ease until 1746, when English forces at the Battle of Culloden, in Scotland, defeated the supporters of the House of Stuart and brought to an end the pretensions of the Stuarts. Twenty years later, in 1766, the death of the 'Old Pretender', James Francis Stuart, brought to an end Rome's support for the Stuart cause. These developments brought relief to the Protestants in Ireland, who began to worry less about the likelihood of rebellion at home. Another factor in ending religious persecution was Britain's need, on the international scene, of the support of Catholic Austria.

Where public office and parliament and ownership of land were concerned, the prohibitions were more entrenched. To enter public office one had to take an oath recognising royal supremacy. This included rejecting even the spiritual supremacy of the pope, the denial of transubstantiation and the repudiation of the Mass – all of which excluded any genuine Catholic from office. Regarding land, a Catholic might not buy land, or lease it for more than thirty-one years. If the eldest son of a Catholic landowner became a Protestant he could inherit the family estate, thereby making his father a tenant. A further provision, known as the 'gavel act', stipulated that on the death of a Catholic his estate would not pass to his eldest son but be divided among all his sons. The overall effect of these laws was that the majority of the Catholic population were left as tenants or landless labourers, political nonentities, hampered in their trades and forbidden to have their own schools. As a result they were frequently evasive, and distrustful of the law and of government. A 'slow process of dismantling this penal code began in 1759 but was marked by no significant progress until the 1770s'.[1]

THE EFFECT OF WIDER EVENTS

Daniel Murray grew up in a period of change at home and of major change overseas. The American War of Independence commenced in 1775, and was followed with intense interest in Ireland and throughout much of Europe. The widespread withdrawal of British troops from Ireland for the war against France and the American colonists provided the Irish Protestant Ascendancy with the opportunity to wrest a more independent parliament and free trade from a beleaguered British government.

During the next twenty years, native industries were promoted and the impact of the industrial and technological revolution was manifested in better roads, the development of canals and generally improved communications. Wide streets, impressive public buildings, numerous and varied horse-drawn carriages, an active interest in politics and rhetoric, and lavish hospitality were noted features of Ireland's capital city. Yet, for Daniel Murray, who spent some of his early years in Dublin, reminders of the reverse side of this gilded, progressive world were easy to find. The contrast was unavoidable. The English traveller, the Revd John Milner, remarked on the disparity between the magnificence of the public buildings 'and the circumstances of the people at whose expense they have been erected'.[2] These people lived in over-crowded tenements in filthy streets, and among them epidemics of fever and plague were frequent. Murray's contact with this side of Dublin life left him with a life-long concern for the condition and the relief of the poor.

The success of the North American colonists, and the concurrence of their proclamation of 'self-evident truths' with the prevailing ethos of the Enlightenment among many in the Irish parliament, prompted two Catholic relief acts in 1782. These were far-reaching. In religious matters, legal recognition was granted to the secular clergy, provided they took the oath of allegiance to the king of England. The regular clergy – members of religious congregations – were allowed to minister without penalty so long as they registered with the state. Many Catholics disliked this provision, but they put up with it as an inconvenience rather than a hindrance. The same applied to the retention of sanctions against the conversion of Protestants, and bans on the addition of steeples or bells to Catholic churches and chapels, on Catholic priests officiating at funerals, on the public wearing of vestments and the assumption of ecclesiastical ranks and titles. The stipulation that Catholics could only establish schools under licence from the Protestant bishop was also unwelcome, but it was accepted as an improvement on the existing situation.[3] In the event, one of the effects of the acts was Rome's appointment of a Dominican, John Thomas Troy (1786–1823), as archbishop of Dublin in 1786. Prior to 1782, he had no legal right to be in the country.

Socially and economically, too, matters had improved for Catholics, who were allowed to own land, and to lease it for long periods. James Caulfeild, earl of Charlemont, commented in his memoirs on the extraordinary increase in tolerance in the Irish parliament. In 1772, the parliament had rejected his proposal to grant Catholics a short lease of land sufficient for a cabin and a plot of potatoes; yet six years later, without any opposition, the same parliament permitted Catholics to take out leases of lands of any extent for 999 years. 'The spirit of tolerance', Charlemont observed, 'was lately gone abroad and had spread itself through all the polished nations of Europe … I should rather suppose that it took its rise from fashionable deism than from Christianity, which was now unfortunately much out of fashion…'[4]

During the second half of the eighteenth century, relatively prosperous Catholic merchants advanced materially by availing of loopholes in the penal legislation and the government's connivance at its non-application. Resentment at the restrictions of the legislation, nevertheless, grew with increased freedom. Middle-class Catholics relished Edmund Burke's reminder to the House of Commons, recently highlighted in Arthur Young's *Tour of Ireland* (1780), that 'connivance is the relaxation of slavery, not the definition of liberty'.[5]

During Murray's youth, his family not only continued to survive as strong tenant farmers through these many changes, as they had through the darker days of the penal laws; they also managed to expand. As reliable, hard-working tenants, they may have been protected by their landlord and by their Protestant neighbours.[6] How effectively the family had survived, and was now flourishing with the easing of the penal laws, is indicated by a surviving indenture, made in 1787, between Lord Wicklow and Thomas Murray of Sheepwalk.[7] It ran:

> Letting town and lands of Ballyvogue otherwise Sheepwalk and part of Raheen now in his possession, containing 102 acres plantation measure excepting all mines, minerals or timber to Thomas Murray his exors, admors and assigns from 25 March 1787 for and during the natural life of Peter Murray, 2nd son of the said Thomas Murray aged 24 years or thereabouts, Daniel Murray, 4th son of the said Thomas aged 19 years or thereabouts, Thomas Murray, 5th son of the said Thomas Murray aged 14 years or thereabouts.

The indenture also provides the only information available about the rest of Daniel Murray's family. Meantime, eleven years prior to the agreement between Lord Wicklow and Thomas Murray, Daniel was sent to Dublin to advance his education.

EDUCATION IN DUBLIN

Daniel, from all accounts, was a bright and pleasant child. His early education was given by his parents or by the parish priest or, perhaps, a local schoolmaster. It must have been of a high standard because, in 1776, at the age of eight years, he was accepted in the remarkable school in Dublin sometimes known as Fr Betagh's 'classical academy'. Thomas Betagh was a former Jesuit, who became a member of the Dublin diocesan clergy in 1774 following the suppression of the Society of Jesus. During the morning hours, he worked in the parish chapel of St Michael and St John in Rosemary Lane. During the afternoon he ran a private school at Saul's Court, situated at the top of Fishamble Street, under the shadow of Christ Church Cathedral. This school had started with an older former Jesuit, Fr John Austin, who, in time, together with Betagh, opened a boarding school adjoining the original foundation. It served, inter alia, as a seminary for the diocesan sees of Meath and Dublin.[8] In addition, Betagh developed a variety of schools providing basic free education for poorer children[9] and evening classes for young apprentices and labourers.[10] On Sundays, Betagh preached to a large congregation who, it is said, held him 'in extraordinary veneration'.[11] At his funeral, the preacher, Dr Michael Blake, a former pupil, told of Fr Betagh teaching children night after night in cold cellars when he was already past seventy years of age, and of his clothing forty of the most destitute each year at his own expense. In Blake's estimation, he educated more than 3,000 boys.[12]

Thomas Betagh

In the afternoon school, Betagh provided a wide education but with particular emphasis on the classical languages of Latin and Greek. He was assisted from time to time by Fr Mulcaile, also a former Jesuit, who worked at St Michan's Church across the river, ran a school for poor boys and was spiritual director to the Presentation Sisters at George's Hill. A writer and translator of a number of works, Mulcaile's skill as a Latin scholar was indicated by his translation of *Gulliver's Travels* into Latin, under the title *Peregrinatio Laputensis.*[13] Many of Betagh's students went on to become well-known Catholic clergy, among them Fr Michael Blake, later bishop of Dromore, Monsignor William Yore, an influential parish priest in the Dublin archdiocese and founder of St Joseph's school for deaf boys, and Fr Peter Kenney, pioneer in Ireland of the restored Society of Jesus (1814). The most celebrated of them all was to be Daniel Murray. As he was a considerable distance from home, Murray stayed initially at the Jesuit house in Cook Street – where former Jesuits lived – and subsequently with a Catholic business family at Merchants Quay.[14] He soon made a deep impression on Betagh by his ability, gentle manner and general amiability. The older man became to him both a friend and spiritual guide.

Daniel Murray's parents may well have viewed their son as a possible future priest. During his eight years in Dublin, he himself decided he had a vocation to the priesthood. Archbishop Carpenter of Dublin had learned about him. He interviewed Murray, and then his parents, before sending him to study philosophy and theology in Spain, at the historic Irish College in Salamanca. He arrived there, after an arduous journey, on All Saints Day, 1 November 1784.[15] By this time, Murray had spent eight years studying in Dublin. He was now about to spend a further eight years in Salamanca. It was to prove a new and formative experience for him.

AT THE IRISH COLLEGE IN SALAMANCA

For Murray, although the journey to Salamanca proved taxing, there was the novelty and excitement of visiting the continent for the first time. Long before the city itself came in sight, the pinnacles of its cathedrals would have been visible. Thereafter would have come the golden gleam of the soft stone buildings, the city's dull yellow walls and the tiers of red and brown roofs rising above the river Tormes. The jostling life of the narrow city streets would have contrasted with the seclusion to be glimpsed behind high walls. Finally arriving in the college itself there would have been, no doubt, a warm welcome awaiting him from his own countrymen and from other fellow students.

Before long, he would have absorbed something of the historical significance of the college: he would have learned of its foundation by Frs Thomas White and James Archer at the end of the sixteenth century, and of its proud record of sending priests to Ireland through the years of persecution. Inevitably he would have become aware of how much the Irish Church owed to the shelter and support of Spain over past centuries, and the benefit of attending the great University of Salamanca, in its heyday one of the chief universities of Europe.

As a student, Murray soon made a mark. In 1789, the rector, Dr Patrick Curtis, in his report to the King of Castile on the personnel of the college, was highly complimentary about Murray:[16]

> Daniel Murray, student, native of the Archdiocese of Dublin, of Catholic and noble family, twenty-one years of age, distinguished himself at home for his knowledge of Latin, Greek and other branches of Humanities. He has been a student of the college for four years. This youth gave proof of a real ecclesiastical vocation, joined with extraordinary piety, talents and application to study. He made rapid progress in his studies and his conduct was most edifying. He surpassed by a great deal all his fellow students, and is of great promise.

This latter testimony takes on additional weight when one learns that Murray's fellow students included future Irish prelates Kyran Marum, (bishop of Ossory, 1814–27), and Patrick Everard (coadjutor archbishop of Cashel, 1814–20, and archbishop of Cashel, 1820–21). Robert Laffan, the latter's successor in Cashel (1823–33), was also a student at Salamanca. Historically, it is of interest to note that the rector of the college during Murray's time, Dr Patrick Curtis, later became the archbishop of Armagh (1819–32), and that, as Daniel Murray left Salamanca, a new student named Oliver Kelly was added to the roll. Kelly later became the archbishop of Tuam (1814–35). Thus, the four archbishops who were to lead the Church during some of the most momentous years in Ireland, were past students of the Salamanca College.[17] Significantly, the influence of that city on these men was not confined to their studies. They also embraced features of its Catholic culture, in which Catholicism was affirmed with solemn dignity and elegance in ornate churches. Unassuming elegance, dignity and ease of manner were features often commented on in the later Daniel Murray.

A NEW ARCHBISHOP FOR DUBLIN

During those years, news of Ireland came from visiting Irish clergy and from the infrequent postage service. In 1786, Daniel would have learned with interest of the appointment of John Thomas Troy OP to the see of Dublin; he could have had no inkling, however, of how that appointment was going to change his life.

Before his appointment to Dublin, Troy had been bishop of Ossory. Before that, he had been superior of the Dominican house of San Clemente in Rome, where he was also dean of studies, specially chosen as the most suitable person to train students not just academically but 'in exemplary manners and conduct'.[18] A fellow Dominican, to whom Troy had written, observed of his letter that it was 'a pretty elegant piece like yourself'. [19] In Ossory, Troy had sought the improvement of clerical discipline and practice, and had established diocesan conferences with a view to renewing the clergy. In Dublin, his priority and practice remained the same. Faced with a diocese of forty-five parishes, he undertook a full visitation, and required the pastors to submit reports on their parishes to him. No doubt, while receiving reports of the new archbishop, Daniel Murray would also have learned of his political astuteness and his efforts to establish good relations with leading figures of the Protestant Ascendancy.

Murray, besides, could scarcely avoid hearing of the liturgies at the chapel of the archbishop in Francis Street, Dublin, where Dr Troy employed a Neapolitan musical director, Tomaso Giordani. He would have heard how the latter, in May 1789, under Dr Troy's direction, composed a grand *Te Deum*, which was first performed in the chapel to mark a thanksgiving service for the King's recovery to health. Troy presided at the altar, assisted by three of his suffragan bishops, before a congregation of three thousand. Included in that congregation were the Duke of Leinster, the Earls of Kildare, Portarlington, Belvedere, Bective and Tyrone, Lord and Lady Arran, Thomas Conolly, Henry Grattan, David Latouche (the attorney general), and the Lord Mayor and sheriffs of Dublin. Never before, and perhaps never again, would so many of the Protestant Ascendancy come to a Catholic service.[20] Murray would have been further heartened had he known of an earlier observation by Dr Troy, when bishop of Ossory, that unlike the French colleges, the 'Roman, Spanish and Portuguese are commonly thought to be the most exemplary, just as they are certainly the most loyal to the Holy See.'[21]

THE IMPACT OF REVOLUTION

As well as the news he received from Ireland that would influence Murray's future, there was, in the last years of his time in Salamanca, dramatic news from France that would affect his political outlook. The French Revolution in 1789, which must at first have appealed with its slogan 'Liberty, Equality, Fraternity', soon took on a more negative and frightening aspect with its blatant anti-clericalism. Church lands were nationalised, religious orders abolished and papal jurisdiction removed by the Civil Constitution of the Clergy in July 1790. By that Constitution, clergy and bishops were to be elected by the laity in a similar way to district and department officials, and at the same time the clergy were obliged to take an oath of loyalty to the new constitution. With the Pope's condemnation of the Constitution of the Clergy, a split occurred between clergy taking the oath and those not doing so.

Expressions of support for the French Revolution would have been subdued in Bourbon Spain, with its close royal links with France. Nevertheless, on 5 May 1791, Dr Troy wrote to Archbishop Butler of Cashel concerning disturbances in the Irish College in Salamanca as well as in the Paris houses. Older students were being called home, Troy explained, and the younger students were being sent to Louvain and Antwerp.[22] Murray, however, appears to have stayed on at Salamanca for another year, since the academic lists of the Irish College indicate his presence there until, at least, May 1792.[23] The date of his ordination as a priest is not clear, but it would appear to have taken place in 1791 or 1792, because he was back in Ireland, as a priest, early in 1793.

Before Murray left Spain, the humiliation of the French monarch had evoked indignation and anger in Spanish society, and the King's subsequent execution, in January 1793, shocked all of Europe. There followed the massacre, not only of priests and nuns, but of thousands of citizens. By then Daniel Murray had returned home. He retained, however, an abhorrence of the excesses of the Revolution, a view that resonated strongly with the Irish bishops, all of whom were trained on the continent and who identified with the sufferings of the Church in France and wherever the Revolution spread. In 1793, Fr Daniel Murray was appointed by Dr Troy as assistant priest in St Paul's Church, Arran Quay.[24]

NOTES

1 P. J. Murray, 'Daniel Murray, Archbishop of Dublin 1823–1852' in *Journal of Arklow Historical Society*, 1986, p.12.

2 Constantia Maxwell, *Dublin under the Georges, 1714–1830* (Dublin: Hodges Figgis & Co Ltd, 1946), pp.264–5, citing Milner, writing in 1807.

3 James Kelly, 'The Impact of the Penal Laws' in J. Kelly & D. Keogh, *A History of the Catholic Diocese of Dublin* (Dublin: Four Courts Press, 2000), pp.170–171. For further reading see: J. Kelly. *Prelude to Union: Anglo-Irish Politics in 1780s* (Cork: Cork University Press, 1992); T.Bartlet. *The Fall and Rise of the Irish nation: the Catholic Question, 1690–1830* (Dublin: Gill and Macmillan, 1992).

4 Hugh Fenning OP 'A time of reform: from the "penal laws" to the birth of modern nationalism, 1691–1800' in B. Bradshaw & D. Keogh, *Christianity in Ireland* (Dublin: Columba Press, 2002), pp.134 –5.

5 Quoted by Young, in A. W. Hutton edition (London, 1892), vol. 1, p.114. The work first appeared in 1780.
6 M. T. Kelly, 'Most Rev. Daniel Murray, Archbishop of Dublin (1768–1852)', in *A Roll of Honour. Irish prelates and priests of the last century* (Dublin: CTS, 1905), p.60.
7 Dublin Diocesan Archives (DDA). Copy of a document from the archives of P. J. Murray. In an article by P. J. Murray 'Copy of a lease of a farm at Sheepwalk, Arklow, in 1787' in *Journal of Arklow Historical Society*, 1984. In the article it is mentioned that Daniel Murray was the last survivor of the names mentioned.
8 A. Cogan, *The Diocese of Meath*, 111, (Dublin, 1870), p.138; see W. J. Battersby, *The Jesuits in Dublin*, p.109, and under Austin and Betagh; also G. A. Little, *Revd John Austin SJ.* (Pamphlet: Dublin, 1910).
9 W. J. Battersby, op. cit., p.109. G.A. Little, *Revd John Austin SJ* lists various centres of education associated with Austin and Betagh.
10 'A short history of the parishes of Ss. Michael and John', in the *Year Book* (1957).
11 S.A. (Mrs Sarah Atkinson), *Mary Aikenhead, Her Life, Her Work, and Her Times* (Dublin, 1879), pp.117–18. See Myles Ronan, 'Archbishop Murray (1768–1852)' in *Irish Ecclesiastical Record (IER)*, (1952), vol. xxvi, p.241.
12 W. J. Battersby, op. cit., p.109. See Warburton, *History of the City of Dublin* (1818), vol. ii, p.811.
13 R. Burke Savage SJ, *A Valiant Dublin Woman: The story of George's Hill, 1766–1940* (Dublin: M.H. Gill and Son Ltd, 1940), p.156.
14 F. P. Carey, *Archbishop Murray of Dublin (1768–1852)*, (Pamphlet: Dublin, 1951), p.4.
15 P. J. Murray, art. cit., loc. cit., p.12.
16 F. P. Carey, loc. cit., p.6.
17 Idem, pp.6–7.
18 DDA. Troy Papers, green file, personal, no. 12 (1765); no.15 (1769).
19 Idem, small green file, 1770-1776: Dr. T. de Burgo, bishop of Ossory, to Troy, 14 April 1770.
20 Faulkner's *Dublin Journal*, 7 May 1789, cit. D. Keogh 'The pattern of the flock: John Thomas Troy, 1786–1823' in J. Kelly & D. Keogh eds., *History of the Catholic Diocese of Dublin* (Dublin: Four Courts Press, 2000), p.227.
21 *Archiv. Hib.* xlix (1995), Hugh Fenning OP, 'Documents of Irish interest in the *Fondo Missioni* of the Vatican Archives': John J. Troy OP, bishop of Ossory, to Cardinal (Leonardo) Antonelli, Prefect, from Kilkenny, 21 August 1780, no. 179.
22 Troy-Butler, 5 May 1791, no. 2. Troy Papers. DDA.
23 D. O'Doherty, 'Academic Lists of the Irish College Salamanca' in *Archivium Hibernicum,* Vols. 6 & 7, cit F. P. Carey, op. cit. p.7; P. J. Murray, art. cit., p.12.
24 Carey, op. cit. loc. cit.; P. J. Murray, idem.

CHAPTER 2

The Impact of Revolution (1793–1800)

On his return to Ireland, Murray worked for some eighteen months in Dublin. There he was surprised at the impact the French Revolution was having, something that was to change the circumstances in which he was to live and work.

MIXED VIEWS OF THE REVOLUTION

The cry of 'Liberty, Equality, Fraternity' had stirred the blood of many middle- and working-class Catholics and Presbyterians. Seven editions of Thomas Paine's *Rights of Man* appeared in Dublin between 1791 and 1792.[1] Some of the Dublin clergy were said to 'canonise … with unqualified praise, the whole proceedings of the late National Assembly of France'.[2] Murray's archbishop, Dr Troy, on the other hand, viewed the prospect of revolution in Ireland as destructive of all that had been achieved towards Catholic Emancipation. He was fearful that what had been obtained from the government could easily be withdrawn.

There were increased grounds for such fears following the further Catholic relief acts of 1792 and 1793. In the former year, university education was made available to Catholics, and the establishment of Catholic colleges was permitted as well as entry to the legal profession. This measure paved the way for the founding of Carlow College, in 1793, and for Daniel O'Connell's emergence as a lawyer. The following year, the British government, facing war with France, obliged the Irish parliament to pass a concessionary act. This extended parliamentary franchise to Catholics, enabling them to hold civil and military offices – with specific exceptions – and removing the statutory bar to university degrees. In addition, because the Revolution had cut off the main supply of priests from the Irish seminaries in France, the bishops pressed for a seminary college at home. The government, wishing to ensure the support of the bishops and uneasy about students coming from the continent, agreed to the establishment of St Patrick's College in Maynooth, Co. Kildare, in 1795.

UNBRIDLED VIOLENCE

The extension of the franchise – by open ballot – to the Catholic majority population, followed by the concession of a Catholic seminary, was seen by many Protestants as a threat to the controlling position of the Protestant Ascendancy. From 1795, certain members, led by John FitzGibbon, the Lord Chancellor of Ireland, determined to safeguard their ascendancy for all time by bringing about a parliamentary union with Britain. The expansion of the United Irishmen, said to have 200,000 members by 1798,[3] together with that organisation's negotiations with France, heightened fear of a French invasion and provided scope for a policy of terror, and for playing the sectarian card. Catholics were represented as likely to be disloyal to the crown, and the arrival of a French fleet at Bantry Bay, on 22 December 1796, engendered further fear, bordering on hysteria. Only very bad weather prevented an actual invasion taking place.

During 1797–98 government forces exhibited unbridled violence. An uprising took place in Meath and Wexford, and martial law was proclaimed. Sir Ralph Abercromby, commander-in-chief in Ireland, observed, on 26 February 1798, that the army in Ireland was 'in a state of licentiousness which must render it formidable to everyone but the enemy'.[4] Under martial law, 'troops continually searched for arms. Those suspected ... were tortured or flogged. Those convicted were hanged ... Each day the bodies of rebels killed in the surrounding countryside were brought into Dublin city in carts, and heaped up in the Castle yard'.[5] With the violations and torture, the uprisings and the reprisals, the year 1798 was probably the most concentrated period of violence in Irish history. By the end of the summer the death rate on both sides, from various causes, was estimated at 30,000.[6] Atrocities and achievements became entrenched in folk memory.

A CONTROVERSIAL STANCE

Dr Troy, during the 1790s, preached respect for 'the constituted authorities' and appreciation of the benefits that had been conferred on the Catholic community. In 1791 he had sided with Lord Kenmare and the aristocratic faction in the Catholic Committee rather than the more democratic element led by Wolfe Tone. This, and his constant opposition to the spread of revolutionary principles, led to much criticism, with Wolfe Tone describing him as a 'great scoundrel'.[7] In December 1793 Troy made clear his priorities in a letter to Luke Concanen, a fellow Dominican who acted as his agent in Rome:[8]

John Thomas Troy

> We are equally indifferent to their praise or censure. We are neither aristocrats or democrats … We have spoken as bishops, without taking notice of any party.

Troy, and Murray after him, was condemned by nationalists as being too friendly with Dublin Castle. The primary concerns of both men, however, were for the interests of the Irish Church and its people. Following the attempted French invasion at the end of 1796, Troy, the following February, offered a solemn *Te Deum* in thanksgiving, and subsequently his sermon was circulated as a pastoral letter in his diocese.[9] It emphasised the excesses of the French Revolution. In opposing Jacobin revolution in Ireland, Troy was not being 'unpatriotic'. In the context of what the revolutionaries were inflicting on the Catholic Church in those large parts of Europe controlled by France, he could scarcely have taken any other stand.

In 1798 Troy condemned the rebellion, and excommunicated the many Catholic members of the United Irishmen. The year, indeed, had opened with the utmost reminder of the anti-Catholic nature of the French Revolution. On 10 February, the Papal States had fallen to French armies. Pope Pius V1 was deposed and then arrested. Murray's friend and mentor, Fr Thomas Betagh, had responded to the fall of Rome by giving, from the pulpit of the church of St Michael, 'a powerful course of lectures against the pernicious doctrines of Tom Paine to overflow audiences with great effect'.[10]

The indiscriminate violence and the reign of terror conducted by government forces in Ireland confirmed for Archbishop Troy the futility of revolution against the might of the British crown. The chief secretary, Viscount Castlereagh, reinforced his fear that what the government had given, the government could take back.

REBELLION IN THE AIR

Daniel Murray, for his part, had experienced personally the brutality and terror perpetrated by government soldiery and militia. In 1795, he had been sent as curate to his native parish of Arklow. In this new role, he seems to have earned the esteem of the parishioners. Revd William Meagher PP, homilist and first biographer of Archbishop Murray, commented devotedly in his historical and biographical notes that the young curate manifested an 'enlightened piety' and left behind him, on his departure in 1798, 'a fame of sanctity long remembered with edification'.[11]

It was not an easy time to be a priest in Wicklow, however. Rebellion was in the air. Murray's two brothers, Tom and Peter, had joined the United Irishmen, but there is no evidence that Daniel was influenced by their views.[12] Any sympathy he may have had for the ideals of the Revolution – the abolition of privilege, and the achievement of equality and freedom – was dispelled by its subsequent course in France, where the widespread terror and attacks on the Church persuaded him and most priests in the Dublin diocese to follow the advice of their archbishop. Under pressure from the government to prove their loyalty, many of them swore allegiance to the crown and, despite intimidation from United Irishmen, tried to persuade their people to surrender arms.

The attitude of bishops and clergy was an important factor in favour of peace. Dublin, a hotbed of United Irishmen activity, had no serious outbreaks of violence, and most of the country remained quiet. Some seventy priests were accused of being involved in the 1798 rebellion. Their number constituted a small proportion of the 1,800 priests in the country at the time, and all were not equally guilty; indeed, some were probably not guilty at all. The bishops generally were highly critical of the rebel priests, Troy calling them the scum of the Church, and complaining that they had greatly damaged it.[13]

Murray, in Arklow, took an oath of allegiance and swore, in the presence of the Revd Bailey, who was local magistrate as well as Protestant rector, that he gave no countenance to the United Irishmen.[14] He is said to have counselled a number of young men against participating in armed conflict. Living between two fires, his stance appears to have led to criticism and hostility from some of Wicklow's rebel leaders.[15] While he was on a pastoral visit in Arklow town, an officer of the militia is reported to have shouted to his men, 'Shoot that papist priest!' Quickly, Murray turned into a shop and escaped through the rear.[16]

In 1798, after continuous government harassment, the United Irishmen began their revolt on 23 May. Its outcome varied from place to place – from defeat at Tara, Co. Meath, to victory at Oulart Hill, Co. Wexford. There were outbreaks in Kildare, Antrim and Down, incidents in Co. Wicklow, and a popular revolt in Co. Wexford. On 9 June the armed struggle came very close to Murray and his parishioners. The Wexford insurgents, advancing towards Dublin, were repulsed by a strong garrison force at Arklow. On 29 June, the insurgents were finally defeated at Vinegar Hill, near Enniscorthy, Co. Wexford.

A PERSONAL EXPERIENCE OF TERROR

Sometime towards the end of June, or during the first days of July, Fr Murray had an experience that seared his life. Different accounts of the occurrence have been published.[17] Some declare that yeomanry or the Antrim militia, returning after the battle of Vinegar Hill, were involved;[18] others suggest that it was ill-disciplined soldiers from the garrison at Arklow who were responsible; others simply speak of English soldiers or military 'ruffians'. Whatever group was involved, they were bitterly anti-Catholic and especially hostile to the Catholic clergy. Their hostility was aggravated, no doubt, by drink and by the prominent part played by priests in the Wexford conflict.

Reconstructing the likely scenario from the different accounts, it is clear that Fr William Ryan, the parish priest of Arklow, while staying at the home of his relatives at Johnstown, near Arklow, was murdered in his bed around midnight by an inflamed military group. Next morning, the perpetrators made their way towards the Catholic chapel in Arklow, which was then situated at the end of the town, in a location later known as Old Chapel Ground. Murray was either preparing for Mass or had finished Mass, when he learned of the murder of his parish priest. Soon, some parishioners came rushing into the building telling him of the rowdy advancing soldiery. It seems that he considered confronting them, but the sound of gunfire and the urging of his parishioners persuaded him quickly to fold the vestments, conceal the sacred vessels, and clamber through the back window with the help of some of the congregation.

He borrowed a horse from the Protestant rector, the Revd Bailey. Then, pursued by some of the militia or soldiery, he made his way along the banks of the Avoca river, crossing it at Shelton Abbey and reaching the family farm at Sheepwalk. There Murray changed horses, and set out on the perilous journey across the mountains towards Dublin. To evade patrols and marauding gangs returning from Wexford, he avoided the main roads. He reached the home of family friends at Glenealy, and with their help he managed to reach Dublin.[19]

Back in Arklow, meanwhile, the soldiery set fire to the parish chapel, completely destroying it, and then proceeded to the Murray's farm at Sheepwalk. There they set fire to all the outhouses, destroying stores of hay and grain, burning four horses alive in their stables, and killing livestock. One of the marauding party, ran through the house determined to kill any male member of the family. He came to a bedroom where Daniel's nephew lay sick of high fever. On being told that the disease was infectious, however, he instantly fled, warning his fellow raiders not to risk their lives. They set fire to the house and left.

The loyalist terror after the rebellion was markedly anti-Catholic. Sixty chapels were burned in the south-east of the country. Lord Cornwallis, now both commander-in-chief and lord lieutenant, was horrified to find that in conservative Protestant circles 'if a priest has been put to death the greatest joy is expressed by the whole company'. A year later, in August 1799, Archbishop

Troy complained to Dublin Castle that no 'priest can appear in the N.E. parts of that distracted county [Wexford] nor in the neighbourhood of Arklow'.[20] Wisely, he did not send Murray back to his Wicklow parish.

As a young man, then, Daniel Murray had been a hunted priest fleeing for his life. His parish priest had been murdered, his own family had been terrorised, their stock and farm provisions had been destroyed and their home torched. He had personal experience of a period when thousands died from violence. The horror of what he saw and heard at this time, the terror he personally experienced and the stories retailed in his own family left an indelible mark on his mind. He was left with a permanent abhorrence of violent revolution, an awareness of its futility against the superior might of the British government and its supporters and first-hand knowledge of the terrible vengeance they could wreak.

THE CHURCH IN DUBLIN

After his escape to Dublin, Murray was welcomed by Dr Troy and appointed as a curate at St Andrew's Church. That church was once part of the stabling attached to the Lord Ely's mansion, and would later become the site of the Theatre Royal, since demolished.[21]

At this time, while some churches in the city area often had statues, fine paintings and a variety of pews, most churches in the archdiocese were poorly built structures. Sometimes they were converted stables, situated in alleys or back streets. In some of the more remote country areas in the archdiocese – in Co. Dublin and Co. Wicklow – conditions were poor both outside and within.

Clergy in these parishes were sometimes unable to survive at all and had to leave. There were no salaries from the state, and the priests were totally dependent on voluntary subscriptions from the people. This helped to make them independent of the government and brought them closer to the people and their acute problems, but these voluntary subscriptions varied considerably, with some better-off parishes providing generously for their priests, while others in poorer areas were unable to provide even basic maintenance. To remedy the situation, John Carpenter, Dr Troy's predecessor as archbishop of Dublin (1770–86), insisted that church door collections should 'be divided equally' among the diocesan clergy to ensure that all were supported with 'that decency which their character required'.[22]

Forbidden by law to use titles and insignia, the secular clergy dressed in a way that was not distinctive, and were officially addressed as 'Mister'. Much of their work was catechetical, as they sought to redress the lacuna in doctrine and values occasioned by the penal laws. Archbishop Carpenter was conscious of the need for more priests to minister to the increasing population.[23] It is not easy to determine the ratio of priests to people in the diocese in those years. In 1802, Archbishop Troy estimated that there were 400,000 Catholics in the twenty-six parishes of the archdiocese, and not enough priests to meet the needs of so many. That remained the way during Daniel Murray's time as priest and his first years as bishop. When, some decades later, a great surge came in the Catholic population, the ratio of priests to laity became critical. Returns available for 1834 were to show a total of 2,156 diocesan clergy in the whole country, endeavouring to serve a Catholic population of 6,436,060: a ratio of one priest to 2,985 people.[24] The ratio in Dublin at that stage was probably somewhat better, and the local clergy, besides, had the assistance of some members of religious orders. Nevertheless, the problem continued to be critical until the decline of population took place in the years after the famine.

THE ACT OF UNION

Meantime, in 1798, Daniel Murray had returned to work among colleagues and friends, but in the aftermath of the rebellion there was a palpable sense of tension. Catholics lived on tenterhooks, uncertain of the future. Blatant chicanery and bribery were involved in the process of terminating the Irish parliament and bringing about an act of union between Britain and Ireland. Because of their influence over the people, the government wanted to secure the loyalty of the Catholic bishops, and with that in view Catholic Emancipation was promised informally in return for their support of the union. The bishops were also required to agree to a government veto on episcopal appointments, payment of the clergy, and some government control over Maynooth College.

The bishops, having consulted Rome, felt they had little option but to agree. Dr Troy believed that the prime minister, William Pitt, was committed to bringing in Catholic Emancipation once the act of union was passed, and he set himself to persuading his fellow bishops and Catholics to support the union. Archbishop Thomas Bray of Cashel assured him on 1 July 1799 that he would cooperate.[25] Troy, meantime, availed of his reputation for loyalty, boldly seeking from Lord Lieutenant Cornwallis the restoration of Catholic chapels destroyed in Wicklow and Wexford. After the bloody repression of the previous years, it is surely ironic that as many as sixty-nine chapels – usually small, mud-walled structures – were replaced, at government expense, by sturdy, barn-like buildings according to a cruciform plan, with flagged floors, galleries and improved sanctuaries.[26]

On 2 July 1800, the British Act of Union was passed in the British House of Commons, and on 2 August, the Irish parliament passed the Irish Act of Union, abolishing itself. Earlier that year, in April, Archbishop Troy had explained his actions in a letter to his Roman agent, Luke Concanen:[27]

> We all wish to remain as we are, and we would so, were it not that too many of the clergy were active in the wicked rebellion or did not oppose it ... If we had rejected the proposal *in toto*, we would be considered here as rebels ... if we agreed to it without reference to Rome we would be branded schismatics. We were between Scylla and Charybdis.

The Union of Great Britain and Ireland came into effect on 1 January 1801. A month later, on 3 February, William Pitt announced his intention to resign as prime minister because of King George III's refusal to agree to Catholic Emancipation.

The result was that Britain was seen once again, in the eyes of the majority, as perfidious, and the bishops as, at the least, over-trusting and misled. The refusal of Catholic Emancipation also had repercussions among the bishops themselves. Murray, like Troy before him, would establish close contact with British officials as a means of benefitting the Catholic people, and he would tend to put a positive construction on British intentions. Some other prelates, however, vigorously opposed him from time to time, reflecting increasing suspicion and distrust of all government plans and initiatives.

For the next twenty years, Catholic representatives, including Daniel Murray, would be involved in denying the government the right to veto episcopal appointments. The restoration of an Irish parliament for the Irish people would dominate Irish politics for the best part of 120 years. Meantime, from 1798 to 1800, Murray worked hard in St Andrew's parish, counselling people in those difficult years, caring for the poor and the sick and manifesting an openness to people and a gift for preaching.

NOTES

1 R. F. Foster, *Modern Ireland, 1600–1972* (London: Penguin Books, 1988), p.265.

2 Dr Plunkett, bishop of Meath, to Fr Betagh, 20 Jan. 1792, cit. by A. Cogan. *The Diocese of Meath*, vol. iii (Dublin, 1870), p.171.

3 Ian McBride. *Eighteenth Century Ireland* (Dublin: Gill & MacMillan, 2009), p.368.

4 T.W. Moody and F.X. Martin eds., *A New History of Ireland* (Oxford: Clarendon Press, 1991) vol. viii, p.289.

5 C. Maxwell, *Dublin under the Georges, 1714–1830* (Dublin: Hodges Figgis & Co Ltd, 1946), p.36.

6 R. F. Foster, op. cit., p.280.

7 Cit. D. Keogh 'John Thomas Troy, 1768–1823' in Kelly & Keogh eds., *History of the Catholic Diocese of Dublin* (Dublin: Four Courts Press, 2000), p.217.
8 Troy – L. Concanen, 24 Dec. 1793, Archives of Propaganda Fide (APF), *Scrittino originali referite nelle congregazioni generali, vol. 899 f 269;* cit D. Keogh art. cit in op. cit., p.219.
9 D. A. Kerr. 'Priests, Pikes and Patriots' in S. J. Browne & D. W. Miller eds., *Piety and Power in Ireland, 1760-1960*, Essays in honour of Emmet Larkin (Belfast/Indiana: Notre Dame Press, 2000), p.21.
10 Irish Jesuit Archives (IJA), 'Suppression and Restoration of the Society of Jesus in Ireland', a notebook with hand-written contributions on the history of the Irish province after 1800, author/authors name and date not given.
11 Revd Wm. Meagher P.P., *Notices of the Life and Character of His Grace Most Rev. Daniel Murray ... as contained in the Commemorative Oration ... with Historical and Biographical Notes* (Dublin 1853), Notes, note 1, p.53.
12 Donal Kerr, 'The Forgotten Archbishop: Daniel Murray, 1768–1852' in Kelly & Keogh eds., *History of the Catholic Diocese of Dublin* (Dublin: Four Courts Press, 2000), p.252.
13 D. A. Kerr, 'Priests, Pikes and Patriots' in op. cit. p.23.
14 Donal Kerr, 'The Forgotten Archbishop …' in op. cit. p.252.
15 F. P. Carey, Pamphlet. *Archbishop Murray of Dublin ...* p.8.
16 Donal Kerr, art. cit., in op. cit., p. idem.
17 Among the accounts are F. P. Carey iam cit.; P. J. Murray. 'Daniel Murray, Archbishop of Dublin, 1823–1852' in *Journal of Arklow Historical Society*, (1983), pp.12–13; an account of the incident said to be given by a niece of Murray, a single page in Murray Papers, Dublin Diocesan Archives. Also Donal Kerr. 'Dublin's Forgotten Archbishop: Daniel Murray, 1768–1852' in Kelly & Keogh' eds, *History of the Catholic Diocese of Dublin* (Dublin: Four Courts Press, 2000), pp.252–3.
18 Donal Kerr. art. cit. idem.
19 Myles Ronan. 'Archbishop Murray (1768–1852)' in I.E.R. Jan–June 1952, vol. lxxvii, p.241.
20 Donal Kerr. art. cit., p.253.
21 F. P. Carey, iam cit. p.9.
22 Cit. James Kelly, 'The Impact of the Penal Laws' in Kelly & Keogh eds, *History of The Catholic Diocese of Dublin* (Dublin: Four Courts Press, 2000), p.166.
23 Idem, p.168.
24 D. McCartney, *The Dawning of Democracy. Ireland 1800-1870* (Dublin: The Educational Company of Ireland, 1987), p.36.
25 Moody & Martin eds., *A New History of Ireland* (Oxford: Clarendon Press, 1982), VIII, p.291.
26 D. Keogh. 'John Thomas Troy …' in *Hist. of Diocese of Dublin*, pp.219, 227.
27 Troy – L. Concanen, spring 1800, DDA, Troy Papers; cit. D. Keogh art. cit. loc cit., p.218.

CHAPTER 3

Esteemed Pastor and Coadjutor Archbishop (1800–12)

Fr Murray's work at St Andrew's attracted Dr Troy's attention. In 1800 he transferred him to the metropolitan chapel of St Mary in Upper Liffey Street, where Archbishop Troy was parish priest. There, Murray was to establish a reputation as a very special pastor.

AN INFLUENTIAL CURATE

For all its title as 'metropolitan chapel', St Mary's was a humble outhouse penal chapel. It was hidden away among a cluster of houses and could only be approached by a narrow passage. Inside, the light was dim, as the windows, which were small, were ranged on only one side of the building. Despite a low ceiling, there was a gallery. A painting of the Virgin and Child, copied after Raphael, hung over the altar. The chapel was not half large enough for the congregation. On Sundays the little yard, the narrow passage and the street itself were filled with a pious crowd trying to get as close as possible to the chapel, even to its external wall. From shortly before noon until one o'clock, times for the last Masses to begin, there was a clatter of hoofs and the roll of wheels as, in the fashion of the day, all who had carriages rode in state to chapel. It was considered only right and appropriate to have one's best horses and liveries seen in the labyrinth of lanes surrounding parochial and conventual chapels. The pedestrian part of the congregation, according to one commentator, did not take umbrage at all this show but rather gave it their approval.[1]

Dublin in the years after the union was in a state of depression. Most of the fine houses were shut up. The splendid buildings with colonnades of Portland stone and sparkling granite fronts were looking tarnished, 'monuments of a prosperity untimely ruined'. Amidst the gloom, however, many Catholic middle-class people continued to do well. Their opening to advancement had been through trade. A considerable number of Dublin merchants and traders, despite their Catholicism, had amassed wealth and attained high social positions, while remaining politically unimportant. They were fortunate in being to a great extent engaged in branches of business hardly affected by the union, such as brewing, distilling, discounting and provisioning the troops on service abroad; consequently they safely negotiated the crisis that had proved the ruin of so many of their fellow-citizens.[2] At Sunday Mass, these well-to-do middle-class people asserted their religious beliefs in style, providing a contrast in their opulence to the small and shabby chapel buildings and the poverty of the greater part of the congregation. Fortunately, however, as Murray soon learned, many of these wealthy people were generous in their support of the poor and of the church ministers and buildings.

Murray at this time was in his late thirties. A handsome man of 'erect carriage, elastic step and graceful movements', he was described by a female admirer as having clear and dark eyes, a fine forehead, and hair 'disembarrassed of powder' falling loosely behind.[3] He had a commanding presence, and at the altar he offered Mass with devout recollection. In addition, he became celebrated for his sermons and their distinctive style. He was asked to deliver a number of charity sermons in aid of schools, convents and churches dependent on the financial assistance provided by such occasions. Murray drew large crowds, including many wealthy patrons. What was different was that his language avoided the ornate rhetoric then in vogue. He spoke simply and in a quiet, clearly enunciated voice, very much at variance with the stentorian style of orators common at the time. During his lifetime, in his sermons for charity, he raised the equivalent of hundreds of thousands of pounds in today's money. Daniel O'Connell later had this to say of his sermons:[4]

> Others amazed the … nation by their profound erudition, by their overwhelming eloquence … but for the good archbishop of Dublin it was reserved to lead not only the intellect of his auditors captive, but their hearts also, showing up the dogmas of faith, not only as irrefragably true, but divinely amiable and beneficent.

In the words 'amiable and beneficent', O'Connell identified two of Murray's principal characteristics, features already much in evidence in his years as curate in Liffey Street. Significantly, Murray would often be compared to St Francis de Sales, whom he regarded as his patron. Like de Sales, he believed that more could be achieved by a spoonful of honey than by a barrelful of vinegar.

Murray's zeal and unostentatious work for his parishioners, especially the poor, and his good relations with his fellow clergy, led to his becoming a dean of the diocese while still a curate. This occurred around 1804. The following year, in a bizarre concatenation of events, he found himself briefly a parish priest. The parish of Coolock and Clontarf became vacant when its pastor, Canon Patrick Ryan, was appointed bishop of Ferns. In such cases, the appointment of the succeeding parish priest was reserved to the Holy See, and Dr Troy duly forwarded three names to Rome, placing Fr Paul Long first. Assuming that the Holy See would accept his first nomination on the list, as was usually the case, Archbishop Troy appointed Long to the parish, where he assumed duty in January 1805. When the Apostolic Letter reached Dublin three months later, however, it bore the news that Canon Daniel Murray had been appointed, and that canonically he had been parish priest of Coolock and Clontarf since 24 March. Murray, much to the relief of the embarrassed Dr Troy, voluntarily resigned the Coolock pastorate. In such a case, the right of appointment reverted to the archbishop, who forthwith regularised Long's position. Canon Murray continued as a curate in Liffey Street for another three years, years that proved important for the Church in Ireland.[5]

VALUED FRIENDS

Among the parishioners with whom Murray became friendly were John O'Brien and his wife Anna Maria, *née* Ball. John O'Brien was a partner in a well-established business engaged in foreign import trade. His brothers and sisters, and also his partners, were all described as 'in good circumstances', as were many of his friends. They were all were described as 'remarkable for their charity to the poor and their liberality in supporting the clergy, the chapels and the few institutions which it had been possible to establish' in those difficult times.

Anna Maria O'Brien was one of a number of remarkable women influenced by Murray and devoted to him. Attractive, with a strong personality and very definite views, she was given strong moral and financial support by her husband. As someone who was close to Murray, it is relevant to note the comments of a near contemporary. 'She had very decided notions concerning the duty of Catholics at that particular time; they should not any longer hide in back streets, nor wear that cowering expression that distinguished them in public places from their Protestant fellow-countrymen, nor allow themselves to be jostled off a path to which they had as much right as any of their countrymen.' She was assertive in her lifestyle and she dressed in the best taste. 'Her house was elegantly appointed, her carriages and horses unexceptionable, her own presence singularly imposing.' And with it all, 'her interests were those of the

Mary Aikenhead

Catholic community, and everything connected with the poor, the helpless, the afflicted'.[6] It was through Anna Maria O'Brien that Murray was to meet Mary Aikenhead, founder of the Irish Sisters of Charity.

Mr and Mrs O'Brien used to attend Fr Murray's daily Mass. Afterwards, on occasion, he would walk with them to their home in Mountjoy Square and join them for breakfast. 'A good deal of charitable business work', it appears, 'was discussed and organised on these occasions.'[7] Through the O'Brien and Ball families, Murray's influential contacts extended beyond his parish in Dublin to other parts of the country. The contacts, for the most part, were with people committed to a Christian way of life and especially to working for the poor.

During 1807, Murray accompanied the O'Briens to Cork. The occasion was the religious profession of Anna Maria O'Brien's sister, Cecilia Ball, at the Ursuline Convent in Cork city. Also in the party was another sister, Frances (or Fanny) Ball. It was on this occasion, through a friend – a Miss Lynch, who was due to join the Poor Clare Sisters in Dublin – that Mary Aikenhead first met with Anna Maria O'Brien, who invited her to spend time with her in Dublin. At the time of her visit to Cork, Mrs O'Brien was about twenty-two years of age, and was described as 'strikingly handsome, with a tall, slight figure, stately carriage, and dressed in the fashions of the day'.[8] Despite appearances, however, she was feeling less than well. This is indicated in a letter written from Cork on 2 July 1807 by a Mr Donnellan.

Murray and the O'Briens had visited this man during their stay in Cork. Subsequently, Murray wrote to thank him for his hospitality and, to Donnellan's surprise and gratification, expressed the hope that he had recovered from his cold. (It was in such small, thoughtful ways, that Murray endeared himself to many.) In Donnellan's reply, he told of his pleasure in receiving Fr Murray and Mr and Mrs O'Brien on their visit to Cork, and how delighted he was to learn that Mrs O'Brien 'had somewhat recovered her spirits as from that very great depression she laboured under', adding that, as far as he could judge, she was 'most amiable and answers the excellent character I always heard of her'. Donnellan also reported that 'Miss Ball is perfectly well' and that his sister, Mary Donnellan, 'pays her constant visits'. If Miss Aikenhead were in town, she would commission him to say something for her.[9] Already, at this stage, it is evident that the curate from Upper Liffey Street had a network of middle-class contacts with whom he shared spiritual interests and who were prepared to assist him in his work for the less well-off.

COADJUTOR IN DUBLIN

Archbishop Troy, who had followed Murray's career with interest, decided in 1809 that he no longer had the energy of past years. During 1808 and 1809, he had to curtail confirmations because of illness, and he decided to ask the Pope for a coadjutor with the right of succession. He petitioned Pope Pius VII for the appointment of Canon Murray, whom he described as 'a doctor of theology … a canon of Dublin and a most celebrated preacher … held in high regard by both the clergy and people'.[10] Further considerations in Murray's favour were his urbanity, his circumspection in judgement, his fluency in Latin, Spanish and French, his zeal and energy, and his appreciation of religious life. It did not seem to matter that Murray was still only a curate. Neither Murray nor the chapter of the diocese was informed by the archbishop of this request at the time it was made.

Some time before the response came from Rome two months later, Dr Troy informed the senior clergy of his choice of coadjutor. They, it appears, expressed their approval. When the decision arrived from Rome, Murray was named titular Archbishop of Hierapolis and Coadjutor Archbishop with right of succession. Murray himself, however, was shocked and dismayed by the appointment. He approached his old friend and mentor, the influential vicar-general, Dr Betagh, 'and with tears' requested him to intervene to protect him against this 'judgement from heaven for his sins'. Betagh listened sympathetically, and then counselled him not to question the decrees of God. 'Who are you,' he is said to have asked, 'that you should resist the Holy Ghost?'[11] Thus counselled, Murray submitted to the appointment.

On 30 November 1809, in the small stable chapel of St Mary, in Upper Liffey Street, the consecration of Coadjutor Archbishop Murray took place. The ceremony was conducted by Dr Troy, assisted by the archbishop of Armagh, Richard O'Reilly, together with Bishop Patrick Ryan of Ferns and Bishop Daniel Delany of Kildare and Leighlin. The packed congregation included the Earl of Fingal, Thomas Moore (viewed as 'our national poet'), Henry Grattan, the young Daniel O'Connell, John Philpot Curran (father of Robert Emmet's Sarah), the Protestant Lord Mayor of Dublin and the City Fathers.[12] Troy authorised the publication of an English translation of the rite of consecration, not for the benefit of the Catholic congregation alone, but for their 'fellow-Christians, who, though estranged from the Roman Catholic community, might, however, desire to inspect … [its] ceremonies'.[13] The distinguished ecumenical gathering was a tribute to the standing and work of Archbishop Troy, and to the unaffected charm of Daniel Murray and his interest in people irrespective of religion or class. The consecration sermon, appropriately, was given by Dr Betagh.

After the ceremony, Archbishop Murray remained on in Liffey Street for another two years, performing the ordinary duties of a priest and, occasionally, deputising for the archbishop at confirmations and visitations of parishes. He continued his interest in the education of poorer children. In that year, on 9 July, he received a vote of thanks from the governors of Booterstown Female Orphan School for agreeing to preach the annual charity sermon for the school on Sunday, 6 August.[14] As bishop, his attraction as a preacher drew larger crowds to the benefit of the schools concerned.

THE VETO CONTROVERSY

Shortly before Murray's consecration, the matter of a veto on episcopal appointments became a major issue. It was an issue that was to concern him deeply. With the King's rejection of Catholic Emancipation and Rome's opposition to the clergy being paid by the state, the arrangements made in 1799 had fallen through. In 1808 these arrangements came up again, but this time centred on one element, a veto on the appointment of bishops being granted to the king. The Irish Catholic bishops, in full session, rejected it. Troy was dismayed at this, because he felt that the veto, in better circumstances, might still be an option.[15] His coadjutor, Daniel Murray, was to show himself strongly against the veto.

The controversy about the veto, which raged between the years 1808 and 1815, widened from being an episcopal issue to one with vigorous social and political dimensions. The Catholic Committee, which was largely run by Irish Catholic gentry, was anxious to placate government and Protestants by offering the right of veto on the appointment of bishops, as had been granted in 1799. This was something accepted by the Papacy in many countries. An increasingly vocal middle class, however, did not want to give any concession to the government. There was a strong sense of grievance that the privileges granted in 1793 and the further concessions promised by the union were seldom put into operation, and that discrimination was still widely practised.

The division among Irish Catholics came sharply to the fore in May 1808. Henry Grattan, on 25 May, introduced a Catholic petition in the House of Commons, stating that he had been authorised by Catholics to introduce a scheme whereby future appointments to vacant bishoprics would require the approval of the king. His concession made little difference in the House of Commons, where the petition was rejected by 281 votes to 128.[16] The concession, however, stirred up strong feelings at home, especially among those whom George Ponsonby, former chancellor of the exchequer and supporter of Catholic claims, described as 'the people of the middling orders, in this (city) and in the country towns'.[17] The concession of a veto was represented extravagantly as likely to bring about the ruination of the Catholic Church in Ireland.

On 1 August 1808, Bishop John Milner, vicar apostolic of the midland district of England and agent of the Irish hierarchy in London, published a letter to 'A Parish Priest in Ireland' – in reality to Dr William Coppinger, Bishop of Cloyne – in which he vigorously defended his support of the veto in 1799. In doing so, he was supporting the statement of the Irish bishops at that time in relation to the veto, whose approach was in keeping with regular practice. 'In Catholic countries,' Coppinger wrote, 'the prince nominates without any control, and the pope gives jurisdiction as a matter of course.' [18]

The Irish bishops in September 1808 gathered in full session, as noted above, and came out against granting a veto. Milner learned from one of the bishops that, of the reasons which weighed with the prelates, 'the chief was that the government would in all probability not be content with the veto, but would use any concession as a lever to ask for more, and for things which a Catholic could not concede'. Perhaps even more important, Milner understood, was 'the apprehension that in view of the excitement of the people, the bishops would lose all influence over them if they consented to the veto'.[19] In a letter to Sir John Coxe Hippisley, a voluble English Catholic, written on 17 September 1808, Milner further commented that at the Irish bishops' conference some of the prelates 'were obliged to yield to the majority'.[20] Subsequently, he observed, 'our friends complain that the old and experienced bishops let themselves be bullied by the younger ones; and they mention one in particular, a coadjutor, who harangued the assembly for three hours together against the concession.'[21] In the event, Milner changed his public attitude to the veto in deference to the bishops' declaration.

The critical outlook of some of the Irish bishops is conveyed in a letter by Bishop William Coppinger of Cloyne to the bishop of Cork, Dr Francis Moylan, on 11 November 1808:[22]

> With regard to the discontent of our Catholic Aristocracy at the late resolution of our bishops, it proves ... that these gentry are more interested in their individual aggrandisement than they are in the existence of Catholicity in Ireland. The more I have reflected on this matter, the more settled is my conviction that even the *negative* interference would destroy our Religion here. The King certainly neither knows or cares anything about the fitness or unfitness of our priests for the prelacy.

> Governors of counties, parliament squires, Duignans [*a reference to the secretary of the Grand Lodge of Ireland and bitter opponent of Catholic Emancipation*] would be exclusively active for the respective objects of their choice. The very qualities which Catholic electors would look to: zeal, piety, learning, rigid virtue and exemplary conduct, would be sufficient grounds of rejection with these men, for this obvious reason that bad bishops would be more efficient in the projected ruin.

He added that such was the people's indelible distrust of the government, that a bishop seen as a government appointment would not be respected. He trusted that His Holiness would be 'fully and fairly put in possession of the real state of the case by prelates of more weight' than himself.

Following his changed stance on the veto, Milner found himself under attack from fellow bishops in England. Writing to Bishop Peter Collingridge on 27 November 1808, he defended himself, referring to an earlier public vindication, on 13 November, in the *Morning Chronicle*, which was copied in *The Globe* and other papers. In the course of his presentation, Milner indicated the passionate feelings that had been stirred in Ireland by the veto question. 'The common people in Ireland are mad upon the subject', he wrote. 'They consider the matter in a political view, and are determined to have a something, be it what it may, which has no connection with the hated English. The bishops have been forced to yield to their prejudice.' Nevertheless, he was going to stand by the Irish bishops. His parliamentary friends in England had threatened to give him up if he did not give the bishops up. 'This I have refused to do,' he said, 'as I refused to sacrifice the bishops to the democrats of Ireland …'[23] Later, Dr Troy felt it necessary to defend Milner's change to Bishop William Poynter of the London district, a leading advocate of the veto among English Catholics. Milner, as agent of the Irish bishops, had complied with their instructions to their satisfaction. He added that 'the change of opinion is not an invariable proof of inconsistency'. The archbishop concluded quietly but firmly that 'whatever Dr Milner says or does precisely as agent of the Irish prelates under their instruction, is sanctioned by them'.[24]

In all of this, Daniel Murray, prior to his consecration as bishop in November 1809, took no active part. The participants would have been known to him, at least by reputation, and the general trend of events and the issues involved were so widely publicised as to be part of general knowledge among the clergy in Dublin. Following his consecration as bishop in late 1809, Murray would become privy to all episcopal dealings regarding the veto.

Even before Murray's consecration as bishop, however, a more serious event of universal import occupied Catholic attention. On 6 July, Pope Pius VII was arrested by the French, deported to Savona, near Genoa, and later to France. The confusion in Church affairs resulting from the Pope's imprisonment was reflected on 25 January 1810, in a letter from Dr Troy's Dominican correspondent in Rome, Luke Concanen. After expressing his delight at Troy's news about Dr Murray's consecration, Concanen explained that with regard to the veto, the 'Irish prelates must decide what they thought best'. No direction or advice can now be expected from Rome on that or any other subject. 'Propaganda is closed, like all other Church tribunals. The archives and papers were yesterday sealed up. All are to be sent to Rheims, with the officers of each tribunal. It's not known what will happen to the students.'[25] On 18 April, Concanen confirmed that all papal tribunals had been closed down.[26]

Caught up as they were in serious local matters, the Irish bishops nevertheless displayed a solidarity that looked beyond Irish affairs to the universal Church. On 3 March 1810, they sent a joint letter to the bishops of the universal Church, protesting strongly against the violation of the rights of the Holy See and on the indignities the Pope had been made to suffer.[27] These developments abroad, incidentally, added an extra dimension to the veto problem at home. Now, the appointment of Irish and English bishops lay not just with the papacy as 'a foreign power', but with the papacy in the power of an enemy of Britain!

With the stalemate over the veto still unresolved, Dr Troy was relieved to pass on to his coadjutor another issue demanding serious attention: Maynooth College and its on-going problem of student indiscipline.

CONCERN FOR MAYNOOTH

Maynooth, like other colleges, tended to manifest in its student body the unease present in the national scene. In 1798, ten students were expelled for their sympathies for the United Irishmen. On 8 January 1803, Archbishop Troy informed Archbishop Bray of Cashel that 'a most unwarrantable and scandalous spirit of insurrection has lately manifested itself in Maynooth College by a general and public disobedience of the students to their superiors and professors'. He had instructed his 'vicar in that district' to repair to the college and initiate to the subjects of the Dublin diocese 'that if they did not immediately ask pardon on their knees and promise to withdraw from all tumultuous meetings' they would be withdrawn from the college. All except four had obeyed. 'I shall allow a week to these four for reflection,' Dr Troy continued, 'and I shall positively remove them from the college should they continue longer obstinate. I hope they will not.'[28]

On 27 January, he reported to Bray that peace had been restored in Maynooth since the 16 January. The students acknowledged their error and promised good conduct in the future.[29] Little more than a week later, however, on 4 February, Troy commented that five bishops had written to him urging a speedy meeting to elect a president of Maynooth and to adopt the necessary measures to put down 'the wicked spirit of insubordination which is smothered rather than extinguished'.[30]

Then, as if to confirm the views of the five bishops, Troy, five years later, on 17 November 1809, had to inform Bray that the forthcoming meeting at Maynooth on 1 December 'will investigate the causes of the recent scandalous riots in the college and punish the leaders'. Arthur James Plunkett, earl of Fingall, Dr Richard O'Reilly of Armagh, Dr Patrick Plunkett of Meath and Dr Troy himself had visited the college but had failed to discover the offenders, so they had decided that a general meeting should be called.[31]

It was against this background, that Murray was asked to take responsibility for Maynooth. Fortunately, he was able to report an improved situation within a short time. On 26 July 1810, he wrote to Dr Bray that Dr Patrick Everard, who had arrived to take over the presidency just three days previously, had already effected great improvements and restored order.[32] The next year, Murray was appointed administrator of St Andrew's Church in Hawkins Street; but soon afterwards, in 1812, he learned that Dr Everard's health had broken down and he had to retire from Maynooth. With no president readily available, the bishops turned to Murray to take on the unforgiving task. On 26 June 1812, the Lord Lieutenant approved his election as president. It was to be a memorable year in his life in a number of ways.

NOTES

1 S.A. (Sarah Atkinson), *Mary Aikenhead* … (Dublin, 1879), pp.118–119.
2 Idem, pp.113, 115.
3 Idem, p.119.
4 Donal Kerr, 'Dublin's forgotten archbishop: Daniel Murray, 1768–1852' in Kelly & Keogh, *History of the Catholic Diocese of Dublin* (Dublin: Four Courts Press, 2000), p.262.
5 F. P. Carey, *Archbishop Murray of Dublin*, pamphlet, p.10.
6 S.A. op. cit. pp.116–117.
7 Idem, p.20.
8 Idem, p.112.
9 Donnellan-Murray, 2 July, 1807. DDA. Troy Papers, Green file 4, 1806–1808, no.72.

10 Troy – Pope Pius VII, 28 Nov. 1808. Archives Propaganda Fide (APF), Sc. Irlanda 18, f. 481, cit. D. Keogh. 'The Pattern of the Flock: John Thomas Troy, 1786–1823"' in Kelly & Keogh. *History of the Catholic Diocese of Dublin* (Dublin: Four Courts Press, 2000), p.231.
11 F. P. Carey, op. cit. p.11.
12 Idem.
13 D. Keogh, Art. cit. in op. cit., p.232.
14 Governors of Booterstown Orphan School – Murray, 9 July, 1809. DDA. Troy Papers, Green file 5, 1809–1811, no.16.
15 D. Kerr. 'Dublin's forgotten archbishop…' in Kelly & Keogh, op. cit., p.254.
16 S. J. Connolly, 'The Catholic Question, 1801–12' in W. E. Vaughan, ed. *A New History of Ireland,* V. Ireland under the Union 1: 1801-70 (Oxford: Clarendon Press, 1989), pp.36–7.
17 Idem, p.41.
18 John Milner. 'A parish priest in Ireland…', 1 Aug. 1808. DDA. Troy Papers, Green file 4, no. 103.
19 Milner – Dr Douglas, Sept. 1808. DDA. Troy Papers. Green file 4, 'English Bishops, 1808'.
20 Milner – J. Cox Hippesley, 17 Sept. 1808. Idem.
21 Idem.
22 Coppinger – Moylan, 11 Nov, 1808. The Moylan Correspondence in *Collectanea Hibernica*, no.15 (Dublin: 1972), no. 20, pp.80–82.
23 Milner – Collingridge, 27 Nov. 1808. DDA. Troy Papers, Green file 4, 'English Bishops 1808'.
24 Troy – Poynter, 1810, DDA. Troy Papers, Green file 4, 'English speaking Bishops and Dr Troy', 43.
25 L. Concanen – Troy, 25 Jan. 1810, DDA. Troy Papers, f. 375–6, no.286.
26 Idem, f. 378–79, no.288.
27 Letter to Bishops of Universal Church, 3 March, 1810, DDA. Troy Papers, Green file 5, 1809–10, no.23.
28 Troy – Dr Bray, 8 Jan. 1803. Bishop Moylan's Correspondence, no.34, in *Collectania Hibernica*, No.15 (1972).
29 Troy – Bray, 27 Jan. 1803. Letters of Troy from Cashel files (Thurles archives), 1791–1817, no.20.
30 Idem, 4 Feb. 1803, no.21.
31 Idem, 17 Nov. 1809, no.25.
32 Murray – Bray, 26 July 1810. DDA. Troy Papers, Green file 5, no.27.

CHAPTER 4

Educational Concerns and Initiatives

During the years 1812–13, Daniel Murray advised and assisted three people who were to have a major impact on education and on the spiritual and social life of Ireland in subsequent years: Peter Kenney, Edmund Rice and Mary Aikenhead. Inspired by the example of Fr Betagh, Bishop Murray held as a priority the education of poor children. Before he could devote himself fully to this matter, however, he had to deal with the more immediate problem that had arisen in Maynooth College, the main training ground of the diocesan priests of Ireland.

THE CHALLENGE OF MAYNOOTH

Murray's appointment as president was viewed by the Trustees of the college as a provisional arrangement. They hoped that Dr Everard might be persuaded to return after an interval. Meanwhile, someone like Murray was needed to act with a strong hand. Murray made it a condition of his acceptance of the presidency, that he could appoint Fr Peter Kenney as his vice-president.[1] At that time, the Jesuits had not yet been formally restored universally, but they had been restored in Sicily since 1803. It was there that Kenney studied, took his vows as a Jesuit, and was ordained.

Peter Kenney was assured of a warm welcome from churchmen on his return to Ireland, since Dr Betagh, his old friend and mentor, had spoken highly of him for many years. Before he arrived, however, in the autumn of 1811, Kenney learned of Betagh's death and of the enormous crowd – an estimated 20,000 people – that attended his funeral. On his arrival, he also learned that Betagh had left to him and the Society of Jesus his lodgings (with the rent paid for a year), his furniture and his extensive library. Immediately on his return to Ireland, Kenney set about seeking a site for a large college, something like the Grand College in Palermo or the English Jesuit college of Stonyhurst, Lancashire. His objective was the education of the country's rising Catholic middle class, with a view to their taking leading roles in society. In the interval, he was persuaded that the greater glory of God would be served by his undertaking the position in Maynooth.[2]

It is not clear when Murray and Kenney first met. They both had enjoyed Betagh's favour as students, but now they also discovered that they got on well with each other, that they shared similar values, and were united in their theological and spiritual outlooks. Murray, as a result, felt that he and Kenney would be of one mind in their approach to the challenge of Maynooth.

The college, at this stage, had approximately 205 clerical students. Of these, more than three-quarters were the sons of farmers, with the remainder coming from the ranks of tradesmen and shopkeepers, the lower professions and small-scale businesses.[3] Life within the college's walls, as with most seminaries then and for long afterwards, was spartan. The day commenced at five o'clock, and was fully regulated. Students made their own beds, swept their own rooms, cleaned their own shoes, and so on. Silence reigned, except at certain times. There were no fires in the rooms and heating was provided only in certain areas. Food was simple, even coarse, and students survived from the time of rising until three in the afternoon on what one former student termed a 'sorry breakfast'.[4]

The students were not easy to govern. They had not been through any preparatory seminaries. Most were 'quite unbroken in the ways of discipline and obedience, and were not accustomed to recognise any constituted authorities with sentiments of affection or esteem,' and they tended to resort to 'disorderly scenes … instead of legitimate means of redress'.[5] Student disorders, as noted earlier, tended to reflect the times 'when the public mind was excited'.[6] Most recently, before Everard's appointment, special rules had been drawn up asserting the following as grounds for expulsion: incitement to riot, disorderly noise in the prayer hall, and the circulation of defamatory letters against the president, the professors and fellow students. Following a special enquiry into the state of the college, the President and Dean had resigned in June 1810.[7] A position of responsibility in Maynooth was not something eagerly sought in the early years of the nineteenth century.

REFORM OF THE COLLEGE

As at most seminaries, the students at Maynooth, had, in addition to periods of vocal prayer, what was commonly known as mental prayer. The material for this mental prayer was given the evening before, and was to be the subject of reflection in the morning. From Kenney's extant journals, it is evident that, right

Peter Kenney (1839)

through the year, he provided points for these meditations, preached at daily Mass and gave two retreats of six days or more. Repeatedly, he brought home to his hearers the sacredness of their calling, stressing the wonder and challenge of it. He set the standard high, and conveyed an expectation of a generous response.[8]

During his period in Maynooth, Murray came and went. 'He visited the city regularly each week, preached to his parishioners of St Andrew's every Sunday morning, lent his assistance with the vicars general at the archbishop's council on Monday and returned, the same day, to Maynooth.'[9] Accordingly, much of the immediate contact with the students was through Kenney.

The beneficial effect of their efforts was widely noted. The most comprehensive, if florid, acknowledgement of their achievement was conveyed by Murray's first biographer, his contemporary, William Meagher. 'They found the discipline of the college … sadly relaxed,' he wrote, 'and a spirit anything but ecclesiastical too widely diffused among the inmates – insubordination, and moroseness, and foppish estimates of independence, supplanting the modesty, and docility, and respect for order, and reverence for legitimate authority, which religion demands. The vigour, and vigilance, and high ascetic tendencies of Dr Kenney, together with his reasonableness and moderation, and respectful and friendly bearing towards the students, soon wrought wonders amongst young people naturally so pious and tractable.' The 'suavity' of Murray, and his 'courteous treatment' of all, 'completed the happy revolution … Worldly-mindedness of every sort became unfashionable, discipline was re-established, and studies prosecuted with assiduity.'

Murray himself rarely addressed the students, Fr Meagher continued, and when he did his words were treasured. Kenney, on the other hand, 'very often exhorted the community on their various duties, and in that strain of fervid elocution and lofty sentiment so fitted to kindle up the imagination of his young auditors.' For them, Meagher went on, 'he composed his series of meditations – one of which was produced each evening for almost the entire period of his stay in the college'. Until the time of writing they were 'as prized, by many in far advanced life, and as recently perused as they were listened to in their prayer hall at the college.'[10]

One of the most striking tributes to Kenney was that paid by Murray before the commission set up to enquire into education in Ireland. Asked by the commissioners whether Kenney was being called on frequently to preach in Maynooth because he was a Jesuit or because he was 'a man of very considerable powers', Murray, on 20 December 1825, replied in words that also could be applied to himself:

> Solely in my opinion as being a man of very considerable powers, of

> very extensive information, of ardent and enlightened zeal, possessing an accurate knowledge of the springs which move and the virtues which elevate the human heart, together with a great facility of communicating his sentiments to the public in an impressive manner.[11]

Both men worked closely together, on and off, during the remainder of their lives. Archbishop Murray supported Kenney in his foundation of Clongowes Wood College, and subsequently in the order's opening of a church in Gardiner Street and of a school nearby that later became Belvedere College. He availed of Kenney's services as a spiritual director to the Christian Brothers, the Sisters of Charity and other religious groups in the archdiocese. Kenney, for his part, always had the warmest regard, respect and reverence for the Archbishop.

Murray's perpetual round of journeys to and from Dublin occasioned fatigue, expense and loss of time. There were no railroads in those days, and travel was slow. In addition, his role in the archdiocese was demanding. As soon as it became clear that Dr Everard could not resume his office, Murray was left with no alternative but to resign, which he did in November 1813.[12] The trustees were fortunate to find an able president for the now stabilised college. Bartholomew Crotty ruled as president for nineteen years,[13] until his appointment to the bishopric of Cloyne and Ross in 1833.

THE ADVENT OF THE CHRISTIAN BROTHERS

Very far removed from the world of strong farmers and prosperous merchants was the condition of the children of the poorer families in Dublin. A basic need of these children, in Murray's view, was an education which would help them improve their situation. In 1812, an important step was taken on their behalf. Murray contacted someone able and willing to provide them with free education.

In the last quarter of the eighteenth century there were some forty-eight Catholic schools in the capital city, with 1,300 names on their rolls. Of these schools, however, only eight were free, and these accommodated no more than 255 boys.[14] Meantime, a prosperous businessman in Waterford, following the death of his wife, had determined to provide education for the male children of the poor in that city, much as Nano Nagle was doing for children in Cork. Encouraged by some priests and bishops, Edmund Rice, a deeply religious man, wrote in 1796 to Pope Pius VI outlining his plans to establish a community of male teachers. The Pope encouraged the proposal, as did Edmund's friend, Bishop James Lanigan of Ossory. From such beginnings emerged the religious congregation of the Irish Christian Brothers.

Edmund Rice was born in Callan, Co. Kilkenny, in 1782. As mentioned, he became a successful businessman in the Waterford area, and his business background is reflected in the organisation of his schools. He studied what was effective in existing schools, and examined government reports on education. He read the work of contemporary educationalists and their pedagogical innovations, including those of Richard Lovell Edgeworth (1744–1817), Joseph Lancaster (1778–1838) and Andrew Bell (1753–1832). Rice brought order and discipline into his school and this, together with his management skills, made it possible to cater for large numbers of boys of diverse abilities and little acquaintance with self-control and learning. His first school, at Mount Sion in Waterford, was blessed in 1804 by the new bishop, John Power, who was an old friend. By then it was catering for over 300 boys.

The efforts of the new congregation of men, known popularly as 'the monks', proved successful in imparting knowledge, while also, as will be seen, preserving as a priority the religious and oral formation of the pupils. At Mount Sion, the poorer pupils were also provided with a daily meal of bread and milk. For many years, a tailor was employed to repair tattered clothes and to distribute suits to the needy. Soon there were requests from other dioceses for schools run by 'the monks'. Rice, conscious of the special needs in cities, responded by sending men to Cork and Limerick. In Dublin, Archbishop Troy and Murray were aware of these developments taking place in Munster and, in 1812, Murray contacted Edmund Rice. The two men got on well, their intentions coincided, and Rice agreed to send men to Dublin.

Murray was to play an important role in the development of the new congregation. He provided a location for the school at Hanover Street, amongst the poor of the south docks, and Rice sent a few brothers to it, led by his first disciple, Thomas Grosvenor. The methods used in Munster were successfully applied. The brothers set out to mould the behaviour and character of their pupils, who were quite unused to discipline and regularity. He wanted to enable the boys to obtain work, and so there was an emphasis on basic matters such as cleanliness – clean hands and face – and on self-discipline. Pupils were taught to 'sit, stand, move and address a person with the modesty, gracefulness and propriety which public society expected'.[15] In short, the aim was to provide the pupils with basic numeracy, literacy in English and the necessary social skills to function in an increasingly bourgeois society.

None of this would have mattered to Rice if it were divorced from religion. A striking feature of the schools was the priority attached to the religious and moral formation of the pupils. Time was reserved each day for 'moral instruction' and

Edmund Rice

for lessons from the catechism. There were set times for prayer. The day was punctuated with the Hail Mary as the clock struck the hour. At noon, the students recited the Angelus and acts of faith, hope and charity. At three o'clock the *Salve Regina* and the Litany of the Blessed Virgin were said. Children were prepared for the sacraments, and confessions were available for the whole school at least four times a year.[16] The schools' emphasis on religion invited inevitable criticism from some non-Catholic commentators. Rice remained largely unmoved by criticism or praise, however. He placed his trust in Providence and remained constant to the revealing motto for his schools, 'Catholic and Celtic, to God and Ireland true'.[17]

Murray did all he could to assist the Brothers. 'He preached their charity sermons, and interested several wealthy and benevolent friends of his own to aid them.' He engaged many of the most influential parishioners of St Andrew's parish to form themselves 'into committees of management and trusteeship, attending their meetings in person, and stimulating their zeal … To the Brothers themselves he was accessible at all hours, for advice and consolation, under the grievous difficulties and privations with which they had, for years, to contend.' Their superior, Thomas B. Grosvenor, 'a person of piety … and of considerable scientific and literary acquirements … was never weary of recounting the multiple instances of the archbishop's solicitude for their welfare …'. Grosvenor was later received into Holy Orders in the diocese by Murray.[18]

Archbishop Troy, in his *Relatio* – or annual letter – to the Holy See in 1818, observed:[19]

> Among other schools, one is pre-eminent, due to the very great zeal of Most Reverend Dr Murray, my coadjutor, who about two years ago (*sic*) erected in the parish of St Andrew, of which he had charge in this district, a school where several hundred are daily instructed under the care of pious and efficient lay-masters, generally known as monks, who, in addition to the three customary religious vows which are renewed annually, bind themselves to instruct the poorer boys.

Some 550 boys were enrolled at the Hanover Street school. Due to opportunities at harvest time or other reasons, there was never a full attendance. Nevertheless, the achievements of the school led to an invitation to open a school at Mill Street in 1818, and in James Street in 1820. The Mill Street school transferred to Francis Street when the lease expired in 1838, and from Francis Street the Brothers moved to Synge Street, which became one of the outstanding schools of the congregation.[20]

MURRAY AND THE DEVELOPMENT OF THE CHRISTIAN BROTHERS

In the early years, the members of the congregation in different dioceses were subject to their local bishop. This made it difficult to move men from place to place and to establish new foundations. Murray experienced the problem when he requested some of the brothers for Dublin. Bishop Power of Waterford was reluctant to release any men. Rice was keen to have his men bound together by religious vows but be independent of local prelates, so that they could be transferred from one diocese to another.

With this in mind, both Archbishop Troy and Murray urged Edmund Rice to apply to Rome for approval of a rule and constitutions that would place all the members under one superior general. Murray suggested to him that the members of the congregation might adopt the rule of the De La Salle Brothers. On returning from Rome in 1817, Murray brought with him copies of their rule and of the original papal brief (1680) setting up the Institute of Christian Schools, as it was called. This provided a model of the kind of central government the new foundation needed, and the De La Salle model was accepted by representatives from each of the Brothers' foundations in August 1817.[21]

Among the brothers themselves, however, there was no unanimity about the matter. Some wished to stay under episcopal control, and seemed uneasy about having one of their own as overall superior. Many bishops, likewise, were not happy with the new proposal. Having suffered the loss of two close episcopal friends, Bishop Moylan of Cork in 1815 and Bishop Power of Waterford during 1816, Rice confined his discussions with the bishops to Archbishop Troy and Murray who, in effect, were patrons of the project. An external factor influencing both Rice and Murray was the government's efforts to acquire a veto on appointments to bishoprics, and the possible effect of this on schools. Autonomy, including freedom from a potentially compromised episcopate, was desirable. Among hesitant members of the congregation itself, an additional influence in favour of autonomy was the person of the new bishop of Waterford, Robert Walsh (1817–21), who was domineering, controlling and highly abusive of Edmund Rice and his companions.

Archbishop Troy, meanwhile, worked away at obtaining Roman approval of the amalgamation of the brothers in different dioceses into one autonomous institute. He obtained the approval of sixteen bishops, but they had additions of their own they wished to make to the proposed constitutions. One of these, which prevailed, was a vow to deliver 'gratuitous education'. This provision was not amended until 1872, despite unanimous appeals from the Brothers on numerous occasions to be allowed to charge students who were in comfortable circumstances.[22] In October 1820, Murray was able to write to Rice to tell him that Pope Pius VII had issued a brief recognising its Institute and rules. Murray prayed that God would 'grant stability to an Institute that promises so fairly to be of essential benefit to the interests of religion in this country'.[23] Early in January 1821, Edmund Rice received the brief from Peter Kenney, who had brought it from Rome. This brief, an impressive parchment with official seals, established the first congregation of unordained religious men in Ireland.[24]

An important factor in securing papal approval was Rice's known hostility to proselytising schools. In 1818, the prefect of Propaganda Fide, Cardinal Francesco Fontana, in a letter to Archbishop Troy, outlined papal opposition to these schools, urging the bishops to protect their people, especially the poor, from 'the fatal poison of depraved doctrines', and instructing them to establish Catholic schools to defeat this menace.[25] In time, as the Protestant proselytising movement became more prominent, the Christian Brothers' schools were widely seen as the ideal instrument to counter the threat, although there were some dioceses to which the Brothers were not invited because the bishops disliked their assertive independence.

Not all the brothers accepted the papal brief. Some of the Cork members remained under the local bishop, while others left the congregation to follow different careers. These included some of Rice's earliest companions, Thomas Grosvenor, Thomas Reidy and Ignatius Mulcahy. On 11 January 1822, nineteen brothers assembled at Mount Sion, and began their eight-day retreat of profession conducted by Peter Kenney, now superior of the Irish Jesuits and, as has been seen, an old friend of Edmund Rice. On 20 January 1821, the retreatants made their vows as Irish Christian Brothers. Later that day, the first general chapter elected Edmund Rice as their superior general.

Soon, Rice decided to move the generalate from Mount Sion to Dublin, where he planned to have the curia, a single novitiate and a model school close to the generalate. At a meeting in July 1826, Rice outlined his plans to Murray – by this time Archbishop of Dublin – who was most welcoming and supportive. He invited the Brothers to his own parish of St Mary's, where there were particularly pressing needs which the Catholic school in Liffey Street was incapable of meeting. Many children, in fact, were attending Protestant schools. On Murray's invitation, a number of parishes in the area had combined to form an education committee, whose members now hoped to fund Rice's venture, and they commissioned an architect to find a suitable location. In the meantime, the committee acquired a premises in Jervis Street, where the Brothers opened a school in June 1827. As in other locations, the three brothers did not restrict their activity to teaching; they embarked on a range of apostolic work, visiting the nearby hospital and instructing the Sisters of Charity in Gardiner Street in the skills of teaching large numbers.[26]

Just as the Christian Brothers experienced a welcome and support from Murray, so also the Jesuits, Vincentians and many others enjoyed his favour and encouragement. Prudent and cautious by temperament, Murray welcomed anyone who had something useful to offer the diocese and people of Dublin. He was prepared to provide advice and counsel, and to call on the assistance of his wealthy friends where a worthy organisation sought his help. Having done that, he was then reluctant to interfere or impose. Fr Meagher, his biographer, put it well in his devout style:[27]

> If appraised of any undertaking for God, he hearkened, he aided, he advised – but there his part terminated … he did not overwhelm with a load of patronage; he did not confound by the frequency of his interference; he left the matter in the hands to which providence had entrusted it – to the guidance of minds that had been inspired to originate it.

As well as the Christian Brothers, Murray gave great assistance to various women's congregations involved in educating girls, especially those from poor families. Indeed, nobody could give greater witness to his generosity and breadth of vision than the women founders of religious organisations during his long ecclesiastical career.

THE BISHOP AND MARY AIKENHEAD

As we have seen, it was during his visit to Cork with the O'Briens in 1807 that Daniel Murray first met Mary Aikenhead. Born in 1787 to Dr David Aikenhead, a Scots Protestant, and Mary Stacpoole, a Catholic, Mary was the eldest of four children. She was baptised into the Church of Ireland, and grew up in a middle-class society where Catholics and Protestants intermingled easily.

In 1801 her father died, and the following year she entered the Catholic Church. Soon after her father's death, she took responsibility for the family's financial concerns, for which she displayed a practical aptitude. By the time she met Murray, she was twenty years of age, and described as an amiable young woman, who had a sense of humour, was fond of reading, was intellectually quick, fluent in French, and accustomed to moving in both Catholic and Protestant social circles.[28] The occasion of their meeting in 1807 was the profession of Cecilia Ball, Anna Maria O'Brien's sister, at the Ursuline Convent in Cork. Anna Maria invited Mary to Dublin, and two years later, Mary stayed with the O'Briens at their town residence in the recently built Mountjoy Square.[29]

That year, 1809, Murray became coadjutor archbishop of Dublin. For some time he had had in mind the formation of a group of women who would devote themselves to improving the lot of poor people materially, socially and spiritually, especially by means of education. He discussed this with Anna Maria O'Brien and Mary Aikenhead. Mary expressed a keen interest, but felt that she would not be free to take part until her two sisters were finished school.

In August of that year, her mother died and Mary became head of the family. Murray kept in touch with her and urged her to write regularly to him. He made it clear, however, where her responsibilities lay: 'I never thought it right that you should finally commit yourself on that question until all the obstacles to the accomplishment of your wishes should be removed.' Meanwhile, he advised, 'under every discouragement, attend to your religious duties with all the fervour possible'.[30]

The next year, Mary visited the O'Briens once more, where the plan to form a new religious organisation was discussed in more detail. In 1811, she felt free to commit herself to the new body. Mary was enthusiastic for the venture, and she held lengthy discussions with Murray and Anna Maria O'Brien. She wondered who would lead the sisters, and was taken aback when informed that both Murray and Mrs O'Brien considered her to be the founding superior of the new community. She put off the decision. She consulted Dr Everard, then president of Maynooth, and after assurance from him and renewed assurance from Murray, she finally agreed.

She stipulated, however, that she and a first companion should undergo a novitiate year in a suitable convent to prepare them in the theory and practice of religious life. Murray had anticipated her concern and already had a place in mind: the Bar Convent in York, where Anna Maria Ball and her sister, Fanny Ball, had been at school, and where two of Murray's nieces were currently receiving their education. The convent belonged to the Institute of the Blessed Virgin Mary, a congregation founded by Mary Ward in the seventeenth century. Their rule was based on that of the Jesuits, which was seen as an exemplar of active religious life. Like the Jesuits, their general superior was answerable to the pope rather than to the diocesan bishop.

Archbishop Murray contacted and received the approval of the superior of the convent, Mrs Elizabeth Coyney, as she was known, and Dr Wilson, vicar apostolic of the northern district. On 24 May, Murray accompanied Mary Aikenhead and Alicia Walsh on their journey to York. He realised that for the two women it was a venture not only into foreign surroundings but also into a doubtful future. On 6 June 1812, they commenced their novitiate.[31]

During Mary's and Alicia's time in York, the Archbishop kept in touch by letter and by a number of personal visits. On 13 June 1812, just a week after he left them in York, and suspecting that they might be finding it difficult to settle, Murray wrote a chatty letter outlining some humorous experiences he had had in his travels. Then, saying that he should be back in Dublin in about a week, he asked Mary to write to him there. He requested a detailed account of how she was getting on. 'I am now more than ever interested in your happiness; a new link binds us together in most indissoluble friendship.' And he concluded, 'Give my regards to the little Murrays, and all my other acquaintances in your house.'[32]

Murray did not allow his exalted position to get in the way of his gift for friendship. He was warmly regarded by most of his priests, but he was particularly close to men such as Drs Patrick Everard, a fellow student from Salamanca days, James Doyle of Kildare and Leighlin and, of course, Peter Kenney of whom a contemporary wrote, 'the Archbishop and the Jesuit father were united by ties of intimate friendship.'[33] With women, too, he had many friends, but, as earlier indicated, his friendship with Anna Maria O'Brien and Mary Aikenhead was deeply felt and openly expressed. They shared an intense common interest and commitment.

The mention of the 'little Murrays' in the letter quoted above is of particular interest. They were his nieces, daughters of two of his brothers. He had special regard for them, and two of their letters to him have survived, handwritten in splendid copperplate. Letter-writing was considered an important social accomplishment in young ladies in the first half of the nineteenth century. Rules on how to begin and end a letter, helpful turns of phrase and careful penmanship were taught in many schools. There were instruction manuals which explained that one should use the person's title when addressing the recipient, and finish with 'Respectfully', or 'Faithfully' in the case of someone not well known. The Murray girls followed most of these rules. Archbishop Murray was addressed as 'Hon. and dear Uncle', and they finished with 'I remain your dutiful Niece', followed by their full name, Cecilia or Catherine Murray. In between they don't say much about their lives or study, beyond stating that they are happy at school. They ask him to write to them and – no doubt aware that their letters would be examined – convey the best wishes of the Revd Mother and community. The Archbishop is 'Dear Uncle', which, at least, suggests a certain ease of relationship with his teenage nieces.[34]

In August 1815, a little over three years after their arrival at the Bar Convent, Murray arrived in York to bring Mary Aikenhead and Alicia Walsh back to Dublin. He arranged that they would take temporary vows for one year. A house was obtained to serve as a convent in North William St, and the sisters were placed in the care of Fr Kenney. Under his guidance, they discerned that the rule of the York Convent was the one they wished to have for their congregation.

This was communicated to Murray who was in in Rome at the time, having been commissioned by a plenary meeting of the Irish bishops to plead the case against the veto with the Pope. Pleased with the choice, Murray petitioned the Pope for a rescript 'to erect a congregation of sisters in Dublin' who would live 'according to the Rule of the Convent of York', and with the addition of 'a fourth vow obliging them to devote their lives to the service of the poor'. The rescript, dated 30 November 1815, reached Dublin on 6 January 1816.

On his return in March 1816, Dr Murray had an amount of extra business awaiting him, including confirmations. The temporary vows of the two women were renewed on 1 September, and on 10 September they ventured out to visit the sick, becoming thereby the first 'walking nuns' in Ireland. On 9 December 1816, following an eight-day retreat conducted by Fr Kenney, Murray received the perpetual vows of Mary Aikenhead and Alicia Walsh. The following year, postulants – possible candidates for the congregation – began to arrive.[35]

The accumulation of poor diet and living conditions, on top of continuous work and much stress, led to a breakdown in Mary's health during 1818. She was ordered by her doctor and by Archbishop Murray to go away for rest and a change of air. Anna Maria O'Brien made her country house, Rahan Lodge in Co. Offaly, available to her. This, as it turned out, was a fortunate arrangement. The Jesuits had just opened a house in Tullabeg, located only three miles from Rahan Lodge. Because of his responsibilities for Jesuit activities in Ireland and North America, Fr Kenney was no longer readily available, but the young superior, Fr Robert St Leger, became a life-long friend of Mary. He took on the task of writing constitutions for her congregation, and he provided a detailed system for the training of novices.[36]

After two months, Mary returned to North William St, and then moved to a new convent at Stanhope Street, where she acted as mistress of novices. At this time, the sisters continued to grow in number, and in 1826, Mary was pleased to be invited to open a convent in her native Cork. The bishop, Dr Murphy, was a problem, however, since he considered government from Dublin as 'foreign government'. He was later so difficult that Mary feared he would induce some of the sisters to break away from the parent congregation and, as happened with the Christian Brothers, form a new institute in Cork.[37] She contacted Murray who expressed his concern, and appealed to the Sacred Congregation in Rome for protection. The result was a decree from the Holy See, dated 30 June 1836, stating that sisters who had already joined and those who would join in the future could not pass to any other religious order or institute without the special permission of the Holy See.[38]

Archbishop Murray was keen to have the sisters involved in the education of girls from poor families. He decided to spend a bequest he had received, of £4,000, on a new convent and schools in his cathedral parish. He approached Mary and she agreed. She placed the organisation of the new school in the hands of her own cousin, Sr Xavier Hennessy, 'a former society beauty, and one of the Hennessy brandy clan from North Cork'. Sr Xavier had a rude awakening when the school opened in 1830, however, with all the educational theory and management plans she had imbibed now seeming futile. Hundreds of unruly girls descended on the new premises hopeful of a free meal but with no desire for education. The children, unused to the discipline of a school, were highly resistant to law and order. Almost in despair, Sr Xavier consulted her mother general. Mary listened sympathetically and then said, 'What you need is a man. We'll get you a Christian Brother.'

The following Sunday, when visiting Jervis Street hospital, the sisters met Edmund Rice and his novice master, Br Duggan. Rice had a high opinion of Mary Aikenhead, and once said of her, 'She is such a woman as God raises up once perchance in a hundred years when there is a great work to be done'. He listened to their story and promised to send them Br Duggan. Sr Xavier was not impressed, however. She described Duggan as 'that little boy'. Duggan may have been small and may have looked young but he was, in fact, in his thirties and experienced. He came to Gardiner Street school and established order, but not without considerable effort. He had 'to whistle and shout' to secure silence in the classroom.

The girls attending the new school, it seems, had earlier been attending proselytising schools, and had been given strict injunctions by their parents to eat all they could get, take the clothes that were on offer and be sure to give plenty of trouble to the teacher! They did not know how to distinguish between the Sisters of Charity and Mrs Smyly's proselytising teachers, until Br Duggan came to the rescue. He soon taught the sisters the art of organising classes and controlling pupils. He conducted classes for the sisters for a number of months in the evenings. With his assistance, Sr Xavier compiled a 'Manual of School Government' which dealt with every department of school life. This was found to be of invaluable help for those who came after her. In the course of time, her reputation spread beyond the boundaries of Dublin to England and Scotland, and Mother Aikenhead entrusted to her the training of the sisters who were to be engaged in teaching. Many young lay women were also trained so that they might become teachers in Catholic schools.[39]

In 1830, Mary Aikenhead's health declined. She had difficulty walking and was in pain. The following year she became permanently invalided. Her doctor diagnosed a form of inflammation of the spine. She moved to a convent in Sandymount for the sea air. As her congregation spread to different parts of Ireland, to Preston in England and to Sydney in Australia, she governed for almost thirty years by her pen. With the assistance of her doctor, Dr O'Farrell, a much respected Dublin physician, she planned a Catholic hospital in the city. St Vincent's Hospital opened on St Stephen's Green, Dublin, in 1834, the first hospital in the English-speaking world to be owned and staffed by women.

In her later years, if the pain eased, she was occasionally conveyed to convents by wheelchair to mark a special event. Despite her affliction, she survived her great friends and advisers, Frs Kenney and St Leger, and also Archbishop Daniel Murray, for whom she grieved most of all as a friend and as 'Father and Founder of the Congregation'.[40] She died in 1858.

Daniel Murray was particularly close to Peter Kenney and Mary Aikenhead. Although he was less close to Ignatius Rice, as we have seen he was very supportive of him and his Christian Brothers, bringing them to Dublin for the first time. He was also supportive of Catherine McAuley, whom he assisted in the formation of the Mercy Sisters,[41] encouraging them in their work of teaching poor children in Dublin and across the English-speaking world.

NOTES

1 P. J. Corish, *Maynooth College, 1795–1995* (Dublin: Gill and Macmillan, 1995), p.50.
2 Kenney – Abp. Troy, 31 Oct. 1812, Irish Jesuit Archives (IJA), Kenney Letters, also a copy in brown notebook.
3 Trustee Returns, 1808, cit S. J. Connolly, *Priests and People in Pre-Famine Ireland, 1780-1845* (Dublin: Four Courts Press, 1982), p.39.
4 Eugene France O'Beirne, *An Accurate Account of the Papal College of Maynooth* (Hereford, 1840). O'Beirne was a former student who joined the Established Church.
5 Dr John Healy, *Maynooth College, 1795–1895* (Dublin, 1895), p.250.
6 Idem. pp.231f.
7 Idem, pp.223, 226–7.
8 Thomas Morrissey SJ, *As One Sent: Peter Kenney SJ, 1779–1841* (Dublin: Four Courts Press, 1996), p.95.
9 William Meagher, *Notices of the Life and Character of his Grace, Most Rev. Daniel Murray ...*, Notes, p.108.
10 Idem, pp.90–91, *italics mine*.
11 *Commission of Inquiry into Education* in Maynooth College, Appendix No.51, 20 Dec. 1825, p.411.
12 Wm. Meagher. Op. cit., Notes, p.108.
13 P. J. Corish. *Maynooth College, ...*, p.50.

14 D. Keogh, *Edmund Rice and the First Christian Brothers* (Dublin: Veritas, 2008), p.146.
15 Christian Brothers *Manual of School Government* (Dublin 1845), pp.16–17, 206–7, cit. D. Keogh. op. cit. p.123.
16 D. Keogh, *Edmund Rice, 1762–1844* (Dublin: Four Courts Press, 1996), p.48.
17 D. Keogh, *Edmund Rice...*, p.49.
18 W. Meagher. op. cit. Notes, p.94.
19 Archives Prop. Fide. Scritture Originali Riferite nelle Congregazione, 1818, vol. 919, F. 43-44; cit. M.C. Normoyle. *A Tree is Planted,* p.104.
20 W. Meagher, pp.57f; D. Keogh, *Edmund Rice and the Christian Brothers*, p.145.
21 Idem. *Ed. Rice and Christian Brothers*, p.150.
22 Idem. p.157.
23 Murray – Rice, 3 Oct. 1820, in M.C. Normoyle. (ed.) *Companion to A Tree that is Planted* , p.66. See Keogh. op. cit. p.157.
24 M. C. Normoyle, *A Tree that is Planted* (Dublin, 1975, private circulation), p.136.
25 Cardinal Fontana – Troy, 18 Sept. 1818, A.P.F. LDSC. 1819, vol. 300, E 642-3; cit. Keogh. *Ed. Rice and Christian Brothers*, pp.157–8.
26 D. Keogh, *Edmund Rice,1762–1844*, pp.71–2.
27 Donal Kerr. 'Dublin's Forgotten Archbishop, Daniel Murray…' in Kelly andKeogh. *Hist. of the Catholic Diocese of Dublin*, p.250.
28 S. A. *Mary Aikenhead, her Life, her Work...*, pp.95ff.
29 Idem, p.112.
30 Murray – Aikenhead (in Mrs O'Brien's hand), 6 Feb. 1810, cit. S.A. pp.126–7.
31 Idem, pp 134–7; and D. S. Blake. *Mary Aikenhead (1787-1858)*, Servant of the Poor (Dublin 2001), pp.25, 29.
32 S. A. *Mary Aikenhead...,* p.142.
33 Idem, p.132.
34 Catherine Murray – Bp. Murray, 15 Jan 1812; Cecilia Murray – Bp. Murray, 29 Jan. 1812, DDA, Troy Papers, Green file 6, nos.71, 73.
35 D. S. Blake, op. cit., pp.34–36. Alicia Walsh took the name Catherine in religion.
36 Idem, pp.38–39.
37 Idem, pp.41–43.
38 A Sister of Charity, *The Life and Work of Mary Aikenhead* (London 1924), p.92; cit. M. C. Normoyle, *A Tree is Planted*, p.162.
39 Blake, op. cit. pp.47–8; Annals of the Congregation, 1828–30, and Sr Agnus Murrogh-Bernard to Br P.J. Hennessy, 29 Sept. 1923, in Christian Brothers General Archives, 189/211, cit. D. Keogh. *Edmund Rice and the First Christian Brothers*, p.182.
40 Blake, op. cit. p.88; S. A. op. cit. pp.387–8.
41 M. C. Sullivan. *The correspondence of Catherine McAuley, 1881–1841* (Dublin & CUAP, 2004), pp.44, 45 n.29, 46–7.

CHAPTER 5

A Decisive Decade (1813–23)

Part I: Moving Towards Emancipation

While Murray was actively involved in Maynooth, the quest for Catholic Emancipation had grown in vigour and had been taken up by the people. Already in 1812, a number of public meetings had taken place. After one such gathering in Co. Clare, in March 1812, Daniel O'Connell had written to his wife, 'The spirit is got abroad and it would be impossible to allay it without full emancipation. You cannot conceive how anxious everybody is to press forward'.[1] At the end of 1812, Henry Grattan summoned his closest associates to his house in Co. Wicklow to draw up a relief bill that he would introduce in the next session of parliament.[2] On 24 May 1813, however, Grattan's Catholic Relief Bill was undermined by an amendment from the speaker, Charles Abbot, deleting the clause that permitted Catholics to sit in parliament. The amendment was carried by four votes, and the bill rendered fruitless.

During the discussions on the bill in committee, Canning and Robert Stewart (Viscount Castlereagh), both leading supporters of Emancipation, reintroduced the question of securities for the government in granting Emancipation. Grattan, anxious to maximise support for the bill, accepted the addition of clauses providing for a commission, made up mainly of Catholic peers, that would certify the loyalty of candidates for vacant episcopal sees and scrutinise all documents received from Rome in relation to the appointments. In Ireland, news of these clauses was received with hostility among both clergy and laity. On 26 May 1813, two days after the bill had been effectively neutralised by Abbot's amendment, the Irish bishops issued a joint pastoral letter rejecting its proposals as unacceptable.[3] A marked change had taken place both in the political climate and in the attitude of clergy and bishops. This was to become very obvious the following year, when Rome seemed to come down in favour of a government veto on the appointment of bishops.

THE VETO CONTROVERSY AGAIN

On 6 April 1814, Napoleon abdicated and the Pope was freed from captivity. Pope Pius VII re-entered Rome on 24 May 1814. Two months prior to that date, however, while the Pope was still in captivity, Giovanni Quarantotti, cardinal secretary of Propaganda Fide, issued a papal rescript granting a right of veto to the British monarch in the appointment of bishops. On 16 February, he informed Archbishop Troy of this change, and enclosed copies of the rescript. On the same date, Dr Poynter, representing the English Catholics, told Troy that, after much discussion, it had 'been decreed that the English Catholics may with gratitude and satisfaction accept the veto'.[4] Troy was dutiful in his acceptance of the Roman decision, and on 5 May, he sent a copy of Quarantotti's rescript with an accompanying note to Archbishop Thomas Bray of Cashel. His note was clear: '*Rescripta Roma venerunt. Causa finita est* ... Whatever be our sentiments on this subject, it is our duty to acquiesce in the decision of such authority, and set the example of submission.'[5] Troy asked Bray to send copies of the rescript to his suffragan bishops.

Archbishop Troy's attitude was not reflected in the priests and laity, or in most of his fellow bishops. At a meeting in Bridge Street chapel, on 12 May, eighty-two priests of the Dublin diocese adopted resolutions declaring that the Quarantotti Rescript wanted 'those authoritative marks whereby the mandates of the Holy See are known ... especially the signature of the Pope'. It was also resolved that granting a veto to an anti-Catholic government was 'at all time inexpedient', and that a veto was 'pregnant with incalculable mischief to the cause of Catholicity in Ireland'. As a way forward, the meeting suggested that for episcopal appointments 'arrangements of domestic nomination can be made among the clergy of Ireland'. Similar voices of the clergy were raised in resolutions during May in the dioceses of Ossory, Cloyne and Ross, Clonfert, Cork, Derry, Dromore and Limerick.[6]

On 19 May, there was a strong lay resolution from 'Irish Catholics' against the rescript. The bishops, at a joint meeting on 27 May, refused to accept Quarantotti's document as conveying the mind of His Holiness. Common to all three protests, if not explicitly stated, was a distrust of the policies and action of British governments towards the Irish Catholic population. The bishops, at their meeting on 27 May, deputed Murray to make representations at Rome on their behalf, in conjunction with Dr Milner, who was already there. Milner had arrived in Rome in late May 1814, and immediately began to lobby any cardinal or official he could contact. He had several meetings with Cardinal Litta, prefect of the congregation of Propaganda, and made clear to him, by his words and by copies of his writings, that he was devoted to the Holy See. This helped to counter his assertive, almost aggressive presentation of his case. Milner played a considerable part in reopening the whole question of the veto, as Archbishop Troy's agent, Argenti, reported on 25 June 1814.[7]

MISSION TO ROME AND PARIS

Murray's deputation on behalf of the bishops gave him an active role in a struggle that was to influence Irish history for almost 150 years. On one side of the struggle were those who accepted the right of the state to have an influence on Church affairs by means of a veto that would ensure the loyalty of bishops; this situation was widely accepted by Rome, and had been tolerated by the Irish hierarchy in return for the promise of emancipation prior to the Act of Union. On the other side were those who sought to have Church appointments completely separate from government influence and dependent only on Rome. Popular opinion, which was increasingly anti-English, was clearly on this side of the argument, and was to prevail. It introduced the alliance of an independent-minded Catholic Church with the leaders of strong national feeling, an alliance that was virtually to identify being Irish with being Catholic. It also led, at times, to a split in the Catholic community between supporters of violent assertiveness and a majority more in tune with the views of Church leaders.

Despite being deputed by the bishops on 27 May, Murray was still in Ireland early in July. Much had to be arranged to allow for his absence from Dublin, since Archbishop Troy had left most of the supervision of the archdiocese in Murray's hands. At the same time, the Irish bishops were becoming increasingly concerned about the restoration of the Irish colleges on the continent, and their proper functioning. They wished Murray, in addition to his Roman mission, to investigate the situation at the Irish College in Paris. During the years from the Revolution to the abdication of Napoleon, some of the colleges had been taken over by government departments. All had suffered materially, and those that subsequently reopened to students were faced with problems of discipline, uneven teaching and staff disunity. In July, the Irish bishops petitioned the Holy See for the restoration of the Irish colleges, and they deputed Murray to make this part of his brief.[8] A letter from Troy to Murray, undated but written in 1814, informed him that in dealing with the king's ministers, in relation to the Irish College in Paris, his powers were unlimited.[9]

It is not clear when Murray set out, or how long he spent in Paris en route to Rome. He certainly spent much time at the Irish College on his way home.

He had reached Rome almost certainly by the end of July. On 7 August, he and Milner were special guests at the Jesuit church, the Gesù, for the Pope's announcement of the restoration of the Society of Jesus. Pope Pius VII said Mass at the altar of St Ignatius in the presence of cardinals, the two bishops, some lay guests, and Jesuits assembled from many nations, some of them old and thinking they would never see this day. A number of young Irish Jesuits, who had completed their training in Sicily, were present. They were delighted to have Murray with them on such a memorable occasion.[10]

It was a difficult time for Murray as delegate in Rome. He knew few people, and there were particular cardinals to be met, as well as officials who were relevant to his mission. In all of this, Milner was a great support. Murray's command of languages, his natural ease and dignity and his respectful manner all combined to make a favourable impression, but it was not a propitious time to plead one's case, as an extant letter from Cardinal Litta to Archbishop Troy makes clear. On 11 October 1814, Litta explained that he had met Murray, whom he found delightful company. But, he goes on, owing to the 'universal shipwreck' the Church had just survived and the immense backlog of urgent business, he was sorry he could not have spent more time with 'that patient and docile prelate'.[11]

Murray made a lengthy submission to Litta against the veto. In the course of it, he conceded that fifteen years previously, ten prelates 'seduced by the fallacious promises of the Irish Secretary' were led to believe that some control over the appointment of bishops might be conceded, but having conferred with their brethren, and having heard 'the loud and almost universal clamour of the nation', they had the 'truly Christian fortitude to acknowledge their momentary delusion'.[12]

The pope, in response to advice from Cardinal Litta and other cardinals who believed that Quarantotti had acted ultra vires, ordered the whole issue to be studied afresh. Litta had been sufficiently impressed by Milner's and Murray's case to reproach Paul McPherson, the agent for the English bishops, for using such 'arts and industry' to wrench concessions from the elderly Quarantotti. He charged that the vicars apostolic had sacrificed religion 'to content the unlimited ambition of the Catholic laity'.[13]

Murray had plenty to occupy him. The Irish bishops, and particularly Archbishop Troy, had reminded him to use his time in Rome to have appointments made to a number of vacant dioceses. Murray was able to report on the 29 September 1814 that Dr Patrick Everard had been appointed coadjutor to Archbishop Thomas Bray of Cashel, that Dr Oliver Kelly had been appointed archbishop of Tuam, Dr George Thomas Plunkett to Elphin, Dr Peter Waldron to Killala,

Dr Kyran Marum to Ossory, and Dr Charles Tuohy to Limerick.[14] All had been recommended to Rome byArchbishop Troy.

Towards the end of October, Murray was planning to leave Rome. On 24 October, the Dominican Fr John Connolly, who acted as an agent for Troy and some other Irish bishops, informed Dr William Coppinger, of Cloyne and Ross, that he was sending rescripts for three parishes by Murray, 'who leaves Rome within a few days'. Connolly then added that 'nothing has been published about the Quarantotti Rescript or about its reception in Ireland'.[15]

In Rome, and subsequently in Paris, Murray also conducted business on behalf of the Irish Sisters of Charity. It is, perhaps, from his contacts with the sisters at this time that Aikenhead's biographer, Sarah Atkinson, was able to write that Murray and Milner 'were well received in Rome and had many audiences with the Pope'.[16] On such occasions, the delegates had the opportunity to convey the views and fears of the Irish bishops and people about the concession of the veto. In the event, the Quarantotti rescript was first restudied and suspended, but was not entirely removed from the agenda. The acceptability of the veto was to be reasserted in a formal letter from Cardinal Litta to Dr William Poynter, vicar apostolic in the London district, in April 1815.[17] Murray's overall experience as delegate was mixed. He had been received with respect and friendliness, but tangible results of his and Milner's efforts over many months were difficult to measure.[18]

From Rome, Murray travelled to Paris. He spent more than two months there, including Christmas, faced with conflicting reports and endeavouring to deal with a fraught and complex situation. Eventually he was to return home leaving the problems in the Irish College only partly resolved. They were to demand his time and attention once again later in the New Year. By the 6 February 1815, Murray was in London on the journey home. Milner, meanwhile, had stayed on in Rome, from where he informed Archbishop Troy, on 12 January 1815, that things remained as they had been when he arrived: 'European state affairs take precedence over spiritual matters'. He observed that he missed Murray, 'his manners, his talents, his upright character, and the very respectable way he was enabled to live added greatly to his exertions and to my own…'[19]

DEVELOPMENTS AT HOME

In Ireland, at the same time, Daniel O'Connell had become exercised at the absence of a clear-cut decision from Rome. He feared that the very able Vatican secretary of state, Ercole Cardinal Consalvi, was arriving at an understanding

Daniel O'Connell

with the British foreign secretary, Viscount Castlereagh, according to which, in return for papal approval of the veto, British support for the restoration of the Papal States would be forthcoming at the Congress of Vienna, which had just been convened. On 24 January 1815, O'Connell summoned an aggregate meeting of the Catholic laity of Dublin. At it, he audaciously addressed the Irish bishops and clergy, and even set out the temporal and spiritual limits of the Pope's authority and jurisdiction in the Irish Church. 'I deny', he asserted, 'that the Pope has temporal authority in Ireland.' He went on to insist that 'in spiritual matters too, the authority of the Pope is limited; he cannot, although his college of cardinals were to join him, vary our religion either in doctrine or essential discipline, in any respect.' O'Connell concluded by alluding to the veto: 'Even in non-essential matters, the Pope cannot vary it without the consent of the Irish bishops.'[20]

This remarkable outpouring by O'Connell had a markedly Gallican ring about it, which was deeply unwelcome in Rome, and was a likely source of unease to Archbishop Troy and a number of the Irish bishops. Such oratory, when it came to be coupled with persistent efforts to pressurise the episcopacy by means of strong populist pronouncements at aggregate lay meetings, resulted in Murray maintaining a distance between himself and O'Connell's movement.

Meantime, Murray was caught up in an accumulation of work relating to the diocese, the Sisters of Charity, the Christian Brothers' schools and a range of correspondence from home and abroad. Among his immediate concerns was the collection of funds for a Catholic Metropolitan Church, the planning for which had commenced in 1812 and which Archbishop Troy was keen to see implemented during his episcopate. On 28 March 1815, the foundation-stone of the building that was later to be known as Dublin's Catholic Pro-Cathedral was laid in Marlborough St.

In the midst of Murray's domestic preoccupations, Milner kept him informed of any developments in Rome regarding the veto. On 24 February 1815, it was his view that the Quarantotti Rescript was not receiving papal approval. He assured Murray that he missed him and that he was sorry to hear that his visit to France was not proving successful.[21] A more uplifting message came from a gentleman called Daniel Philips, who indicated an additional dimension to Murray's visit to Rome and Paris. He congratulated him on his conduct of affairs on the continent and on his reception by various courts.[22]

WIDER CONCERNS

At home, meanwhile, feelings about Quarantotti's rescript had become so much a matter of public interest that, on Murray's return, the coal porters of Dublin organised a public celebration for him. Acknowledging their welcome from the balcony of his house at 39 North Cumberland St, Murray commended to their prayers the urgent cause of the liberty of the Church, even in Ireland; and in this connection, he was overjoyed to announce that Pope Pius VII had revoked the suppression of the Society of Jesus, which had been brought about by the enemies of Christianity.[23]

The continent and its courts had by then, however, been thrown into shock and anxiety once more by the news of Napoleon's escape from the island of Elba on 1 March. He arrived in France six days later. Once the news spread, the effect was dramatic. In Rome, the Pope and curia moved once again. On Spy Wednesday, in some disarray, they made their way by Viterbo, Florence, Pisa and Leghorn to Genoa, which was garrisoned by British troops and blocked off by the British navy. Milner tenaciously followed the papal entourage, hoping to get an answer for the Irish bishops. Repulsed again and again by Cardinal Litta, he was eventually dismissed by him. Reporting on this to Murray, on 21 May 1815, Milner mentioned that Dr Poynter and the shrewd agent, McPherson, had stayed with the papal party.[24]

On 26 April, Cardinal Litta issued a formal letter, addressed to Dr Poynter, stating the Pope's readiness to agree to a veto to the British sovereign in the event of Catholic Emancipation being granted. Regarding this 'Genoese Letter', as it became known, there is extant in Archbishop Troy's papers a letter from Litta, also dated 26 April 1815, explaining that his letter to Poynter was, in effect, a formal repudiation of Quarantotti's rescript. The right to scrutinise documents between the Holy See and the local Churches was excluded, and the oaths of allegiance were more innocuous than those accepted by Quarantotti. The Genoese Letter was not formally published for another eight months because of concern, on the part of Troy and Poynter, at the likely responses to the document.

On the wider stage, the Congress of Vienna concluded its deliberations on 9 June. Nine days later, Napoleon was finally defeated at the battle of Waterloo, and he abdicated, for the second time, on 22 June. Britain was on the crest of a wave of achievement and adulation, and it was more difficult than ever for the small voice of Irish Catholics to be heard. Murray, nevertheless, was determined to keep opposing the veto. He believed that Rome was open to change, and that he had the contacts to operate effectively there. Grounds for such expectations were suggested by Milner in his letter to Murray on 21 May: 'Cardinal Litta, the Marquis of Pallevicini, and your other friends at Rome continue to speak of your Grace with the utmost respect and regard'.[25] Milner signed his letter 'your ever faithful and affectionate friend'. Murray's links with powerful foreign connections, and his readiness to avail of them, were illustrated some weeks later in his request on behalf of a certain 'M. Guiness' to the Archbishop of Rheims, Angelos Talleyrand – a powerful family name in Europe during the first quarter of the nineteenth century. Archbishop Talleyrand replied on 17 August 1815. On receipt of Dr Murray's letter, he had written at once to his nephew, the Prince de Talleyrand, in favour of M. Guiness. 'Dr Murray's recommendation is enough to convince Archbishop Tallyrand of the right M. Guiness has to the King's bounty. He was happy to oblige Dr Murray.'[26]

By late July and early August, rumours had become persistent that Rome would grant the veto. Murray was deeply disappointed by the Genoese Letter and believed that 'the Irish prelates should make a strong protest now'.[27] That would require a return delegation to Rome. The need for a delegation to the continent was further indicated by urgent requests for assistance from the Irish College in Paris. On 12 August, Dr Walsh, of the Irish College, writing to Dr Everard, emphasised the importance of retaining the college. He mentioned that Fr Paul Long, former president of Maynooth, who had become president of the Irish College after the fall of Napoleon, had begged Murray to return and rescue the college from a usurper, Richard Ferris. Walsh asked Everard to accompany Murray to save not only the Irish College in Paris but also the Irish College in Bordeaux.[28]

THE BISHOPS' RESOLUTIONS

On 23 August 1815, Murray relayed to the conference of the Irish Catholic bishops an account of his late mission to Rome, and 'conveyed to them the feelings of the authorities in Rome on the … question of the veto'. He explained that 'it was all too evident' that the papal court, being now under greater obligation than ever to the British government, was disposed to make some concession to the ministry: that, in fact, Pope Pius VII, who owed the restoration of his dominions mainly to Britain, might be inclined to grant a veto to the king'.[29] The following day, the bishops adopted a series of resolutions against the veto for submission to the Holy See, and Bishops Murray and John Murphy of Cork were deputed to represent the episcopal conference in Rome.

Regarding the problems in Paris, Dr Patrick Everard, coadjutor of Cashel, was deputed to assist Fr Paul Long in his negotiations with the king's ministers concerning the property of the Irish colleges in France. On the eve of departure, however, Everard fell ill,[30] which meant that Murray and Murphy were required to visit Paris in his place.

As they listened and deliberated about the veto, the bishops were under immense external pressure. O'Connell had called an aggregate meeting for the Catholic laity on 21 August, two days before the bishops' conference. It was resolved at the meeting that a committee, including O'Connell, would meet with the bishops next day to convey their hostility to the veto. It was also resolved to call another aggregate meeting of the laity on 29 August, five days after the episcopal conference, to review the bishops' resolutions.[31]

The bishops issued a joint declaration declaring the veto inadmissible. Among their statements was a remonstrance to His Holiness and an address to the Prince Regent. Dr Murray was entrusted with the task of laying before the Supreme Pontiff, in 'express terms', the sentiments of the Irish Church and people.[32] The express terms were direct and demanding, and they were to occasion disquiet and hostility in Rome. The Irish bishops, in a blend of religious and national emotion, put aside past differences to unite on this question. The change that had taken place among them in less than a decade was personified in the reaction of Archbishop O'Reilly of Armagh. In 1808 he had been a supporter of a veto, but in 1815 he was reported to have said that if he were required to participate in the consecration of a bishop elected under any such arrangement, he would resign his see.[33]

To appreciate the directness and virtual defiance of the bishops' resolutions, it is necessary to view some of their printed statement. On 24 August 1815, 'The Roman Catholic Prelates of Ireland unanimously agreed' the following:

> *Resolved:*
> That it is our decided and conscientious conviction that any power granted to the Crown of Great Britain of interfering, directly or indirectly, in the appointment of bishops for the Catholic Church in Ireland, must essentially injure, and eventually subvert, the Roman Catholic religion in this country.
>
> *Resolved:*
> That with this conviction … unalterably impressed on our minds … we should consider ourselves betraying that portion of the Church entrusted to our care by the Holy Ghost did we not declare most unequivocally that we will at all times, and under all circumstances, deprecate and oppose in every canonical and constitutional way, any such interference.
>
> *Resolved:*
> That though we sincerely venerated the Supreme Pontiff as visible head of the Church, we do not conceive, that our apprehension for the safety of the Roman Catholic Church in Ireland can or ought to be removed by

> any determination of his Holiness, adopted, or intended to be adopted, not only without our concurrence, but in direct opposition to our repeated resolutions, and the very energetic Memorial presented on our behalf, and so ably supported by our Deputy, the Most Revd Dr Murray, who, in that quality, was more competent to inform his Holiness of the real state and interests of the Roman Catholic Church in Ireland, than any other with whom he is said to have consulted.

Two shorter resolutions followed, and all were signed by Oliver Kelly, President, and followed by the signatures of all the prelates.[34]

In the wake of the bishops' conference, Murray set in train the arrangements required in the diocese during his absence, and on 7 September he and Murphy departed for Rome.[35] As they left they were in no doubt as to the mood and expectation of the Catholic laity led by O'Connell. At the aggregate meeting on 29 August, O'Connell exulted that 'we have shown how powerless the Pope is to alter, without the assent of our bishops, the discipline of the Church'. Moreover, the Catholic Board, on the same date, decided to send three deputies of their own to Rome to present a remonstrance to the Pope.[36] Subsequently only one was sent, Richard Hayes, a Franciscan friar, who was to cross swords with Murray and Murphy.

AT THE IRISH COLLEGE IN PARIS

Very little information is available about the journey of Murray and Murphy. They spent some time in England. Then, from London, they travelled to Paris, where they spent a considerable time dealing with the problems of the Irish College in Paris. As the college had already occupied much of Murray's time and attention, and would continue to do so, it is relevant to place in context the situation as he found it.

After the turmoil of the revolutionary years, the French government, in 1801, united the remaining Irish, Scots and English colleges – and their revenues – into a single legal entity, the British Establishments. This led to the Collège des Irlandais, on rue du Cheval Vert, opening its doors to students in 1805. The state established a *bureau gratuit*, which had responsibility for the temporal affairs of the college.

The Irish bishops were unwilling to send students to Napoleonic France, and consequently the rector of the college, Revd John B. Walsh – who, together with Revd Charles Kearney had kept the college in existence during the Revolution – opened the premises to the children of Irish, English and Scottish exiles in

France, as well as to French boarders. Walsh gradually came under pressure from a number of sources but particularly from a section within the émigré Irish community, which challenged his authority. In 1812, they succeeded in having him replaced by a former priest with strong connections to the Napoleonic regime, Richard Ferris. The fall of Napoleon, however, and the restoration of the Bourbon monarchy in the person of Louis XVIII, revived the battle between Walsh and Ferris for the control of the Irish College.

Walsh, as has been seen, corresponded with some Irish bishops. Realising that an opportunity was present to regain control of the college, they had sent the experienced Fr Paul Long as their chosen rector. Murray, on his arrival in the college, encountered a tangled situation. In the negotiations with the French government, the fact that the Irish College was legally part of the British Establishments was a complicating factor. Within the staff and among the students there were political conflicts and different loyalties, while good order and sound teaching needed to be established. During his stay, Murray grew in esteem for Paul Long who, in 1816, was to gain French government recognition of his position. There remained, however, a constant opposition lobby seeking the restoration of Richard Ferris as rector.[37]

DISAPPOINTMENT IN ROME

Because of the delay in Paris, Murray did not reach Rome until late November 1815. Argenti, the Irish bishops' agent, informed Archbishop Troy on 25 November that 'all the papal tribunals were closed for holidays' and that 'Dr Murray arrived, bringing Mr Kendrick with him'.[38] As Murray and Murphy waited for their interview with the Pope, Murray busied himself establishing a sound basis for the Irish Sisters of Charity. On 6 December, he wrote to 'Mrs Aikenhead' in North William St, telling her that he had received permission for the Sisters of Charity to function under the jurisdiction of Troy and Murray according to the rules of the Convent of York, but with the addition of the fourth vow binding the sisters to the service of the poor.[39]

In Murray and Murphy's meeting with His Holiness, any sense of joy at the concession to the Sisters of Charity was soon dissipated by the coolness of their reception as delegates of the Irish bishops. The bishops' strong resolutions were not well received. The delegates met an implacable Pope, seemingly quite committed to the veto. They also experienced that Ercole Cardinal Consalvi, the powerful secretary of state, was a major voice supporting the veto, and that he was diplomatically interested in pleasing Britain.

The situation was such that the delegates felt there was nothing more they could do in Rome. Their disappointment was accentuated when Consalvi presented them with a letter from His Holiness for the Irish bishops. On opening it, they were taken aback by its tone and contents. Subsequently, on 9 January 1816, Murray wrote sharply to the Cardinal in reply, saying that he and Dr Murphy had read with astonishment the letter they had been given to bring back to the Irish bishops. Having received the final response of His Holiness to the Irish bishops' remonstrance, they had regarded their mission to Rome ended. They could not, however, bring back and publish this letter to the Irish bishops because it would endanger the cause of religion in Ireland, especially as their former mission to Rome regarding the veto had failed to produce the expected effect.[40] In addition, Murray pointed out that it was not true, as the Cardinal's letter stated, that he had had recourse to another tribunal, and he also refuted other falsehoods and calumnies circulating about them in Rome.

On the same date as the letter to Consalvi, Murray and Murphy replied to a rather belligerent letter from Fr Hayes, the representative of the Catholic Board. Hayes reported that he had had a number of meetings with Cardinal Litta, and had won him over to accepting domestic nominations of episcopal candidates instead of the unwelcome veto system. Hayes criticised Murray and Murphy for leaving Rome and not staying on to represent their case, and he warned them that he would make their failing public on returning to Ireland. In this letter, Hayes did not mention that he had presented Litta with a lengthy analysis of the Irish Church, which contained a sustained attack on Archbishop Troy's undue influence and suggested that Troy had engaged in certain abuses in favour of his relations. This document appears to have sown doubts in Litta's mind, and subsequently Archbishop Troy's influence was impaired in Rome.[41]

In their response, Murray and Murphy expressed surprise at his criticism of their leaving Rome. Once they had presented the bishops' remonstrance to the Pope, they wrote, their mission was ended. Fr Hayes's threat to publish a calumnious letter in Ireland would not intimidate them. They would explain to the prelates who sent them how they had carried out their mission. They reminded Fr Hayes that his attempts to calumniate them in Rome had failed, and that when the truth became known in Ireland it could only reflect badly on him.

Hayes replied on 17 January 1816. He had received their letter which, he claimed, misunderstood what he had said. He then commented that they had departed Rome leaving the matter of the veto no better than at the time of the Genoese Letter. Their refusal to bring back Consalvi's letter, so insulting to Irish prelates and people, was a mistake. They should have stayed and protested. 'The Pope is upset at the ferment in Ireland', Hayes continued. 'He has ordered

Consalvi to write another, different reply.' In Hayes's view, His Holiness did not regard his concession of the veto as an ecclesiastical decision.

Finally, Hayes charged Murray and Murphy with coldness towards him. He had certain charges to make against them, but not Dr Milner, in Irish newspapers. At the end, he enclosed a letter for Dr Long in Paris.[42] There was an element of truth in Hayes's letter that added to the delegates' sense of failure and to their resentment of Hayes.

THE JOURNEY HOME

Murray and Murphy made their way to Paris where there was still work to be done. While there, the Pope, on 1 February, sent them a revised letter addressed to the archbishops and bishops of Ireland. Drs Murray and Murphy, he declared, had presented him with a copy of the resolutions passed by the Irish prelates at their conference in August 1815. He was grieved and concerned at the manner in which Cardinal Litta's letter was received in Ireland, especially by the bishops. He stated that the concessions he had made regarding the veto simply followed the way laid down by his predecessors. The Irish bishops' fears, he assured them, were groundless. He mentioned some of the benefits granted to the Irish Catholics by the British government, and observed that even should the London government do its worst, the veto, as he had proposed it, could not injure or destroy religion.[43]

On 10 March, while in London, Murray and Murphy composed their report for the Irish bishops and sent it to Troy and the other archbishops. In it they stated that, to their mortification, they were obliged to say that their mission to Rome had not produced the effect which their lordships had anticipated. The remonstrance had not rendered the Holy Father 'fully sensible of the great extent of danger to which the Catholics would be exposed in Ireland', were he to grant to the British government what was proposed in Cardinal Litta's letter. As a result, it was 'the intention of His Holiness to abide by the terms of that letter, should full emancipation be first conceded to the Catholics of Ireland'. The delegates added that it was their duty to observe that, if a security were demanded by the government against the supposed danger of foreign influence, they believed that His Holiness would condescend to give his sanction to what is termed domestic nomination instead of the 'odious measure' of veto, which would open 'an inexhaustible source of discontent in the public mind of Ireland'. His Holiness would not make any proposal of this kind to the British government. Should His Majesty's ministers signify their satisfaction with this arrangement, however,

Murray and Murphy had 'no hesitation in declaring' their 'decided conviction that it would be obtained without difficulty'.

They concluded their report by asserting that 'they employed every means which the most ardent zeal would dictate to give effect to the remonstrance of the Irish prelates', and that they were 'among those who deplore most bitterly, that our efforts' had 'not produced a more favourable result'. They enclosed the Pope's reply to the bishops' remonstrance, and requested that copies of all their enclosures be sent to the suffragan bishops.

The next stage in the veto saga was to be decided by the bishops at a national synod scheduled for Kilkenny on 24 April 1816. Before that, however, the response of Archbishop O'Reilly of Armagh to the delegates' report, on 28 March, gave some indication of what the joint episcopal response might be. He was amazed, he said, at the attitude adopted by the Pope to the 'humble and earnest petition of a whole people, bishops, clergy and laity'. He found it hard to bring himself to Christian submission. He feared the effect this would have on religion, but he was certain that Drs Murray and Murphy could not have done more than they did. He was sending Murray's report to his suffragans, and also notice of the April meeting.[44] Dr Milner informed Murray on 17 March that he had written to Cardinal Litta, lamenting the failure of the two bishops' mission to Rome and that 'the Holy See had exchanged the dominion of Napoleon … for that of Castlereagh'.[45]

A DISGRUNTLED PRELATE

Murray, as he conveyed to Archbishop Troy, deplored 'most bitterly' the failure of their mission. He appears, indeed, to have been personally seared by his second Roman experience – the misrepresentation and innuendoes, the obduracy and lack of understanding in face of coherent argument, the dominance of pragmatism. Accordingly, when he learned on his return that a number of Irish Catholic aristocrats had held a meeting on the 13 February and had signed a petition on behalf of the Roman Catholics of Ireland that publicly welcomed a royal veto, he was incensed. The normally 'patient and docile prelate', to whom expressions of anger seemed foreign, availed of the most solemn day in the Church's liturgy, Good Friday, to make his displeasure felt. In quiet, incisive tones, speaking of the passion of Christ, he commented:

> To this bound and suffering victim I would now implore the attention of those misguided Catholics who seem willing to impose new and disgraceful bonds, not indeed on his sacred person, but on his mystical

> body, that is, his Church, which was ever more dear to him than his personal liberty – more dear to him than even his life … And what virtuous Catholic would consent to purchase the chance of temporal advantages at the price of such a real spiritual calamity.[46]

These remarks on such a solemn occasion, from a man noted for peace and reasonableness, caused a minor sensation and delighted those against the veto.[47] On 14 April, Daniel O'Connell wrote from Cork to his wife, 'Dr Murray's sermon delights us all here. He has marked the name of Judas on the vetoists'.[48] As might be expected, Lords Trimelstown and Bellew and other Catholic gentlemen, whom O'Connellites termed, the 'seceders', protested to Archbishop Troy. On 17 April they informed him that they were mentioned from the pulpit by his coadjutor. They requested him to state if there was anything in their petition, which they enclosed, that a Roman Catholic might not sign.[49] The Archbishop replied that they could sign their petition without breaking the law of the Church or incurring his displeasure.[50] Grattan duly laid the petition of the 'seceders' before the House of Commons, but it was quickly dismissed.[51]

Two days later, as if to round off the Roman mission on a more positive note, Murray received an appreciative letter from the Cork Catholic Association. It contained a resolution thanking Murray and Murphy for their exertions in undertaking the long journey to Rome in midwinter 'to preserve the integrity of our religion and our communion with the centre of Catholic unity by disabusing His Holiness of the impression which our enemies had endeavoured to make upon his mind'.[52]

THE NATIONAL SYNOD AND THE POPE'S LETTER

At the National Synod, on 24 April 1816, the letter of His Holiness was read and discussed. In the bishops' subsequent letter to the Pope, they regretted that he still considered his concession of a veto to make little difference. Their experience of English government over three centuries led them to think otherwise. The Holy Father had pointed out the benefits Catholics had received during the reign of the recent kings, 'but the granting of these reliefs was unavoidable as they were given from ulterior, political motives of security. The granting of the veto would mean that the British government will go further than demanding a say in the appointment of bishops; next they will want to dictate the appointment of parish clergy, awarding pensions to the loyal and nothing to others. They, the Irish bishops, do not think that emancipation itself should be won at such a price.' They proposed, in the place of veto, a form of domestic nomination. Their letter was adjusted to be far more respectful than their previous remonstrance.

Murray, who sent the letter through Cardinal Litta, also took care to enquire after Litta's health, who he knew had been unwell. He explained that the bishops had also resolved to petition both Houses of Parliament, through Lord Donoughmore and Sir Henry Parnell, 'praying them to resist any application which may be made to the legislature to give to the Crown … any *legal power* to interfere in the nomination of Roman Catholic bishops in Ireland'.[53] Murray was also careful to point out that the projected domestic nomination would require that all chosen candidates take a solemn oath of allegiance to His Majesty.

CARDINAL LITTA'S REPLY AND DOMESTIC NOMINATION

The reply to Murray and the Irish bishops was not sent until 29 August 1816, when Cardinal Litta wrote to Murray thanking him for his letter. He apologised for the delay, and then reported that he had given the bishops' letter to His Holiness, who was much more satisfied with it than he was with the previous letter. Are the bishops and the diocesan clergy, Litta asked, all agreed on the significance of domestic nomination? People little animated by true patriotism could profit by dissensions that might arise, so it was most important that the views of the Catholics should not be divergent on this matter.[54]

Two months later, on 28 October 1816, Murray responded to Litta's two questions.[55] Would the British government be satisfied with domestic nomination in place of the veto? To this Murray replied that if the government were not satisfied, then the proposal would fall. As to what was to be understood by 'domestic nomination', Murray replied at some length. He began by making clear that 'whatever the Holy See deigns to expound as to the kind of domestic nomination it would be ready to approve in the event of emancipation, we will be satisfied with it'. Since Litta had asked if the bishops and priests were agreed on the meaning of domestic nomination, he, Murray, on the advice of Archbishop Troy, had researched the matter. He had written to the bishops and had spoken to some of the most learned and zealous of the priests, and had come up with the rough sketch of the plan he was now submitting to His Eminence. No plan will please everybody, but this will please the greater part.

He then outlined the plan. On a vacancy occurring, the chapter of the diocese would name three subjects that it believed to be the most worthy to replace the defunct bishop. Before commencing the election, each canon priest of the chapter would swear that he would not vote for anyone whom he believed might be disloyal to His Majesty, or anyone unworthy to be raised to the episcopate.

The list of the elected would then be submitted to the bishops of the province, as convened by the archbishop. The majority of the bishops, so convened, would have a right of veto with regard to the three chosen names. Before exercising that right, however, the bishops would have to take an oath similar to that of the canons, but with the addition that they would not reject anyone on the list except 'this be only for reasons purely of conscience'. The list of the three individuals, as approved by the bishops and the chapter of the vacant diocese, would then be forwarded to Rome 'so that the Holy See may deign to choose one among them for appointment to the vacant diocese'.

Murray then observed judiciously, 'No one understands better than your Eminence that this plan ought to satisfy a most jealous government with regard to the loyalty of the bishops, and at the same time it would give to His Holiness the greatest assurance that it would place only worthy subjects in the dioceses of Ireland'.

Murray added a question and an urgent request. 'Would the Holy Father,' he wondered, 'really approve a law that would give us emancipation conditional on domestic nomination such as I have just marked out?' He then asked Litta to send a short and confidential reply to the archbishop of Dublin or to himself. It was a surprisingly naïve request to make to a leading cardinal in the Roman curia, even if, as seems to be the case, Murray viewed him as a friend.

THE CLOSE OF A DIFFICULT YEAR

A final letter on the veto in 1816 came, appropriately, and in familiar tones, from Dr John Milner. Writing on 8 December, he was grieved that Drs Murray and Murphy had not answered his repeated letters, and he wondered if he had offended them. He was working day and night to defeat the machinations of those who were bent 'on enslaving and ruining our insular Churches'. He would die happy opposing Castlereagh, Canning and company. 'I will go to London at the time of the contest', he wrote, and he hoped that Murray could come also. He would take lodging for them both. 'You and I together, under the protection of the Most High, will defeat all our combined enemies.'[56] It was a challenging, if romantically defiant, note on which to end a very difficult year for those seeking Catholic Emancipation.

Even O'Connell seemed subdued. He had become the dominant figure within the Catholic agitation, based on ability, exceptional energy, oratorical skill, political judgement and a flamboyant political style. His capacity for brinkmanship and intimidation accorded well with the militant mood of a large section of the Catholic population. The Catholic bishops, as noted, did not escape his hectoring style, but O'Connell depended on publicity to be effective. In 1816, however, the government, using the wide power that the law provided for the suppression of hostile newspaper comment, closed press publicity to him. The *Evening Post*, well disposed to him, was silenced. Other newspapers were unwilling to publish anything that might expose them to prosecution.[57]

On top of all that, 1816 had been a year without a summer and the autumn brought no relief. A report from Drogheda in October spoke of ducks swimming among the oats and potatoes in the flooded fields.[58]

Part II: Emerging Divisions

The 'time of the contest' envisaged by Milner seems to have been Henry Grattan's proposal in the House of Commons in 1817, calling for a committee to enquire into Catholic claims. There was talk of the issue of the veto arising, and the Irish bishops were sufficiently concerned that they elected Bishops Murray and Everard as their deputies in London. Milner was delighted at their appointment and invited them to stay with him.[59] The proposal was defeated by 245 to 221 votes, but the margin was an improvement on previous motions. Milner, writing on 2 July 1817, thanked God that the exertions of the two Irish prelates 'warned off the threatened danger (of a veto), at least for the present', and he sent his regards to the Irish bishops. He would 'always respect their stand, to which English Catholics owe so much'.[60] A day later, in Dublin's Clarendon St chapel, the tired Catholic Association gave way to a new Catholic Board.

TENSION WITH THE CATHOLIC BOARD

The first meeting of the reorganised Catholic Board took place on 12 July. At that stage news and rumours had reached Dublin about the expulsion from Rome of the Board's representative, Fr Richard Hayes. At the meeting, O'Connell moved 'that a sub-committee be appointed to prepare … a Letter of Complaint and a Remonstrance to the See of Rome, upon the indignity offered by the temporal authorities of the court of Rome to the very respectable delegate of the Catholics of Ireland, the Revd Mr Hayes'.[61] On 19 July, Edward Hay, the secretary of the Catholic Board, was instructed to forward the Board's motion to Cardinal Litta for presentation to the Pope.

Furthermore, O'Connell wrote and sent a circular letter to the bishops, and a separate circular to the clergy.[62] His letter to the bishops bespoke a type of Gallican autonomy. It expressed the alarm of the Board at the dangers to the Irish Church suggested by the expulsion of Richard Hayes from Rome. The Board objected to Catholic discipline in Ireland being submitted to Propaganda Fide 'as if this were a mere missionary country without a national Church'. The bishops were urged to take steps 'to obtain the concurrence … of the pope in such a concordat as shall establish fully and forever Domestic Nomination [in the appointment of bishops] which shall secure institution after each election, and confirm the Irish Church in her national independence'.[63]

Feeling it necessary to respond firmly to O'Connell's pressure and strategic intimidation, Archbishop Troy and Murray sent a joint reply to Edward Hay, as secretary of the Board, and then presented it for publication. 'To the matters urged on their attention', they explained that they deemed it proper not to respond further than to express their conviction 'that those Prelates need not the admonition of the Catholic Board to be deeply impressed with a sense of the awful trust' which, in virtue of their sacred office, had been invested in them, 'and that they will be ever ready to pursue with a firm and steady step the path of duty which their conscience shall point out.'[64]

The *Dublin Evening Post*, acting as the voice of the Catholic Board, declared that this was not what 'the Catholics of Ireland had a right to expect from *Doctor Murray*. He opposed the veto from the pulpit, and when the crisis had come, as it has, when addressed, as he was, respectfully, by his flock, he should not have given a cold, formal and equivocal answer to their representation. We speak out – this is no time for equivocation – no time for temporising; and Doctor Murray may be assured, that the Catholics of Ireland *expect from him*, and speedily, a more decisive, a more distinct, a more direct line of conduct.'[65] The paper went on to contrast the response of the archbishops of Dublin to the enthusiastic and appreciative replies of Drs O'Shaughnessy of Killaloe, Marum of Ossory, Coppinger of Cloyne and McLoughlin of Raphoe.[66]

Murray, and especially Archbishop Troy, were used to having considerable influence in the appointment of bishops. The current system was now in danger of being eclipsed if, under domestic nomination, it was replaced by the diversified voice of the clergy, influenced by public pressure and intercession. Cardinal Litta had warned about this and, following the decision of the cardinals of Propaganda, he was to emphasise the difficulties present in domestic nomination and to express regret that some bishops were deceived.[67] Already, on 16 March 1816, Archbishop Troy had made explicit his fears regarding such a system. He wrote strongly to Litta about the assembly of priests at Waterford, who came together to recommend a successor to the late bishop, John Power.[68] He complained that 'not only the parish priests, as was the custom, but the curates, all the regulars, and even the seminarians, including the deacons and subdeacons, assembled together in the principal chapel in Waterford and *postulated* (demanded) for the Rev Mr Flannery, the parish priest of Clonmel, as successor to the bishop, he having the majority of the secret ballot'. 'Hitherto', Troy explained, 'where there was not a chapter, the recommendation, not the postulation, belonged only to the parish priests and the provincial bishops. To extend this to others, it seems to me, is an intolerable abuse, productive of cabals and democracy in the government of the Church, an act encouraging the laity to meddle in ecclesiastical affairs, as they unfortunately interfered recently on the occasion of the royal nomination to the episcopacy. It is very necessary', he advised, 'to remedy this dangerous innovation'.

O'Connell had broken new ground by bringing the populace into political and ecclesiastical affairs in a coordinated manner. It was a development that was difficult to control and was open to major abuse. Troy was uncomfortable with the development as it had been used regarding the royal nomination or veto, and he clearly feared a similar mass involvement in domestic nomination. It was the manner in which domestic nomination was exercised in Waterford that concerned him, rather than the controlled form of domestic nomination proposed by Murray, his coadjutor archbishop. The situation in Waterford – in terms of the range of people involved, and the postulation that their choice be accepted – appeared to greatly limit the role of the bishops and of the pope himself.

O'CONNELL'S EXPLOSIVE RESPONSE

O'Connell, for his part, was angry and vituperative at what he viewed as the Archbishops' flouting of his control and authority. In a letter to Edward Hay, as secretary of the Catholic Board, he interpreted the Archbishops' response as 'support for the veto', and he attributed Murray's involvement to Archbishop Troy, 'the pliant Trojan'. 'Their publication of their letter to you', O'Connell judged sweepingly, 'was intended to intimidate other bishops from that zealous opposition to the veto which the people look for and the times require.' He was dismayed at Hay for 'not instantly counteracting the poison by publishing all such replies as you received reprobatory of the veto and favourable to domestic nomination'. He continued in the same vein, 'As the war began at the other side, you ought at once to have published every publishable letter.' He then urged Hay to publicise the warm acquiescence to the address of the Catholic Board by

Bishops Coppinger of Cloyne and O'Shaughnessy of Killaloe.

As regards Murray's defection – for that is how he saw it – O'Connell expressed astonishment and disparagement:

> I am, I own, greatly shocked at the part Dr Murray is taking. I had the highest opinion of him and the greatest respect for him. But I see he wishes, with Dr Troy's See, to inherit the patronage of the Catholic Church of Ireland. Oh! It is melancholy to think of his falling off – he who compared the vetoists to Judas.

'As to Dr Troy,' O'Connell continued contumaciously, 'better could not be expected from him. His traffic at the Castle is long notorious. But the sneer at the Board and the suppressed anger of those prelates would be ludicrous were the subject not too important and vital.' Then, with improved insight, he asked, 'Are they angry because we urge not the *name* but the reality of domestic nomination? Alas, the fact is, that is just the cause of their ill temper and the source of their attack upon us.' O'Connell then assured Hay that he would be unable to conceive the abhorrence 'of these vetoistical plans amongst the people at large. I really think they will go near to desert all such clergymen as do not take an active part on the question. The Methodists were never in so fair a way of making converts.'[69]

The storm passed. O'Connell's readiness, in pursuit of his objectives, to cause division between the people and their bishops, between clergy and bishops and amongst the bishops themselves remained particularly unwelcome to Archbishop Troy and Murray, and to many other bishops too. Nevertheless, they valued his commitment and powerful advocacy in the cause of Catholic emancipation, and they were reluctant, even afraid, to criticise him openly. O'Connell, in turn, conscious of the respect the public had for Murray, refrained from public criticism of him.

Some six months after its remonstrance to the Pope, and its complaint about the treatment of Fr Richard Hayes, the Catholic Board received a firm response from Pius VII. In a letter dated 21 February 1818, which appeared in the *Freeman's Journal* on 8 June that year, the Pope explained that, if the government passed an act of emancipation, he would be induced in his decision regarding any arrangements about the appointment of bishops 'by no temporal considerations or political counsels (of which it would be criminal even to suspect us) but we had solely in view the interests and well-being of the Catholic religion'. Then, turning to the Board's appeal about Richard Hayes, he did not mince his words about their delegate. He charged Hayes with having 'furnished us with many and weighty causes of grief and vexation' unbecoming in a member of a religious order. He added that Hayes's calumnies against himself and the Holy See, together with his arrogance and audacity, had reached such a pitch that he could no longer suppress his sentiments without abandoning his personal dignity. Referring to Hayes's report to them the previous December, he concluded that it too was full of falsehoods and calumnies, and therefore not deserving of any credit.

MORE PROBLEMS WITH THE IRISH COLLEGE IN PARIS

As the summer of 1817 passed into autumn, the problems of the Irish College in Paris impinged once more on Murray's time and energy. Complaints about the president, Fr Long, as well as charges of corruption against him, were levelled by Bishop Coppinger. Murray strongly defended the president, and the charges and complaints proved unfounded.

Long, indeed, had achieved a great deal. He succeeded in having the Irish College detached from the English and Scots colleges and, with Murray's assistance, he persuaded the Irish bishops to begin 'sending students to Paris for the first time since the 1790s'. The college, moreover, despite the depletion of revenues since before 1789, was sufficiently healthy financially to allow it remain open. Despite Long's successes, however, the opposition associated with Richard Ferris did not disappear. In 1820, Ferris was once again named president. After a short time, however, he was replaced by the veteran, the Revd Charles Kennedy, who had been in charge more than three decades earlier when the Revolution commenced.[70]

ROUTINE CONCERNS OF OFFICE

A daily feature of Murray's life was the pressure of correspondence. A brief sample of letters conveys something of their diversity. The provincial of the English Jesuits, Revd Charles Plowden, wrote from Stonyhurst College asking Murray to ordain two English Jesuits, who had been refused ordination by the English bishops. The reason for their refusal is unclear. Leaving aside any influence more remote historical issues may have played, the decision may have been prompted by a fear many of the English bishops seem to have had that the restoration of the Jesuits would displease the English government and delay Catholic Emancipation. Murray evidently agreed to the request, however, because Plowden wrote to him on 19 June, and again on 18 July 1819, thanking him for ordaining the two men – Revds Newsham and Bridges

– which was 'so much in keeping with the Pope's wishes'.[71]

Towards the close of 1820, on 15 December, there came news of the death of Dr Thomas Bray, archbishop of Cashel. He was succeeded by his coadjutor, Patrick Everard, but the succession was brief. On 31 March 1821, Everard died. On 1 April a letter was sent to Murray which indicated Murray's closeness to the deceased. Fr Molloy, of Cashel diocese, wrote to Murray to say that he was 'needed to arrange about the funeral and about Dr Everard's affairs'.[72] Murray had been named as executor of Everard's will.

On a different note, Murray's pastoral care was exemplified in 1821 in the form of a letter to the 'Foremen and Gentlemen of the Grand Jury' concerning the hardship experienced by Roman Catholic prisoners in the absence of a chaplain of their faith. He was concerned, Murray explained, for this 'most important part of my flock'.[73]

Following the death of Dr Everard, Murray experienced one of the difficulties of being an executor. On 30 April 1822, a certain Judith Everard wrote from Fethard to Mr Molloy in Dublin, in connection with Bishop Everard's will and the legacy to which, she claimed, her children were entitled. A month later, on 29 May, she wrote to Murray stating that she had been to see the Lord Chancellor, and that she would leave her four children with Dr Murray if she got no more than the £14.17s that Murray had sent her.[74] It is not clear what was the outcome.

In very few instances are Murray's replies extant. What seems evident is that people from all walks of life – the poor, the well educated, the aristocracy – felt able to approach Murray, who appears to have been at ease with all sections of the population. On 3 February 1820, Lord Gormanston wrote to Murray thanking him for his sympathy on the death of his wife, continuing at some length to speak about her qualities and how much he missed her.[75] More than a year later, on 11 July 1821, Gormanston expressed his concern to Murray about his 'deficient son'.[76]

While such ecclesial and personal matters were occupying Murray's attention, Catholic agitation for emancipation had quietened in Ireland, but support for it had increased in the House of Commons.

A DIVIDED HIERARCHY ON THE RELIEF BILL

On 2 April 1821, a Catholic relief measure, proposed by William Conyngham Plunket, was passed in the House of Commons. It established Catholics' eligibility for membership of parliament and for appointment to the professions. Catholics were required to take the oath of supremacy, but in a modified form that didn't demand the rejection of transubstantiation and of devotion to Our Lady and the saints. There were also requirements in terms of securities, reviving the idea of government commissions that would certify the loyalty of candidates for vacant Catholic sees and would examine correspondence with Rome. The measure, with its legislative explanation of the oath of allegiance and supremacy, was deemed to permit Catholics to take it without compromising their religious beliefs, and it passed its third reading by a majority of nineteen votes.

Meantime, the Irish prelates had been taken by surprise by the favourable vote. They endeavoured to come to grips with the securities and, more particularly, with the modified oath of allegiance and supremacy. Archbishop Troy and Murray had a new suffragan bishop, Dr James Doyle, who succeeded to Kildare and Leighlin in 1819. Murray greatly valued the new bishop's assistance. Doyle's rather audacious and assertive manner, combined with his competence as a theologian and skill as a writer and preacher, seemed to attract the gentler, more cautious Murray. Doyle, for his part, was drawn to Murray's calm assurance, his aura of spirituality and inner peace. Though he was impatient at times with Murray's over-leniency towards erring clergy or laity, he held the Coadjutor Archbishop in respect and warm regard.

On 14 March 1821, Murray sought Doyle's 'speedy advice' on the nature of the oath of allegiance and supremacy in the Catholic relief bill. He asked if the proposed oath could be taken by Catholics, or if it was heretical. Doyle replied that he would wish to see the terms of it softened, but in its present form he would not say that it could not be taken.[77] On the very date of Doyle's reply, 15 March, however, Archbishop Curtis, of Armagh, informed Murray that Catholics would object to the wording of the oath of supremacy.[78]

The support of the House of Commons for Catholic relief, combined with the modified oath of allegiance and supremacy, seemed to shift the focus of many bishops towards concessions in return for emancipation. This was more marked in Dublin, where there was a clearer appreciation of the advances that had been made in parliament and government. The response to the bill in the other three provinces was very different. To the oath and the securities there was open hostility. On 30 March, Dr Doyle, writing from Murray's residence at 41 Cumberland St to Sir Henry Parnell, deplored the harsh spirit of the clerical reaction in the ecclesiastical provinces of Cashel, Tuam and Armagh. By comparison, he considered that the resolutions of the Dublin province were couched in measured language, which nonetheless did not disguise their difficulties with the securities.[79]

O'Connell's open opposition to Plunket's bill, because of the concession of the veto, accentuated the division among the bishops. A further factor was Dr

Milner's antagonism to the measure. On 1 April, the day before the third reading of the bill in the House of Commons, Milner replied to a letter from Murray that mentioned the division among the Irish bishops over the oath of supremacy. Milner expressed his concern at the division, and then asserted that the form of the oath issued on 17 March was no better 'than that for refusing which your Archbishops O'Hurley and Creagh and our Fisher and More, with a hundred more victims in each island, suffered glorious martyrdom'.[80] Eight days later, he again deplored the disunity, and warned that Archbishop Troy and Murray might lose their popularity because of their stance.

The bill, however, was defeated in the House of Lords on 17 April 1821 by 159 votes to 120. It is worth noting that in that vote a number of members who in the past would have opposed such a bill voted in favour of emancipation. Reflection on the attitude of both Houses to the bill suggests that henceforth the main opponents to Catholic Emancipation would be from the representatives of hereditary power, namely, the House of Lords and the king. Nevertheless, the advent of a new king, George IV, in 1821, evoked renewed hopes. Murray, meantime, was able to assure Milner, much to the latter's delight, that the Irish bishops were united once more.[81]

WELCOMING THE NEW KING

The arrival of King George IV to Ireland was a major event, which evoked popular enthusiasm for the monarchy and inevitably impinged on the religious hierarchies. In July 1821, the Irish Catholic hierarchy, at Murray's suggestion, agreed to present an address to the king, who was expected in Ireland during August. The idea was favourably received by the government. Dr Doyle set about writing the address of welcome, but the result was too blunt for Murray. It reminded the monarch of the intolerance and pain experienced by Catholics in the absence of emancipation. Lord Donoughmore and Murray agreed that the address should be kept to a 'hearty welcome', disallowing all other sentiments.[82] Dr Doyle concurred, and Murray asked Donoughmore to draft the address.

The King arrived at Howth on 12 August. His public entry into Dublin, on 17 August, was attended by a procession of carriages and horsemen stretching for a mile in length and was greeted by cheering crowds. On 21 August, in Dublin Castle, eleven of the bishops, clad in their episcopal robes, led by Archbishop Curtis and including Drs Troy, Murray, Doyle and Kelly of Tuam, presented their address to George IV.[83] Murray read the address, which welcomed a sovereign who 'comes to his people with the olive branch of peace in his hand'. It pledged the bishops' 'undivided allegiance',[84] and all the prelates kissed His Majesty's hand.[85] The King's visit was marked by intense popular excitement. As he left from Dunleary – which was shortly afterwards renamed Kingstown in his honour – the enthusiasm was such that some of the crowd followed the royal barge until they stood up to their necks in water. The King, for his part, responded warmly, announcing to the cheering crowds that his heart had always been Irish.

George IV's arrival and behaviour raised hopes among Catholics, including O'Connell, of a new openness to Catholic emancipation. These seemed further confirmed towards the end of 1821 by the appointment of Marquis Wellesley, elder brother of the Duke of Wellington, as lord lieutenant. O'Connell, writing in January 1822, viewed Wellesley as 'the harbinger of emancipation'.[86] The King, in fact, was to show himself firmly opposed to Catholic political claims, and the change in the executive in Ireland had no connection with the royal visit. But these chastening facts were to remain hidden from Irish minds and hearts for some time.

CULTIVATING GOODWILL FOR THE PEOPLE'S BENEFIT

As they sought to avoid a repetition of the divisions that arose over Plunket's bill, the bishops, led by Curtis and Murray, sought to arrive at an agreed system of episcopal nomination and appointment. As a result, the whole issue of domestic nomination came to the fore again and was actively debated between 1821 and 1823. Edward Hay, former secretary of the Catholic Association, viewed the bishops' approach with suspicion, however, and felt that they might concede on the veto for their own ends. A letter of his in the *Dublin Evening Post*, on 7 January 1822, was highly critical of Murray. Hay alleged that Murray had conceded the veto in 1817 in return for emancipation and episcopal nomination of the bishops. Murray responded strongly on 9 February, stating that Hay's statement was 'unsupported by fact' and that 'the public know how to appreciate fully that poor gentleman's reveries'. Stung by Murray's reply, Hay published a letter that O'Connell had written to him long before, on 27 July 1817. In that letter, O'Connell claimed that Murray was supporting the veto, adding, 'as to Dr Troy, better could not be expected from him – his traffic at the Castle is long notorious'. For O'Connell, this was a most embarrassing exposure of what was a private letter. The *Dublin Evening Post,* which published it, was engaged in a row with O'Connell at the time, holding him to be ill-mannered and haughty. On 23 February, the *Dublin Evening Post* published a letter from O'Connell to

Archbishop Troy apologising for his letter to Hay in 1817 and imploring His Grace's pardon. He similarly apologised to Murray.[87]

Despite prejudice about their closeness to the Castle, the bishops now found themselves elevated in popular and governmental estimation following their reception by the King. They pursued this advantage by attending in official dress at the Lord Lieutenant's levees and similar functions. Wellesley had intimated that he would welcome an address from the Irish bishops in the style of their presentation to the King, and it was in that spirit that Drs Curtis, Murray, Kelly, Marum and Doyle presented their address at Wellesley's first levee in Dublin Castle, on 8 January 1822.[88] The bishops, as usual, pledged their loyalty to the king and obedience to the laws. They also deplored those 'atrocities which have totally outraged all religion, in some parts of the country'. Wellesley replied that he had full confidence in the bishops' principles of affectionate loyalty towards their King, and he, for his part, would administer the law with a 'firm, but even and temperate hand'.

Murray viewed such occasions as an opportunity for the bishops to confirm 'the footing which we have already obtained and of securing the favour of the new government'.[89] The hope was that by cultivating a good understanding with government, the interest of religion would benefit. 'I hope this may be the case,' Doyle commented to his brother, 'and though I don't like the parade of attending every new viceroy on his arrival (which must now be done as a matter of course), yet I am glad that we are thus considered.'[90] In March 1823, O'Connell wrote to his wife about a large gathering at the Castle, where 'the crowd was nearly as great as at the King's levee, and Dr Troy and Dr Murray were there in full canonicals'.[91] It was to be Archbishop Troy's final levee.

Meanwhile, the issue of domestic nomination remained dependent on the approval of both Rome and London, and would continue formally unresolved until 1829.

THE END OF AN ERA

At the end of 1821, and into January of 1822, Archbishop Troy was seriously ill. On 14 January, however, Milner expressed to Murray his satisfaction at the news that Troy was out of danger.[92] Indeed, Troy appeared to recover well but, on 11 May 1823, he died, at the age of sixty-four. His death received surprisingly little public notice, but one of those who spoke of him with unexpected regard was Daniel O'Connell, who had been at times a very severe critic of his. Writing to his wife, then at Tours in France, he commented:

> You have I suppose seen by the newspapers that Dr Troy is dead. He arrived at a fine old age and died in the sentiments of purest religion. May the great and good God be merciful to his soul. Dr Murray succeeds as a matter of course but cannot take the archiepiscopal throne until a notification is made to Rome. However, his right of succession is long since decided. Dr Troy died without a guinea. He was a most charitable man and never was known to refuse giving what he could to a person in distress. He governed the Catholic Church in Ireland in a stormy period and was very much beloved by his own clergy…[93]

One of Archbishop Troy's ambitions had been the erection of a great cathedral. He had laid the foundation stone in April 1815, and it was fitting that his obsequies took place within the walls of his unfinished building. The office of the dead was led by the primate, Dr Curtis, assisted by five bishops and the clergy of Dublin. Following High Mass, Archbishop Troy's remains were brought to the vaults of George's Hill convent, where they remained until their translation to the Pro-Cathedral in May 1824.[94]

John Thomas Troy had led an influential section of the Irish Church through the era of declining penal laws. In his early years, Catholics worshipped in small primitive chapels in back streets; now imposing churches were being built and a cathedral was under construction. During his time, the violence and humiliation of 1798 had gradually given way to an assertive demand for full political emancipation. Perhaps Troy's greatest gift to the Irish Church was his choice of committed bishops to many dioceses, not the least of which, it would have been generally agreed, was his choice of his successor, Daniel Murray.

NOTES

1 Maurice R. O'Connell, *The Correspondence of Daniel O'Connell, vol.1, 1792–1814* (Irish University Press, 1972), p.285.

2 S. J. Connolly, 'The Catholic Question, 1801–1812' in W. E. Vaughan (ed.), *A New History of Ireland, vol.v Ireland under the Union I, 1801–70* (Oxford: Clarendon Press 1989), p.47.

3 S.J. Connolly. 'Union Government 1812–23' in W. E. Vaughan (ed.) op.cit., pp.49, 51–52.

4 Poynter – Murray, 16 Feb. 1814. DDA. Troy Papers.

5 Troy – Bray, 5 May, 1814. (Thurles Archives), Copy in Troy Papers, Green file 7, no.24.

6 Brendan Clifford. *The Veto Controversy*, p.184.

7 Argenti – Troy, 25 June 1814, DDA; Macpherson – F Dr Poynter, 15 June 1814, Westminster Diocesan Archives, cit. Ambrose Macauley. *The Catholic Church and the Campaign for Emancipation in Ireland and England*, (Dublin: Four Courts Press, 2016), pp.216–17.

8 Troy – Murray, July 1814, Troy Papers, no.23.
9 Idem, no.25.
10 S. A., *Mary Aikenhead...,* p.148. See T. J. Morrissey, *As One Sent: Peter Kenney SJ., 1779–1841,* pp.112–13.
11 Litta – Troy, 11 Oct. 1814. Troy Papers.
12 Murray to Propaganda, Vatican Archives, Archives of the Secretariat of State (formerly the congregation of Extraordinary Ecclesiastical Affairs), Rome, Inghilterra 1814, Pos. 9, fasc.4, ff, 73r–77r (undated), cit. Macauley. op. cit. p.219.
13 Macauley, op. cit., pp.222–3.
14 Troy – Bray, 26 Oct 1814. Troy Papers (from Thurles Archives).
15 Connolly – Coppinger, 24 Oct. 1814. Troy Papers (from Cloyne Archives).
16 S.A., *Mary Aikenhead ...,* p.148.
17 B. Clifford, *The Veto Controversy,* p.185.
18 S. A., op. cit. , p.148.
19 Milner – Troy, 12 Jan. 1815, Troy Papers. f. 436, Green file 7, no.329. It is incorrectly dated 12 July.
20 John O'Connell, *The Selected Speeches of Daniel O'Connell, M.P.* (Dublin 1865), p.448, cit. Emmet Larkin. *The Pastoral Role of the Roman Catholic Church in Pre-Famine Ireland, 1750–1850* (Dublin: Four Courts Press, 2006), p.89.
21 Milner – Murray, 24 Feb. 1815. Troy Papers, Green file 7, no.82.
22 D. Philips – Murray, 12 April 1815, Troy Papers no.72.
23 F. P. Carey, *Archbishop Murray of Dublin* (Dublin: Messenger Publications, 1951), pp.14–15; Myles Ronan. 'Archbishop Murray (1768–1852)' in *IER,* April 1952, p.247.
24 Milner – Murray, 21 May 1815, Troy Papers.
25 Idem.
26 A. Talleyrand – Murray, 17 August 1815, Troy Papers, no.79.
27 Milner – Murray, 31 July, 1815, no.84.
28 Walsh – Everard, 12 August 1815.
29 S. A., *Mary Aikenhead...,*pp.153–4.
30 Troy Papers, no.75 Troy – Bray, 15 Sept. 1815, Troy Papers, Green file 7, no.78. no 78.
31 E. Larkin. op.cit., p.90.
32 S. A., op. cit., p.153.
33 Bp. Jn. Power – Bray, 9 Sept. 1815, Bray Papers, Cashel Diocesan Archives, cit. S.J. Connolly in 'Union Governmnet, 1812-23' in W. E. Vaughan (ed.) op cit., p.52.
34 Resolutions of Bishops, 24 Aug. 1815, printed statement. Troy Papers.
35 S.A. *Mary Aikenhead ...,* p.153–4.
36 Cit. E. Larkin. op. cit., pp.91–2.
37 Liam Chambers. *The Irish Colleges in Paris, 1578–2002: History* (*Centre Cultural Irlandais, Paris), Historique 4.* Online.
38 Argenti – Troy, 25 Nov. 1815, no.55 Troy Papers. The Mr Kendrick may have been Francis Kendrick, future Bishop of Philadelphia.
39 S. A., op. cit., pp.155–7.
40 Murray – Consalvi, 9 Jan 1816 (draft letter), Troy Papers, Green file 8, no.65.
41 E. Larkin. op. cit., pp.98–102.
42 R. Hayes – Murray & Murphy, 17 Jan. 1816, Troy Papers 1816, no.14.
43 Letter of Pius VII, 1 Feb. 1816, Troy Papers 1816–17, no.1.
44 O'Reilly – Murray, 28 March 1816, Troy Papers.
45 Milner – Murray, 17 March 1816, Troy Papers.
46 Donal A. Kerr. 'Dublin's Forgotten Archbishop: Daniel Murray, 1768–1852' in Kelly & Keogh, *History of the Catholic Diocese of Dublin,* p.254.
47 *Dublin Chronicle*, 15 April 1816.

48 O'Connell – Wife, 14 April 1816, in M.R. O'Connell. *Correspondence of Daniel O'Connell*, vol. II.
49 Trimelstown & Bellew – Troy, 17 April 1816, no.257.
50 DEP. 23 April 1816.
51 Ibid. 28 May 1816.
52 A. O'Connor – Murray, 19 April 1816, Troy Papers, nos.66–7.
53 E. Larkin. op. cit., p.95.
54 Card. Litta – Murray, 29 Aug. 1816. Troy Papers.
55 Murray – Litta, 28 Oct. 1816, Acta SCP, vol.179 (1816), fols.75–78, cit. Larkin. op. cit., pp.96–7.
56 Milner – Murray, 8 Dec. 1816. no.47.
57 S. J. Connolly. 'Union Government 1812–23' in W. E. Vaughan ed. op. cit. p.56.
58 A. Trant. 'Government Policy and Irish Distress, 1816-19', MA Thesis, (UCD, 1965), p.1, cit. S.J. Connolly in art. cit., op. cit., p.61.
59 Milner – Murray, 26 Feb–10 March 1817, Troy Papers.
60 Milner – Murray, 2 July, 1817, idem.
61 M. R. O'Connell, *The Correspondence…*, vol. II, notes p.157.
62 Idem; and see E. Larkin. op. cit., pp.107–109.
63 D. O'Connell – Wife, 23 July, 1817, in M.R. O'Connell. op. cit., no.712, pp.158–9.
64 *Dublin Evening Post*, 22 July 1817, cit. in M. R. O'Connell, op. cit., no.712, pp.158–9, note.
65 *Dublin Evening Post*, 24 July 1817, cit. M.R. O'Connell, op. cit., p.160. Italics in text.
66 Idem, 24 July. 'Catholic Affairs'.
67 Litta – Troy, 3 Dec. 1817. Troy Papers, Green file 8.
68 *ACTA Sacra Congregationis Propaganda, vol. 179 (1816), fol. 93, cit.* E. Larkin, op. cit., pp.97–8.
69 O'Connell – Edward Hay, 27 July 1817 in M.R. O'Connell. op. cit., no.713. pp.159–60.
70 L. Chambers. *The Irish Colleges in Paris…Historique 4&5.* For issues raised: Coppinger – Murray, 8 Nov. 1817. Troy Papers, no.90; Murphy – Murray, 15 Nov. 1817, idem, no.95; Coppinger – Troy, 11 May 1818, Troy Papers, Green File, 9, no. 19; Charles Sughrue – Murray, 12 May 1818, idem, no.20; Coppinger – Murray, 23 May 1818, idem, no.22; Idem, 15 June 1818, no.24.
71 Charles Plowden – Murray 19 June and 18 July 1819, Troy Papers, Green File 9 (1818–1819), no.4.
72 Fr Molloy – Murray, 1 April 1821, idem, no.57.
73 Murray – Grand Jury, 1821, idem, no.76.
74 J. Everard – Murray, 29 May 1822, idem, Green file 11, no.45.
75 Lord Gormanston – Murray, 3 Feb. 1820, Green file 10.
76 Idem, 11 July, 1821, idem, no.116.
77 Bp Doyle – Murray, 15 March 1821, DDA. 30/5, no.84, cit. Thomas McGrath. *Politics, Interdenominational Relations and Education in the public ministry of Bishop James Doyle of Kildare & Leighlin, 1786–1831*, (Dublin: Four Courts Press, 1999), p.1.
78 Abp. Curtis – Murray, 15 March 1821, Green file 10, no.85.
79 Doyle – Sir Henry Parnell, 30 March 1821, cit. McGrath. op. cit., p.4.
80 Milner – Murray, 1 April 1821, Green file 10, nos.96, 97.
81 Milner – Murray. 9 April 1821, Troy Papers, File 30/5, no.34, misdated as 1820.
82 Donoughmore – Murray, 27 July 1821, file 30/5, no.79.
83 *Dublin Evening Post* (DEP), 21 Aug. 1821.
84 *Preston Chronicle,* 1 Sept. 1821.
85 *DEP,* 23 Aug. 1821.

86 M.R. O'Connell. *O'Connell Correspondence*...vol. ii, 347, cit. Connolly. 'Union government 1812- 23' in Vaughan (ed.). op. cit pp.68–69.
87 *Dublin Evening Post* (DEP), 21 Aug. 1821.
88 Idem, 10 Jan. 1822.
89 J. Doyle – Rev Peter Doyle, 3 Jan. 1822, KLDA, cit McGrath. p.10.
90 Idem.
91 O'Connell – Wife, 5 March 1823; *O'Connell Correspondence* ,vol II, no. 983, p.444.
92 Milner – Murray, 14 Jan 1822, Troy Papers, Green file 11, no.16.
93 O'Connell – Wife (at Tours), 25 May 1823, *O'Connell Correspondence*.... Vol. II, no.1023, p.447.
94 D. Keogh. 'John Thomas Troy, 1786-1823' in Kelly & Keogh. *Hist. of Catholic Dioceses of Dublin*, pp.233–35.

CHAPTER 6

Early Years as Archbishop of Dublin (1823–26)

The year 1823 was particularly busy for Murray. Apart from the illness of Archbishop Troy, which was followed by his death and funeral, there was a welter of letters and requests from bishops, priests, government officials, professional people and a variety of lay men and women, seeking advice, financial aid or some form of advancement for themselves or members of their family. With Archbishop Troy's death, Murray found himself very much in the foreground. He was now archbishop of a diocese that was expanding almost daily in population and, unlike Troy, he had no coadjutor prelate to assist him. Even before his formal appointment had arrived from Rome, people looked to him for comment, advice and decisions. In dealing with his early years as archbishop of Dublin, this chapter will consider his performance as a pastor, and then outline two of the major developments that faced him in those years: the resurgence of Protestant evangelisation and the emergence of a powerful popular movement for Catholic Emancipation.

AN UNEXPECTED START

Perhaps the most significant test of the new archbishop in 1823 was an event for which he had no preparation. He was confronted with evidence of a miraculous cure in the case of a very ill woman religious at the Carmelite convent in Ranelagh, Dublin. The cure was attributed to the intercession of Prince Alexander Leopold Emerich of Hohenlohe-Waldenburg (1794–1849). He was a German priest who had gained a reputation as a miracle worker. His first alleged miraculous cure was of Princess Mathilde Von Scharzenberg in 1821, who had been a paralytic for some eight years. As his reputation for miraculous healings spread, crowds from different countries flocked to where he was stationed to benefit from his remarkable powers. Many cures were attributed to him in Europe and North America. In Dublin, his intercession was sought for Mary Stuart of the convent of St Joseph, Ranelagh, who had been paralysed in body and speech. Her instantaneous recovery obliged Archbishop Murray to examine all the evidence carefully. On completion of this task, he issued a pastoral letter, on 15 August, proclaiming the cure and giving thanks to God for it. It deserves attention as an unusual historical document issued by a man noted for his caution and his sensitivity to anything that might offend unionist opinion. Addressed 'To The Catholic Clergy and Laity of the Diocese of Dublin',[1] it began:

> With a heart at once struck with awe, and inflamed with gratitude to 'the God of all consolation', we proclaim to you a new and wonderful manifestation of his goodness, which we have just had the happiness to witness. Mary Stuart, of the Convent of St Joseph, Ranelagh, has … been restored instantaneously to health, from a state of grievous and hopeless infirmity, for the relief of which, all the resources of human skill had been expended in vain.

Murray then related that he had learned of the cure from a letter of the prioress of the convent, Mary Catherine Meade, which he received on 2 August. The letter described how Mary Stuart had been afflicted by a sickness for four years, during which she had suffered bouts of paralysis, and how for several months past she had been confined to bed, wholly deprived of the power of assisting herself or of moving from the position in which she lay. When moved gently by attendants, she suffered much pain and a temporary loss of speech. For five weeks she had entirely lost the power of articulation. 'Up to the morning of the 1st instant,' wrote Murray, 'she continued in this deplorable state, without any symptoms of amendment, and apparently beyond the reach of human aid'.

The Archbishop then went on to give an account of the happenings on 1 August, the dramatic nature of which breaks through the narrative.

> On a certain hour that morning, as had been settled by previous arrangement, she (Mary Stuart) united her devotion (as did also her numerous friends) with the Holy Sacrifice of the Mass, which was to be offered by Alexander, Prince of Hohenlohe, in the hope of obtaining immediately from God that relief which no human means could afford; – with this view, she received, though with much difficulty, the Divine Communion at the Mass, which was celebrated at the same hour in her chamber for her recovery; – Mass being ended, and no cure as yet effected, she was in the act of resigning her self, with perfect submission, to the will of God, when instantly she felt a power of movement and a capability of speech; – so that she exclaimed with an animated voice – 'Holy, Holy, Holy, Lord God of Hosts!' – raised herself without assistance, to offer on bended knees, the tribute of gratitude to heaven.

Murray then tells how she called for her clothes, dressed and walked 'with firm step' to the convent chapel where, with the members of the religious community and friends, she offered a solemn thanksgiving to God 'for this wonderful and manifest interposition of his goodness'.

'Faced with this statement', Murray explained, 'we felt it a sacred duty to examine the grounds on which it was made, that if it originated in a mistake, we might endeavour to dispel the delusion, but, if founded on fact, we might proclaim the glory of God.' He visited the convent and met Mary Stuart, who presented the details of her story as given above, making a sworn attestation on the matter. Her friends and attendants confirmed the account in all its details. They did so, Murray observed, 'with a degree of candour and simplicity, which could not fail, even then, to produce on our mind the clearest conviction, that the restoration of the said Mary Stuart to the state of health in which we saw her, was beyond the reach of human power'.

Aware of the great responsibility he carried in making an announcement on such a matter, Murray revisited the convent after several days. He described his approach to the investigation:

> We subjected all the circumstances to a new and rigid inquiry; we collected information on the spot, from every source within our reach; we weighed it in the presence of the God of Truth; we called in to our aid the wisdom andintelligence of our Reverend Brethren of the Roman Catholic Clergy of this city, and we have the consolation of knowing that our judgement is supported by their unanimous opinion, when we declare, as we hereby declare, on what appears to us the most unquestionable evidence – that the cure which was effected in the person of the said Mary Stuart, on the 1st of August, instant, is the effect of a supernatural agency, an effect which we cannot contemplate without feeling in our inmost soul an irresistible conviction 'that this is the finger of God'.

Among his papers, together with the pastoral itself, Murray included doctors' certificates in the case and the evidence of nine persons.

Not all of Murray's fellow bishops were pleased with his pastoral letter. On 20 August, Dr Curtis, the cautious archbishop of Armagh, referring to the publication of Murray's letter in the press, thought it unwise to publish it, considering what those who attack the Church say about miracles and the belief of Catholics in them.[2] As if to confirm his fears, the Belfast weekly, *The Irishman*, on 29 August, carried letters and an editorial comment denying the possibility of miracles and deriding the alleged miracle in Dublin.[3] It should be mentioned here that Dr Curtis was a man of definite views, and that these were often of a critical nature. On 19 August, he had written to Murray that he had lost a curate from typhus, a fine man whose health was not equal to his zeal. Then Curtis added that the two remaining curates were zealous and proper, 'but like all coming from Maynooth, they cannot bear much fatigue'![4]

Murray, as indicated previously, had been close to Dr Everard, the late archbishop of Cashel. Not surprisingly his successor, the archbishop-elect, Robert Laffan, sought his advice. During April, Murray responded to a letter from him; and on 1 July, he assured Laffan that he would be coming down to his consecration by mail coach and would like to be met at the stopping place in Littleton.[5] The new archbishop continued to seek Murray's advice for some months.[6] In October, Murray joined the other Irish archbishops in sending congratulations to the new pope, Leo XII.[7] The year drew to a close with Cardinal Somaglia, on 20 December, forwarding to Murray the bull of appointment to the archbishopric of Dublin.

RELIGIOUS AND SOCIAL UNEASE

The New Year brought a range of problems which added to the pressure Murray already felt in his new role. On 20 March 1824, he requested Cardinal Consalvi that he might defer his *ad limina* visit to Rome, due at the end of the year, because his flock was 'exposed to grave dangers'. He also asked that he might delay the sending of his account of the diocese until 1825.[8] Both requests were granted.

The 'grave dangers' to which Murray's flock were exposed were related to the prevailing deep divisions in Irish society during 1824–5. The Crown, along with Tory and Orange organisations, remained strongly opposed to concessions to Catholics. Agrarian violence threatened to build up opposition to the Catholic community, and to bring about repression and further violence. The sectarian bitterness created by the Protestant evangelical societies had deepened denominational ill-feeling and social division. That division acquired an added edge from the fact that the 'Second Reformation' of 1822–7 – when Protestant evangelical preachers were making great efforts in Ireland to evangelise not only children in schools but also adults – received strong support from such prominent landlords as Lords Farnham, Roden, Powerscourt, Lorton and Gosford.[9]

The evangelical movement stemmed from England. It had its headquarters at Exeter Hall in London, and chose Ireland and its Roman Catholic people for a great missionary crusade. It was well supported financially and was to remain active into the 1860s. The medium of the Irish language was used to reach the people in remoter parts of the country. The Protestant crusade changed the atmosphere of accommodation between Catholics and Protestants to one of virtual spiritual warfare. In Ireland, the crusade took on particular prominence with the declaration in 1822 by William Magee, the new Church of Ireland archbishop of Dublin, that the time had come for the established clergy to throw aside the cloak of compromise and accommodation and proclaim the truth to all those sunk in religious error. They must boldly denounce the claims of both Roman Catholics on the one side and of Presbyterian dissenters on the other.[10] In a time of heightened tensions, the irenic Archbishop Murray struggled to preserve good relations.[11]

In addition to all the foregoing, there was the widespread poverty and unemployment in the cities and countryside that added to the aura of gloom and hopelessness. Murray was aware that the movement for Catholic rights had been stalled both by the efforts of the Chief Secretary, Robert Peel, from 1812 to 1818, and by continuous divisions among Catholics themselves, and that the popular sense of grievance and frustration was deepened by the Catholic population's awareness of how greatly it outnumbered the favoured Protestant minority. By 1823, Richard Lalor Sheil observed that 'a general stagnation diffused itself over the national feelings'.[12] It prompted him and O'Connell to come together to create a nationwide movement that would make use of the numerical superiority of the Catholic population. Daniel Murray as archbishop would continue to distance himself from political involvement, but this did not exclude him from a deep desire for Emancipation, which he viewed as a means towards improving the lot of the less well-off and providing better educational opportunities for their children.

A NEW CATHOLIC ASSOCIATION

Daniel O'Connell, reflecting on the bleak overall situation in Ireland, decided that the Catholic population needed protection, attention to their grievances and a boost to their morale. In May, he and Lalor Sheil announced the formation of a new society, which anyone could join who paid one guinea per year, clergy being free of charge. The Catholic Board, which it replaced, was constituted towards organising petitions. O'Connell insisted that the new organisation concern itself with the wider grievances of the Catholic people, thereby providing a broader base and evoking wider support. Less than a year later, O'Connell proposed extending the membership of the association to all who would contribute one penny a month. He envisioned collecting this 'Catholic rent' by means of committees in the towns, and by means of the clergy over the greater part of the country. The assistance of the clergy was essential, and to that end he sent a circular letter to the Catholic bishops on 10 March 1824, expressing the hope that the objects of the association might be deserving of their 'sanction and countenance' and be worthy of their approbation.[13] The role of the clergy, it was made clear, was not to collect the contributions but to supervise those collecting them, so that all would be done as instructed.

The association highlighted the numerous grievances it wished to combat, including the influence of Orangeism, the abuses of power by landlords' agents and tithe proctors, and the biases of the magistrates. Among the practical issues it raised in rapid succession were the alleged proselytism of the Kildare Place Society and other bodies, the lack of a Catholic chaplain at Newgate Jail, disputes over burial grounds, bias in the judiciary, and the problem of tithes. Attention was drawn to these in order 'to take the strongest measures the law will allow to enforce our cause on the attention of parliament'.[14] The movement successfully crossed divisions between town and country, and embraced the 'men of no property'.

To O'Connell's delight, the new body won the general approval of two of the bishops he greatly admired, and whose support would carry considerable influence, Archbishop Daniel Murray and Bishop James Warren Doyle of Kildare and Leighlin. They jointly viewed the association as a support for their work for Catholic schools and against proselytism. Bishop Doyle's powerful responses to attacks on Catholics were encouraged by Drs Murray and Curtis, and his *Vindication of the religious and civil liberties of the Irish Catholics* made headlines at a national level. At a meeting of the Catholic Association in Doyle's diocese, on 10 April 1824, a lengthy letter of his was read. It detailed the educational situation in his diocese, and defended the endeavours of the Catholic clergy to provide and supervise schools for the Catholic children. He also commended parishioners for collecting the monthly fee of the association, thereby giving powerful support to that body.[15]

The monthly rent brought about a strong sense of involvement, an expansion of membership, and an increase of finances. From the large sum collected, the sum of £5,000 was to be set aside for Catholic schools, to help them compete with the proselytising schools conducted and financed by the Kildare Place Society; a further £5,000 was to pay for the education of priests destined to serve the Irish emigrants in America; and another £5,000 was intended to be applied to the provision of churches and parochial houses for priests in Ireland.[16]

The provision for Catholic schools and for clerical needs was calculated to appeal to bishops and priests, and to encourage their vital support for the association. The £5,000 for Catholic schools was inadequate, but it was very welcome to clergy in poorer areas, who were under pressure to develop schools for Catholic children and to discourage attendance at the growing number of proselytising schools. Murray and a number of other bishops were also drawn to the association by the very scale of the inequality Catholics endured in the administration of justice. In this connection, it has been estimated that there were 257 posts, from Lord Lieutenant to sub-sheriff, that were barred by law to Catholics; of the 1,314 lower offices for which Catholics were eligible they held only 39 by 1828; they were excluded from 655 offices of civil rank or honour, such as MPs or officers of corporations; and of the 3,033 minor offices to which they could aspire, they held only 134.[17]

BISHOP DOYLE'S DISCOMFITING INITIATIVE

Murray's friend and stout supporter, James Warren Doyle, created problems for him and his fellow prelates during June 1824. In a letter to Alexander Robertson, an English MP, he agreed with him that an 'ecumenical' union between Catholic and Protestant Churches would serve as a solvent of political antagonisms, and he observed that such a union would not be difficult to accomplish and should be attempted. He added to the unreality of his statement by describing the king as 'wise, liberal and enlightened'. The crowning embarrassment for his fellow bishops was his claim that if a rebellion were raging in Ireland, 'no sentence of excommunication would ever be fulminated by a Catholic prelate'.[18] This evoked from five professors at Maynooth a strong disagreement. They issued a manifesto proclaiming the duty of obedience to lawful authority and the allegiance of Maynooth to its sovereign. Archbishop Curtis sought to mend fences by writing to the Duke of Wellington, with whom he had been in occasional contact since they met at Salamanca in 1812. He assured Wellington that, in all of Bishop Doyle's writings, there was no passage 'as harsh, unreasonable or reprehensible'. He added, however, that 'if the aggressor does not come forward and make speedy, full and sincere amendment for his error', he would be disavowed or suspended by his fellow bishops.[19]

In the event, the Irish bishops made no public comment. Doyle realised that he had overstepped the line of obedience to constitutional authority and, perhaps, regretted making the proposal for 'reunion' without consulting the Roman authorities or fellow prelates. He wrote a letter of resignation to the Pope – but did not send it.[20] It is most likely that he consulted Murray in his predicament. He would from time to time express his appreciation of the advice and kindness he received from the Archbishop, whom he described as 'the most holy and prudent man I know'.[21] This personal response to Murray raises the question, even this early in Murray's career as archbishop, how effective he was as pastor of the diocese. After all, by 1826 he had been a prelate already for sixteen years and under Archbishop Troy had been given considerable authority and room.

MURRAY AS DIOCESAN PASTOR

A bishop, as the leading pastor in his diocese, may be assessed under three headings: his Christian witness, his preaching of the gospel, and his ability to create the right pastoral structures for his people.

As regards pastoral structures, Murray, while still coadjutor archbishop, identified the much-neglected education of the people as a major need and, as has been seen, he set about finding religious men and women who would undertake that work. He asked Mary Aikenhead to set up schools and undertake charitable work for the poor, and he asked Frances Ball to start a congregation for the education of better-off girls, known as the Loreto Sisters. He persuaded Edmund Rice to send Christian Brothers to Dublin, and encouraged Peter Kenney in his leadership of the restored Society of Jesus in Ireland and in his foundation of Clongowes Wood College. In each case, Murray offered counsel and support, but otherwise he did not interfere.

Now, in 1824, as archbishop of Dublin, he encouraged Catherine McAuley to begin what was later to become the largest congregation ever established in the English-speaking world, the Sisters of Mercy. They opened schools, orphanages and hospitals in Ireland and abroad. Murray was available in the difficult early stages, providing advice and assistance.[22] These different charismatic founders, and especially those of the three women's organisations, were due to give a new impetus to religious life in Dublin and in much of Ireland. Murray would later promote the establishment of the Vincentians in the diocese who, together with some Jesuits, would introduce public missions and pave the way for the subsequent 'devotional revolution'. At the level of key lay involvement, Murray was to introduce the Society of St Vincent de Paul as a support to Dublin's poor. Other pastoral objectives, such as the provision of sufficient and adequate churches for the people, became a major concern during his years as archbishop, as will later become evident.

As already noted in an earlier chapter, Murray as preacher and teacher avoided the lengthy sermons and rhetorical flourishes that were common at the time and, instead, appealed to his congregations by a simple style delivered in a low but distinct voice. At times he could electrify, as in his exceptional Good Friday

Catherine McAuley

sermon regarding the veto, but this was all the more noteworthy because of his normal quieter style, in which, nevertheless, he manifested an ability to appeal to the heart as well as the intellect, in Daniel O'Connell's view.[23] Something of Murray's simple, direct style is in evidence in his public letter on the recovery of Mary Stuart, and it also appears in his first Lenten pastoral as archbishop, in which can also be found signs of the amiability and beneficence that appealed to O'Connell.

On 24 February 1824, his Lenten letter[24] encouraged his people to join in the penitential season with their brethren throughout the whole Catholic world. He commented that it was 'a humiliating fact … that (due to) the relaxed custom of modern times little now remains of what our forefathers held necessary for the Christian observance of Lent'. Following this opening, a return to former stricter times seemed heralded; but, instead, Murray stated that, because of the variety of afflictions which 'the numerous poor of this city and its neighbourhood have to suffer', he had been induced to permit 'to his entire beloved flock, during the approaching Lent, the use of flesh-meat at dinner only, on every Sunday, Monday, Tuesday and Thursday from next Sunday until Palm Sunday, both included, and also the use of eggs for the same period of time on every day, Friday excepted.' It was a typically sympathetic gesture towards the poor, even if those most likely to benefit were the middle-class who could afford meat.

As archbishop, Murray took care to continue the clerical conferences initiated by Archbishop Troy. The programme for conferences during 1824 was printed in Latin and it presented for each month, from May to October, the themes for consideration and discussion.[25] These focused on areas of key interest, or issues that might arise for priests in parish ministry. The material was presented in the form of questions. In May, the theme was Easter Communion: 'For what reasons can it be deferred? Can it be fulfilled by a sacrilegious communion? What is to be thought of daily or frequent communion? Exclusion from sacred communion … what of the reputation of public sinners? On communion in *viaticum* (the last rites) and its obligation? How often in the same illness? What dispositions of soul and body are required to receive the Eucharist fruitfully?' In June and the succeeding months the focus was on the Sacrifice of the Mass. The detailed questions continued each month into October in an attempt to clarify Church teaching and practice, to bring together men isolated in busy or scattered parishes, and to revive and stimulate them mentally and spiritually.

With respect to Murray's 'Christian witness' as bishop, this was well established before his succession as archbishop. He was known, as has been observed, for his gentleness and edifying lifestyle, while remaining amiable and approachable. His friend, the very able, but rigorist, Bishop of Kildare and Leighlin, James

W. Doyle, spoke of Murray as timid and over-indulgent towards erring clergy. On reproaching the archbishop on the matter, however, he was reminded of St Francis de Sales's advice that firm gentleness is more effective than severity and punishment. There is much evidence of Murray's clergy responding to this behaviour, so that they avoided giving any offence or pain to their archbishop.

As a prelate, Murray avoided any personal manifestations of wanting to be perceived as *Sacerdos Magnus*. Significantly, his consecration ceremony as archbishop took place quietly in the Liffey Street chapel.[26] From all accounts, his priests were heartened by his personal witness and by their ready access to him. He actively encouraged public and private devotions among them and throughout the diocese. The promotion of devotions to the Sacred Heart of Jesus and to Mary, Mother of God, had been a feature of his ministry for many years, and even more markedly as archbishop. His devotion to Mary was such that he was to obtain from the Holy See the extension to Ireland of several feasts of the Blessed Virgin that were well known in Europe but had not functioned in Ireland during penal times. Though the dogma of the Immaculate Conception had not yet been pronounced by the Church, Murray had already for many years promoted devotion to Mary under that title.[27]

During his long tenure as archbishop, the most striking demonstration of diocesan devotion and fervour occurred in 1826. The occasion was the extension of the jubilee year, which had been inaugurated in Rome by Pope Leo XII in 1825, to all Catholics. In 1825, at the dedication of the metropolitan church to the Immaculate Conception – the church later known as the Pro-Cathedral – Archbishop Murray preached on the significance and nature of the forthcoming jubilee. The jubilee indulgence, Murray explained, 'imparts the remission not of sin, but of the temporal punishment that often remains due to sin'. Before receiving the indulgence, he explained, one must first be forgiven for one's sins in the Sacrament of Penance, and this must be followed by reception of the Eucharist.[28]

The language and teaching on indulgences sounds foreign to us nearly two hundred years later, but at the time, according to William Meagher, Murray's friend and biographer, those who 'smiled scornfully at the attempt, as they called it, to engraft on to the enlightenment of the nineteenth century the inanities and follies of the twelfth', had 'miscalculated egregiously'. He explained that 'from Europe's remotest boundaries, and from regions remoter still' people thronged to Rome, and that 'the same devout enthusiasm was felt … in the capital of Ireland'.[29] On 8 March 1826, the jubilee was opened by Archbishop Murray, in the Church of the Immaculate Conception, 'with extraordinary splendour and solemnity'.[30]

The jubilee devotions were conducted in certain named churches. William Meagher captured something of the atmosphere of the week. 'The public devotions commenced each morning at 7 o'clock, consisting of prayers and instructions from the pulpit, and were renewed again at mid-day, and a third time in the evening.' The confessionals 'were crowded almost without interruption by unprecedented multitudes'. Men and women of every rank and age came as penitents. The jubilee had to be extended again and again to meet the demands of other churches, and 'the archbishop renewed, in person, the same imposing ceremonies in each church.' The good effects of the jubilee continued, according to Fr Meagher. 'For a long time, the attachment of the metropolitan Catholics to the observance of their religious duties' had been 'anything but edifying', but now, thanks to the graces of the holy year, there had been for many years an 'amazingly increased frequentation of the sacraments.'[31]

A BUILDER OF CHURCHES

Just four months before the jubilee, the majestic church that Archbishop Troy had envisaged was ready for dedication. Murray was said to have hastened the final stages of the construction, and he was often seen lingering at the scaffolding, encouraging the contractors and labourers.[32] The dedication took place on 14 November 1825, the feast of the patron of the diocese, St Lorcan O'Toole. The occasion evoked much public interest. The ceremony was carefully prepared, and a special choir sang Mozart's Great Mass in C Minor. 'Admission tickets brought in the considerable sum of £2,346.'[33]

A few months later, the contrast between this fine structure and the normal places of worship was evident. The archbishop, in response to the unprecedented outpouring of public fervour and devotion, brought the jubilee to crowded chapels located in outhouses, converted stables or other inadequate structures, set among Dublin's lanes and back streets. The need of fitting churches for his people became an objective of Dr Murray's episcopate. By the time of his death, some ninety-seven commodious churches would be constructed across the archdiocese.[34]

THE CONTINUING QUEST FOR EDUCATION

Apart from these exciting happenings, life for Murray continued in its more humdrum fashion. During 1824, together with a number of other prelates, he signed a petition to be presented by Henry Grattan to the House of Commons, seeking government aid for Catholic schools for the poor. The chief secretary, Henry Goulburn, informed Murray on 18 March 1824 that the petition would not have his support, since he always considered 'that the establishment of a separate and exclusive system of education for the Roman Catholic poor in Ireland was not calculated to promote the welfare of that class of the community nor the general interests of the community'.[35]

After an exchange of letters, a disappointed Murray wrote on 22 April 1824, saying that he had thought from earlier statements of Mr Goulburn that the Irish bishops could look forward to the day when their poor could participate in the benefits of education; but circumstances since then had 'soon dissipated this pleasing illusion'. He deplored the bishops' lack of success and considered that the government's decision could only cause trouble. He concluded mordantly that, while waiting for better days to dawn, the Catholics would continue to do the best they could out of their own scanty resources and with the help of liberal-minded Protestants and others who had always aided them.[36]

Nevertheless, there were some hopeful signs. On 2 March Murray had received notice from the Lord Lieutenant's office that he was receiving a grant of £100 from the schools' fund for the building of a poor school in Townsend Street.[37] Indeed, on the very day Murray had written to Goulburn, the Lord Lieutenant sent word that he was considering the matter raised in the bishops' petition, and that he hoped the Commission of Enquiry to be set up would satisfy all classes. If the bishops wished to present a memorial, he would appoint a time to receive it.[38] In the draft of a reply from Murray, he expresses his thanks for the letter with its news of the intention to set up a commission to enquire into the state of education in Ireland. In welcoming this, he thanked the Lord Lieutenant for his efforts in the matter and also for the grant for poor schools.[39]

ROME'S CONCERN FOR CONVENT LIFE

The year could scarcely end without a request from Propaganda in Rome to look into some matter for them. As usual, it arose from adverse reports they had received. 'It was reported to the pope', Cardinal Somaglia informed Murray on 4 November 1824, 'that the discalced Carmelite nuns, at Ranelagh, have relaxed discipline, are not keeping the rule of their order, are admitting and conversing with seculars etc'. He asked Murray to investigate this matter personally and very discreetly, and to report if there was any truth in the allegations. If there was, Murray was to suggest remedies for the abuses and propose the most prudent method of restoring true observance of the rule and constitutions.[40] The convent concerned was the one where the cure of Sr Mary Stuart had taken place.

Archbishop Murray could never be accused of responding with undue haste. It took him more than a year to reply, which he did on 11 November 1825. He had received, he stated, Pope Leo's command to make confidential enquiries concerning the Ranelagh nuns. As it would be impossible for him personally to conduct such an investigation secretly, he had arranged with a prudent and pious priest, on whom he could depend and on whom he enjoined secrecy, to do so. This priest would make a full report to Murray, who would transmit it to the Holy See.

Murray then went on to say that he thought the reports that reached Rome had little or no foundation. The nuns lived piously and as good religious should, and they had little to do with externs. He felt it necessary to explain, however, their particular circumstances, namely, that they ran two schools. In one school, many poor girls were educated free of charge. 'If that school were not available the girls would in all likelihood go to the Protestant schools and yield to the incentives put before them to abandon their own religion'. The nuns' other school catered for girls of well-to-do parents, who paid fees. Without this school, the nuns could not exist or maintain their poor school. 'According to the custom in Ireland,' he added, 'these parents are allowed to speak to the nuns at certain times and not a breath of scandal has arisen from this'. Some small differences may have arisen among the sisters themselves, but 'the Father Visitor' would settle these when he had heard both sides.[41]

EDGING TOWARDS EMANCIPATION

During February and March 1826, much excitement was generated in Ireland, as the prospect of emancipation seemed imminent. On 3 March, Archbishop Murray was instructed to come to London to attend the House of Commons Committee on the State of Ireland;[42] and on the 18 March he was asked to attend the Bar of the House of Lords.[43] Also on 3 March, Henry Parnell wrote to Murray from the House of Commons, urging him in 'the strongest manner' to comply soon with the request from the House of Commons Committee 'as it is of the greatest importance to have your Lordship's witness given to the persons who have been appointed to prepare the bill for repealing the Penal Laws … I can assure you that there is a most sincere disposition to consult and attend to the opinions of the Catholic bishops'. Henry Parnell concluded, 'I am happy to acquaint [you] that there is every appearance of success.'[44]

Five prelates from Ireland were examined by the Committee, Murray on 22 March and 7 May. Four prelates were examined by the select committee of the House of Lords, with Murray appearing before them on 24 March.[45] In a gracious bridge-building gesture, Dr Poynter hosted Drs Curtis, Murray and Doyle during their time before the Committee.[46]

Daniel O'Connell, meantime, was even more optimistic than Henry Parnell. In February, supported by William Cobbett and Francis Plaice, the radical reformer and agitator, O'Connell held public meetings in England as he endeavoured to overcome prejudice among the worker middling class. 'I am quite vain of my success,' he told Jane Sugrue in exuberant mood on 25 February. 'It is here that the great battle is to be fought. I must make a missionary trip to England every year until Emancipation is achieved…'[47] By the 2 March, he was telling James Sugrue, 'I may venture to say that *we are to be emancipated.* The tide has turned in our favour…';[48] and two days later, he informed his wife, 'I have the happiness to tell you that Emancipation is, I believe, at hand … Indeed, I am sure it is'.[49] In that same letter, written from the House of Commons where he was waiting to be examined by the Committee, the thought of sharing his success with Archbishop Murray caused him to exclaim:

> How anxious I am that the bishops were here! Doctor Murray has not an hour to lose. Darling, go to him yourself in your carriage and tell him I respectfully solicited his immediate coming. I wrote to him myself yesterday. In short, we have won the game.

O'Connell continued, in less than modest terms, 'May I thank Heaven that it was your husband, Sweetest, that won it. If I had not been here, nothing would have been done. I *forced* Sir Francis Burdett to bring on his motion.'[50]

On 1 March, Burdett had presented the petition for Emancipation. On 23 March he introduced the Emancipation bill to the House of Commons. Subsequently two measures (known as 'wings') were added to placate opposition. These disenfranchised the forty-shilling freeholders, and provided remuneration for the Irish Catholic clergy. The House of Commons passed the Emancipation bill, with its wings, but it was rejected by the House of Lords on 17 May 1825. The measures known as 'wings' fell with the bill.

COMMITTEE ON THE STATE OF IRELAND

The 'wings' were not popular with many of the hierarchy, and O'Connell's support for them led to a decline in his reputation. Nevertheless, there were many who were disappointed and dismayed at the bill's defeat by the Lords.[51] Murray,

Doyle and others, meantime, had continued to work with the Committee on the State of Ireland. On 25 April, Murray received a request from the Committee for 'an account of the number of religious houses in each diocese of your province – the order to which they belong, and the number of persons belonging to each, distinguishing men and women – and by what funds they are maintained, and whether any considerable increase or decrease of number had taken place within the last ten years'.[52] Murray set about meeting their request.

The prelates before the Committee were queried about papal power, the appointment of bishops, payment of the clergy and the correspondence of churchmen with Rome. The bishops again stressed that papal authority was limited to the purely spiritual sphere, and they emphasised their full allegiance to their sovereign and the inability of the pope to absolve subjects from that allegiance. They objected to any interference by the Crown in the appointment of bishops. Murray and Doyle claimed that Protestant rulers were never permitted to appoint bishops directly or to exercise a veto over these appointments, but they agreed that compromises had been found in Prussia and Russia. Asked about state payment for the clergy, all the bishops agreed that in the absence of Emancipation it was unacceptable. They preferred the voluntary system, but were prepared to discuss state payment if it were part of the concession of Emancipation. Strangely, neither Murray nor Doyle had serious objections to submitting official Roman documents – bulls, briefs and rescripts – to the scrutiny of the government, provided highly personal and confidential material of a spiritual nature were excluded.[53]

TENSION BETWEEN O'CONNELL AND BISHOP DOYLE

In March 1825, the introduction of new legislation led to the dissolution of the Catholic Association. By July, however, O'Connell had managed to found a new Catholic Association within the law. By the first of November, feeling that he was recovering his reputation, he informed his wife, 'We are beginning to agitate again. Tomorrow we will hold a little aggregate and if that shall succeed we shall hold one every Wednesday'.[54] It was the beginning of a new concerted drive towards Emancipation. In the same letter, he commented to his wife on the stir caused by the Lord Lieutenant's marriage. Marquis Wellesley had married a 'regular Catholic', who 'always goes to Mass publicly'. At the ceremony, 'Dr Murray was attended by two other priests'.

The following day, 2 November, Bishop Doyle wrote to thank Murray for his many kindnesses and to state that he would be at Murray's disposal for the dates mentioned. Doyle was to preach on Sunday, 14 November, at the solemn opening and consecration of the metropolitan church in Marlborough Street, the Pro-Cathedral. Dr Doyle, formerly a champion of O'Connell, was, by then, openly displaying a definite coolness towards him. The occasion of the distance between them appears to have been O'Connell's defence of Burdett's bill with its two wings. Under criticism, O'Connell had maintained, on 9 July, that his entire conduct had 'the entire concurrence and sanction' of Bishop Doyle and Archbishop Murray.[55] On 14 July, Revd Professor William Kinsella of Carlow College wrote a public letter denying that Bishop Doyle had given any sanction to O'Connell's acceptance of the 'wings'.[56] O'Connell responded that he had been misrepresented, and that the concurrence of the two prelates related only to the measure of provision for the clergy.[57] Doyle, however, at a formal dinner in Carlow College in December, just before the provincial meeting of the Catholic Association, made a speech in which he vigorously condemned the 'wings', especially the measure for clerical provision which he described as a 'paltry bribe'.[58] Rightly concerned at the loss of so powerful an advocate, O'Connell, on 18 December, sought the assistance of Dr Jeremiah O'Donovan, a former professor of classics at Carlow College, asking him to find out why Dr Doyle was displeased with him.[59]

A JOINT PASTORAL ADDRESS

Whatever about the distance between Doyle and Murray, on the one hand, and O'Connell on the other, both men joined with the rest of the hierarchy in producing a joint pastoral address, on 25 January 1826,[60] which forwarded the case for Emancipation and pleased O'Connell. Murray and Doyle played a major part in drafting the document, which issued a number of resolutions on the education of Catholic children and a further set of resolutions aimed at counteracting the 'grievous misconceptions regarding certain points of Catholic doctrine' that 'are still unhappily found to exist'. The bishops presented these last resolutions 'that all may be enabled to know with accuracy the general principles of those men who are proscribed by law from any public participation in the honours, dignities and emoluments of the state'. In this part of their address, prior to dealing with public issues relating to political allegiance and related matters, the combined hierarchy dealt with basic matters of doctrine which had been misunderstood.

Having dealt in some detail with these, the bishops went on to reiterate in vigorous form the statements made by their colleagues before the Commission on the State of Ireland regarding their loyalty to the king, the pope's lack of any temporal or civil authority within the realm, their attitude to state provision for the clergy, and so forth. Thus, as their twelfth resolution declared, 'The Catholics of Ireland swear, that they will be faithful, and bear *True Allegiance*, to our most gracious sovereign lord *King George the Fourth*,[61] that they will maintain, support and defend, to the utmost of their power, the succession of the crown to His Majesty's family, against any person or persons whatsoever'.

They further declared that it is not an article of the Catholic faith, nor were Catholics required to believe, that the pope is infallible They added, with a view to allaying fears and countering hostile rumours, that Catholics, far from claiming any right or title to forfeited lands resulting from any right, title or interest which their ancestors may have had therein, declare upon oath 'that they will defend to the utmost of their powers, the settlement and arrangement of property in this country, as established by the law in being'. They also 'disclaim, disavow and solemnly abjure any intention to subvert the present Church establishment', further swearing not to 'exercise any privilege to which they are or maybe entitled to disturb and weaken the Protestant religion and Protestant government in Ireland'. In conclusion, the bishops expressed their readiness to provide 'authentic and true information upon all subjects connected with the doctrine and discipline' of their Church.[62]

This earnest, almost servile, submission was succeeded by Dr Poynter, at the behest of the British Catholic Association, drawing up a statement, signed by all the vicars apostolic of England and Scotland, which asserted their loyalty to the king and also disclaimed any intention of infringing the rights or properties of the established Church.[63]

A SIGNIFICANT ELECTION

By the middle of 1826, there were some signs of renewed optimism in Catholic ranks. The response of the Irish bishops at the parliamentary enquiry and the statements of both hierarchies had gone some way to clearing prejudices about Catholic doctrine and claims. The optimism on the Catholic side received a huge boost as a result of the general election, called for June 1826. In that election, it was decided to challenge the entrenched power of the Beresford family in the Waterford area. A liberal Protestant, favourable to Catholic Emancipation, Henry Villiers-Stuart, was put forward to oppose the dominant Lord George Beresford. Villiers-Stuart's supporters enlisted the parish clergy, who motivated the Catholic voters, especially the forty-shilling freeholders. The clergy denounced the bribery being used by the Beresford side and also the harsh tradition of the Beresford family. Despite fears of reprisals, the Catholic voters stood firm and the pro-Emancipation candidate had a resounding success.

There followed a hasty mobilisation of the Catholic voters in Louth, Westmeath, Monaghan and Armagh, with the result that pro-Emancipation candidates gained victory over the anti-Emancipation members who had held those seats. Richard Lalor Sheil, who had campaigned in Louth, exulted, ' We have awakened the people to the noble consciousness of their religious and political duty ... We have kindled this great, this wide, this expansive flame, which envelops the country.'[64] The Catholic Association had become aware of the power it possessed through the votes of the forty-shilling freeholders, and the expectations of the traditional ruling class had been overturned. In the large majority of county elections, only supporters of Emancipation could expect to win seats. The British Catholic Association recognised the historical significance of the Waterford result. Its members sent their thanks to the bishops, clergy and the forty-shilling freeholders for their electoral victory.[65]

How was all this viewed by Archbishop Murray? The awakening of the people 'to the noble consciousness of their religion' was something Murray and the other bishops welcomed. He, and some of the other bishops as well, felt uneasy about the clergy's involvement in politics, however. The sight of thousands of excited and enthusiastic Catholics led by Catholic priests evoked in Murray, with his memories of 1798, concern about its effect on the Protestant population. He was not alone in his concern. Already in 1824, the Duke of Wellington, viewing the expansion of the Catholic Association, envisaged the prospect of 'civil war in Ireland sooner or later'.[66]

More immediately, in 1826, Murray and his fellow prelates were facing a plan for national education, which the Commission of Enquiry, set up by the Lord Lieutenant, had produced. Murray, it will be recalled, had welcomed the First Lieutenant's initiative in promoting the enquiry, and he was more ready than many of his colleagues to work with the government to arrive at a solution that would benefit Catholic children.

THE HIERARCHY AND NATIONAL EDUCATION

The bishops, in their pastoral address of January 1826, made it clear that, having 'considered attentively' the plan of national education submitted to them, they resolved 'that the admission of Protestants and Roman Catholics into the same schools, for the purpose of literary instruction, under existing circumstances, be allowed, provided sufficient care be taken to protect the religion of the Roman Catholic children, and to furnish them with adequate means of religious instruction.'

This positive response, however, was hedged around with resolutions aimed at protecting the religion of the Catholic children. Thus, in a school where a majority of children were Catholic, it was deemed necessary to have a Catholic headmaster, and where Catholic children were in a minority, a permanent Roman Catholic assistant should be employed. Moreover, it was required that the said headmaster and assistant be appointed on the recommendation, or with the express approval, of the Catholic bishop of the diocese, and that they, or either of them, could be removed on the representation of the said bishop. Also, in conformity with the principle of protecting the religion of the Catholic children, it was required that 'the books intended for their particular instruction in religion' should 'be selected or approved by the Roman Catholic prelates'. Moreover, no book or tract for instruction in literature should be introduced into any school, in which Catholic children were educated, if the book or tract were objected to on religious grounds by the Catholic bishop of the diocese in which the school was established. Looking ahead, the bishops considered it improper that masters or mistresses intended for the religious instruction of Roman Catholic youth should be trained or educated under the control of personnel professing a different faith; and they considered it desirable that a male and female model school be established in each province in Ireland, supported at the public expense, for the purpose of qualifying such teachers. Finally, on a solemn note, in their sixth resolution, the bishops declared:

> As appointed by divine providence to watch over our flocks, we will, in our respective dioceses, withhold any concurrence and support from any system of education which will not fully accord with the principles expressed in the foregoing resolutions.[67]

Concerned as ever about education for the poor, Murray in 1826 availed of the support of Catholic gentry and friends to establish, at the close of the year, an Education Society with a view to founding free schools for the doctrinal, moral and useful instruction of the poor. It had as its president Lord Cloncurry and as its vice-presidents Lords Dungannon and Killeen and Sir Thomas Esmonde.[68]

SADNESS AND REGRET

At the close of Daniel Murray's early years as archbishop of Dublin, the combined Catholic hierarchy had made important statements on national education and had made a wholehearted contribution towards easing the way to emancipation; and Murray, as archbishop, had grown further in esteem among his fellow prelates.

There was one occurrence in 1826, however, which must have aroused in Murray feelings of sadness and, perhaps, twinges of regret, even of guilt. The death of the vicar-apostolic, John Milner, took place at Wolverhampton on 19 April 1826. An outstanding champion of Catholic Emancipation, and deeply devoted to the Holy See, he had been more at home with Irish churchmen than with most of his fellow Englishmen. He was mentor and friend to Murray on the latter's first visit to Rome on the veto issue. He much admired the young Murray.

By 1817, however, Murray had drawn away from him. He was slow to respond to Milner's letters, much to Milner's distress. Murray's temperament, with its practice of a honeyed and gracious attitude towards opponents, was at odds with Milner's more black-and-white approach, whereby opponents were viewed as villains to be buffeted by voice and pen with polemic and vituperation. The opponents in question included Dr Poynter and many English Catholics as well as government ministers. He had become something of an embarrassment to Murray, especially in relation to his contacts with English Catholics and with representatives of the government. To a man as sensitively perceptive as Murray, the pain he caused to his old friend was likely to have challenged him on hearing of John Milner's death. This was probably exacerbated when Dr Curtis, who had the settlement of Milner's affairs, informed Murray that certain stocks were in his name and a bequest had been left to him.[69]

Soon, however, the momentum of the Catholic movement was to occupy Murray's attention and relegate his anti-veto protagonist to prayerful memory.

NOTES

1 Wm Meagher. *Notices of the Life and Character of His Grace Most Rev. Daniel Murray* (Dublin 1853), 'Public Letters of Dr Murray', pp.144–48. Italics in text.
2 Curtis – Murray, 20 Aug. 1823, file 30/7, no.12.
3 *The Irishman*, 29 Aug. 1823, ref. idem, no.55.
4 Curtis – Murray, 19 Aug. 1823, idem, no.10.
5 Murray – Laffan, 4 April 1823, no.5, 1 July 1823, no.3.
6 Laffan – Murray, 31 Dec. 1823. Laffan – Murray, 6 Aug. 1824, file 30/8, no.4; idem 10 Aug. 1824, no.5; idem 14, 27 Aug. 1824, nos.7, 6.
7 Pope Leo XII – Irish Archbishops, 22 Nov. 1823, file 30/7, no.14.
8 Murray – Card. Consalvi, 20 March 1824, idem, no.80.
9 Cit. A. Macauley. *The Catholic Church and the Campaign for Emancipation in Ireland and England* (Dublin: Four Courts Press, 2016), p.327, n.7, from I. Whelan. *The Bible War in Ireland: the 'Second Reformation' and the polarization of Protestant – Catholic relations, 1800–1840* (Madison,WI: University of Wisconsin Press, 2005), pp.134–70.

10 Stewart J Brown. 'The New Reformation Movement in the Church of Ireland, 1822–1829' in S. J. Brown & D. W. Miller (eds) *Piety and Power in Ireland, 1760–1960, Essays in honour of Emmet Larkin* (Belfast: Institute of Irish Studies, 2000), pp.180–81.
11 Patrick J. Corish, *The Irish Catholic Experience, a Historical Survey*, (Dublin: Gill and Macmallin, 1985), p.157.
12 Richard Lalor Shiel cit O. McDonagh. *The Heriditary Bondsman: Daniel O'Connell,1775-1829* (London 1988), p.205, cit Bartlett. *The Fall and Rise of the Irish Nation,* p.304.
13 O'Connell – Abp. Robert Laffan, 10 March 1824, a model of his letters to the Irish Catholic prelates, *Correspondence of Daniel O'Connell*, vol. iii, no. 1110 and notes 1 and 2, pp.51–2.
14 *O'Connell's Speeches*. Ii, 411 (May 1823), *O'Connell's Correspondence,* ii, 465–6; cit. Bartlett, p.329.
15 *Freeman's Journal*, 31 May 1824. See Macauley op. cit., p.327.
16 Macauley, op. cit., p.327.
17 Idem, n.11, pp.328–9, cit. S. J. Reynolds, *The Catholic Emancipation Crisis in Ireland, 1823–1829* (Newport CT, 1970), p.65.
18 *Dublin Evening Post (DEP),* 24 June 1824.
19 Cit. T. McGrath. *The Public Ministry of Bishop James Doyle* ... (Dublin: Four Courts Press, 1999), pp.24–5.
20 Macauley. op. cit. p.330.
21 D. Kerr. 'Dublin's Forgotten Archbishop, Daniel Murray, 1768–1852' in J. Kelly & D. Keogh. *History of the Catholic Diocese of Dublin*, p.260.
22 Idem, p. 248.
23 Idem, p. 262.
24 DDA. Murray Papers. Printed Pastoral Letter, 24 Feb. 1824, file 30/8/1.
25 Idem. Printed Program in Latin, May – October 1824, file 30/8/2.
26 F. P. Carey. Archbishop Murray of Dublin (1768-1852), p.15.
27 Myles Ronan. 'Archbishop Murray, 1768-1852', in IER, April 1952, p.246.
28 Wm Meagher. op. cit. 'The Great Jubilee of 1825', pp.102–5.
29 Idem, pp.102-3.
30 Idem, p.103.
31 Idem, pp.106–7.
32 F. P. Carey. op. cit. p.16.
33 Myles Ronan, art. cit. op. cit. p.243.
34 F. P. Carey. op. cit. p.16.
35 H. Goulburn – Murray, 15 March 1824. DDA. Murray Papers. File 30/8, no.58.
36 Murray – Goulburn, 22 April 1824, idem, no.60.
37 W. Gregory (Dublin Castle) – Murray, 2 March 1824, File 30/8, no.33.
38 Lieut. Col. Shane – Murray, 22 April 1824, idem, no.64.
39 Murray – Ld. Lieutenant, April/May 1824, idem, no.43.
40 Card. Somaglia – Murray, 4 Nov. 1824, f. 30/8, no.107.
41 Murray – Propaganda, 11 Nov. 1825, f. 30/9, n.51.
42 House of Commons Committee – Murray, 3 March 1825, f. 30/9, no.8.
43 House of Lords – Murray, 18 March 1825, f. 30/9, no.9.
44 Henry Parnell – Murray, 3 March 1825, f. 30/9, no.10.
45 *O'Connell Correspondence,* vol. iii, no. 1185, no.2.
46 Macauley. op. cit., p.341.
47 *O'Connell Corresp.* O'Connell – J. Sugrue, 25 Feb. 1825, no.1177, p.124.
48 Idem. O'Connell – James Sugrue, 2 March 1825, no. 1179, p.127. Italics in text.
49 Idem, O'Connell – His Wife, 4 March 1825, n. 1180, p.128.

50 Idem, p.129.
51 Abp. Curtis – Dr Poynter, 25 May 1825, cit. Macauley, op. cit., p.342.
53 Committee of House of Comm. – Murray, 25 April 1825, f. 30/9/12.
53 Macauley. op. cit pp.343–4.
54 *O'Connell Corresp.* O'Connell – Wife, 1 Nov. 1825, no.1258, p.197.
55 *Freeman's Journal*, 11 July 1825.
56 Idem, 20 July 1825.
57 *O'Connell Corresp.* O'Connell – J. Donovan, 18 Dec. 1825, no.1273, no.2.
58 Idem, no.1273, no.4, p.216.
59 Idem, no.1273, p.215.
60 Murray Papers. Printed Pastoral Address of the R.C. Archbishops and Bishops to the Clergy and Laity of their Communion throughout Ireland. File 30/9, Irish Bishops no.49.
61 Italics in place of large Capital Letters in text.
62 Same Pastoral Address, Resolution XIV.
63 Macauley, op. cit. p.351.
64 Cit. idem, p.354.
65 Idem.
66 Wellington-Peel, 3 Nov. 1824. *Peel Correspondence*, i, 348–9, cit. Bartlett, p.333.
67 Pastoral Address cit. n 60 above.
68 *O'Connell Corresp.* vol.iii, no.1441, no.7.
69 DDA. Curtis – Murray, 27 April 1826, f. 30/9, no.44.

CHAPTER 7

The Years to Catholic Emancipation (1827–30)

Public events impinged on Daniel Murray as archbishop early in 1827. During February he was a prime mover in the archbishops' petition for Emancipation to the House of Lords. In their petition, the bishops emphasised their loyalty to the king and pointed to their pastoral address of 1826 as disclaiming any suggestion of disloyalty.

Shortly afterwards, Sir Francis Burdett's motion that the House of Commons set up a committee to consider Catholic claims was defeated. Peel added to the disappointment of Catholic clergy and laity by stating that Catholics did not observe the second commandment. The insulting nature of Peel's comment was further impressed on Murray by Eneas McDonnell, the Irish Catholic Association's agent in London. He referred him to a newspaper report in which Peel accused the Irish bishops of being untruthful in their address of January 1826 since, contrary to their claim that Catholics observed the Ten Commandments, their catechism showed that they did not accept the second commandment. Murray found it difficult to accept that Peel could have held such an opinion, but he felt it necessary to demonstrate in the public forum how mistaken that view was. He did so in the form of a public letter to Eneas McDonnell, which appeared in the *Freeman's Journal* of 25 March 1827.

CORRESPONDENCE AND ANNOUNCEMENTS

Overall, the year 1827 was relatively free of stress for Murray. Correspondence, as usual, must have taken much of his time. Some of the correspondence addressed to him in March and April reflected conditions in the city and country. Many letters contained appeals for financial assistance, some sought posts as teachers, and some carried complaints about neighbours or clergy. Unfortunately, Murray's replies to these and most other letters have not survived.

In March, Murray received a significant printed address from the Catholic

Association. It highlighted an ongoing problem for the political progress of the Catholic movement, expressing concern about violent outbreaks that weakened the campaign for emancipation. Addressed to the people of Ireland, it warned them to avoid secret societies and gave reasons for doing so. It was signed by Daniel O'Connell and O'Gorman Mahon.[1] The following month, another printed item carried the welcome announcement of the founding and aims of the Catholic Book Society. Set up to counter the publications of the Bible societies, Murray and Doyle took a great interest in its establishment and development.[2]

The Archbishop's friendly attitude towards government officials, often criticised by opponents, was acknowledged in a letter of appreciation from the Irish Office in London, on 22 July. The writer was William Lambe, subsequently Lord Melbourne and prime minister. He wrote:[3]

> I shall not again visit Ireland in the character of Secretary. When I was last in Dublin I called upon your Grace to thank you for the friendship and assistance which I received from you during my continuance in that office. In whatever station I may be placed, I shall ever retain a potent sense of it, as well as an anxious desire to promote by every means the religious peace and civil prosperity of Ireland.

Despite the prohibition of episcopal titles to Irish Catholic prelates, Lambe clearly had no difficulty addressing Murray as 'your Grace', and valuing his friendship – which says something significant about both men.

Towards the end of 1827, Murray received news of the death of Dr Poynter. The latter's successor as vicar apostolic of the London district, Dr James Bramston, wrote to the archbishop of Dublin, on 30 November, to announce that 'the last days' of the lamented friend 'were in conformity with the whole of his excellent life'.[4] Then, in the following month, welcome news arrived regarding Murray's plans for the education of Dublin's poor.

PROSPECT OF A MODEL SCHOOL

In the Catholic Association, on 8 December, Daniel O'Connell recommended that £1,500 be appropriated for establishing in Dublin a model school in opposition to the proselytising establishments which, he claimed, were in operation there.[5] Resolutions to that effect were carried by O'Connell at the Association's aggregate meeting on 19 December. The news of a model school gave rise to questions about its location. O'Connell received very clear advice and much information on education in the city in a letter from a Michael Hickey, of 40 Jervis Street, Dublin.[6] Writing on 15 December, Hickey urged that the site for the new school be located on the north side of the city. No part of the archdiocese of Dublin or of the country at large had a greater claim, he said. There was 'an extremely numerous and poor school population' in that area, an 'almost total lack of free school education', and there was 'the baleful and destructive influence of nearly forty fanatical and proselytising establishments'. There were 'thirty-six of these establishments in Murray's united parishes, to which upwards of a thousand Catholic children are attending'.

The writer went on to observe that 'Doctor Murray's Education Society, since its establishment this time twelve months, has done wonders. It has five schools superintended by efficient masters and attended by between six and seven hundred boys. These schools are crowded to excess. Still, they are unable to stem the torrent of proselytism pouring in upon the people in this part of the city.' Having compared the greater need of the north side of the river Liffey compared to the south side, the writer went on to suggest a suitable site in King's Inn Street, for which he felt that he had 'made out a good case'.

The year ended with the idea of a mission to England to combat anti-Catholic popular prejudices, and 'to unweave those webs of calumny and deceit of which the Bible and Tract Missionaries have been the dishonest artificers'. The idea was proposed at the meeting of the Catholic Association on 22 December 1827.[7] It is not clear that Murray was consulted about the venture, and it is not clear that he would have welcomed an enterprise likely to be unacceptable to Protestant friends and acquaintances, as well as to many English Catholics. In the end, disagreement within the Irish Catholic Association resulted in the mission never setting out.[8] Nevertheless, the degree of confidence and enthusiasm suggested by the envisaged mission to England was an expression of the powerful wave of public enthusiasm for Emancipation being expressed during 1828. Murray and the bishops were borne along by it.

Among the other demands on Murray's time, requests from Rome could not be neglected. They were tokens of esteem.

REQUESTS FROM ROME

Like Troy before him, Murray was approached on occasion by Rome, requesting his advice on certain matters, or instructing him to fulfil specific roles. In June, he was consulted about the appointment of a coadjutor archbishop for Armagh. Dr Curtis had recommended three names from which the appointment ought to be made, and Propaganda wished Murray to forward, in strict confidence, his own opinion as to which of these should be promoted, in view of the discord that existed among the Armagh clergy.[9] Later that year, in September, Propaganda once again contacted Murray, asking his opinion about a matter raised by Dr Doyle.[10] In August, Doyle had written to Propaganda seeking a reduction in the number of holidays of obligation or, as an alternative, permission for Irish Catholics who attended Mass on those days to be relieved of their obligation to abstain from servile work.

A month later, Murray was asked for his opinion once again, this time about a situation that had arisen in the diocese of Ossory. On Murray's recommendation, the Holy See had appointed Fr Miles Murphy as bishop of Ossory. Since then, Murphy had written to Propaganda, refusing the appointment, saying that he was unequal to the task and was repugnant to the priests of the diocese. This was very displeasing to Propaganda, who had thought that tranquillity would be restored in Ossory by following Murray's advice. In strictest confidence, Murray was asked to inform Propaganda of his opinion. Should the refusal be accepted? If it should, who should be chosen in Murphy's stead?[11] Murray advised that Murphy's offer be accepted and he recommended a Fr William Kinsella in his place. He was duly appointed.

POPULAR PRESSURE FOR EMANCIPATION

During 1828, Murray was concerned at the swell of popular enthusiasm and the perceptible sense of repressed violence, and he feared an armed response from Orange and government agencies. O'Connell maintained pressure on the government, and at the last meeting of the Catholic Association in 1827, proposed that there should be petitions ready for the opening of parliament on 22 January 1828. In order to show that Irish Catholics were friends of civil and religious liberty, these petitions would be for the emancipation of Catholics and also of the Dissenters of England.[12] On 13 January, as a challenge to government, the Association organised 'simultaneous meetings' in some 1,600 of the 2,500 parishes in the country.

That the government was going to adopt a strongly negative attitude seemed indicated nine days later, when the Duke of Wellington was appointed prime minister and Robert Peel home secretary. The rising demand for emancipation continued in public meetings, however. The general enthusiasm was such that Archbishop Curtis, at the end of January 1828, felt obliged to agree to an invitation to preside at an Emancipation meeting in Drogheda, which was within his archdiocese of Armagh. He did so, he declared, as a resident of the town, not as archbishop, lest opponents might claim that the clergy were dictating the political agenda.[13] Archbishop Curtis, were it known, was privately opposed to Emancipation. On 22 October 1828, he would make this remarkable disclosure to Sir John Sinclair, a Scottish acquaintance: 'My own firm opinion is … that … Emancipation is a contemptible thing and not worth the tenth part of the struggle, labour, expense and irritation it has cost already'.[14]

EDUCATION A PRIORITY

Murray, meantime, had education as his immediate priority. In February, the Irish bishops joined with him in petitioning parliament for improved education for the poor of Ireland. Murray contacted William Lambe, asking him to present the petition to the House of Commons. On 12 February, Lambe declared that while he would always be ready to help in anything concerning Ireland, in 'the present circumstances' he thought it better not to present the petition. The 'present circumstances' seemed to relate to the recent death of his wife.

There was more positive news on 11 March, with the appointment by the House of Commons of a select committee on Irish education. A frequent contact of Murray's on educational matters, Thomas Spring Rice, MP for Limerick, contacted him on 16 May to announce that Rice's report on education had been almost unanimously adopted by the select committee, and would be presented to the house on the coming Monday where he hoped it would be well received. It was framed with the desire to act impartially and justly.[15] Three days later, both men would have been well pleased when the report of the select committee of the House of Commons on Irish education recommended the establishment of a government body to control elementary schools. Further good educational news came for Murray three weeks later when, on 9 June, Daniel O'Connell laid the foundation stone of the Catholic Model School in Richmond Street, on the north side of the city of Dublin. The school later became known as O'Connell School.

HOPEFUL SIGNS AND TROUBLESOME RUMOURS

While these developments were taking place, there were some hopeful signs where emancipation was concerned. The appointment during March of Henry Paget, Marquis of Anglesey, as Lord Lieutenant was viewed as a favourable omen, as he was considered to be a friend of religious liberty. Then there was the repeal of the Test and Corporation Acts. These acts dated from the seventeenth century, and required officials in boroughs, military officers and other crown officers not only to take the oath of supremacy and allegiance, but also to receive the sacrament according to the rites of the Church of England. The repeal of these acts enabled Dissenters to take their place in parliament, which was welcomed by Irish Catholic leaders as a further advance towards civil liberty.

In April, rumours came from Rome of a concordat being arranged between the British government and the Papacy. O'Connell, for whom they conjured up a recurrence of the veto, took these rumours very seriously. The Irish people, he declared in April 1828, 'would not allow the pope or any spiritual authority to interfere with their civil rights'.[16]

Murray soon became the recipient of letters on the matter. Michael Blake, who had reopened the Irish College in Rome in 1824, informed Murray, on 10 May 1828, that he had been assured by the prefect of Propaganda, Cardinal Bartolomeo Capellari, that no negotiations had taken place between the British cabinet and the Holy See on that subject.[17] Nevertheless, a short time later, Robert Gradwell, who had been rector of the English College in Rome and was recently appointed coadjutor bishop in the London District, let it be known that he had to hurry back to England, because the Pope and the congregation wished that he might be their agent in any negotiations regarding a concordat.[18]

In October, Christopher Boylan, who had taken over at the Irish College in succession to Fr Blake, informed Murray rather alarmingly that he and all the Irish bishops should be ready to fight against any restrictions on their rights that might be made with the consent of Rome. In his view, the Irish bishops did not enjoy much prestige at the Vatican, with most of them being 'looked upon as too deficient in their qualities of coolness, sagacity, and penetration to entitle their opinions to much weight in the … contemplated statement of the Catholic grievances'. These impressions, Boylan largely attributed to the influence of Gradwell.[19]

It was not until 2 April 1829 that Boylan was able to report happily to Murray that the danger had passed.[20] The whole matter had been blown out of proportion. Indeed, Dr Ambrose Macaulay observes in his recent book on the period, that 'there is no mention of a concordat in the relevant Roman archives. Such proposals as there were probably got no further than friendly discussions with some cardinals or Roman officials'.

THE SIGNIFICANT CLARE ELECTION

While rumours of a concordat were receiving attention in Rome, England and Ireland, the issue of Catholic Emancipation had been raised to a new level by a by-election in Co. Clare. The member for the county, Vesey Fitzgerald, had been appointed president of the board of trade, and had to vacate his seat pending an election. The Catholic Association decided to put forward a candidate, but no agreed candidate was forthcoming. Then, on 24 June, two weeks before the election, Daniel O'Connell put his name forward. If elected O'Connell, as a Catholic, could not take the oath required of members of parliament, so that his challenging presence in the contest infuriated opponents but stimulated and excited his supporters. He campaigned with vigour. His electoral opponent, Vesey Fitzgerald, was in favour of Catholic claims, but he was attacked brutally by O'Connell, denouncing him as the ally and colleague of Peel and Wellington, 'the most bitter, persevering and unmitigated enemies of Catholics'.[21] Backed by the priests of the diocese of Killaloe, who rallied the forty-shilling freeholders and helped maintain discipline, O'Connell won the contest by an overwhelming majority: 2,057 votes to 982. His victory made news throughout the country, as well as in Britain and on the Continent. Bishop Doyle, who had sent a letter of encouragement before the election, rejoiced at the result, as did most of the Catholic bishops and clergy. The British Catholic Association extended its warmest thanks to the Irish Association, congratulating it on advancing the cause of Emancipation, and congratulating the Irish Catholics too 'on their most exemplary forbearance under unparalleled provocation'.[22]

Although Peel and Wellington did not publicly comment on the Clare election, they were conscious of the significance of the result. Peel was aware of the difficulty of resisting a movement that did not use violence or break the law. At the same time, he was also conscious of the increasing hostility of the Brunswick Clubs, an Orange organisation formed to oppose Emancipation. The peace of the country was clearly endangered, and Wellington informed the King on 1 August 1828 of the deepening risk of rebellion in Ireland. He received permission to discuss the concession of emancipation with Peel and the chancellor, Lord Lyndhurst. They agreed that it had to be granted.[23]

Expectation of emancipation was widespread in Ireland. O'Connell was given added encouragement by the support in Dublin of influential Protestants, including several noblemen, who declared for an end to the disqualifying laws against Catholics.[24] During October and November 1828, however, the danger loomed of a split between the Irish and English Catholic Associations. Some members of the English Association, led by the Duke of Norfolk, stated that while desiring unconditional emancipation they were prepared to agree to certain acceptable securities. This was unacceptable to O'Connell and the Irish Association. The danger of an actual severance between the two associations was averted by the government not pursuing the need for securities of an ecclesiastical nature.

Towards the end of 1828, Archbishop Patrick Curtis, alarmed by the depth of popular feeling for emancipation, decided to write to the Duke of Wellington to hasten the recognition of Catholics' rights. He had met Wellington when he was rector of the Irish College at Salamanca, where he had permitted his students to act as guides to British forces. The Duke replied on 11 December. He was, he remarked, 'sincerely anxious to witness the settlement of the Roman Catholic question', but he saw no prospect of a settlement as the matter was bedevilled by party passions which prevented the matter being considered disinterestedly.[25]

The response indicated some movement on the Duke's part, but Catholics were no longer prepared to be put off by further delays. Curtis showed the letter to a few friends and to O'Connell. Lord Anglesey, the Lord Lieutenant, who was supportive of the Catholic claims and was friendly with Archbishop Murray, also learned of Wellington's reply and recommended that it be published widely in the newspapers. In a letter to Curtis, he advised that 'the Catholic should trust to the justice of his cause – to the growing liberality of mankind', and he regretted that the Catholic had 'lost some friends and fortified his enemies within the last six months by unmeasured and unnecessary violence'.[26] At this stage, Anglesey knew that he was to be removed from office because of his attitude towards the Catholic agitation.[27]

The dismissal of Anglesey, with suggestions of failings as Lord Lieutenant, caused serious disappointment to churchmen and Catholic politicians in Ireland. The *Freeman's Journal*, of 12 January 1829, reported that Archbishop Murray attended a meeting of the Catholic Association at which an address was presented to Anglesey. According to the report, the archbishop asserted that it was not by 'personal or irritating insinuations' that the retiring viceroy should be honoured or the interests of the country promoted. 'A more steadying hand', Murray insisted, 'never held the destinies of Ireland.' The viceroy's recall was 'a national misfortune, and a new infusion into the cup of Irish calamity'.

THE ARRIVAL OF EMANCIPATION

In January 1829, Wellington informed the King of heightened agitation in Ireland, and sought his permission to have a solution, satisfactory to Protestants and Catholics, discussed in cabinet. As Peel had withdrawn his threat to resign if emancipation were granted, George IV reluctantly gave his consent. Proposals for emancipation could now be drawn up.

O'Connell decided to go to London to influence the situation. It was agreed to dissolve the Catholic Association and, at the last meeting of that body, before his departure on 6 February, O'Connell enthused about the bill for emancipation, claiming – inaccurately – that it was already prepared. Confident that it would be free of conditions, O'Connell declared that he would rather 'die on the scaffold than ever consent to an abolition of that brave, that noble, and generous body', the forty-shilling freeholders.[28]

When parliament met on 5 February 1829, the King's speech outlined the government's plans. The House of Commons supported the proposal to link emancipation with the dissolution of the Catholic Association and the disfranchisement of the forty-shilling freeholders. Many Protestant bishops strongly opposed the measure, and 720 anti-Catholic petitions, containing more than 100,000 signatures,[29] were sent to parliament. Nevertheless, the bill passed its third reading on 10 April and, on 13 April, the King signed it into law. Bonfires blazed on Irish hills, and O'Connell put aside his promise to die on the scaffold rather than consent to the abolition of the 'noble and generous forty-shilling freeholders'.

EFFECTS OF THE EMANCIPATION ACT

Catholics could now enter parliament. All offices, civil and military, were open to them except the monarchy, the lord chancellorships of England and Ireland, and the lord lieutenancy of Ireland. The former, offensive oath repudiating Catholic beliefs was replaced by a general oath of allegiance. The basic elements of the previous oaths remained: the royal succession, the pledge not to disturb or weaken the Protestant religion or government, the denial of papal power to depose princes, and the denial of papal jurisdiction in the civil or temporal affairs of the realm. As a sedative to the Protestant opposition, Catholic bishops were forbidden to use the title of their sees, and the Jesuits and other religious orders were forbidden, with unseemly autocratic intent, to enter the country; those already resident were obliged to register, and were prevented from admitting new members.

On 6 March 1829, O'Connell had written to Murray about three aspects of the bill. The first concerned the change in the Catholic oath. It was now to run, 'that I will not use my privileges etc. to disturb *or* weaken the Protestant religion *or* government'. In the earlier oath there was *and* where the *or* now stood. In O'Connell's view, this change did not make any essential difference but he submitted his private opinion to his 'lawful superiors'. As regards episcopal titles, a law against their use already existed, but if Murray thought the matter important he would, of course, oppose it. As to 'the proposed law against monastic extension' – the prevention of admission to religious orders – it 'will be, I think, one of those statutes against which we lawyers delight to drive four in hand'.[30]

Murray and the Dublin clergy signed a joint petition seeking a repeal of the law against Jesuits and other religious orders, and sent it to the Duke of Wellington on 6 April. He replied on 18 April stating that he would 'take an early opportunity of presenting the letter to the House of Lords'.[31] A similar letter and petition had been sent by Murray to Robert Peel at an earlier date. Peel replied on 23 March acknowledging receipt of the letter and petition, and stating that he had 'presented same'. He joined in the hope expressed by the signatories that 'the result of the measure now before parliament may be the establishment of religious peace and the renewal of mutual confidence'.[32]

Peter Kenney, superior of the Jesuits in Ireland, had been concerned at the attitude and language of the document regarding the religious orders. On 1 April he was deeply moved to receive a letter from his friend, Archbishop Murray, together with a copy of the joint petition. He replied from London a week later expressing heartfelt feelings 'for the honourable testimony rendered to us in common with the other religious of the archdiocese of Dublin by your Grace and the clergy of the archdiocese'. He would feel gratified 'at any opportunity of testifying to the clergy of Dublin how much this splendid proof of their charity, piety and ecclesial spirit has increased the affection' he had 'ever felt for them'. The tribute of the archbishop and the secular clergy to the regular clergy, Kenney added, had done much good in England, as it showed the union and good feeling that existed in Dublin between the different bodies of clergy. He regretted that the petition was not now going to the Lords; and he suggested that some influential peer say a few words supporting the anticipated amendments to the Duke of Wellington's bill.[33] The amendments Kenney hoped for did not prevail.

LETTER FROM THE HIERARCHY

The oath of allegiance prescribed in the act was forwarded to Rome for approval. Its examiner, Carlo Vizzardelli, had reservations about certain parts of the oath, but it was accepted by the recently elected Pope Pius VIII.[34] In Ireland, on 9 February 1830, the hierarchy issued a letter to the Catholic population about these developments. Largely written by Dr Doyle and approved by Murray, it conveyed lavish praise of the King and Prime Minister Wellington. At a time of upheaval 'our gracious and beloved Sovereign, walking in the footsteps of his royal father (whose memory be ever cherished) commiserated the state of Ireland, and resolved to confer upon her the inestimable blessing of peace. This great boon became the more acceptable to this country, because, among the councillors of his Majesty, there appeared … the most distinguished of Ireland's sons, a hero and a legislator … a man raised up by Providence to confirm thrones, to re-establish altars … and to staunch the blood and heal the wounds of the country which gave him birth. An enlightened and wise parliament confirmed what the sovereign and his councillors commanded'.

In view of all that, the bishops went on, was not the king, whom they were bound to honour by the law of God, now entitled to all obedience and gratitude? And did not his ministers merit from the Catholic people 'all confidence commensurate with the labours and zeal evinced by them'? And was not that legislation, 'which raised you up from your prostate condition, entitled to your reverence and love'? Moving on to the attainment of emancipation, the bishops took care to join themselves with the lay population in that achievement. 'We united our efforts with those of the laity in seeking to attain their just rights and to obtain them without a compromise of freedom of the Church. Success attended our efforts because reason and justice, and religion, and the voice of mankind were on our side.'

The bishops rejoiced at the result, the letter continued, regardless of the provisions which injuriously affected not only themselves 'but those religious orders which the Church of God, even from the apostolic times, has matured and cherished'. These revisions constituted a sacrifice required 'not by reason or policy, but by prejudices holding captive the minds of some honest men'. They rejoiced, nevertheless, at the overall good affected for the country, but also because they were now discharged 'from a duty which necessity alone' had allied to their ministry and which they hoped that they, or their successors, would never have to resume. These, the bishops declared, 'are the sentiments which the spirit of our calling inspires … and which our clergy, always obedient to our voice, will cherish along with us'.[35] This last, was more an aspiration than an objective representation of the bishops' relations with their clergy.

HIGH HOPES AND OMINOUS SIGNS

The adulation of the king and prime minister was part of the choreography of the period, and was meant to impress and win goodwill. It did so to some extent; but if the bishops were hoping for long-term benefits from the King and Wellington, their hopes were soon greatly undermined. Five months later, on 26 June 1830, George IV died, and in August Wellington was voted out of office.

Emancipation was viewed as a panacea by many Catholics. Bishop Doyle had stated that once emancipation was granted 'the whole of the Catholic population would consider their grievances, as it were, at an end'. He anticipated the cessation of religious strife, a surge of internal improvements, and an influx of English capital.[36] The Catholic hierarchy, as noted, looked forward to a dignified retreat from political agitation and a return to the primacy of its spiritual mission. All were to be proved wrong, though this was not yet perceptible.

What soon became apparent, however, was the government's grudging and mean-spirited enactment of the law. O'Connell, despite his resounding victory in the Clare election of 1828, was required to stand for election again before being allowed sit in parliament. Nevertheless, he embarked on his parliamentary career with high hopes and intent. On 3 August 1829, he wrote to Murray announcing that he was now an MP and that he would be honoured to do his utmost to forward the bishops' wishes with respect to Catholic charities and Catholic education, matters to which he had devoted much thought. Now that emancipation had been granted, measures should be taken to place Church endowments in a state of perfect legal security. He would be glad to do everything he could to assist in this.[37]

O'Connell hailed the gaining of emancipation as 'a bloodless revolution more extensive in its operation than any other political change that could take place'.[38] At the end of his long, exhausting and successful campaign, he retired to his home at Derrynane, Co. Kerry. From there, on 22 October 1829, he wrote in high spirits to the utilitarian philosopher, Jeremy Bentham, declaring that 'the change of scene – of house – of habits – of exercise gives a new tone to my mind, and I leave this place with a new impulse, and with my mind new strung for … my winter campaign'.[39] The 'winter campaign', in a hopefully bright new era, was to prove difficult and crepuscular.

A SOLUTION TO EPISCOPAL APPOINTMENTS

While public attention was centred on the struggle for emancipation and its achievement, a solution was found, almost unnoticed, to the formerly disputed question of Irish Catholic episcopal appointments. A sub-committee of the bishops examined the issue from 5–12 February 1829, with a view to submitting a proposal to the Holy See. Its report was accepted by the hierarchy on 12 February, and forwarded to Rome by three of the archbishops, Curtis, Murray and Laffan. The fourth archbishop, Oliver Kelly of Tuam, was already in Rome, ready to recommend the episcopal proposal, which conveyed what had become the practice in Ireland.[40]

The letter of the three archbishops proposed that when a see became vacant, the names of three persons would be recommended by a section of the clergy of the diocese, and three names by the bishops of the province. Each group would separately meet and forward its proposals to Rome. On 20 June, Propaganda Fide accepted the archbishops' proposal subject to five modifications. Of these, the most important was the stipulation that the proposed recommendations were informative only, and not obligatory on the Holy See. On 17 October 1829, Cardinal Capellari wrote to Murray reiterating the prescriptions to be observed and enclosing the decree, which settled the method of Irish Episcopal appointments.[41] For the first time since the end of the Stuart influence, the voice of Irish Catholics in the selection of Irish bishops had been formally recognised by Rome.

As 1829 passed, however, there was in view for Archbishop Murray and Bishop Doyle the pursuit of a system of education sponsored by the government that would benefit the less well-off across the country.

NOTES

1 Printed address to people of Ireland, DDA, f.30/10/18.
2 Catholic Book Society leaflet, idem, f.30/10/26.
3 Wm Lambe – Murray, 22 July 1827, f.30/10/37.
4 Bramston – Murray, 30 Nov. 1827, f.30/10/10
5 *Dublin Evening Post (DEP)*, 11 Dec. 1827.
6 Ml. Hickey – O'Connell, 15 Dec. 1827. *O'Connell Correspondence*, vol.iii, no.1441, pp.366–67.
7 *DEP* 24 Dec. 1827.
8 O'Connell – his Wife, 24 Dec. 1827, note 1. *O'Connell Corresp.* vol.iii, no. 1441.
9 Propaganda – Murray, 28 June 1828, f.30/11/59.
10 Idem, 21 Aug. 1828, f.30/11/64 and 30 Sept. f.30/11/70.
11 Idem, 4 Oct. 1828, f. 30/11/72.Murray recommended that Murphy's refusal be accepted. He and Dr Doyle recommended in his stead William Kinsella, who was appointed on 15 May 1829 – Propaganda to Murray, 28 May 1829, f. 31/2/19.
12 *Freeman's Journal,* 1 Jan. 1828.
13 Idem, 23 Jan. 1828.
14 Curtis – Sir Jn. Sinclair, 22 Oct. 1828, cit. T. McGrath. *The Public Ministry of Bishop James Doyle,* p.66, and see A. Macauley *The Catholic Church and the Campaign for Emancipation* ... p.376.
15 Spring – Rice-Murray, 16 May 1828, f. 30/11/4.
16 *Freeman's Journal,* 17 April 1828.
17 Blake – Murray, 10 May 1828, DDA. Cit. Macauley, op.cit., p.363.
18 Macauley, op. cit., p.363.
19 Boylan – Murray, 28 Oct. 1828, DDA., cit Macauley, p.366.
20 Idem, 2 April 1829, DDA, cit Macauley, p.365.
21 *F.J.* 26 June 1828.

22 *DEP*, 14 Oct. 1828.
23 Macauley, op. cit. p.370.
24 *DEP* 7 Oct. 1828.
25 *F.J.* 26 Dec. 1828. Wellington's letter was dated 11 Dec. cf. Macauley, p.377.
26 Anglesey – Curtis, 23 Dec. 1828; *F.J.* 2 Jan. 1829.
27 Macauley, p.379.
28 *F.J.* 4 Feb. 1829.
29 Macauley, op. cit. p.381.
30 O'Connell – Murray, 6 March 1829, *O'Connell Corresp.* vol iii, supplementary letters 1829, no. 3410a.
31 Wellington – Murray, 18 April 1829. DDA. f. 31/2/51. He is responding to a letter and petition from Murray.
32 Peel – Murray, 23 March 1829, DDA, f. 31/2/52.
33 P. Kenney – Murray, 8 April 1829, f. 31/2/55.
34 Macauley, pp.381ff.
35 Bishops' Letter to Catholics of Ireland, 9 Feb. 1830, DDA.
36 James W. Doyle, Evidence before the Select Committee, p.394, cit. Bartlett, p.343.
37 O'Connell – Murray, 3 Aug. 1829, DDA, f. 31/2/30 and *O'Connell Corresp* vol. iii, no. 3414.
38 T. McGrath. *The Public Ministry of Dr Doyle*, p.74.
39 O'Connell – J.Bentham, 22 Oct. 1829, *O'Connell Corresp.* no.3416.
40 T.McGrath, *Politics, Interdenominational Relations and Education in The Public Ministry of Bishop Doyle*, Appendix, p.255.
41 Capellari – Murray, 17 Oct. 1829. DDA. f.31/2/27. The proposal to Propaganda and its replies are contained in brochures etc in this one file.

CHAPTER 8

The Arrival of National Education (1830–32)

While much of the archbishop's time and attention during 1830 and 1831 was taken up with educational matters, the round of daily contacts and the demands of correspondence continued unabated. Looking through a cross-section of Dr Murray's correspondence during these years, his visitation of parishes and the reports he received from each one are particularly striking. In 1830, between the months of May and October, he visited eighteen parishes, many of them, such as Maynooth, Athy and Celbridge, quite a distance away. The following year, twelve parishes are recorded; some of these are the same as the previous year, while others – such as Wicklow, Blessington and Skerries – are different.[1] In the era before the railways, such visitations made considerable demands on time and energy.

LETTERS FROM FAR AND WIDE

During 1831 the number of letters from France greatly increased. Murray was evidently the most widely known of the Irish bishops, not only because of his role in Dublin, the capital city, but also because of his earlier contacts with the Irish colleges in France. In 1831 there was a particular reason for the increase in the number of letters. Already in January that year, Fr Myles Gaffney wrote from Beauvais that 'the new Parisian journal *L'Avenir* has published three articles on Ireland', where one of the editors had been on a visit. The author eulogised the Catholic clergy and the faithful, and praised Drs Murray and Doyle.[2] He also drew attention to famine conditions in the west of Ireland.

Among Murray's letters are some twenty-three from the editors of *L'Avenir* – de Montalember, de Caux, Lacordaire, and de Mennais – who made stirring and successive appeals to the Catholics of France for relief of those suffering from famine in the western dioceses of Ireland. From June to the end of September

1831, thousands of francs were raised and sent through Murray for distribution.[3] One of those writing to him was Philippe Carron, bishop of Le Mans and nephew of the Abbé Carron, who was known to Murray. Bishop Carron opened a diocesan relief fund, and sent 5,000 francs with the observation that the response of his own people surprised him; they were poor themselves and had little to give, but they gave with a good heart that pleased God.[4]

By August, the situation had improved. Dr John MacHale in Ballina contacted Murray on 6 August, acknowledging that they were all under a great obligation to the French clergy, the French Catholics and to Murray for aiding then in their distress. 'The worst is over', MacHale remarked. 'The harvest is early and good, but some will need relief until the end of September.' By way of contrast, MacHale found fault with the way government aid was given.[5] On 27 October 1831, the western bishops passed resolutions thanking *L'Avenir*, the French Catholics and Murray. They explained that alms that had come late would be channelled into education; and £50 was sent to Murray for the Catholic Book Society or any other charity he wished to choose.[6]

In that same year, there is mention of certain health difficulties Murray was having, and of Fr John Hamilton as his secretary. From then on, the gracious and efficient Hamilton became invaluable to Murray. He was the medium through which many, including some bishops, contacted the Archbishop. Hamilton's presence reflected Murray's involvement in a myriad of activities, and also the increased incidence of illness in Murray's life at this time. Dr Peter Baines, vicar apostolic, writing from Bath on 26 October 1831, expressed pleasure that Murray's health had improved and his regrets at the unexpected death of Fr Glynn of Marlborough Street, who was attached to Murray's pro-cathedral.[7] Similarly, four days later, Archbishop Curtis was glad that Murray's health had improved, but noted that Murray's letter to him suggested that he was depressed over Fr Glynn's unexpected death.[8] The following year, correspondents would mention that Murray was still at Leamington Spa in Warwickshire, celebrated for its mineral springs.[9] This was a location frequented by other Irish bishops from time to time.

In addition to the usual correspondence from government and Roman sources, there was the familiar blend of requests from clergy, religious sisters, writers of a different religious persuasion, and bishops from as far away as Buenos Aires. Letters from clergy conveyed a variety of problems. Fr J. Deane, parish priest of Blanchardstown, requested an impartial enquiry to settle disputed parish boundaries between himself and three other priests of the diocese.[10] Another letter came from Fr William Young, curate at Howth and Baldoyle, who complained that his income from 23 of May to 12 September totalled only

£7.16s and that he could not live on what he got. His parish priest, Fr Keogh, was very old, did little work and had not celebrated Sunday Mass for eighteen months, yet he kept the fees for all marriages and 'respectable christenings'. A week later, on 23 September, Young wrote to Murray telling him that 'through sheer necessity' he had left the parish. He sought another appointment, or proper provision 'for the working clergyman' in the Howth/Baldoyle parish.[11] From well beyond the Dublin diocese, on 23 October 1830, Fr Thomas Foley, parish priest in Dingle, Co. Kerry, appealed to Murray regarding his dispute with his bishop, Cornelius Egan who, he alleged, had infringed his rights as a parish priest and had suspended him.[12]

A letter from a religious sister must have come as a relief from such difficult situations. Sr M. M. Power, of the Presentation Convent in Thurles, wrote to Murray about a relation of the late Archbishop Everard, a girl for whose training she had some responsibility. Murray, it will be remembered, was executor of Archbishop Everard's will. Having mentioned the training being received by the girl in her charge, she suggested that Murray ought to let all the Everard children know that they cannot expect any more help from him. They seemed to be under the impression, she said, 'that you are still to do wonders for them'.[13]

From Buenos Aires, the vicar apostolic, Mgr Marianus, sent news of Fr Patrick O'Gorman, who had been sent there by Murray. A man of zeal who had done fruitful work in the city, O'Gorman had earned the enmity of certain Protestants, and Marianus was writing to Murray to forestall and counteract any calumnies these people might spread about Fr O'Gorman.[14] Back home, a concerned citizen, who made it clear that he was not of Murray's Church, expressed a very special plea on 25 January 1831. Mr F. J. Atkinson, of Moore St in Dublin, wrote of the poverty and uncomplaining goodness and patience of a family living in the forge he had lent them at the rear of his house. The father, a blacksmith, was unemployed. Their one child, a little girl, had contracted measles and, because they could not afford remedies, she had died. They had no money for the child's interment. Atkinson knew that Murray helped people of all creeds and classes. The fact that this family were members of his own flock should make him more anxious to help them with some money in their present affliction. He personally would try to find employment for the father, and he hoped that Murray would do the same.[15]

While the Archbishop contended with pastoral problems like the foregoing, there remained a variety of letters from Rome and from government representatives.

OFFICIAL CORRESPONDENCE

Among the letters from Propaganda Fide one, dated 2 July 1831 about the Irish College in Rome, called for immediate attention. The letter complained of a deterioration in discipline and constant quarrelling in the college. This situation was hindering the work of the students, and it was considered necessary to recall the rector, Fr Christopher Boylan. In fact, Boylan had already written to Murray asking to be recalled on health grounds. The letter suggested that Murray would be wise to accept Boylan's resignation for reasons of health, and to appoint a successor capable of establishing good order and concord. This was urgently needed in the college.[16]

Some three months later, on 30 October 1831, Archbishop Curtis thanked Murray for his letter regarding Fr Boylan. He was pleased that Murray had asked Cardinal Capellari to appoint Dr Paul Cullen in Boylan's stead, as rector of the Irish College and also as agent of the Irish bishops.[17] Cullen was to prove a marked success in Rome, a circumstance that paved the way for his later eminence. It is ironic that John MacHale and Paul Cullen, both of whom were recommended by Murray for their elevations – as coadjutor bishop of Killala and rector of the Irish College, respectively – would subsequently display vigorous opposition to Murray.

From the government side, Murray received word from Lord Anglesey, still Lord Lieutenant, that he was pleased with the bishops' letter of 9 February 1830, which Murray had sent him.[18] On 22 February, he also acknowledged receiving from Murray the hierarchy's memorial on education, adding that he would give most anxious attention to this important subject.[19] When, however, Murray recommended a certain Mr Hamill for a particular post at the disposal of the Lord Lieutenant, he received the response that, while anyone recommended by the archbishop would be a most worthy candidate, unfortunately, in the present case, the government did not intend making any appointment of the kind Mr Hamill solicits.[20]

Another person to whom Murray sent the bishops' pastoral address of 9 February was George Leveson-Gower, 2nd Marquis of Stafford and Chief Secretary of Ireland. He, too, was pleased with the address.[21] Subsequently, he also received a letter from Murray regarding education, this time inviting him to present a petition from the Irish bishops on national education. On 23 February 1830 he agreed to do so, subject to certain conditions.[22] Murray replied on the same date, accepting the conditions, and then adding deftly, 'The Irish bishops do not wish nor is it in their province to dictate, but whatever system of education is adapted they, and the laity as well, would want the religious instruction of

Paul Cullen

Catholics to be under the control of their own pastors; everyone in the Catholic body would be grateful for such a system'.[23]

During 1830 and 1831, Murray's hopes of providing education for the poorer classes seemed about to be realised in a government-sponsored education system. Recognising the depth of Murray's commitment, Lord Lieutenant Anglesey sent him £100 for education purposes on 6 December 1830. About to leave Ireland, he thanked Murray for his support in maintaining peace, and paid his respects.[24] He had no idea that he would return quite quickly under a new administration. On 26 June 1830, George IV had died and was succeeded by William IV. In August there was a general election, and Wellington's government was defeated. On 22 November 1830, Earl Grey became prime minister in a Whig administration. A major development in the education of the majority population of Ireland was soon to be realised.

EDUCATION IN REVIEW

At this point, it may be helpful to review Murray's long struggle to provide education for his people, and to place it in the context of the time.

Faced with shortage of money, no government aid, a fast-growing Catholic population and the absence of trained teachers, it was a daunting task to provide any form of education for Catholics. The situation in the cities was exceedingly difficult; in the country areas it was almost impossible. Hedge schools arose to provide education in rural areas. Frequently, they were run by poorly educated masters, teaching in hovels which were often damp and dark and with little or no furniture. Schools for the Protestant population of the Established Church, by contrast, were aided by the state and had trained or better-educated teachers.

In December 1811, the government sought to benefit both sectors of the population by the establishment of the Kildare Place Society. Its task was to run non-denominational schools with well trained teachers, which pupils of different religious persuasions could attend without danger to their religious beliefs. The venture started well but then became focused on evangelisation, with emphasis on the Bible as a class text for all pupils. The teachers were almost entirely Protestant with a particular way of presenting the Bible. Such circumstances, as has been seen, evoked opposition from Catholic bishops and prominent laity such as Daniel O'Connell and the sympathetic Lord Cloncurry. The bishops made it a condition for the attendance of Catholic children at such schools that the Bible not be used as a school subject, and that children should only be taught religion by a teacher of their own persuasion. The Bible, it was argued, was too complex to read without guidance. Bishop Doyle put the Catholic position succinctly: 'Without the authority of the Catholic Church to interpret scripture, spiritual anarchy inevitably resulted'. In addition, the Catholic Church's reverence for Scripture and her anxiety to prevent its misuse 'would induce her to keep it out of the hands of children, either in or out of school'.[25] On the Protestant side, this was seen as obscurantist, a determination to deprive children of the great gift of the Bible. Murray had a heated exchange on such an issue with a Church of Ireland headmaster, Thomas Ellis of Abbotstown, Co. Dublin, during August and September 1825.[26]

Meantime, Murray had sought to expand possibilities for education in Dublin by helping to found the Irish Sisters of Charity, and by promoting the work of the Sisters of Mercy and the Christian Brothers. Also, with the help of wealthy Catholic business people, he set up other schools to meet the overflowing population of young children. During all this time, Murray and the other bishops kept the educational needs of the Catholic population before successive governments. This practice received renewed vigour with the appointment of James Doyle to Kildare and Leighlin, and from the support of prominent lay people, Catholic and Protestant.

Murray's vision, indeed, extended to plans for university education, according to Bishop Doyle. When the Catholic Association in 1827 came up with a proposal to erect a model school to train Catholic teachers, Doyle viewed it as ground-work for a university that would devote particular attention to the study and teaching of science. In a letter to his brother Peter, written on 30 November 1827, Doyle declared, 'I am engaged … in an effort to commence an Irish university under the name of the Model School in Dublin. Doctor Murray will co-operate with me as will O'Connell, and they are both very able co-operators … Our ulterior motive must for a time be concealed…'[27]

FINAL STEPS TOWARDS NATIONAL EDUCATION

In December 1830, Thomas Wyse, MP for Waterford and a Catholic, produced a comprehensive plan for national education. He corresponded with both Murray and Doyle, who had been feeling concern lest their hopes for government-sponsored education be put aside under the new government. Wyse kept pressing the matter. On 12 January 1831, he told Murray that he was introducing a motion in parliament on the subject of national education, and he asked Murray's view on a number of questions. Should there be separate Protestant and Catholic parish schools? Should the teachers or pastors of different persuasions be responsible for teaching religion in the schools? How should the schools be financed? And what provision ought to be made for continuing education, which should be mainly technical?[28]

A month later, on 25 February 1831, the Chief Secretary, Edward Stanley, assured Archbishop Murray that he aimed to provide the benefits of education to all children, and wished to remove 'the slightest grounds of a design of proselytism'. The cooperation of the Catholic hierarchy, he declared, was vital to the success of such a measure.[29] Many Catholics at the time, however, felt that he was procrastinating. At the end of July 1831, Thomas Wyse brought a bill before the House of Commons on the establishment and upkeep of a national system of education. His action put pressure on the Chief Secretary, whose eventual plan was to bear considerable resemblance to that of Wyse.

On 9 September 1831, Edward Stanley moved a vote for £30,000 to be placed at the disposal of the Lord Lieutenant for educational purposes. It provided for a national system of education in Ireland. In November, the Duke of Leinster received a letter from Stanley with the final draft of his guidelines for the scheme of national education. It was to be operated by appointed commissioners, assisted by inspectors of the schools. On 27 November, Archbishop Curtis, in a letter to Murray, expressed his delight at the appointment of Murray and Mr Blake as the Catholic representatives among the commissioners. Curtis commented also on the appointment of the new Protestant archbishop of Dublin, Richard Whately, and the contrast he presented to his predecessor.[30]

The appointment of Murray and Blake, however, was not without its moments of uncertainty and annoyance. It was known that the membership of the board of commissioners would be representative of the main religious denominations. How this would be arranged, and the likely names of the representatives, was a topic for discussion. In early November 1831, Murray was displeased to hear that Catholic representatives had been chosen without his being consulted. He had agreed to serve on the board himself, and he had in mind as another Catholic representative someone who was knowledgeable on educational and political issues, his friend, the able lawyer, Anthony Richard Blake. Murray now learned – from Blake – that there were to be three Catholic representatives on the board, Murray, Dr Bartholomew Crotty, president of Maynooth, and a layman who had not yet been named. Angry at what he thought was happening, Murray wrote almost petulantly to Doyle:

> If such is the constitution of the Board, I think it is better for me to decline having anything to do with it. Dr Crotty could give no efficient assistance … I think that if people at headquarters meant honestly, I should have been consulted about the persons who would have the name

> of watching over Catholic interests at the Board. But I believe that on this point we are not to expect honesty.

'The omission of Blake's name', Murray continued, 'was proof of this. He is much and justly incensed.' Murray found it hard to believe that the board, from which so much was to be expected, would be constituted 'in the very inefficient and unsatisfactory way' that Blake had heard. 'But should this turn out to be the case,' he put it to Doyle, 'ought I not to decline accepting a place in it? I think I ought.'[31]

Whatever Doyle's response, Murray was able to report to him in better form on 26 November. The Education Board was formed and 'our friend Blake is again in his glory'. Murray declared himself pleased that 'as yet there appears to be great fairness intended, as far as religion is concerned'.[32] The board was constituted as follows: three members of the Established Church (Dr Richard Whately, Archbishop of Dublin, the Hon. Maurice Fitzgerald, 4th Duke of Leinster, and Revd E. Sadlier, Provost of Trinity College); two Dissenters (Revd James Carlile, Presbyterian, and Robert Holmes, Unitarian); and two Roman Catholics (Dr Daniel Murray, Archbishop of Dublin, and Mr A. R. Blake). Murray had consulted the hierarchy before accepting Stanley's invitation to join the board.

The mixed religion of the projected schools and of the board was far from the ideal that the Irish Catholic prelates would have liked, but there was no practical alternative. Stanley had put it plainly to Bishop Doyle on 13 January 1831. He was pleased, he said, to find the Catholic hierarchy in favour of a system of 'uniting the children of different religious persuasions in the same schools'. It was the only system to which, 'under the peculiar circumstances of Ireland', parliamentary aid ought to be applied.[33] Doyle echoed this in a circular letter to the clergy of his diocese on 26 December 1831. The terms on which the state grant was being given, he observed, were not perhaps the best possible, but at the same time they were well suited to the circumstances of Ireland. He exhorted his clergy to apply to the Board for aid, and he gave directions about how to do so.[34]

In the board as finally constituted, there were just two Catholic representatives instead of the mooted three. This was a point of later criticism of the national system. Nevertheless, at this point, Murray's appointment was recognised as historically significant. He was the first Catholic bishop appointed to a state board since the treaty of Limerick. The Education Board also offered the unique opportunity for both archbishops to work together.

On the vexed question of the teaching of religion in the schools, it was agreed that one or two days of each week were to be set aside for such separate religious instruction as might be approved by the clergy or other representative of the different persuasions. Religious instruction could also be given before or after ordinary school hours on other days of the week. There was envisaged some combined religious instruction based on selected extracts from Scripture. This was prepared by the Revd Carlile and was so chosen as not to raise difficulties for the different denominations.[35]

Mr Stanley's hopes of the religious denominations working together, however, received a serious setback when the Established Church refused to take part. Some Church of Ireland bishops, nevertheless, did avail themselves of the benefits of the national system. The Presbyterians were critical of the system, but then argued their case and gained concessions to meet their special requirements. The Catholic hierarchy followed the lead of Murray and Doyle, and the public approval of O'Connell, in accepting the government measure as the best available. There was one dissenting voice, nevertheless. John MacHale, the Coadjutor Bishop of Killala, in a letter to a priest of the diocese on 8 March 1832, described the national system as 'narrow, bigoted and insulting', the defects of which should be exposed.[36] Already he was a well-known figure with strong anti-government views, but not yet the formidable force he was to become as archbishop of Tuam.

DUTIES OF A COMMISSIONER

The commissioners had the task of administering state aid to the school committees. This aid was to cover: (a) annual repairs to school houses and furniture; (b) permanent salaries for teachers; (c) the purchase of books and stationery at half-price; and (d), where necessary, one-third of what was required to provide a new schoolhouse, the building being vested in the commissioners.[37]

In addition, the commissioners 'issued a list of approved texts for use in the schools and made associated regulations for the conduct of the schools. Inspectors were appointed to see that the approved practices were followed. The commissioners published a series of school texts that proved so successful that they were used throughout Britain and its empire.' The textbook series reflected the curriculum of the national schools. Their use was not compulsory, but they were almost universally adopted because of their high standard and because they were cheap. The most important, as the system progressed, were the six reading books, which formed a logical, integrated sequence of instruction, taking the child from elementary literacy to fairly sophisticated lessons in geography, science and literature. Most pupils stayed only for the first two books. The fourth and fifth books contained material up to secondary-school level. Pupils, therefore, could receive the basis of a secondary-school education if they had competent teachers and parents that allowed their children to remain at school.[38] Unfortunately, the attendance level of many pupils was low, due to parents requiring them to earn some income to allay the family's poverty.

THE WORKING OF THE SYSTEM

As the system operated, each school was under the control of a local manager. In schools that were largely Catholic, the manager was almost always the parish priest, and in mainly Protestant schools the rector, minister or landlord. The manager's powers were quite extensive. He was entrusted with the daily oversight of the school. He had the right to appoint teachers, subject in theory, but seldom in reality, to the commissioners' veto. In practice, he could dismiss teachers whenever he pleased; there was no appeal against arbitrary dismissal until late in the century. The manager chose which of the several textbooks the school would use and, within broad limits, arranged the school timetable. Thus, as has been observed, 'the national system of education was both highly centralised and strongly localised'. Tensions were inherent in the relationship, but open conflict seems to have been rare. Teachers and parents had little say in the system. The commissioners themselves were appointed, not elected, and hence the entire educational mechanism was insulated from local civic influence.[39]

To ensure the availability of trained teachers, a model school was established in Dublin in 1833, and other such schools were planned for different locations around the country. The school subjects consisted mainly of spelling, reading, writing (on slates or on paper), grammar, geography, geometry, arithmetic, book-keeping and, in the case of girls only, needlework. For the fourth and fifth years there was a more advanced curriculum in science, mathematics and literature. The school day ran from 9.30am to 3.00pm in the winter months, and until 5.00pm in the summer.[40]

THE RELIGIOUS ORDERS AND THE NATIONAL SYSTEM

Already on 12 September 1831, before the bill on national education was published, Edmund Rice enrolled seven of the twelve Christian Brothers' schools in the new scheme. He did so out of financial necessity, encouraged, it seems, by his friend, Murray. Strangely, the brothers gave little consideration to the differences between the national system and their own system, in which religion was integrated into every subject and between subjects, and in which religious symbols were widely used. Moreover, they laid great emphasis on their own independence as distinct from being subjected to another's system.

Within a few years, in 1836, despite the dire financial circumstances of many of their communities, the brothers in chapter voted '*una voce* condemning the Commission' because of 'its inconsistency with our system'.[41] The inconsistency they found was not only related to religion and independence of operation, but also arose from political grounds. Without state funding, the Brothers became less attractive to bishops and other prospective patrons. The most recent biographer of Edmund Rice judged that the Brothers entered the national scheme with little apparent understanding of its workings or its potential for development. Their 'failure to engage with the national system assured that not only was their effectiveness as a teaching order seriously circumscribed but, as a consequence of their hasty withdrawal, future generations lost sight of their driving principles which have been obscured by the myth of the brothers' nationalism'.[42] Externally, the argument against the national system took on a political hue, suggesting that the system neglected Irish history and was hostile to 'faith and fatherland', a semi-hallowed phrase associated with O'Connell and with the Brothers' aims.

By contrast, the Presentation Brothers and some twenty-six convent schools were affiliated to the national system in 1838. 'Their experience reflected the popular consensus that the only major restriction which the national system imposed was the limitation of religious instruction to the hours timetabled by the school manager.'[43] Catherine McAuley, founder of the Sisters of Mercy, expressed the views of many when, observing the educational benefits of the national system for poor children, she judged 'that under the right conditions – proper textbooks, strict observance of the end-of-day regulations about religious instruction (both Protestant and Catholic), good relations between teachers and inspectors, and attentive oversight by the commissioners of national education of whom Dr Murray was a member – the potential danger of proselytism by textbooks or teachers, could be averted'.[44]

Br Rice's withdrawal from the national system dismayed and annoyed Archbishop Murray. He knew of the brothers' financial difficulties. He had contributed financially to them, and had sought support from others for them. He now learned of their withdrawal, not from Rice himself, but from the commission, to whom Rice had written before writing to Murray. In pique, the Archbishop withdrew his annual donation of £40 to the Hanover Street School and the aid obtained by charity sermons. His anger was short-lived, however, and his goodwill was back in place by 1840, when he allowed charity sermons, once more, and renewed his donation.[45]

Part of Murray's annoyance over the brothers' dismissal of the national system was caused by his deep appreciation of the work of the commissioners and of the positive ecumenical spirit that prevailed amongst them. Sir Thomas Redington, under-secretary at Dublin Castle and a Catholic, 'used to say, that in the absence of Dr Murray the rights of Roman Catholics were ever ready to be defended by Dr Whately, who was accustomed to remark: "we have no security for the system being impartial as regards ourselves, unless we can afford the same protection to others"'.[46]

Ironically, the fiercest attack on the national system and on Murray's commitment to it, came from within the ranks of the Irish Catholic episcopacy. It proved of major significance for future relations within the Irish Catholic Church. It is the subject of a later chapter.

NOTES

1 Visitations, DDA. f. 31/2/136.
2 Myles Gaffney – Hamilton, 23 Jan. 1831. DDA. Hamilton Papers, 1831, no.12.
3 DDA. 31/3/ 17–33.
4 Philippe Carron – Murray, 15 July 1831; DDA. 31/3/ 26, 28.
5 DDA, MacHale – Murray, 6 Aug. 1831, f.31/3/6.
6 Dr Kelly – Murray, for western bishops, 27 Oct. 1831, f.31/3/8
7 Baines – Murray, 26 Oct. 1831, DDA. f.31/3/ 15.
8 Curtis – Murray, 30 Oct.1831, idem f.31/3/ 9.
9 Fr L. Dunne – Hamilton, 16 Aug. 1831. DDA. Hamilton Papers, no.71. The spa was said to be beneficial for muscular and rheumatic complaints and sundry other disorders.
10 J. Deane – Murray, 28 Jan. 1830. DDA. f.31/2/90.
11 Wm Young – Murray, 15, 23 Sept. 1830. f.31/2/ 116, 117.
12 Thomas Foley – Murray, 23 Oct. 1830. f.31/2/ 131.
13 Sr M. M. Power – Murray, 19 July 1930. f.31/2/ 111.
14 Mgr Marianus - Murray, 19 Dec. 1831. f. 31/3/16.
15 F. J. Atkinson – Murray, 25 June 1831. f. 31/3/ 55c.
16 Propaganda – Murray, 2 July 1831. f. 31/3/ 70.
17 Curtis – Murray, 30 Oct. 1831. f. 31/3/ 9.
18 Archdeacon Singleton – Murray, 12 Feb. 1830. f.31/2/92.
19 Idem, 22 Feb. 1830. f. 31/2/ 93.
20 Idem, 17 Feb. 1830. 31/2/ 93.
21 Leveson-Gower – Murray, 14 Feb. 1830. f.31/2/ 93.
22 Idem, 23 Feb. 1830. f. 31/2/ 98.
23 Murray – Leveson-Gower, 23 Feb. 1830. f.31/2/97.
24 Singleton – Murray, 6 Dec. 1830. f. 31/2/ 129.
25 Cit. T. McGrath. *The Public Ministry of Bp. James Doyle. 'The Kildare Place Society and the National System of Education'*, p.160.
26 T. Ellis – Murray, 26 Aug – 30 Sept. 1825. f. 30/9/ 18–26.
27 Bp James Doyle – Peter Doyle, 30 Nov. 1827. Kildare & Leighlin Diocesan Archives

(KLDA), cit. T.McGrath in *Pastoral and Educational Letters of Bp.Doyle*, no.24, p.254.
28 T. Wyse – Murray, 12 Jan. 1831. f. 31/3/48.
29 E. Stanley – Murray, 25 Feb. 1831. f. 31/3/92.
30 Curtis – Murray, 27 Nov. 1831. f. 31/3/11.
31 Murray – Doyle, 11 Nov. 1831. KLDA, cit. McGrath in *Politics, Interdenominational Relations and Education in the Public Ministry of Bp. Doyle* (Dublin: Four Courts Press, 1999), pp.229–30.
32 Idem, 26 Nov. 1831. KLDA, in op. cit. p.230.
33 Stanley – Doyle, 13 Jan. 1831. KLDA, cit McGrath in op. cit. p.221.
34 DDA. Bp Doyle circular, 26 Dec. 1831. f. 31/3/13.
35 Ignatius Murphy, 'Primary Education' in *Catholic Education. The Church since Emancipation* which is part of P.J. Corish (ed.) *A History of Irish Catholicism* (Dublin 1971), pp.6, 8.
36 MacHales' letter in *Freeman's Journal*, 9 March 1832.
37 Mins. of National Commissioners, 1 Dec. 1833. NLI. Ms.5529, cit. Norman Atkinson. *Irish Education* (Dublin 1969), p.94.
38 D. H. Akinson. 'Pre-University Education, 1792–1870' in W. E. Vaughan (ed.) *A New History of Ireland*, vol.v., p.530.
39 Idem.
40 Norman Atkinson, op. cit., p.99.
41 Bp Joseph Murphy – Tobias Kirby, 17 Sept. 1841. Irish College Rome archives, Kirby papers, KIR/80, cit. D. Keogh. *Edmund Rice and the First Christian Brothers* (Dublin: Veritas, 2008), p.219.
42 Keogh. op. cit., p.211.
43 Idem, p.220.
44 Mary C. Sullivan (ed.) *The Correspondence of Catherine McAuley, 1818–1841* (Dublin & CUPA, 2004), p.166, no.45.
45 Keogh. op. cit. p.223.
46 T. Ellis – Murray, 26 Aug – 30 Sept. 1825. f.30/9/ 18–26.

CHAPTER 9

Illness, Hospitality, Pastoral Care and Defence of the Faith (1832–40)

Issues of health, at both a public and personal level, concerned Murray in the 1830s. In 1832, Dublin was afflicted by a cholera outbreak. The Archbishop responded with a pastoral letter, which evoked praise not only because of its spiritual message and its call to prayer at a critical time, but also because of its practical advice to people about steps they should take to avoid contagion. He encouraged the two religious congregations with which he was closely associated, the Irish Sisters of Charity and the Sisters of Mercy, to care for the plague-stricken people, especially the poor, and to help others to cope with illness in the family, while avoiding occasions of infection themselves. The sisters won high praise for their fearless and generous work, as also did some of the Irish Christian Brothers.

A NEW HOSPITAL IN DUBLIN

It would seem that, following his close involvement with the cholera epidemic, Murray, in conjunction with Mary Aikenhead, decided on the need for a large Catholic hospital that would be available especially to the poor. It was difficult to obtain financial aid for this project from wealthy Catholics. They were reluctant to get involved in an operation that would draw the public notice of Protestants, especially if the hospital were run by nuns. Anna Maria O'Brien and her husband, however, backed the project; and when Aikenhead sent three sisters over to Paris in May 1833 for nursing training at the Hospice de la Pitié, administered by the Sisters of St Thomas of Villanova, Mr and Mrs O'Brien and Archbishop Murray accompanied them on their journey.[1]

Murray subsequently made a further effort to contact a number of wealthy Catholic friends for financial assistance. He and Aikenhead found a suitable location at 56 St Stephen's Green: a large vacant Georgian house of four storeys over a basement, the former town house of Anthony Brabazon, 8th Earl of Meath. Mary Aikenhead set about transforming the fine airy rooms for the benefit of patients, while allocating the confined attic rooms to the nursing sisters. Murray objected to this latter arrangement and, despite the delay and additional cost, insisted that the ceiling be raised in the attic rooms so that the occupants would have more light and comfort.

In 1834, Mary Aikenhead opened the Centre of Catholic Charity, which became known as St Vincent's Hospital. The opening of the hospital attracted much public interest 'as it was the first hospital organised and staffed by women to open in these islands'. The benefit of the hospital was widely extended by its regulations to 'present to individuals of every sect and every creed equal advantages and equal attention'.[2] The Archbishop continued to take a keen interest in the hospital, and assisted with subsequent enlargements.[3]

PERSONAL HEALTH PROBLEMS

While concerned with the health of others, Murray's own health was seriously impaired during the 1830s. He had a succession of illnesses which necessitated his absence from work and the delegation of much diocesan business to Fr John Hamilton. Hamilton, who was administrator of the Pro-Cathedral from 1831–53, was a remarkably able man. He managed a very busy pastoral life of his own, while also assisting in the running of the diocese.

William Meagher, whose eulogy is a main source of personal information about Murray, as we have seen, observed that he came from a long-lived family and that he inherited a sound, though not a robust, constitution. He valued health as of particular importance in a priest's career and, consequently, took great care of his own health. When he felt it to be 'seriously attacked … he summoned his medical adviser' and followed his advice. Far from being excessively anxious about his health, however, he continued working except when seriously indisposed.

As to the nature of Murray's illnesses, Meagher commented that at the earlier stages of his episcopacy, and at intervals throughout, 'he suffered much from bilious derangement especially, and great liability to catch cold'.[4] According to a modern medical dictionary, biliousness is a vague term referring, among other symptoms, to headaches and vomiting, and a form of stomach disorder. In Murray's case, one wonders if he was suffering from a gastric ulcer or some such condition. Whatever the explanation, the attacks were such that, on more than one occasion, his friends believed he was in danger of dying. Examples of recorded references to Murray's health, from 1832 to 1840, will convey the frequency, and perhaps the unexpectedness, of the bouts of illness he suffered and the disruption they caused.

On 24 July, and again on 16 August 1832, we learn that Fr L. Dunne, 'an old friend of Dr Murray', asked John Hamilton if Murray had yet returned from Leamington Spa.[5] In 1833, there is no record of an illness, but the following year there was concern that his sickness might prove fatal. In the early summer all seemed well, and Dr Nicholson,[6] in a letter to Hamilton on 20 June 1834, noted that Hamilton and Murray were going to Rome. By 25 November, however, Nicholson was expressing concern because he had heard that 'our beloved archbishop had a feverish attack and that you were with him all night of Thursday … O Good God, what should we do without him! Ages may come and roll away, and another Daniel Murray may not be found. He seems to have been specially designed by Providence for the times in which we live.'[7] On 5 December in that same year, Nicholson was delighted to learn that Murray was recovering.[8] Two days later, John MacHale was relieved to hear 'that Dr Murray was out of danger'.[9]

The following year, on 31 March 1835, Nicholson was 'grieved to hear of Dr Murray's illness', and he prayed that he might be saved.[10] That year, Murray seems to have been ill into November. On 19 November, Nicholson hoped the Archbishop was recovering from his illness.[11] Fr Meagher singled out this year as a particularly bad one for Murray. 'In 1835, while on his way home from Italy, his life was placed in imminent peril by one of those attacks, which detained him for several weeks an invalid in the little town of Lanslebourg, in Savoy.'[12] It is possible that Meagher has confused 1835 with the following year in his account. Murray, as will appear later, was particularly active in 1835, whereas, in the following year, he definitely went to Rome and was absent from his diocese from April to September. In April 1836, Murray and Hamilton were at Leamington Spa,[13] and subsequently went on to Rome. On 16 June 1836, Dr Walter Meyler, of the Pro-Cathedral, wrote to Hamilton that he was glad that they had arrived in Rome and hoped that they had received all his letters.[14] On 19 July, Meyler reported that he had received Murray's letter from Genoa.[15] Meantime, on 16 July, Fr Woods, also of the Pro-Cathedral, had written with the sad news that Daniel O'Connell's wife was dying.[16]

Shortly afterwards, while in Italy, Murray had an attack. Hamilton wrote from Turin to a doctor describing the symptoms and asking advice on medication. Dr Louis Barralta replied in French on 29 July 1836, prescribing for the stomach ailments and cough from which Murray was suffering.[17] Also in July, while on their travels, Hamilton received a letter from Sir Augustus Fortis, who was staying at a hostel in Savoy. He was sending 'some bottles of Drogheda ale and some bottles of old Sherry that Dr Murray may find more palatable than the wines of the Savoy inns'. He had heard that Murray was not well and he hoped that the illness was not serious.[18]

While they were away, Hamilton's brother, Frank, sent him news of a more racy nature from Dublin. In August 1836, he reported that 'a local paper had jibes about Dr Murray's return; he was called "His Meekship, with Mrs O'Brien, the Head of the Church, accompanying him"'. Murray's long-standing friendship with Mr and Mrs O'Brien, as well as their support for his work, was a well-known feature of his life. The *Register*, Frank Hamilton continued, also stated that there was no truth in the rumour that Murray went to Rome to receive the cardinal's hat, 'a dignity he has twice refused'.[19]

By the second half of August, Murray and Hamilton were on their way home. On 28 August, Fr Woods informed Hamilton, now at Leamington Spa, about the situation at home: 'funerals numerous, collections down, Dublin is empty'.[20] Murray and Hamilton were still there on 14 September 1836, when Meyler requested Hamilton to let him know when they would arrive home, so that Murray might not find them napping but at their posts.[21]

In 1837, the saga continued. Murray informed Nicholson, on 14 February 1837, that he was in bed with a fever when Nicholson's letter had arrived.[22] Later in the year, Murray was staying at Rahan Lodge in the midlands. The O'Briens, his close friends and owners of the property, wrote to Hamilton on 1 November 1837, asking him to use his influence with Murray to induce him to remain another week at Rahan Lodge before the winter set in.[23] The request seems to have had a favourable response.

On 3 November, Murray sent word that he could not leave for Dublin for another ten days or so. Hence, 'the conference is postponed until 24th, also the office for the deceased clergy'.[24] Five days after that letter, Murray approved the suggestions for clerical changes proposed by Drs Hamilton and Meyler, and instructed that Fr Mathew and the vicars and priests of the parish be invited to dine with him on 16 November.[25] Despite such indications of renewed energy, however, there were further references, on 16 and 19 February 1838, to the Archbishop being ill and not available.[26] His health problems continued for some time. On 28 April, Dr Kirby, in a letter from the Irish College, commented that 'all in the college were glad to hear of Dr Murray's recovery'.[27] The improvement seems to have continued throughout 1839, but once again, on 1 June 1840, Fr Taylor, of Carlow College, announced that 'they were sorry to hear that Dr Murray is ill and hope it is nothing serious'.[28]

His illness in 1840 seems to have been the last assault on Murray's constitution.

'Thenceforward, to the close of life,' Fr Meagher asserted, 'he was blessed with, comparatively, uniform good health. It was remarkable, indeed, that as years accumulated on him, his health became, if not stronger, at least more equable, while on his mental health time appeared incapable of inflicting the slightest injury.' Meagher remarked on how 'the people marvelled at the upright stature and the light and firm step, with which, to the last, he hastened on his way through the street'. It was said, moreover, that the diffidence in his own opinion, which in his earlier life caused annoyance to those who sought guidance from him, seemed to disappear in later life, when he delivered lucid views with 'unfaltering confidence'.[29]

During Murray's periods of illness and recuperation, clergy meetings and confirmations were deferred, and inconvenience was caused to many;[30] but the remarkable thing was the amount of work he nevertheless managed to undertake and bring to conclusion between 1833 and 1840, sometimes in the face of bitter opposition and public criticism. It would appear that the pastoral duties of his office, and his particular commitment to the education of the poor, drove him on.

AN AMIABLE AND HUMOROUS HOST

Despite the pressures of work and the trials of illness, Daniel Murray always found time to relax with others. He welcomed company to his table and, on a fairly regular basis, he invited all the priests of the diocese – and others as well – to dine with him. Thus, on 10 March 1841, he wrote to Hamilton from his house in Mountjoy Square, inviting him and the priests of the diocese to dinner on Friday, adding that 'Dr Cullen will be there'.[31] More frequently, he invited the priests of the Pro-Cathedral to be his guests, often just a few of them. Notable among these were John Hamilton and Monsignor William Yore. The latter was a former student of Betagh's and a contemporary of Kenney's, whose ill health prevented him becoming a Jesuit, as he had hoped. Instead, he joined the diocese, where he was noted as a good priest and became Vicar General. On these social occasions, it is said, the Archbishop put aside any sense of distance from others and took a boyish pleasure in being a friend among friends, enjoying good food and wine.[32]

He also enjoyed inviting close lay friends to dine with him, among whom was John Richard Corballis QC. His invitations not infrequently carried a current of urbane humour. An invitation to Corballis ran:

> Come here on Wednesday evening next the 23rd inst at six o'clock and we can have our chat enlivened by an occasional recourse, in spite of

> Father Mathew, to a drop of the fruit of the vine. In other words, come and dine with Yrs etc, D Murray.

The reference to Fr Theobald Mathew's teetotal movement was playful, not derogatory, for Murray was a friend of the temperance leader and had welcomed him warmly to his diocese. On another occasion, a birthday invitation to Corballis was also gently humerous:[33]

> If I live until Thursday next, the 18th inst. I shall enter on the 77th year of my earthly pilgrimage and if you wish to ascertain how an old stomach (not a teetotaller one) can do its duty, come on that day at six o'clock … and partake of that very plain kind of fare which you prefer.

Such warm friendships with lay friends could have their drawbacks, as Fr Peter Cooper intimated to Dr Cullen. Cooper, a curate in Murray's church in Marlborough Street and a strong repealer, was one of Murray's fiercest critics. He complained that once Murray had given his friendship he could see no wrong in his friends. The particular friend Cooper had in mind was Anthony Blake, who has been previously mentioned as a member of the Education Board of the National Schools. He was a lawyer, whom Cooper viewed as a Machiavellian figure leading the Archbishop astray.

With close clerical friends, such as Hamilton and Yore, Murray's humour often took the form of raillery or leg-pulling. In this vein, he cautioned Hamilton, who had difficulty with some pious women who looked after St Mary's chapel, to stay clear of 'the pious ladies who have made a Holy Hobby of the statues. Depend on it … they are a sturdy race and when the interests of piety appear to them to be concerned, it is not safe to come into collision with them'.[34] Hamilton was not amused on this occasion! In a gentler vein, he poked fun at the error in the text of a pastoral letter that was being prepared for circulation: 'Be sure you draw your pen over the i in *grievious,* I mean of course the abominal second i with which our friend Meagher used to annoy us so *grieviously.'*[35]

PASTORAL CARE OF THE FAITHFUL

Murray's papers for 1834, as we have seen, give us information about a visit to Rome and a long and very serious illness he had. In that same year, however, he visited twenty-five parishes,[36] some of which required considerable travel – for example Arklow, Athy, Wicklow and Celbridge. Some of these, moreover, involved a union of parishes. Thus, Wicklow was a union of Wicklow town, Killcommon, Gleneally, Rathnew, Drumkey, Killpool and Ballinahinch, while Clontarf included Cooloch (*sic*), Killester, Raheny, Santry, Ballymun, and

Fairview. Each parish had to complete a report on a range of questions concerning such matters as the number of vestments and altar vessels, the number of confraternities and their work, the number of schools and students, the number of public Masses each Sunday and the attendance at them, the number of those receiving communion, the condition of the church and its lease, whether there was a library and, if so, the number of its volumes.

The report from Clontarf as a union of parishes conveys some indication of the trend of these reports. There were four chapels serving the union – at Clontarf, Cooloch, Ballymun and Fairview. Public Masses on Sunday were balanced across the chapels: Clontarf had Masses at eight and twelve o'clock, Fairview at eight and eleven o'clock, Cooloch at half past nine, and Ballymun at half past eleven. The report gave the number of ciboria, chalices and vestments. It mentioned that some of the vestments were bought by the parish priest, Fr James Callanan. There was no lease for the chapels at Ballymun and Clontarf. The lease at Cooloch was in the hands of the agent of Sir Compton Douvelle, while that at Fairview was in the hands of Fr Callanan. There were two parish libraries: at Ballymun there were one hundred volumes, at Cooloch some forty volumes. There were 'no confraternities but numerous teachers of catechism in each chapel every Sunday'. There were about 120 weekly and monthly communicants. The numbers not attending Easter duties could not be ascertained, but the greater number of absentees was in Clontarf and Ballybough Bridge. In the parish union, there were five free schools; four of these were supported by contributions, mainly from the parents of the children, and one was a national school. The average number of pupils attending each school was eighty to one hundred. Two priests served the entire parish area: Fr James Callanan PP and Fr Charles Boyle PCC. There was a priest's house at Fairview.

In many parishes the Christian Doctrine Society played a major role in providing religious instruction or catechism classes on Sunday, between Masses or after Mass. By the end of the 1830s, the overall pastoral condition of the archdiocese appears to have been healthy, and it was so well organised that the Archbishop could feel confident that daily ecclesial life would continue smoothly during his long absences through illness. The *Catholic Directory* of 1840 commented 'on the state of religion in the Archdiocese of Dublin' in a very positive vein:[37]

> We have already said much in the Registry for 1836, and in our subsequent series. Convents, colleges, confraternities, libraries and religious and charitable societies of every kind abound. In almost every parish within the last fifteen years, new churches have been erected; or the old ones have been repaired. The Metropolitan church in Marlborough Street is now in every respect nearly complete.

Much emphasis was placed on promoting the Church's teaching through publications. The Catholic Society for Ireland was established with the intention of 'promoting the dissemination of Catholic works of piety, moral and religious instruction, and the formation of parochial lending libraries in Ireland'. According to the *Catholic Directory,* the Society had granted, since January 1836, 'upwards of forty thousand volumes of moral and religious books of the value of £1,200 to various parts of the British Empire, viz. to Newfoundland, Madras, The Cape of Good Hope, Malta, Gibraltar, Ionian Islands, Trinidad, St Vincents etc. The principal part, however, was granted to one hundred and seventeen parishes in Ireland, in many of which religious lending libraries are now established owing to assistance from this institution.' The account went on to give reports from various parts of Ireland, including distant and unexpected locations such as Rathlin Island in Co. Antrim, Newmarket-on-Fergus in Co. Clare, and Kilmainham Gaol in Dublin, from where, in December 1838, the convicts thanked the Catholic Society for the books it had sent, remarking how gratifying it was 'to witness the change that has taken place here since we received them'.[38]

In the Dublin archdiocese, the Catholic clergy, presided over by their archbishop, formed a Diocesan Library at 5 Essex Bridge, Dublin. 'Several thousand volumes' had been bequeathed for this purpose, and most of the clergy had liberally subscribed. A committee was set up to run the library, and every effort was being made 'to render this library useful and agreeable to subscribers at large'.[39]

WIDER CONCERNS

Murray's pastoral concerns were not confined to Dublin or to Ireland; his was a worldwide vision. For many years, Rome had looked to him for advice and personnel to fill positions in the Church across the English-speaking world, and to assist with various problems that had arisen. On 3 December 1833, for example, Propaganda sought his advice about the appointment of a vicar-apostolic for Madras, India, where six English-speaking priests were also needed.[40] Some months later, on 10 April 1834, Propaganda informed Murray that the Holy Father had accepted the recommendation he and Dr Doyle had made, and had appointed Fr O'Connor, provincial of the Irish Augustinians, as vicar-apostolic of the Madras mission.[41]

On another occasion, 14 July 1835, Propaganda expressed concern about the many Irish soldiers stationed in Gibraltar whose children were attending

Protestant schools. They requested Murray to send 'two pious and learned priests' and two Christian Brothers to establish schools.[42] This required much time and negotiation on Murray's part but, on 19 September, Propaganda wrote to say they were pleased to receive his letter of 28 August announcing that two priests and two brothers would be sent.[43] Murray, in fact, had particular difficulty obtaining two priests. On 7 November he informed Propaganda that Fr Meehan and two Christian Brothers were going to Gibraltar. This generated a reply, on 12 December, saying that one priest would not be enough.[44]

A week later, on 19 December, Propaganda asked Murray for his help once again. They wanted him to recommend a vicar-apostolic and some missionaries for the island of Madagascar, which had been colonised by the British.[45] On 6 February 1836, a draft reply by Murray proposed thirty-seven-year-old Fr Patrick Griffith OP, who had worked in the Dublin diocese for many years, as vicar-apostolic. He also suggested 'a very zealous priest', Fr Corcoran, as another suitable person.[46] On 11 July 1837, Propaganda informed Murray that they wished to appoint Fr Griffith as vicar-apostolic of the Cape of Good Hope instead of Madagascar. They included the required apostolic letters which they requested Murray to forward to Griffith.[47]

These represent but a few of the numerous requests that came Murray's way, all of which consumed time and energy. They also frequently required negotiation with individuals and sometimes with religious orders. Moreover, once appointments had been made on Murray's recommendation, he was thereafter expected to assist them with difficulties that arose in their foreign roles.

Apart from Rome itself, there was much correspondence from France and Britain. During 1834 and 1835 there was correspondence also with Belgium, especially with the archbishop of Malines, following the introduction of government laws detrimental to the Irish colleges in Belgium.[48] And, of course, there was correspondence on a regular basis with bishops and Irish people living in the United States of America.

FURTHER DEMANDS ON HIS TIME

On the home front, a certain amount of Murray's pastoral care was influenced by requests from Rome. For example, Propaganda sometimes called on Murray to investigate problems arising within religious houses and within other Irish dioceses, with requests to him to report on these situations. On 23 March 1833, he was asked to inquire into the state of religion among the Carmelites in Dublin.[49]

On 23 May 1835, Propaganda was concerned that the Poor Clares in Kingstown were reported to be in difficulties with their Franciscan superiors, arising from a controversy about ownership of temporal goods. Murray was asked to investigate 'and to report back to Propaganda as soon as possible'.[50] On a vacancy occurring in Tuam, Murray was asked to recommend a suitable candidate as archbishop, in which case he supported the clergy's recommendation of Dr MacHale. He was subsequently asked to investigate problems arising with the successor to MacHale at Killala. This proved a long and difficult ordeal, involving much correspondence and causing distress for more than one person.[51]

In addition, there were roles and functions that Murray was expected to perform on the death of fellow prelates. Two such occurred in the early summer of 1834. The first of these was Oliver Kelly, the Archbishop of Tuam, who died in Rome. Murray received news of his death on 14 May.[52] That involved attending the funeral and giving support to clergy in the Tuam archdiocese as they set about recommending a *terna* to Rome for a replacement. Then he had to make his own recommendation to Rome as well. Murray's greatest loss and sadness at this time, however, was caused by the death of his close friend and suffragan bishop, Dr James Doyle, who had been unwell on and off for two years. On 10 March 1832, Doyle had written to Murray from Bath, saying that he had stomach trouble and was depressed.[53] Despite the appearance of recovery, serious illness followed. When Murray heard the news of his friend's death from Fr Maher in Carlow, on 17 June 1834, his reply was dispassionate. The news of Dr Doyle's death was not unexpected, he wrote, but was much regretted. He would be in Carlow for the obsequies, and he would also preside at the nomination of the vicar-general. He asked Maher to ascertain the wishes of the clergy in this.[54]

Subsequently, on 21 October 1834, Murray presided at the meeting of the clergy of Kildare and Leighlin, where three names were submitted to Rome as possible successors to Bishop Doyle: Dr Edward Nolan, Fr Michael Flanagan (the vicar-general), and Fr Denis Lalor.[55] Edward Nolan was subsequently appointed.

In November 1835, Murray sent his usual *Relatio Status* – the account of his diocese – to Rome. On 9 January 1836, Propaganda replied that this had been received and perused with the greatest satisfaction. His work was praised, and particular notice was taken of the studies undertaken by the clergy, which 'leads to an increase of religion and offers great hopes for the future'. Propaganda also noted his difficulties with the Belgian king over the Irish foundations in that country. Murray was granted permission to nominate Dr Cullen to make the visit to the restored basilica of SS. Peter and Paul in his place.[56]

His desire not to make this visit, presumably because of his precarious health, changed when he was told that His Holiness was disappointed at not having the opportunity of meeting with him, and he decided to set out for Rome. His meeting with Gregory XVI established a bond between them, which resulted in the Pope telling Murray that if ever there was a matter of special concern to him he should not hesitate to write directly to him.[57] The price of Murray's visit, however, was that long bout of illness, mentioned above, which laid him low for weeks before he felt able to return home.

MURRAY AS APOLOGIST

A feature of life in the 1830s was a campaign by an evangelical wing of the Protestant Church to denigrate and ridicule Catholics and their beliefs. The campaign was also availed of by Ultra-Tories to attack the Whig Government's national school system, from which the Anglican Communion had formally retired, and which was portrayed as of special benefit to Catholics. The climate of the time was conveyed by Lord Acton in a letter to Murray on 21 September, 1835. He and some Roman Catholic gentlemen from near Worcester had decided to publish a pamphlet containing the more important points of the Catholic faith which had been so misrepresented. They requested that Murray allow his name to be used in their enterprise. It was necessary to act without delay, he wrote, 'as the country is being deluged by hostile tracts'.[58]

Murray's direct participation in the defence of Catholic beliefs occurred when his own name and Catholic teaching were traduced in the public press and even in the House of Commons. He viewed it as part of his pastoral duties to defend such attacks in public. The criticism in the House of Commons was occasioned by a Flemish Catholic theologian, Peter Dens (1690–1775), whose textbook was being used in Maynooth College. Some of its teaching had been singled out for attack by the Protestant Association, revived by the Ultra-Tories in 1835, as part of a 'No Popery' campaign.[59] As Maynooth was part of the Dublin archdiocese, and Murray was a major patron of the college, he was depicted as approving of all of Dens's teaching. Such views were expressed vehemently at a public meeting in Exeter Hall in London.

On 2 July 1835, Murray addressed a public letter to the Prime Minister, Viscount Melbourne, who had been friendly with Murray during his earlier official posting in Ireland. He wrote, he explained, because of a statement in the House of Commons attributing to him 'certain doctrines contained in a theological work of Dens, on the ground that I directed the publication of that work, and appointed it as a textbook for the Conference of the Catholic Clergy'.

It appeared, Murray added, that an attack was being made to injure, through him as a commissioner, the system of national education in Ireland.

Murray declared emphatically that the said imputations, as reported in the newspapers, were 'wholly devoid of any foundation, in fact. I do not entertain the doctrine attributed to me … I did not direct the work of Dens to be published; it was undertaken by a respectable bookseller as a speculation in trade'. It is 'a work that contains a large mass of very valuable matter', while 'containing, too, some obsolete opinions, wholly unconnected with any article of Catholic faith,' opinions that 'hardly any one, at the present day, would think of defending'. Finally, Murray asserted, 'I did not make it a text book for our Theological Conferences; for such conferences, we have no such book'.

Forcefully, yet in a personal and acceptable manner, Murray then addressed certain opinions of Dens which had been attributed to him and the Catholic Church. 'The opinions of Dens regarding the right of Temporal States to compel their subjects, by confiscation and other punishments, to embrace religious doctrines of which their consciences could not approve, were unfortunately too prevalent throughout Europe at the time he lived; and, I must add, nowhere more prevalent than where the Reformation was established.' He continued smoothly, but with a caustic edge:

> And why are the Catholics of Ireland now forced by this unprovoked taunt, to remember that those desolating opinions were but too deeply imbibed, and too cruelly acted on by their Protestant rulers, during those centuries of religious persecution from which they are but just recovering, and the horrors of which they are desirous to forget?

Murray then turned his attention to his critics:

> Blessed be God! Those doctrines are now little more than a record of by-gone intolerance … They are yielding everywhere to that better and more scriptural spirit of mutual forbearance, which has grown up and is spreading through all Christian communities; and they seem to have found almost their last resting place in the minds of those misguided, though otherwise (let me hope) respectable individuals, who lately exhibited such a miserable display of fanaticism in Exeter Hall, and a few (let me again hope) very few fiery zealots, who have allowed themselves to be so far blinded by passion as to participate in their anti-social opinions.

As regards Irish Catholics, Murray concluded, their doctrine on this subject was thus solemnly attested by oath:

> I, A. B., swear that I do abjure, condemn and detest, as un-christian and impious, the principle that it is lawful to murder, destroy, or in anywise

injure any person whatsoever, or under the pretence of being a Heretic.

He ends the letter courteously, as always: 'I have the honour to be, with the most profound respect, your Lordship's faithful humble servant'.[60]

LETTER 'TO THE PROTESTANTS OF GREAT BRITAIN'

The attacks on Murray and the Catholic Church continued to gain publicity through the aegis of Exeter Hall and the efforts of two men in particular, Revds Robert M'Gee and Sebastian O'Sullivan. They demanded that Murray and other members of the Irish hierarchy come to England to face questions. Rather than pretend to ignore the effrontery of the demand, Murray courageously decided to respond by means of a public letter addressed 'To the Protestants of Great Britain'. Written in a personal, informal, fluid style that reached out to the reader, this long and trenchant document, running to nine printed pages, reveals a fresh perspective on an archbishop so frequently thought of as gentle, mild and amiable.[61]

The letter began with an appeal to the fair play and love of justice said to be a feature of the British public. There followed a restrained but devastating blend of argument and ridicule against the bigotry and inaccuracy of his detractors. 'A Protestant clergyman, of the name M'Gee', he wrote, had induced other members of his profession 'to join in a citation, through the public papers, to me, and other Roman Catholic bishops of Ireland, to proceed to London, and there answer, before a public meeting, certain undefined charges which would be brought against us. What these charges were he did not yet condescend to explain.'

Murray continued in the same vein. 'Pause for a moment to consider the nature of this proceeding,' he wrote. Were he to summon the Bishop of London to suspend his various duties and come over to Dublin to answer before a public meeting of Catholics some unspecified charges to be levelled against him, would it not be viewed as 'matchless effrontery', and would not the originator of such a venture be judged to be labouring under some strange mental aberration? For Mr M'Gee, however, such an excuse could not, at least as yet, be offered. He might not have high powers of understanding, but 'he had enough of that low cunning, which belongs to narrow minds, to perceive that such a summons would … not be attended to, and that he would therefore be enabled to advance such statements as would suit his purpose without the risk of contradiction.'

'Well,' Murray observed sardonically, 'when the important day arrived, when the workings of Popery were to be revealed', what was produced was 'the hitherto concealed work of Peter Dens', which was exhibited as a great discovery, even though an associate of M'Gee admitted that it 'was publicly for sale in a Protestant bookseller's shop', and could have been purchased by anyone for a number of years. This book, nevertheless, Murray stressed, was 'the grand discovery, which collected in Exeter-Hall whatever could be found of the deepest shade of bigotry to witness the overthrow of Popery, and to denounce his Majesty's Roman Catholic subjects of Ireland as unfit … to enjoy any of the principles of social life.'

Murray then observed that it had been proved already to the public that the book of Dens was, in no sense of the word, a standard of Catholic belief. The author himself had never viewed it as such; and he would have been horrified to find attributed to him a doctrine of assassination of those who differed from him in religious belief. 'Search his volumes from beginning to end,' Murray pronounced, 'and you will nowhere find a single trace of this abominable doctrine.' Indeed, Dens had not 'written one line to countenance the atrocious opinion that it would be lawful for any individual either to murder or in any manner to injure another, under the pretence that he professed a different creed'. Yet, this was the false ground on which men, assuming to be ministers of the gospel of peace, thought it fitting to become missionaries of discord. They went about 'scattering the seeds of hatred and un-charitableness', and a whole class of men, the Catholic priesthood of Ireland, was denounced, with the most unscrupulous disregard of truth and decency, as 'a band of deceivers' who 'inculcate in secret to their deluded followers' the most 'antichristian principles, perjury, persecution and murder'.

While he pitied the fanaticism which could have suggested such a desperate course of calumny, Murray thought that perhaps some palliative excuse might be offered for Mr M'Gee. He might have imbibed his erroneous notions of the Catholic religion from the nursery, but no such excuse could be admitted for the Revd Mr O'Sullivan. He was trained up, by his own admission, within the Catholic Church. He knew, Murray declared, that 'he was never taught in that Church' the doctrines which were now attributed to it. 'If he was, where, when, and by whom? Let him come forward and denounce the wretched being to execration and scorn.' Murray, at this point, quoted from the catechism approved by the Irish hierarchy, where the responses to the questions, 'Who is my neighbour?' 'How am I to love my neighbour?' 'Am I obliged to love my enemies?' were all based on texts from the New Testament, so different to the teaching attributed to Catholics.

Murray next proceeded to show up the unfairness that characterised the proceedings of his accusers, taking Mr O'Sullivan severely to task. At Worcester, he wrote, the Revd O'Sullivan 'openly perverted a parliamentary document' for the purpose of representing the evidence which Murray gave before a committee of parliament as directly the reverse of what it really was. Again, when it came to representing the teaching of a general council of the Catholic Church, O'Sullivan, in the report of his speech at Paisley, given in the *Paisley Chronicle*, declared that 'before the conclusion of the 14th century, the Nicene Creed had been adopted, and in 1546 the Council of Trent set aside the Creed'. This very Creed, Murray easily demonstrated, was 'adopted and amplified by the first General Council of Constantinople in 381'. With an addition agreed between the Latin and Greek Churches at the Council of Florence in 1439, it 'was actually embodied in the decrees of the Council of Trent on 4 February 1546', and was 'set forth in the 3rd session of that council, as a rule of Catholic faith'. 'After this,' Murray queried, 'what fact can be so public or so authentic as to be safe from perversion?' Even more to the point, Mr O'Sullivan had himself often heard this very creed recited during the Mass in Catholic churches; and he knew that it formed an important part of the Catholic Church service on every Sunday throughout the year.

'Generous Britons,' Murray concluded, 'will you not at length open your eyes to the expediency of examining … the imputations cast upon us and upon our Church, rather than receive them without inquiry, as true, upon testimony which you must now perceive is of the most questionable character? In the doctrine of millions, there can be no secrets.'

Although addressed 'To the Protestants of Great Britain', this letter was unlikely to influence those set in the ways of anti-popery, but Murray hoped it would be read by educated, less prejudiced Protestants, and that it would also give heart to Catholics in Britain. He received a number of letters commenting on the likely good the letter would do. Thus, Philip Howard of Corby Castle, Carlisle, one of the old British Catholic families, wrote to Murray on 19 October 1835, that he believed Murray's address would do great good. He added that the main opposition to the Irish Church question – the tithes controversy – 'comes from the landed and agricultural classes', and that O'Connell's 'coarse, personal vituperation undermines the good effects of his great talents, vitality and zeal'.[62] These were sentiments with which, in private, Murray was likely to concur.

CHALLENGING THE LORD BISHOP OF GLOUCESTER

Before the year concluded, Murray was in a further jousting contest.[63] This time, it was against a very different opponent, the Bishop of Gloucester. The occasion, however, was not dissimilar: he was defending the reputation of the

Irish Catholic clergy. The *Gloucester Journal*, on 12 December 1835, quoted the Bishop as stating that several of the Protestant clergy 'had been murdered, others had been brutally assaulted or denounced as objects of vengeance from the altar by many of the Irish Roman Catholic priests … encouraged by the hierarchy of the Roman Catholic persuasion'.

Murray took up 'this calumnious charge' on 29 December 1835. It was a charge, he suggested, 'too uncharitable to have issued from the lips of a Christian Bishop, and too destitute of any foundation, in fact, or any semblance of probability, to leave the author of it a chance of escaping from the imputation of deliberate slander'. The words used constituted a sweeping condemnation of the whole body of the Catholic clergy of Ireland. No one individual had been designated out of the entire body. Murray wholly acquitted his lordship of 'the crime of originating this foul and calumnious charge', but he had waited in vain for him to disavow these foul expressions which meanwhile 'have been borne in triumph on the wings of a slanderous press to every hamlet throughout the empire … Next to the guilt of inventing the calumny, is that of giving it an implied approval.'

His Lordship was also reported as saying that some of the highest of the Irish Catholic hierarchy, after exulting in the destruction of ten of the Irish Protestant bishoprics, expressed a hope 'that the whole of the nuisance, as they were pleased to call the Protestant Church, would shortly be extinguished'. To this Murray responded that the reduction of the Irish Protestant bishoprics had been executed by the Legislature, which was almost wholly Protestant, and could not be used as a complaint against Catholics. As regards the word 'nuisance', it was true that some Catholic clergy, who had strong feelings about the injustice and cruelty of the tithe-system as it worked in Ireland, did apply this term, not to the Protestant Church but to the Protestant Establishment and its mode of levying support for the Protestant clergy, often by violence and bloodshed. He gave examples to illustrate how Catholic clergy might use such a term as 'nuisance'. Murray concluded strongly, 'My lord, your lordship's character is at stake. Save it from the degrading imputation of encouraging this slander which is circulating in your name'.

The Bishop of Gloucester replied reasonably and astutely on 5 January 1836.[64] He had just read Murray's letter in the previous day's *Standard.* Murray had done him justice when he expressed the belief that the passage quoted was never uttered by him. 'I never made the assertion there attributed to me,' Gloucester stated, 'and the words which I did use are distorted to a meaning and purport totally different from what I expressed.' So far as he could remember his words, he said that some of the Protestant clergy had been murdered; others brutally assaulted and their lives threatened. He observed that some were unable to obtain their dues, the payment of which had, in some instances, been forbidden by priests from the altar. He also remarked that their consequent distress had been made a subject of ridicule and insult by certain of the highest of the Roman Catholic hierarchy; and in so saying 'I mentioned some of those expressions which had proceeded from an individual of your body. And which, being notorious, fixed the allusion upon the person who had himself published them'. The report in the *Gloucestershire Chronicle*, and the recollections of members present, he said, would bear out his account. As to his not disavowing the fictitious paragraph, he had not read the report of the meeting as given in the *Gloucester Journal* of 12 December, and his 'whole time and attention since the meeting have been absorbed by public matters'. Had it been otherwise, he added, it did not follow that it was in his power 'to have procured a correction of the misrepresentation'.

There were weaknesses in Gloucester's response but he had touched a nerve with his reference to the 'notorious expressions' from one of 'the highest of the hierarchy', a phrase that implied an archbishop. Another nerve was touched by the reference to instructions from the altar by individual priests with respect to the sensitive issue of tithes to the Established Church. The tithes were an additional tax imposed on the Catholic population for the upkeep of Protestant clergy, whose services they neither sought nor wanted. It was enforced by law and had to be paid before the landlord's tax. Those who failed to pay were liable to have their stock and goods seized. The tithes bore heaviest on tillage farmers, as pasture and its produce were exempt. Most agrarian uprisings from the 1760s had tithes among their grievances.

The sense of grievance became particularly strong in parts of Munster, Connacht and Leinster – areas of poverty and bare survival – when potatoes were also subjected to tithe. On 22 June, 1831, O'Connell had told the government, 'You take from the poor man often in time of scarcity his tenth potato for that Church'.[65] In the 1830s, as the Bishop of Gloucester was writing, a tithe war waged in Ireland, and feelings ran high among clergy and people, deeply affecting one archbishop in particular. Serious collisions took place between police and peasantry, and people were killed on both sides, even in Archbishop Murray's province of Leinster. In these circumstances, the issue of tithes raised by the Bishop of Gloucester was not one that Murray wished to pursue.

With this in mind, he wisely decided to conclude their interchange as graciously as possible. He replied on 9 January 1836,[66] in a diplomatic exercise that sought to justify both his lordship of Bristol and Murray himself:

> I owe to your lordship my sincere acknowledgements for the honourable and Christian-like manner in which your lordship has disavowed the

> calumnious expressions which the editor of the *Gloucester Journal* had the temerity to impute to your lordship, and to which, in my letter of the 29th ult., I took the liberty to call your lordship's attention. The assurance that the authorship of the passage in question belongs not to your lordship but to the reporter of the journal, is a gratifying confirmation of the opinion which I had previously the honour to express.

Then, playing a card similar to that used by Gloucester, he added, 'Having said so much, I am desirous to abstain from all comment on the statements which your lordship really made on that occasion, trusting, however, that I shall not therefore be supposed to admit the accuracy of the information on which they rested'. In conclusion, Murray assured his lordship that it was not necessary for him 'to appeal to the *Gloucester Chronicle*, or the recollection of others' in support of his assertion, 'as no testimony, how respectable so ever, could increase the conviction which that assertion is calculated to produce'.

At the end of this exchange of letters, the identity of the archbishop who uttered the 'notorious expressions' remains unclear. There is no immediate evidence but, considering his belligerence, his outspokenness on behalf of the people of his poor and populous province, and his strong national views, the likely candidate is John MacHale, Archbishop of Tuam.

THE CURIOUS CASE OF DR MacHALE

With respect to John MacHale, there are two curious letters from Propaganda to Murray, written prior to the confirmation of MacHale's appointment to Tuam, which deserve our attention. On 26 July 1834, Propaganda informed Murray that the priests of Tuam diocese, along with Dr William O'Higgins of Ardagh, had unanimously recommended Dr MacHale of Killala to be Archbishop of Tuam. There had been suggestions, however, the letter continued, that Dr MacHale had not expressed abhorrence at certain disturbances, plots and criticism of civil authorities that had taken place, and Murray was asked to investigate the matter immediately, in strict confidence, and to report back to the Holy See.[67]

Surprisingly, one week later, on 2 August, Propaganda wrote again to Murray, stating very definitely that all doubts referred to in their previous letter had been set at rest, that Propaganda had that day notified Dr MacHale of his promotion to Tuam, and that Murray should abstain from the requested investigation.[68] Why such a change within a week? Rome is not known for its rapid judgements, but time would show that MacHale had some good friends in Rome, including Dr Cullen at the Irish College. In Ireland itself, he had become friendly with Daniel

John MacHale

O'Connell and was very popular in nationalist circles. The growing national spirit among people and clergy had become evident in the wake of Emancipation.

THE ASSERTIVE NATIONAL FACTOR

Already in 1830, MacHale and O'Connell were exchanging letters on repeal of the union as the panacea for Ireland's ills. Meantime, O'Connell hoped to achieve extensive reforms in Ireland by means of an alliance with the Whig government.[69] By January 1834, the Irish hierarchy, very conscious of the active role played by the clergy in the struggle for emancipation, and concerned lest they continue to be active in politics, passed resolutions addressing the issue. In future, it was decreed, chapels were not to be used for any public meetings except those wholly concerned with charity or religion, political subjects were not to be alluded to from the altar, and priests were not to join or aid political clubs, meetings, etc.[70]

On a visit to Ireland in 1835, Alexis de Tocqueville described a meeting he had on 10 July with some Irish bishops and several priests. Present were Edward Nolan (whom he wrongly identified as 'the bishop of Carlow'), Michael Slattery (whom he called 'the archbishop of Munster'), and three bishops from the west of Ireland (not the Leinster area, as de Tocqueville thought) – Patrick MacNicholas of Achonry, Patrick Burke of Elphin and George J. P. Browne of Galway. He found them 'extremely democratic' in the sentiments they expressed. They exhibited contempt and hatred for the great landlords, love for the poor and confidence in them, bitter memories of past oppression and profound hatred of Protestants and, above all, of their clergy. He found 'a certain exultation at present on approaching victory' but 'little impartiality'. In de Tocqueville's view, they were 'clearly as much the heads of a party as the representatives of the Church'.[71] While taking into account the difficulty of a foreigner in understanding the situation, reflected in the mistakes he made, and acknowledging too the Irish tendency to exaggerate for the benefit foreigners, nevertheless there comes across the sense of men in a changing society reacting against the past, with some of them feeling the need to take part in politics both for the sake of the Church and of their people.

The same Bishop Nolan mentioned by de Tocqueville, whom Murray had recommended for bishop, wrote on the eve of the general election of 1835 that although he wished all his clergy to eschew all political activity whatever, this was not practical immediately. With the Tories working to promote Protestantism and holding back necessary social and economic reforms, the clergy had no option but to explain to the electorate the real nature of the question and to muster every Catholic vote behind the Whigs. 'This pious apologia should not blind us to the fact', historian Oliver MacDonagh commented, 'that a roaring political animal had been awoken in many priests and bishops.'[72]

The role of the Archbishop of Dublin in that changing, but still veiled, situation was suggested by Dr Nicholson in his rather *distrait* letter of 25 November 1834, when he lamented Murray's illness and expressed the loss it would be to Church and country were he to die.[73] He commented that while Dr Troy's times necessarily generated timidity and prudence, 'our own dearest Bishop's times almost – at least of late – as necessarily created Confidence, and ... were calculated to create a Daring, which though noble in itself, would not have been dictated by the Wisdom which proceeds from above. And yet, see, how amidst these difficulties, he (Murray) has conducted numerous affairs in Religions, Politics etc. in which he has been engaged. May the great God in his mercy to poor Ireland spare him to us in health, strength and spirits for many years...'

At the end of the 1830s, the status, reputation and wisdom of the Archbishop were to be challenged for the first time by a number of fellow prelates. A mixture of national feeling, desire for change and inherent suspicion of the British government was to place in jeopardy the system of national education so dear to Archbishop Murray. Any expectation, however, that the gentle aging archbishop would give way under pressure was to be confounded by the toughness and resourcefulness of his response.

NOTES

1 D. C. Black, *Mary Aikenhead (1787–1858). Servant of the Poor.* (Dublin: Caritas, 2001), p.54.
2 E. O. C. Meenan, *St Vincent's Hospital, 1834–1994*, pp.15–17.
3 Murray Papers, Centenary panegyric, 26 Feb. 1952, by Mons. Boylan.
4 Wm Meagher, *Most Rev. Daniel Murray ...*, pp.128–9.
5 L. Dunne – Hamilton, 24 July, 16 Aug. 1832. DDA. Hamilton Papers (3), no.71.
6 Nicholson – Hamilton, 20 June 1834. Hamilton Papers (4). Francis Joseph Nicholson (1803–1855), a Carmelite friar, exiled from his community in Clarendon Street, Dublin, stayed with the More O'Ferrell family as chaplain. He was ordained in 1829, spent much of his time in Paris and Rome, was an admirer of Dr Murray and strove to support his case on national education and on the Bequests Act. He was made coadjutor archbishop of Corfu in 1846, became archbishop in 1852, and died in 1855.
7 Nicholson – Hamilton, 25 Nov. 1834. Hamilton Papers (3).
8 Idem, 5 Dec. 1834.
9 John MacHale – Hamilton, 7 Dec. 1834. Ham. Papers (3), f.10/34.
10 Nicholson – Hamilton, 31 March, 1835. Idem (3).
11 Idem, 19 Nov. 1835. Idem.

12 Wm Meagher, op. cit., p.129.
13 Walter Meyler – Hamilton, 23 April 1836. Ham. Papers (3), no.64.
14 Idem, 16 June 1836. Idem, no. 66.
15 Idem, 19 July 1836. Idem, no. 68.
16 Fr Woods – Hamilton, 16 July 1836. Ham. Papers (4), no.24.
17 Dr Barralta – Hamilton, 29 July 1836. Idem, no.94.
18 Sir Augustus Fortis – Hamilton, July 1836. Idem, no.9.
19 Frank Hamilton – Hamilton, 8 Aug. 1836. Idem, no. 30.
20 Fr Woods – Hamilton, 28 Aug. 1836. Idem, no.33.
21 W. Meyler – Hamilton, 14 Sept. 1836. Idem, no.69.
22 Murray – Nicholson, 14 Feb. 1837. Murray Papers, no.93.
23 Mr/Mrs O'Brien – Hamilton, 1 Nov. 1837. Hamilton Papers (4), no.149.
24 Murray – Hamilton, 3 Nov. 1840, Hamilton Papers (1), no.113.
25 Idem, 8 Nov. 1840. Idem, no.116.
26 Hamilton Papers (5) 16, 19 Feb. 1838, nos.24, 27.
27 Kirby – Hammond, 28 April 1838. Ham. Papers (5), no.2.
28 Fr Taylor – Hamilton, 28 April 1840. Ham. Papers (7), no. 63.
29 W. Meagher, op. cit. p.129.
30 Taking two examples: 25 July, 1838, Fr Wm Young, parish of Baldoyle/Howth, writing to Hamilton, hoped the Archbishop would soon be better – 'It is a long time since this parish had confirmation. If some old people are not confirmed soon they will hardly live to the next year.' Another example is given in the Mary C. Sullivan (ed.) *The Correspondence of Catherine McAuley 1818-1841* (Dublin, 2004), pp.63-64: the reception of novices and their profession was deferred for several months because of Murray's illness. Elsewhere it is noted that for a long period Catherine McAuley wished to consult him on a very serious matter but he was not available for months
31 Murray – Hamilton, 10 March 1841. DDA. Hamilton Papers (1), no.122.
32 *Catholic Register 1853*, p.358.
33 Donal Murray, 'Dublin's Forgotten Archbishop, 1768-1852' in Kelly & Keogh (eds). *History of the Catholic Diocese of Dublin*, p.262.
34 Idem, pp.262–3.
35 Murray – Hamilton, no date. DDA. Hamilton Papers (1), no.323.
36 DDA, Murray Papers. Parish Reports 1834.
37 *The Catholic Directory 1840*, p.265.
38 Idem, pp.270–71.
39 Idem, p.266.
40 Propaganda – Murray, 3 Dec. 1833. DDA., Murray Papers, f.31/4, no.54.
41 Idem, 10 April 1834, idem, no.96.
42 Idem, 14 July, 1835, f 31/4, no.167.
43 Idem, 19 Sept. 1835, idem, no.169.
44 Idem, 12 Dec. 1835, idem, no.172.
45 Idem, 19 Dec. 1835, idem, no.173.
46 Murray – Propaganda (draft), 6 Feb, 1836.
47 Propaganda – Murray, 11 July 1837, f. 31/5 no. 107.
48 Dr Higgins, Bp of Ardagh – Abp.Malines, 10 May 1835, no.107, enclosing letter of Irish hierarchy, 13 Feb. 1835, to Abp. Malines, no.108. Abp. Malines-Murray, 21 Jan. 1835, file 31/4, no.112.
49 Propaganda – Murray, 23 March 1833. F. 31/4, no.45.
50 Idem, 23 May 1835, f. 31/4, no. 163.
51 Idem, 2 July 1837, f. 31/5, no.103. Again 18 Nov. 1837, no. 111 –'Killala causes Propaganda more worry than any place in Ireland'; Murray – Propaganda, 12 Dec. 1837, no.112.

52 DDA, Murray Papers, notice to B. Burke, dean of Tuam chapter, announcing the death, 14 May 1834, f. 31/4, no.62.
53 Bp Doyle-Murray, 10 March 1832, f. 31/3, no.133.
54 Murray – Fr Maher, Carlow, 17 June 1834, f. 41/4, no.93.
55 Priests of Kildare & Leighlin – Holy See, 21 Oct. 1834, f. 31/4, no.94.
56 Propaganda – Murray, 9 Jan. 1836, f. 31/5, no.29.
57 Murray – Pope Gregory XVI reminding him of his instruction to contact him in person, given in W. Meagher. *Most Rev. Daniel Murray…*, Notes, p.58.
58 Lord Acton – Murray, 21 Sept. 1835, f. 31/4, no.152.
59 The Ultra-Tories within Robert Peel's Conservative Party reactivated the Protestant Association in 1835, and between 1835 and 1841 successfully used the 'No Popery' cry against Peel when he attempted to carry the grant for St Patrick's College, Maynooth. Peel split the Conservative Party in 1845. See G.A. Cahill. 'The Protestant Association and the Anti-Maynooth Agitation' in *Catholic Historical Review,* Oct. 1957, p.273.
60 Murray – Rt. Hon. Viscount Melbourne, 2 July 1835, in Meagher. op. cit., pp.170–173.
61 Meagher, op.cit. pp.171–9.
62 Philip Howard – Murray, 19 Oct. 1835, Murray Papers, f. 31/4, no.145. Philip Henry Howard (1801–1833).
63 Meagher. op. cit., pp.179–183.
64 Idem, pp.183–4.
65 M F Cusack (ed.) *Speeches and public letters of the Liberator* (Dublin 1875), I 127 (22 June 1831), cit. D. McCartney, op. cit., p.134, Idem, pp.184–5.
66 Idem, pp.184–5.
67 Propaganda – Murray, 26 July 1834, Murray Papers, f. 31/4, no.102.
68 Idem, 2 Aug. 1834, Idem, no.103.
69 Daniel O'Connell – MacHale, 3 Dec. 1830, in A. O'Day & J Stevenson (eds.) *Irish Historical Documents since 1800* (Dublin 1992), pp.43–4.
70 Printed extracts of resolutions passed at bishops' meeting, 28 Jan, 1834. Murray Papers, f. 31/4, no.58.
71 Emmet Larkin (ed.) *Alexis de Tocqueville's Journey in Ireland, July-August 1835,* pp.46–47, but see notes 7–8 in Introduction where it is made clear who were the bishops that de Tocqueville met.
72 O. MacDonagh. 'Politics Clerical' in *States of Mind. A study of Anglo-Irish Conflict 1780–1980* (London 1983), pp.90–91.
73 Nicholson – Hamilton, 25 Nov. 1834. Hamilton Papers, f.35/5/96 (1).

CHAPTER 10

Rejection by the RDS (1835) and Conflict over National Education (1838–41)

In the 1830s, as has been seen, national feeling found expression in the growth of democracy in Irish politics. It was accompanied by a challenge to the control of the Ascendancy and to the forces of authority that supported the Ascendancy. Associated with this impetus towards democracy was anger at oppressive rents imposed on the agricultural population, especially, as noted, in the form of tithes for the support of the clergy of the Established Church. A virtual tithes war broke out in different parts of Ireland, erupting at times in violence and death.

A NATIONAL ETHOS

O'Connell, meanwhile, had formed an Irish party in the House of Commons, which won thirty-nine seats in parliament in the election of 1832. With an eye to achieving the repeal of the Act of Union of 1800, he put down a motion for repeal in 1834, but it was routed in parliament. Viewing the Tories as enemies of reform, he then turned towards achieving reforms in Ireland by means of an alliance with the Whigs and Radicals. In 1835, he invoked the widespread hostility to the tithes in his election strategy, with his party machine successfully using the slogan, 'No Tithes, No Tories'. In the process, a combination of peasant agrarianism and middle-class politics was fostered against the Established Church and its government allies – the magistracy, military and police.

In February 1835, the first meeting of Whigs, Radicals and O'Connellites was held at Lichfield House in London, resulting in a pact that led to a government led by Viscount Melbourne. O'Connell joined the others on the understanding that reforms and good government would be provided for Ireland. 'I am opposed to repeal,' he declared, 'if justice is done for Ireland'.[1] The effect of his campaign for reform and of his vituperative rhetoric was to engender fear and hostility in the unionist population, and the Catholic clergy were included in that hostility.

In the Emancipation campaign, O'Connell had actively engaged the support of the diocesan clergy. Despite the opposition of the Irish hierarchy as a body, some bishops and many clergy, including some in the Dublin diocese, continued to support O'Connell politically, and to help in the operation of his party machine. Many also combined this with opposition towards the collection of tithes. Following violent eruptions in Co. Clare from January to June 1831, the *Dublin Evening Mail* – with which the conservative *Clare Journal* agreed on 28 February 1831 – complained that the Catholic Association, the priesthood and the press had taught the peasantry to believe themselves to be slaves, their landlords oppressors, and their liberation to lie in their own hands. It was not surprising, therefore, that, finding their expectations after Emancipation not realised, they should resort to rebellion.[2] It was also not surprising that among many conservative Irish Protestants, the new situation reinforced their long-held prejudice against the Catholic clergy, finding additional grounds for antagonism and fresh opportunities to vent their spleen. Daniel Murray was to experience this in a very public way in the summer of 1835, when he found himself the unexpected target of politics wedded to religious bigotry.

MURRAY AND THE ROYAL DUBLIN SOCIETY

The indirect occasion for this development was the decision of the British Association of the Advancement of Science to hold its annual meeting in Dublin from 10 to 15 August 1835.[3] There was considerable excitement in intellectual and social circles in Dublin at this honour being conferred on their city, and it was suggested that citizens of eminence should enrol their names amongst the members of the Association. Archbishop Murray's friends, most notably John Richard Corballis, urged him to add his name to the list of those who sought the honour of aggregation. Feeling it the appropriate thing to do, Murray assented. As a condition of membership, however, the Association required that all applicants should previously belong to some local scientific or literary body. Accordingly, Mr Corballis gave notice that he would propose Murray for membership of the Royal Dublin Society on a certain date, with Dr Sandes, senior fellow of Trinity College Dublin and admirer of the Archbishop, claiming the honour of seconding the nomination. On the day specified for the ballot on membership, the unexpected happened. The Archbishop's nomination was rejected.

There was widespread surprise, followed by indignation. Murray had gone out of his way to mingle with and assist government representatives and prominent Dublin Protestants. By his calm, dignified presence and courtesy towards all, he had disarmed much prejudice and ignorance regarding Catholics and their clergy. In Britain, as has been seen, he had won admirers across the religious divisions. At the time of his rejection parliament was in session, and in both houses the action of the Royal Dublin Society was castigated. In the Commons especially, the affront to Murray was resented in cutting terms, and it was suggested that such bigotry should be denounced by withdrawing the grant which the Royal Dublin Society enjoyed. It was agreed that an enquiry be held into the objects and proceedings of the Society. Subsequently, members of the Society who had not voted on the occasion but who were embarrassed by the outcome, sought to lay the blame on a few fanatics who, taking the Society by surprise, sought to vent their hostility towards Catholics by their treatment of the Catholic archbishop. They urged a renewed ballot, assuring Corballis of a favourable result. Corballis sent a note to Murray explaining the new situation, and requesting his views on the matter. The answer he received became a classic of its kind, manifesting deep reflection and the most careful choice of words. Written from Mountjoy Square and dated 7 December 1835, the letter in full reads as follows.

My dear Corballis,

> It is to me a subject of unaffected concern, that I have become most unintentionally a source of disagreement amongst the members of the Royal Dublin Society. It has been my object thro' life to conciliate, not to disunite; and it could not, of course, fail to be peculiarly distressing to my feelings to be an occasion of dissension in a body, which, if united, is so well calculated to do extensive good, and the combined efforts of all whose members are so much wanted for the improvement of the country. As far as I am concerned, all future discussion on the subject of the late ballot would be entirely useless. The decision come to on that occasion was final. It has disclosed the fact that my co-operation for the advancement of the purposes of the Society would not, in the opinion of a considerable number of its members, be likely to prove beneficial. This is quite sufficient to render it impossible for me to entertain the slightest wish to take a part in the proceedings of that body. As far as regards me, therefore, the renewal of a discussion on that subject could lead to no possible advantage; and would but distract the attention of the members from the immediate and practically useful objects of the Society.
>
> I need hardly say how deeply I feel indebted to you, to Doctor Sandes, and to the numerous other members of the Society, who evinced towards me a warmth of kindness which I cannot but consider exceedingly

flattering. I pray you to convey to them what you know to be my feeling on the subject, together with my earnest solicitation, that in the future transactions of the Society, I may be wholly lost sight of; that the recent cause of momentary disagreement may be forgotten; and that the whole body may join in cordial union to promote the great objects of National improvement for which the Society was established.

I have the honour to remain, with affectionate regard, my dear Corballis, most faithfully yours,

+ D. Murray

A majority of members, reacting to the letter, agreed to have it inserted in the minutes of the Society,[4] where it remained as a witness to forbearance and a reminder of the Society's proper role as a promoter of national improvement.

This experience of hostility from a society long associated with Protestant ascendancy was not nearly as upsetting to Murray as the opposition that awaited him three years later from amongst his fellow prelates. Politics of a different hue framed discussion on the national system of education from 1838–41.

A REVOLUTIONARY EXPERIMENT

It will be recalled that in 1826 the Irish bishops had enunciated their preferred educational system: one in which Catholic teachers, educated in Catholic training colleges, under the secular and moral control of the episcopacy, would be present in every school. It was an ideal picture that had no chance of acceptance under a British Tory government. In 1831, however, under a Whig administration, pressure from the Irish Catholic community led to a plan which, while far from the bishops' desired system and developed without consulting them, was still an acceptable alternative in the circumstance of the time. Chief Secretary, E. G. Stanley, explained to the Duke of Leinster in October 1831 that it was 'a system of education from which should be banished even the suspicion of proselytism, and which admitting children of all denominations should not interfere with the peculiar tenets of any'.[5] As part of the new scheme, the government grant to the Kildare Place Society – associated with proslytism in education – was withdrawn, and a seven-person board of education was established, two of whom were Catholics, to superintend the system. It brought with it, as a result, a weakening of evangelical proselytising with its varied interpretations of the Bible. Although the new system was non-denominational in principle, and the Irish bishops had no final voice in either the texts published by the board or the appointment or dismissal of teachers and inspectors, they accepted it as a means of educating the poor and as the best available option. Daniel Murray, as has been seen, led the way in accepting one of the Catholic places on the board of commissioners, the other being filled by his friend, Anthony Blake, the prominent Dublin lawyer.

The system of national education, in the context of the United Kingdom in the 1830s, was a revolutionary experiment in state planning, management and secularity. In terms of secularity, however, it soon faltered. Because of its benefits to Catholics and its discouragement of proselytism, the Church of Ireland pulled out of the system. The Ulster Presbyterians proved very hostile at first, and several national school houses were burned down,[6] but before long they negotiated terms which ensured their active participation. By and large, the advice of Bishop Doyle of Kildare and Leighlin to Michael Slattery, parish priest of Borrisoleigh in Co. Tipperary and later archbishop of Cashel, proved both practical and prophetic from the Catholic point of view. 'The terms setting up the national system of education … are well suited to the particular circumstances of this distracted country … The Protestant clergy … have abandoned the field entirely to us and (this) will have the effect of throwing the education of the Catholic youth of the country into our hands.'[7] By 1838, some six years after the introduction of the system, 'the government was spending £50,000 annually on some 150,000 children in 1,600 schools, 1,200 of which were managed by Catholics … Given the complexity … of so vast a social experiment, the national system functioned efficiently and fairly.'[8]

EPISCOPAL OPPOSITION

Despite the sound operation of the national system and the practical educational benefits it provided for the poorer sections of the population, a few bishops declared themselves unhappy with it at the annual episcopal conference in February 1838. The leaders of the criticism were William O'Higgins, bishop of Ardagh, and especially the formidable John MacHale, archbishop of Tuam. The latter was a national figure. For many years he had been an outspoken critic of government policy and of many of its actions. He combined a spirit of national fervour with an ingrained suspicion of any apparent benefits coming from the hands of government. In the popular mind he was the patriot bishop, second only to O'Connell in public esteem.

Shortly after their criticism had met with little support at the episcopal conference, MacHale appealed over the heads of his fellow prelates by publishing two public letters in the *Dublin Evening Post,* on 13 and 24 February 1838, addressed to Sir John Russell, then chief secretary, denouncing the system of national education. In doing so, he was both implicitly critical of Archbishop Murray, a member of the system's governing board from its inception, and jeopardising a fundamental principle of the episcopal body – unity in action, if not in thought. MacHale's public attack was taken up in different newspapers. It appealed to the native tendency to find fault with the government, and many of his supporters were less than restrained in their criticism.

On the date of the second of these letters, MacHale made sure to keep Rome favourably informed by forwarding the two letters to his friend, Dr Paul Cullen, the president of the Irish College in Rome and acting agent for the Irish bishops. He reminded Cullen that when he was in Rome both of them had looked with 'disapprobation' on the board of the national education system then in its infancy. 'It has since become more obnoxious,' he explained. 'Dr Murray does not, I think, see the extent of its danger', he continued, and 'I felt it my duty lately to express my opinions on its dangerous tendency.'[9] By mid-April, he was reporting to Cullen that he had mobilised his clergy, and that more than 120 priests had 'expressed their unanimous concurrence in the resolutions of all the bishops of Ireland some years ago not to permit the Scriptures to be made a school book for children, and not to relinquish the control which belongs to them over the selection of books and the choice of masters'.[10]

In fact, all clergy were prepared to agree with the bishops' ideal system, but the reality was that it was unattainable. MacHale realised this, yet he kept trying to undermine the actual national education system, approved by a majority of his fellow bishops, by emphasising its difference from the unattainable ideal. Writing to Daniel O'Connell, just three days after his letter to Cullen, MacHale encouraged O'Connell to procure a grant 'for the separate education of Catholic children', which he described as the only subject on which 'the Catholic bishops of Ireland have expressed their solemn and unanimous approval'. A resolution on the matter at their last episcopal meeting was adjourned due to 'the lamentable indisposition of Dr Murray'. The implication was that the resolution would likely have been passed had a vote been taken. In the same letter to O'Connell, MacHale acknowledged that 'a grant for the separate education of Catholics' was not attainable. 'I know that separate education would not be relished at present by the government. I know, too, that many, with an erroneous feeling of liberality, cherish the plan of mixed education. I like religion to be as free as air which is the only true liberality.'[11]

To what exactly was MacHale objecting in the national education system? And why had he delayed his criticism until 1838? It seems that he was objecting primarily to the state's encroachment on the rights of the Catholic Church in religious education, particularly a state with such an anti-Catholic history. His objection was sharpened by what he perceived as the neglect of his diocese by the board of education. Despite these factors, he observed that he might still have remained silent 'were it not for a fundamental change, affecting the best interests of religion'.[12] The 'fundamental change', as he viewed it, was in the Fourth Report of the education commissioners, 1837. He contended that the commissioners had received government approval for the use of the Scriptures as a national school textbook. He cited paragraph 38 of the Report:

> We therefore propose modifying the letter of the rule, so as to allow religious instruction to be given, and the Scriptures to be read, or the Catechism learned, during any of the school hours, provided that such an arrangement be made so as no child shall take part in, or listen to any religious reading or instruction to which their parents or guardians object.[13]

MacHale also objected to the absence of any reference to the Catholic clergy. If paragraph 38 indicated that Sacred Scripture was being used as a textbook, then the national system was in open conflict with the views of the Irish bishops enunciated in 1826.

Murray, however, believed MacHale to be quite mistaken in interpreting the paragraph in terms of a textbook. He had remained silent in the face of the publicity accorded MacHale and his supporters, and he was reluctant to involve Rome in matters of the Irish Church when he felt the Irish bishops were competent to deal with such. He decided, nevertheless, to let Cullen know something of the reality of the situation, which was being obscured by emotion and misrepresentation. He had occasion to write to Cullen, on 28 April 1838, concerning a theological chair at Maynooth, a subject that occupied most of the letter. After dealing with that, he continued:

> Doctor MacHale, you will have perceived, is making a violent outcry in opposition to the sentiments of the great majority of his episcopal brethren, against our national system of education. But what is most surprising is that he bases his principal argument on an evident *misstatement*, namely, that the Bible is, under this system, made a school book.

'We were long struggling', Murray commented, 'to obtain public aid, which could be safely applied towards the education of our poor; and, when obtained, he seems desirous to wrest it from us and throw it back into the hands of those who would employ it against us. As for his pretended hope of procuring a separate grant for the education of the Catholic poor, it is so utterly visionary that no rational person could entertain it for a moment.'[14]

The Bible had an important role in children's education in nineteenth century Ireland. The government and the Protestant Churches insisted on it being part of children's study at school. The Catholic church tended to view the Bible as too difficult for young children, and if used it should be in an annotated edition, such as the Douay version, approved by the Holy See. Without such safeguards, it was seen as open to all kinds of individual interpretations and widespread confusion. The government and the Protestant Churches, on the other hand, did not approve of such annotated versions. Moreover, the suggestion that the Catholic children use the Douay version of the Bible and the Protestant children the St James version, or some other chosen version, was not permitted by the government, which insisted on Protestant and Catholic children being educated together in the chosen form of mixed education. The eventual result was a compromise: selected readings from the Bible which did not conflict with the teachings of the respective Churches, and which also imparted agreed moral values to the children. The work chosen was by a Presbyterian, Revd James Carlile. Entitled *Scripture Lessons*, it was modelled on texts in the Catholic Book Society, and it had the page-by-page approval of Murray and his fellow commissioner, the Protestant archbishop of Dublin, Richard Whately (1787–1863).[15] A further book, used later, was by Archbishop Whately himself, *Lessons on the Truth of Christianity;* it, too, was approved by the commissioners.

The Irish Catholic bishops had unhappy memories of the Bible being used as a proselytising tool by evangelical preachers and also in the Kildare Place system. To MacHale and Higgins, any use of Scripture approved by the government was open to suspicion. Carlile's *Scripture Lessons* was represented as promoting latitudinarianism, or the notion that 'provided one accepts Christianity as the true religion, it makes little difference to what particular denomination one adheres', reflecting 'the view … that there is no creed definitely set forth in Scripture.'[16] Thus, Mr Dillon Browne MP, apparently much influenced by MacHale, informed Dr Slattery, the archbishop of Cashel, on 1 June 1838, that Mr Carlile's work would leave the simple-minded youth of Ireland with the impression that what had been the vital differences between the two Churches were only the hypocritical distinctions of schoolmen.[17] In reality, the youth of Ireland remained unaware of the dangers. Throughout the controversy, MacHale was unable to point to a single conversion from Catholicism to Protestantism as part of his indictment of the national system of education.

In an effort to gauge the level of support among the bishops for the national system, Archbishop Murray addressed a circular letter in early March 1838 to all his episcopal colleagues, with the exception of Archbishop MacHale. In a letter to Archbishop Slattery, on 6 March 1838, Murray indicated the importance to him of the support of his fellow bishops. He stated that he was prepared to resign from the position of commissioner were Slattery opposed to the national system.[18] The following day, Slattery observed that there were numerous national schools throughout the diocese of Cashel and Emly, and that they worked well. He was prepared to give the national system his support until he saw 'something in it more objectionable' than he had 'yet been able to discover'.[19] Murray received only three unfavourable replies. Hence, at this stage, only four out of twenty-six bishops had serious reservations about the national system.[20]

MURRAY AND MacHALE IN CONFLICT

Meanwhile, the controversy continued in the public press, much of it fuelled by ardent partisans. Following MacHale's fifth public letter to the Chief Secretary, in May 1838, Murray, while refusing to participate in the public controversy in Ireland, felt obliged to defend the national system in Rome. He submitted a 'long history' of the system to Cardinal Franzoni, prefect of Propaganda, and at the same time he forwarded the rules of the national system to Cullen for him to translate into Italian.[21] A few weeks later, Murray wrote once more to Cullen, with a view to his contacting Propaganda regarding some of MacHale's charges against the commissioners of the national education system. 'The commissioners', he pointed out, 'do not appoint school masters; but accept or approve of those who are proposed by the local managers throughout the country; and as by far the great majority of these local managers are priests, it follows that no master can be appointed without their approbation. All that the commissioners have to do with the teachers is to see that they be competent persons – of moral character – and that they do not attempt any undue influence with regard to the religion of their pupils.'[22] When Cullen, in reply, requested copies of the school books and the *Scripture Lessons* for the inspection of Propaganda, Murray forwarded them straightaway. He explained that the Scripture extracts being used were intended for 'moral instruction' and were translated directly from the Hebrew and the Greek. They differed in no way from the Vulgate as 'affecting faith or morals'.[23]

By August 1838, the eloquence and powerful personality of John MacHale had persuaded his six suffragan bishops of the possible dangers of the national system and of its inadequacy in light of the 1826 resolutions of the entire Catholic hierarchy. A letter from Bishop George J. P. Browne of Galway, dated 1 August 1838, alerted Murray to his own change of heart and that of the other five bishops of the western province. Previously, on 11 March, Browne had written that such was his 'unbounded confidence' in Murray's 'vigilance and zeal for the maintenance and preservation of the best interests of religion' that he could 'have no possible hesitation in giving the national board my most warm support.' Now, five months later, 'after a week of solemn spiritual retreat,' he was notifying His Grace, 'previous to any public declaration' of the complete alteration of his sentiments regarding the system of national education. 'I am almost perfectly convinced that in the system recommended and adopted by the insidious enemies of our holy faith are laying wily snares to undermine it and gradually destroy that sacred influence which Catholic bishops and pastors should ever possess over their respective flocks.'[24] Recognising the language of MacHale in Browne's sentiments, and the weakness of the individual examples he gave of failings in the system, Murray replied in forthright terms.

He wrote, he explained, from Rahan Lodge, Tullamore, where 'I have been staying for some days for the recovery of my health'.[25] That Dr Browne would exclude from his flock any system he judged injurious to them was a duty, he said, that he would expect from his lordship. He then examined the faults in the system which Browne had outlined in his letter. He observed that some of them could be easily rectified and others were without foundation. Having dealt firmly with these last, Murray mentioned that 'the schools have now been for some years established in your lordship's diocese,' and goes on to enquire rhetorically if 'your lordship found any practical mischief resulting from them?' He continued: 'In the North,' where danger to the Catholic religion in the national system was likely to be most formidable, 'the bishops, far from showing your lordship's alarm, are most anxious to expand the acknowledged benefits of the system as widely as possible among their people. What, in the name of goodness, have you to fear in Catholic Connaught, where there could be so little interference with you?'

Finally, Murray asked Browne to pause before he took the final step his letter intimated. Such a step would prove of lasting regret to him, Murray believed. Should he take it, however, Murray would hold himself at liberty to publish their present correspondence. His Lordship, in that case, would reject in future the aid which the national system offers for the education of his people. This would be a great loss to them.

Murray then instructed his secretary, John Hamilton, to forward to Rome the letters written in March by the Connaught bishops, so that if their sentiments had undergone change the reasons which produced it would be better understood. Murray's stiff letter to Browne had an effect. On 26 August 1838, Hamilton informed Cullen that at a recent provincial meeting of the prelates of Connaught, chaired by Archbishop MacHale, 'it was unanimously resolved not to publish any document against the national system, without having consulted all the bishops of Ireland'.[26]

For several months more, the partisans of both sides conducted a furious polemic. Finally, on 22 October, an exasperated Murray, fearing that repeated misstatements might be accepted as true, published a detailed reply to the objections made against the national system. Appearing in the *Dublin Evening Post* on 23 October 1838, he concerned himself with the issues, avoiding personalities. MacHale replied on 3 November. He made no effort to deal with the issues, but instead took Murray personally to task and launched into a generalised attack on the system. 'From a feeling of respect for him,' wrote MacHale of Murray, 'we suffered much to pass over in silence which would have called forth our earlier animadversion and remonstrance.' He then explained that 'it was only when we saw the vicious system teemed with evils, which no zeal or piety on the part of any individual member of the body, however active, could correct, that we raised our feeble voice to protest against a scheme of education which threatened such serious dangers to the fold.'

To this response – disingenuous and less than honest in his view – Murray replied trenchantly. He took the criticisms MacHale had raised about the operation of the system, such as the inspectors' regulation of the quantity of religious instruction, and, having demonstrated their lack of reality, he asked if MacHale could possibly be serious in drawing the conclusions he did from such premises. Then cutting through MacHale's rhetoric about his respect for Murray deferring his response to the system until he saw its many evils and dangers, Murray commented pointedly that Archbishop MacHale only began to complain about the national system after an application of his for a grant for a school in his diocese had been refused by the commissioners. 'What new light', Murray remarked, 'this disappointment may have thrown upon the national system is not for me to guess.' And then he added, as if addressing MacHale, 'But it appears that, on the following February, in a meeting of the bishops, from which a severe illness compelled me to be absent, and after some of the prelates had retired, your Grace, as I am informed, thought proper, without any previous communication with me, to animadvert on the commissioners, in no very measured terms, for their imputed partiality in the distribution of the education grant, and to harangue the meeting on the dangerous tendency of the system which they administered.'[27]

Despite these cutting charges, MacHale once again refused to deal with them or the other issues raised. He insisted on talking about what the system might become rather than what it actually was, thereby presenting the state once more as an evil manipulator, an image welcome to his supporters and to a wide section of the populace. 'From the extraordinary power now claimed by the state over mixed education,' MacHale asserted sweepingly, 'it would soon claim a similar despotic control over mixed marriages, and strive to stretch its net over all ecclesiastical concerns.' And, he commented insultingly, 'it would never want subservient instruments'.[28] It was, perhaps, the first insinuation by a fellow prelate that Murray was anti-nationalist and a lackey of the Dublin administration.

The public exchange only served to increase the bitterness of the contending partisans and to highlight the division within the Catholic hierarchy. Rome was scandalised and upset by the public quarrel. Paul Cullen conveyed this to Murray, who replied on 12 December 1838 that he, too, lamented the continuation of the controversy. He then explained that he and the great body of the bishops had been assailed for eight long months in the public press and, to the great astonishment of everyone, had remained silent. He eventually wrote, he said, because people were beginning to think that charges so often repeated and never denied must have some foundation.

Having refuted the charges, Murray continued, his part of the controversy was now at an end. If the Holy See even hinted its disapprobation of any part of his proceedings in this affair, he would at once retire from the board and leave the education grants entirely in the hands of Protestants, as before, conscious that in union with the great body of the bishops he had done all in his power to avert the mischief to religion which would inevitably follow.[29] With respect to the *Scripture Lessons*, Murray assured Cullen that they need not be used by those who chose to reject them. No bishop had yet complained of any practical mischief produced by them; and all felt at perfect liberty to reject them if the danger of any mischief should arise. A formal judgement to exclude them from the schools would be 'a gratuitous insult' to those bishops who had admitted them, and would render abortive all Murray's endeavours to keep the education grants out of the hands of the enemies of the Catholic faith and 'to raise our poor out of their degrading inferiority to a level in the scale of education with their Protestant neighbours'.

In conclusion, Murray emphasised that he was but the servant of his brother bishops. He had acted with them, and would continue to do so unless Rome otherwise decreed, 'notwithstanding the *noisy opposition*' which had been partially raised against him – some of it, he feared, more 'from personal feelings than from any motive that is deserving of praise'.[30]

The key figure in the 'noisy opposition' remained MacHale, whose volatility was so well known that Daniel O'Connell found himself embarrassed by it. Writing from Galway to his staunch supporter, P. V. Fitzpatrick, on 19 November 1838, he expressed his pleasure that Archbishop MacHale had come to Galway to honour him, but he feared that at dinner that evening something 'adverse' to Murray might be said. If it happened, it would be directly contrary to

O'Connell's wishes, but he could not prevent an archbishop making a speech. He asked Fitzpatrick to explain the situation to Fr John Miley, another staunch supporter of O'Connell and a prominent priest at the Pro-Cathedral, and to let him know 'that I would rather cut off my right arm than show any disrespect to Dr Murray, a prelate who above all living men, I venerate'.[31] Happily, the dinner passed without the expected embarrassment.

Among the episcopal supporters of Murray, there was considerable disquiet by December 1838 over the national education issue. Responding to a letter from Archbishop Michael Slattery, Dr William Kinsella of Ossory argued that 'the cause of religion has seriously suffered by the collision of the two archbishops'. He suggested that, in order to render Archbishop MacHale 'incapable of doing serious mischief', the majority of the prelates should come to the annual meeting, in January 1839, 'prepared to act resolutely on the matter'.[32]

VERDICT FROM PROPAGANDA FIDE

Two very different accounts of the bishops' annual meeting were sent to Dr Cullen. On 23 January an excited and less-than-detached letter was sent to him by Bishop O'Higgins. He explained that because there was division among the bishops about the present system of national education, MacHale had proposed that the matter 'be referred to the Holy Father for his decision'. Sixteen bishops opposed this, O'Higgins wrote, thereby refusing to consult the successor of Peter. They were set in their 'secular views'. He urged Cullen to put 'the Cardinal Prefect (of Propaganda) or His Holiness (in) possession of all the details, that they may stand on the alert.' He then added, 'If the others write their communications should be received with caution … as, heretic like, they change or modify these things *ad captandum.*'[33]

It is evident that O'Higgins, and indeed MacHale, viewed Cullen as sympathetic to their point of view. Murray, for his part, was more circumspect in his letter. Writing to Cullen on 28 January 1839, he dealt with other Church affairs, such as the administration of the diocese of Killala, and only on page three did he mention the bishops' meeting and the national system of education. When a large majority of the prelates were about to pass a resolution in favour of the national system, Murray reported, 'Dr MacHale urged that the matter was before the Holy See, and that they were not therefore competent to come to a decision on it'. In this MacHale was supported by his provincial prelates, the vicar general of Killala (in the absence of a bishop), and three other bishops. 'But sixteen others', Murray commented, 'including three archbishops, stood firm in their decided approval of the national system of education, and considered it quite unnecessary to annoy the Holy See on a subject which they found by experience to be not only safe but advantageous to religion.'[34]

On 30 January, O'Higgins wrote again. 'We have ample reasons', he claimed, 'for believing the system to be the last effort on the part of England to abolish the Catholic religion in this country'. Arianism was being taught in the text books, he claimed. 'For God's sake, [bring to the attention] of the Pope and cardinals the awful character of this audacious system.'[35] The following day, he wrote again about Arianism in the books approved by the commissioners, focusing in particular on a book by Archbishop Whately, himself a commissioner, entitled *Lessons on the Truth of Christianity*. 'Whatever may result from our application,' Higgins concluded, 'we have with us the Catholic feeling of Ireland, and the honour of counting amongst our opponents, all the bad priests, luke-warm and Castle-hack Catholics, as well as the heretical or Victorian liberals of the empire.'[36]

MacHale, too, wrote to Rome complaining about Dr Whately's *Lessons on the Truth of Christianity.*[37] He did not know – nor did Rome, perhaps – that Murray, as commissioner, approved of Whately's book only on condition that it was used exclusively for Protestant children.[38] Murray, nevertheless, when questioned by Cullen about Whately's *Lessons* came stoutly to its defence. 'With respect to the little book on the truth of Christianity which you mentioned', Murray replied tartly, 'it is quite clear that you did not read it … In the third page the object for which it was written is truly stated to be, not what you were told, but "to suggest such reasons to those who believe in Jesus Christ as may serve to protect them from the insidious artifices of Infidels, and enable them to strengthen the faith of others, or to restore those who may have fallen from Christian profession".'[39]

The national education issues remained under consideration for several months. On 13 March 1839, Murray sent a strong letter to Cullen. He explained that he had forwarded to the cardinal prefect, on 25 February, his answers 'to the animadversions on the national system in general and the Scripture Extracts in particular.' He explained that 'to some of those objections I was obliged to answer in strong language', but hardly any language could be strong enough 'to mark, as it deserves, the dishonesty which pervades them.'

Then turning to Cullen himself, Archbishop Murray remarked that he wished Cullen would ask to see the letters that he had sent, so as to explain whatever obscurity might be in them. For, although the opponents of the national system did not scruple to reckon Cullen on their side, Murray himself believed that Cullen's judgement would be an honest one. 'In the meantime,' Murray continued, 'I cannot withhold the expression of my opinion, that whoever is intimately acquainted with the state of the country, the difficulty we have had in procuring the present system, the utter hopelessness of obtaining aid from parliament for anything better, the danger of allowing the education funds to go back to the exclusive management of Protestants, the experience which the Catholics have had of the beneficial effects of the system … whoever I say is acquainted with all these things must, in my opinion, be convinced, if he be an unprejudiced person, that any attempt, from whatever quarter it may come, to upset the present system would not only be imprudent in the extreme, but would ultimately fail, after having, in the fruitless struggle, inflicted a wound upon religion, from which it would not for a long time recover.'[40]

In late June 1839, Propaganda decided to condemn the Scripture extracts and the national system of education. Having been informed of this by Cullen, Murray replied on 12 July that he had been in possession of the sentiments of Propaganda before receiving Cullen's letter. In his letter to Cullen, Murray explained that the Lord Lieutenant, Lord Ebrington, had obtained the intelligence that Dr O'Higgins was the bearer of a verbal assurance from Propaganda to MacHale 'that the Sacred Congregation disapproved the system of national education altogether, disapproved of the books used for Catholic instruction, and would immediately direct me to retire from the Board'. Upon learning this, Murray continued, the Lord Lieutenant, 'a thinking and benevolent man' without 'the least tincture of bigotry', sent for him and presented him with a letter, which Murray now enclosed for Cullen. The letter stated that Catholics would 'have no hope of public aid for education on terms more favourable than those on which the national system was conducted'. Murray requested Cullen to translate the letter into Italian and submit it to the Holy Father.

If the national system was put down, Murray continued, the consequences would be disastrous. 'It would delight our enemies; it would degrade our hierarchy'; it could lead to 'more violent discontent against the Holy See' than was manifested on the question of the veto. The poor themselves would be the greatest sufferers. He informed Cullen that he had made a further appeal to the Holy Father 'in the hope that the calamities which were threatened … may be still averted'. In conclusion, he drew Cullen's attention to the negative public statement on the national system by his vice-president in the Irish College in Rome, Fr Tobias Kirby. Regarding the system, Kirby seemed to be 'supremely ignorant', Murray commented, and yet he went ahead with his severe criticism despite the fact that his bishop, Dr Nicholas Foran of Waterford, was one of the system's 'most zealous patrons'.[41]

PERSONAL APPEAL TO THE POPE

Faced by the likelihood of a formal pronouncement from Propaganda against the national system of education, Murray decided to resort to a suggestion made to him many years previously by Pope Gregory XVI. In the translation provided by Fr Meagher, his friend and biographer, Murray wrote in early July 1839:

> When on the vigil of the Holy Apostles SS Peter and Paul in the year 1836 … your Holiness condescended to command me, that, whenever there occurred to my mind, any matters, which I might chance to deem serviceable to religion or otherwise, I should lay them with perfect freedom before your Holiness in person. Emboldened by such kindness, I presume to submit to your Holiness a matter in which the interests of religion are deeply involved.[42]

Murray went on from there to outline the problem and to ask that, before any further steps from the Sacred Congregation be taken, a legate might be sent to Ireland to examine the national system with his own eyes. If that were considered inexpedient, he went on, at least one or two of the Irish prelates favourable to the system might be permitted to go to Rome for the purpose of conferring more fully with the authorities there on the matter.[43]

On 22 August 1839, in a letter to Cullen, Murray 'rejoiced to find that the Supreme Guardian of our Faith has himself vouchsafed to look into the nature of our education system'.[44] When the Pope eventually took action, he simply reopened the whole question, asking both parties not to send two bishops to Rome to present the case, which, 'it was feared, would create too much observation',[45] but rather two ecclesiastics of a lower grade, deputed by the contending parties.

Regarding Cullen, meanwhile, there was disquiet among the episcopal majority. In a letter to Murray on 4 August 1839, an irate Dr Crolly, archbishop of Armagh, observed,[46] 'The reports from all who have been lately in Rome are calculated to convince us that our agent, Dr Cullen, has betrayed the confidence which we reposed in him, and in this particular and unfortunate case has endeavoured to injure us in the estimation of the Sacred Congregation'. Crolly then added, 'I am persuaded that the letter which I wrote to him, for the information of the Holy Father, has not been fairly submitted to the consideration of his Holiness, which would have prevented an unfavourable decision against a system of education so advantageous to our religion. If the other prelates will agree with me, Dr Cullen will be troubled no longer with the labour of our agency.'

The removal of Cullen from the position of agent went no further, partly because of Murray's noted clemency and also because Cullen significantly changed his attitude.

PREPARING THE CASE FOR ROME

Towards the end of September 1839, a diplomatic letter from Cardinal Franzoni, Prefect of Propaganda, announced that the Sacred Congregation had deferred for a time 'the formal manifestation of their intentions ... as a renewed testimony, on our part, of your Grace's pre-eminent virtues'. The representatives from both sides should be sent to Rome.[47]

In preparation for the Roman negotiations, Murray circulated a number of query sheets to each bishop regarding the operation of the national school system in his diocese. The individual priests who were managing schools were to be consulted. Responses were to be sent to Murray or to the two representatives at Rome, Frs Ennis and Meagher, who had been chosen by Murray for their ability and their fluency in Italian. All the bishops consulted declared themselves supportive of the national system, though many were very slow in getting the query sheets returned from their priests. A few of them sought additional query sheets in light of the number of schools in their dioceses.[48]

Among the quickest and most decisive in replying was Dr Cornelius Denvir, of Down and Connor who, on 30 October, sent back completed documents, all unanimously for the system. The documents were destined for Propaganda through Frs Meagher and Ennis, he noted, but he was also writing personally to the pope.[49] Even earlier, on 10 October, Archbishop Slattery, of Cashel and Emly, sent the handwritten views of his priests to the pope, in which they unanimously acknowledged the benefits to their people from the national schools, 'not only pertaining to secular literature but also to the Catholic religion itself'. He informed Pope Gregory XVI that when he visited the schools for confirmation, he found the boys in the national schools 'very well catechised'.[50] He reminded His Holiness that almost all Protestants opposed bitterly the national schools on the grounds that they were biased in favour of Catholics, 'which certainly would not have happened if they had thought the system either non-Catholic or anti-Catholic'. A practical result of their activity, Slattery concluded, 'has been that the education of the young has fallen almost entirely into the hands of the Catholic clergy'.[51] Slattery also warned of the 'very grave damage' to the Irish Church if the Holy See, because of the opposition of a few, condemned a system which had been so long approved by the majority of bishops and priests.[52]

THE SEARCH FOR COMPROMISE AND FURTHER DISAGREEMENT

From Rome, in the final months of the year, there came a recommendation to the Irish bishops to see if a compromise could be reached by them at their annual meeting in February 1840. The bishops, in response, set up a six-man subcommittee, composed of Crolly, Kinsella and Ryan in support of the system, and MacHale, O'Higgins and Keating of Ferns opposed to it. MacHale suggested that a mixed-education system would be acceptable, based on the resolutions of the hierarchy in 1826. This would require the appointment of a Catholic clergyman who would have powers to appoint and dismiss teachers, and also to control the times of religious instruction and the books used. He would be a patron of all mixed schools. In addition, the lecturer in religion, morals and history at the training college would be Catholic; a bishop and two laymen from each province would be appointed to the board of commissioners; and, finally, there would be a model school in each province.[53] All this was agreed and put before the assembled bishops, who approved that the proposal be put to the Lord Lieutenant, Earl Fortescue. They could hardly refuse to do so without compromising themselves with Rome. The Lord Lieutenant rejected the proposal, a result that had to be expected by many of the hierarchy.

MacHale now claimed that the support of the entire episcopate for the proposal indicated that they were not satisfied with the existing system. [54] In his Lenten pastoral letter, he publicly stated that the hierarchy were now unanimous in their disapproval of the national system. The majority protested, saying that while they had supported a Catholic solution they considered ideal, they had not expected change.[55] They also pointed out that it had been agreed that if their memorial to the Lord Lieutenant were rejected each of the bishops was free to return to his preferred side, and also that there should be no publication by either side.[56] Archbishop Slattery declared roundly that he 'never witnessed anything so unwarranted, nay so undisciplined, as MacHale's attempt to fasten upon us an abandonment of our former position and an adoption of all his views'.[57]

Prior to such protests, Murray had written two trenchant letters to Cullen, which probably had a definite effect on Cullen's attitude to the national education system, if he were still wavering on the matter. Writing on 24 February 1840, Murray commenced by recounting that 'the project of an amicable arrangement between our prelates on the education question has failed'. He then explained that he and the supporters of the national system met with the ten discontented prelates and agreed to put their views to the government. The ten gave up their claim for a separate grant for the education of Catholics as unattainable, but apart from this 'the changes in the national system which they suggested, would not, and indeed perhaps under present circumstances could not be acceded to. We have, therefore, no hope of being able to educate safely the whole Catholic people, as far as the poorer classes are concerned, without availing ourselves of the aid afforded by the present system.' This result, Murray commented ironically, does not constitute any danger to the flocks of the discontented prelates since, despite their public denunciations, they have not withdrawn their schools from the national system. He went on to provide examples of their double standards.

Referring to the diocese of Ferns, whose bishop strongly opposed the system, Murray pointed out that there were thirty-three national schools in Co. Wexford. Two were 'nunnery' schools and two had Protestant gentlemen as patrons, but the remaining twenty-nine had priests as principal patrons, and whatever aid the board of commissioners supplied passed through their hands. In reference to bishop O'Higgins's area, Murray said that 'the county of Longford is a skirt of the diocese of Ardagh. In that county there are 22 national schools, of which 21 are under Catholic priests.' Yet, Murray commented, 'the prelates of Ferns and Ardagh are among the warmest opponents of the board, the heretical tendency of which they have the other day denounced in the public papers.' Murray then went on to provide other instances of double standards on the part of the bishops of Elphin (Patrick Burke, 1827–43), Kilmacduagh and Kilfenora (Dr French), Clonfert (Dr Coen), and Meath (Dr Cantwell), all critics of the national school system. 'The schools which are daily spreading in their dioceses with their permission', Murray added, 'bear testimony against them if they think the system bad.'[58]

Four days later, Murray wrote further on the issue and, in the process, delivered a virtual ultimatum to Dr Cullen. The apparent double-dealing of so many prelates, Murray observed, 'who denounce in word what they encourage in practice, has exceedingly scandalised the intelligent portion of the Catholic body; and lowered in the minds of Protestants, to a most humiliating degree, the character of our prelacy.'

Murray then proceeded to speak of the government's interest in the current developments and its implications for Cullen. 'What is certain is that they are watching the present state of the education question at Rome with much interest. And I think they are acquainted with every step that is taken. I hope, however, that all the information which they receive is not accurate. I lately saw a letter addressed to the government by one of the diplomatic agents in Italy (a Protestant) which stated that nothing could be decided on the education question until the arrival of Dr MacHale's deputy; but that in reality he did not want one, for that, all through, he had a most efficient one in the president of the Irish

College.' Murray then added pointedly, 'I need not tell you how galling this information would be to the great majority of the Irish prelates, if they could place the slightest reliance on a piece of information, which, for many reasons, they could not possibly anticipate.'[59]

THE REPRESENTATIVES IN ROME

The representatives of Murray and the episcopal majority, Frs John Ennis and William Meagher,[60] arrived in Rome during November 1839, both fluent in Italian. There was, as yet, no sign of representatives from the MacHale party. The Archbishop of Tuam had hoped that he himself or O'Higgins could present their case, but Rome remained insistent against episcopal representation. In the long interim, as they awaited representation from Tuam, the two delegates, Ennis and Meagher, tried to present the case in support of the national school system, and found themselves caught up in the slow-moving drama of Propaganda's varying reactions to and knowledge of the Irish situation.

Fr Meagher, writing to Murray's secretary, John Hamilton, on 16 November 1839, noted that they had instructions not to inform Dr Cullen, or anyone else, about their mission. Three days later, however, he reported that Cullen knew of their arrival and purpose.[61] On 29 November, Fr Ennis informed Hamilton that Cullen's influence with the Pope was spoken about. 'I fear the story is true', he remarked. 'We do not lose sight of what the Bishops have written about D.C. Yet, he is a great puzzle, and I think he may be converted by reasoning and instruction, for he is most ignorant of Ireland and its situation.' As regards their own work, Ennis explained that they had put together a presentation of their case in Italian, embodying in it Archbishop Murray's first letter. Although they were doing little in public, they were doing much in private, explaining things from the start to convince the cardinals, 'who are quite ignorant of the question.'[62] Two months later, on 25 January 1840, Ennis wrote to Murray reporting that everything was delayed by the fact that MacHale's deputy had not arrived, adding that in the meantime they 'draw up explanatory reports and interview various cardinals, many of whom have changed their former adverse opinions on the national education system'. They also had a meeting with His Holiness, he reported.[63]

Even as Ennis sent this positive news, Meagher was commenting on a less pleasant development. The writings of Fr Thaddeus O'Malley[64] in support of education controlled by the state had caused unease in Rome and, since he was associated with the Pro-Cathedral in Dublin, Murray's support of the national education system had come under a cloud. After O'Malley's article and pamphlet on the subject had been translated into Italian and sent to Propaganda, the delegates were made to feel Propaganda's displeasure. They visited the Sacred Congregation to explain that O'Malley was a foreigner and not a member of the Dublin diocese but they were 'shamed and humiliated' by the reception they received. 'Indignation and threats were hurled at them by the secretary of Propaganda.' In the same letter, Meagher expressed his sadness that Murray was ill again, 'and just at such a time!'[65]

A month later, both men were dismayed that so many bishops appeared to support MacHale and the possibility of a compromise at the bishops' annual meeting. 'What an encouragement to future prelates to agitate!' commented Meagher.[66] Two days later, Meagher reported that MacHale had instructed Cullen to inform the Pope of the unanimous agreement of the Irish bishops to present a fresh plan to the Lord Lieutenant.[67] Earlier, on 5 February, Ennis had informed Murray that the cardinals had the idea 'that Catholics in Ireland are all powerful, an idea reinforced by the Bishop of Ardagh's letters to them'.[68] Meagher, in his letter on 29 February, also mentioned that MacHale's deputy, Fr Loftus, had arrived, that he knew no Italian, and that Ennis and Meagher, as a result, had been asked to rewrite their expositions in Latin or French. This would mean further delays.

Some three weeks later, Meagher, who was feeling dejected at this stage, wrote to Hamilton that Archbishop MacHale was viewed in Rome as 'the champion of the Irish Church' and that no matter what he and Ennis could do 'they cannot counter the argument against the text books'. Also, he explained that 'O'Malley's writings had reinforced the belief that loose and very dangerous doctrines were being published in Ireland by priests'.[69]

By 9 April, however, Meagher was in a more positive frame of mind. Ennis had had an interview with Cardinal Franzoni, who showed himself very sympathetic to Murray and said that Propaganda always had complete confidence in him. Franzoni suspected that the decision about the national system of education would be delayed.[70] A fortnight later, on 23 April, Meagher expected a decision in May.

SLANDEROUS RUMOURS

May brought a rash of hostile rumours concerning Murray to Rome. On 2 May, Meagher said how he deplored these calumnies, and thought that Murray should complain to Propaganda about them at once. Murray, however, according to

Meagher, disagreed. The bishops, nevertheless, should condemn these 'shocking accusations'.[71] Five days later, Murray wrote to Cardinal Franzoni. He was dismayed and saddened to learn that a report was circulating in Rome that his reasons for supporting the national system of education were to seek favours for himself and his relatives from the government. Never in his life had he done so, Murray claimed. In fact, his relatives think him hard and unfeeling in their regard. He shrinks from giving instances to prove how unjustified are such reports. He, and the bishops, supported the national system for the sake of the poor and to save them from dangers to their faith. They accepted the system as the best being offered for the time being, and hoping for an improvement in the system at some future date. In conclusion, he reiterated that the good of religion was their only aim and motive.[72]

MOVING TOWARDS A DECISION

In the fluctuating scene, where one mini-crisis after another arose and faded, Meagher was the more regular correspondent of the delegates. In Ennis's fewer letters, however, there was an effort to praise Dr Cullen, who had evidently made an impression on him. Already on 5 February, he had informed Murray that 'Dr Cullen has been very attentive to us', and now, on 30 May, he reported that Cullen spoke very highly of Murray to Dr Kyle of Scotland and to the Pope. Cullen was leaving Rome – presumably for Ireland – Ennis commented. Turning to their daily schedule, he observed that each day they expected Loftus to come up with a copy of his 'tardy defence', although they would not be allowed access to it.[73] A week later, nevertheless, Meagher was able to report to Hamilton that they had received a copy of the document, but it was so full of blots and erasures that another copy had to be requested,[74] involving more delay. On a more uplifting note, Meagher reported, on 9 July, that they had received the document and had returned it within four days as requested. They sent to Propaganda twenty-five closely written pages in response to it. 'Loftus is now quite depressed', Meagher added. 'He came to Rome sure of success, but he is now in the lowest degree of melancholy.' The end cannot now be long delayed, Meagher hoped.[75] Two weeks later, on 25 July, Ennis sent word to Murray that it was now more than six weeks since their papers and those of their antagonist were submitted. A decision was expected early in August, but that depended on the printers. 'The weather is unbelievably hot', he added and they both longed to go home.[76]

August passed, and the early days of September, and Meagher descended into melancholy. And then came the news. 'Great News', he exulted. 'All has ended in success.' Cullen had so effectively switched sides as to be viewed now in heroic terms. 'Dr Cullen, who in the beginning was misled on the national system of education, has proved himself a man of great magnanimity and intrepidity. He sent a letter to Palma giving unqualified approval to the system.' Meagher mentioned that Ennis had written to Murray by the same post informing him of the result. But, he cautioned, 'as Rome will not make the matter public for three months, it must be kept a profound secret; if this is not done all the fruits of the endeavour will be neutralised'.[77]

A word about the process leading to Rome's decision is in order. When the cases of the respective deputies were forwarded to Propaganda, they were, in turn, passed over to an independent consultant, Cornelius Van Everbroeck, a Dutch Jesuit, to review the matter from beginning to end. He came up with an opinion, extending to 118 pages, and including a nine-page postscript. Van Everbroeck concluded that 'the system is neither positively approved nor positively condemned, because in either case the most serious consequences are to be feared'.

This unusual opinion advised, in effect, leaving matters as they were while attempting to secure all appropriate safeguards. Van Everbroeck's presentation contained suitable selections from letters Cullen had sent from Ireland.[78] Cullen, on setting out for Ireland, had been asked by the secretary of Propaganda, Mgr Cadaloni, to supply some information on the national education system after his return. Six weeks after his arrival, Cullen reported to Cardinal Franzoni, the prefect of Propaganda, 'In the dioceses of Dublin and Kildare I have seen a good number of schools and I have noticed that they could not be more Catholic than they are. The teachers are Catholic, the pupils are Catholic, and the principal occupation of the children is learning Christian doctrine.' He concluded that 'I dare not think there is any danger to the Faith.'[79] On 13 September 1840, Cullen sent a long letter from Dublin to Mgr Cadaloni, by which date the Irish delegates had heard confidentially of Propaganda's verdict. Cullen's views coincided with the eventual pronouncement. 'To all appearances', he wrote, 'the system appears very satisfactory and for this reason it has quite a few defenders … Therefore it would seem that it would be very dangerous to condemn it as *undequaque malum* [entirely bad].' He then counselled, 'The best and safest way to deal with this whole matter, as I see it, would be to allow things to remain as they are now, even though in some schools there may be some abuse as a result of the nature of the teaching.'[80] Word of Cullen's input reached the delegates in Rome, as Meagher's high praise indicated.

The cardinals of Propaganda made their formal decision at their monthly meeting on 22 December 1840.[81] It was promulgated in the form of a circular letter to the four archbishops of Ireland on 16 January 1841, under the signature of Cardinal Franzoni. The Sacred Congregation, the circular stated, 'has resolved that no judgement should be pronounced in the matter and that this kind of education should be left to the prudent discretion and religious conscience of each individual bishop, whereas its success must depend on the vigilant care of the pastors, on the various precautions to be adopted and on the future experience which time will supply.'[82]

A DAMAGED REPUTATION

The struggle appeared to have resulted in a victory for Murray and the episcopal majority, but the defeated minority remained resolute in its opinion and ready to oppose Murray should opportunities arise. That a minority of bishops came so close to destroying the national system of education is, on the face of it, quite remarkable. After all, as the late Professor Emmet Larkin observed,[83] Murray had for thirty years been coadjutor and then archbishop of Dublin. His piety, zeal and learning were as much appreciated in Rome as they were in Ireland. His archdiocese, in terms of economic resources and political influence, was probably greater than that of the archbishop of Tuam and his six suffragan bishops combined. Moreover, in the light of the fearful poverty of a greatly expanded peasant population and a decline in the supporting merchant class, the Irish Catholic Church could not afford to finance a primary school system. Given the financial situation, Murray's personal standing, and moral authority and the support of a majority of bishops, including the Primate of All Ireland and the Archbishop of Cashel, how did MacHale almost convulse the country and come so close to achieving his goal? The main part of the answer suggests that MacHale drew his main strength from the transcending Irish theme of national feeling linked to confessionalism. Threats to religion, real or apparent, from an oppressive, foreign government were viewed as a threat to national identity. MacHale was ideally suited to make full use of this combined force, all the more so since he felt he could rely on the conservatism of Rome and the influence of Dr Cullen and some others.

For twenty years, John MacHale, as noted earlier, had been a persistent and bitter public critic of British rule in Ireland, and had built up in the public mind the image of a patriot bishop. By 1839–40, he was, after Daniel O'Connell, the most popular figure in Ireland. Add to this popularity his forceful personality, his facility with words and his unscrupulous behaviour towards all who disagreed with him, and there appears a very formidable demagogue, whose influence and power were enhanced by his office as archbishop of a populous diocese and by the contacts and image he had formed in Rome. In the end, the defection of a key Roman contact played a role in his defeat.

A comment by Dr Ambrose Macaulay about the effect of MacHale's policy on his own archdiocese, is sadly pertinent. 'Without state subvention on the scale provided by the national system the Catholic Church would not have been able to create a *de facto* denominational system of education, and one that came to be recognised as the essential pastoral arm of the clergy for catechising their youth. MacHale's successor was later to complain bitterly of the pastoral opportunities that had been neglected in the archdiocese, and of the attendance of Catholic children at proselytising schools.'[84]

In the overall conflict, Murray's peerless reputation and standing had been weakened by slurs, slanders and public criticism which implied that he was not truly patriotic, that he was a 'Castle Catholic'. The smear was to be applied again and again during his principled stands in the years ahead, until it came to be widely held to the point of his being removed in the popular mind from the gallery of great Irish churchmen. In addition, it should be remembered that, with the years, a declining number of bishops were prepared to give the government credit for good intentions, and among the younger men suspicion of government combined with pervading national feeling to increase the division between Church and state.

Finally, it is appropriate to note some of the effects of the national system of education. Between 1830 and 1845, popular education grew faster than the growth in population and in poverty. One result of this was 'the fall in the national illiteracy rate. By 1841 it had dropped to fifty-three per cent of those aged five and over, and by 1851 to forty-seven per cent, impressive figures by contemporary European standards, especially in the light of the composition and distribution of the Irish population.' By 1845, a considerable majority of the Irish children attended the national schools, although many irregularly.[85] A further result of this was that it enabled generations to escape from rural poverty to life in cities at home, and in Britain and North America. Among the massive tide of overseas emigrants in the 1840s, the great majority, it appears, were able to speak English and thereby start a new life with an advantage over other foreign emigrants. On the reverse side, the processes of depopulation and deracination had a role in the decline of Gaelic culture and language, although such effects were not deplored in the years 1830–45. Rather, the emphasis was on availing of the schools as necessary ladders towards escaping the pit of endless poverty.[86]

NOTES

1 Cit. D. McCartney. *The Dawning of Democracy: Ireland 1800-1870* (Dublin: Helicon, 1987), p.124.
2 Idem, p.131.
3 For the account that follows see Wm Meagher. *Most Rev. Daniel Murray…*, pp.69–71. N.B He gives the year as 1836, instead of 1835.
4 Idem, p.71.
5 Stanley – Duke of Leinster, Oct. 1831, cit in *Reports of the commissioners of National Education in Ireland* (Dublin 1865), vol.1, p.1.
6 D.H. Akenson. *The Irish Education Experiment* (London: Routledge and Kegan Paul, 1970), p.179, cit. Thomas McGrath. 'Archbishop Slattery and the Episcopal Controversy on Irish National Education, 1838–1841', in *Archivium Historicum, XXXIX* (1984), p.16.
7 Doyle sent to Slattery a copy of the circular letter addressed to his clergy, which was published in the *Dublin Evening Post*, 12 Jan. 1831, cit. T. McGrath,article cit. in loc. cit. p.18.
8 Emmet Larkin. 'The Quarrel among the Roman Catholic Hierarchy over the National System of Education in Ireland, 1838-1841' in *Humanities*, no.68, Dept. Humanities, MIT, Cambridge, Mass.,1965, p.122.
9 Mac Hale – Cullen, 24 Feb. 1838, Cullen Papers (C.P.)
10 Idem, 19 April, 1838, C.P.
11 Mac Hale – O'Connell, 27 Feb. 1838, in M.R. O'Connell(ed.) *The Correspondence of Daniel O'Connell*, vol. vi, 1837–1840, no.2508, pp.138–9.
12 John Mac Hale. *The Letters of Most Revd John Mac Hale, D.D.* (Dublin 1847), p.416.
13 Idem, pp.416–17. See *Fourth Report of Commissioners of Education Ireland,* for year ending 31 March 1837, p.6. H. C., 1837–8 (110) xxviii. The concession had been in response to pressure from the Synod of Ulster. See T. McGrath. art.cit., fn.18, p.30.
14 Murray – Cullen, 28 April 1838; C.P. no.423.
15 D.H. Akenson. op. cit., p.244, cit. McGrath. art. cit. p.19, fn.35.
16 *Catholic Encyclopedia* (N.Y. 1913), vol.vii, p.760, cit. McGrath. art cit. p.20, fn.38.
17 Slattery – Murray, 1 June 1838, DDA, Murray Papers, contains a copy of Dillon Browne's letter, f.31/6, 1838; cit. McGrath. art. cit. pp.20–22, fns.39, 42.
18 Murray – Slattery, 6 March 1838, Cashel Archives, Slattery Papers, cit. P. Mac Suibhne (ed.) *Paul Cullen and his Contemporaries*, vol.iv, no.10.
19 Slattery – Murray, 7 March 1838, DDA. Murray Papers, f.31/6, 1838.
20 Murray Papers. Irish Bishops. 34 letters in reply to Murray's query re. their views on national educ. system; f.31/6, 1838.
21 Murray – Cullen, 13 June 1838.
22 Murray – Cullen, 3 July 1838. C.P. ; cit. Larkin, art. cit., pp.124–5.
23 Murray – Cullen, 28 July 1838; C.P.
24 G. J. Browne – Murray, 1 Aug. 1838, Murray Papers, f.31/6, 1838.
25 Murray – Browne, 6 Aug. 1838, C.P. no.451, cit. Sr. M.A. Bolster. 'Correspondence concerning the System of Nat. Education between Archbishop Daniel Murray of Dublin and Bishop George J. Browne of Galway' in *Journal of the Galway Archeological and Historical Society,* vol. 37, 1979/80.
26 Hamilton – Cullen, 26 Aug 1838; C.P.
27 *Dublin Evening Post,* 24 Nov. 1838, cit. Larkin, art. cit. pp.126–7.
28 Idem, 24 Nov. 1838; cit. Larkin, p.127.
29 Murray – Cullen, 12 Dec. 1838; C.P.
30 Murray – Cullen, 24 Dec. 1838; C.P. No. 477, cit. Bolster, art. cit. p.61.

31 O'Connell – P.V. Fitzpatrick, 19 Nov. 1838; in M. R. O'Connell (ed.) *Correspondence...*, vol vi, no.2572.
32 Kinsella – Slattery, 7 Dec. 1838; CDA. 1838, cit. McGrath, art. cit. p.21, fns. 43, 44.
33 Higgins – Cullen, 23 Jan. 1839; C.P. CUL/483.
34 Murray – Cullen, 28 Jan. 1839; C.P. CUL/485.
35 Higgins – Cullen, 30 Jan. 1839; C.P. CUL/487.
36 Idem, 1 Feb. 1839; C.P. cit. Larkin. art. cit. pp.129–30.
37 T. McGrath, art. cit. p.22.
38 Idem, quoting Akenson. op. cit. p.244.
39 Murray – Cullen, 1839 (no precise date), cit. Larkin, art. cit., p.130.
40 Murray – Cullen, 13 March 1839; C.P. CUL/496.
41 Murray – Cullen, 12 July 1839; C.P. CUL/530.
42 Wm Meagher, op. cit., p.58.
43 Idem, p.61.
44 Murray – Cullen, 22 Aug. 1839; C.P. cit. Larkin, art. cit., p.133.
45 Meagher, op. cit. p.61.
46 Crolly – Murray, 4 Aug. 1839; DDA. Murray Papers, f.31/7/ 49.
47 Meagher, op. cit., p.61.
48 DDA. Hamilton Papers (6), Irish Bishops, no, 7, 1839, f.36/2.
49 Idem, nos.8, 9.
50 Slattery - Pope Gregory xvi, 10 Oct. 1839; CDA. 1839/20.
51 Idem.
52 Ibidem.
53 McGrath, art. cit., pp.24–5.
54 Mac Hale – Cullen, 22 Feb. 1840; C.P. CUL/583
55 Kinsella – Murray, 13 March 1840; DDA., f. 31/8, cit. McGrath, p.25.
56 Crolly – Murray, 9 March 1840; DDA cit. McGrath idem.
57Slattery - Murray, 13 March 1840; DDA. f. 31/8, 1840.
58 Murray – Cullen, 24 Feb. 1840; C. P. CUL/584.
59 Murray – Cullen, 28 Feb. 1840; C.P. CUL/ 585.
60 John Ennis (1792-1862), educated Maynooth and St. Sulpice. Curate at Westland Row, Dublin, 1818; later built Blackrock church and several schools. Committed to national school system. Appointed P.P. of Booterstown, 1838. Served in Italy in 1848 also, on university question.Wm Meagher (1796–1881), ordained 27 Nov. 1820, curate in Pro-Cathedral 1830–48. P.P. Rathgar 1848–81. Vicar General, Monsignor, D.D. biographer of Abp Daniel Murray.
61 Meagher – Hamilton, 16, 19 Nov. 1839; Murray Papers, f.31/7, 1839.
62 Ennis – Hamilton 29 Nov. 1839; f.31/7, no.78.
63 Ennis – Murray, 25 Jan. 1840; Murray Papers, f.31/8.
64 Thaddeus O'Malley had previously been excommunicated for siding with the laity in Philadelphia against his bishop, subsequently pardoned in Rome. He came to Ireland, was allowed to celebrate Mass in the Pro-Cathedral. 'Mr O'Malley', Murray explained to Cullen, on 28 Jan. 1840, 'is not one of our priests and is less under control than if he were. He got leave to say Mass 'as it was hardly safe in Ireland to drive a priest of some talent and strong feelings to extremities without a real necessity'. The 'real necessity' came with the criticism from Rome. O'Malley left Dublin. Subsequently, he became an advocate of Home Rule and of a form of Christian Socialism. He died in 1877 at the age of eighty.
65 Meagher – Hamilton, 25 Jan, 1840; f.31/8, no.62.
66 Idem, 27 Feb. 1840, no.63.
67 Idem, 29 Feb. 1840; no.64.

68 Ennis – Murray. 5 Feb. 1840; f.31/8, no.55.
69 Meagher – Hamilton, 21 March 1840; f.31/8, no.65.
70 Meagher – Hamilton, 9 April 1840; f.31/8, no.66.
71 Meagher – Hamilton, 2 May 1840, no.68.
72 Murray – Franzoni (draft letter), 6 May 1840; f.31/8, no.93.
73 Ennis – Murray, 30 May 1840; f.31/8, no.56.
74 Meagher – Hamilton, 6 June 1840; no.70.
75 Meagher – Hamilton, 9 July 1840; f.31/8, no.71.
76 Ennis – Murray, 25 July 1840, idem, no.58.
77 Meagher – Hamilton, 8 Sept. 1840; f.31/8, no.74. 'Palma' was Giovanni Battista Palma, priest and clerk in the Sacred Congregation of Propaganda, with whom Cullen was friendly.
78 Archives Propaganda Fide, Rome, Acta, vol.203, pp.410–11; cit Larkin, art. cit., p.141.
79 Cullen – Franzoni, Ballitore, 7 Aug. 1840; Archives Prop. Fide *Scritture Riferite nei Congressi*, vol.27 (1839–42), ff.274–5, cit. Larkin. art. cit. p.140.
80 Cullen - Cadaloni, 13 Sept. 1840; idem, Acta, vol. 203, ff.270-71, cit. Larkin, pp.140-41.
81 A. P. Fide. Acta, vol. 203, f.412.
82 Idem. *Scritture...*, f.427, cit. Larkin, art cit., p.141.
83 Larkin, art. cit. p.142.
84 Dr John Mac Evilly to Tobias Kirby, 20 Oct. 1879. AICR., cit. A. Macauley. *William Crolly, Archbishop of Armagh, 1835–49* (Dublin 1994), p.225.
85 Oliver MacDonagh. 'The Economy and Society 1830–1845' in W.E.Vaughan (ed.). *A New History of Ireland*, vol. v. *Ireland Under the Union, 1, 1801–1870* (Oxford: Clarendon Press, 1989), pp.234–5. Also Census figures. *Census Ireland*, 1841, pp.438–9 [504], H.C.1843, xxiv, 546–7; *Census Ireland,* 1851, pt. iv, pp.184–5 [2053].
86 MacDonagh. art cit. in loc. cit., pp.234–5.

CHAPTER 11

Repeal and the Bequests Act (1842–45)

During the conflict over the national schools and the subsequent tumultuous events of 1842–45, the daily work and correspondence of the archbishop of Dublin continued. In fact, Murray's weight of correspondence expanded during the 1840s. A brief overview of his papers for 1842–45 reveals him receiving appeals for aid from individuals not only in his own diocese, but from the west of Ireland, and even from Scotland. He had to deal with letters from French bishops and directors of colleges regarding individual Irish priests. We find him responding to appeals from Cardinal Franzoni to examine the suitability of named candidates for bishoprics or the appointment of provincials for religious congregations experiencing disunity. In addition, Rome sought recommendations for bishoprics in Corfu, Ceylon and Bengal, and requested Murray's intercession with British ministers or officials in their regard. There were frequent communications regarding religious sisters' congregations, including the unusual request for nuns to be sent to Tibet, a request that met with a ready response and proceeded well, at least initially.

TIME-CONSUMING ISSUES

Some issues took up much time and consideration. One such issue was the situation of the Catholic Church in Gibraltar, where Irish priests and Christian Brothers were badly treated by the authorities. Their church building had been closed, while some people suffered imprisonment and others were beaten by a mob. Murray was involved in much correspondence, seeking clarity about the situation and appealing to Sir John Russell and others to intervene.

His relations with the Christian Brothers at this time carried its own burdens. When the strain caused by the Brothers' decision to leave the national school system was eventually resolved, a further strain arose in Murray's relationship with them. Having assisted the Brothers to obtain permission from Rome to run some fee-paying schools, which operated successfully, he then found the Brothers, under Br Riordan as superior, closing down these schools. Rome ordered the schools to be reopened. Murray found himself caught in between, communicating with both sides. The tension between the Archbishop and the leadership of the brothers prompted Br Riordan to remove the congregation's headquarters from Dublin to Cork, and thence to Waterford.

A not infrequent correspondent with Murray was Lord Clifford, usually in relation to the work of certain convents and in support of particular works in the west of Ireland, for which he was publicly criticised by MacHale. Correspondence with Rome over the appointment of a bishop in Clogher proved to be less than satisfactory, ending with the appointment of Fr McNally despite advice to the contrary from both Murray and Archbishop Crolly. Inevitably, too, there was a stream of individual letters for Murray's attention, seeking one thing or another. All of these, as noted earlier, were dealt with by Murray, often in consultation with John Hamilton, especially when Murray was laid low by sickness or a severe cold.

In dealing with so many and varied pressures, which included at times public political issues that impinged on himself and his clergy, it is said that Murray endeavoured to follow the advice of the saint he greatly admired and to whom he was compared by his own priests, Francis de Sales. Murray learned much from the gentle, gracious and astute bishop of Geneva, who once observed that 'nothing is so strong as gentleness, nothing so gentle as real strength'. Murray's calm and peaceful manner, so often mentioned by contemporaries, also reflected the advice of the saint: 'Do not lose your inner peace for anything whatsoever, even if your whole world seems upset'. And this inner calm was to be reflected in outward order:

> Undertake all your affairs with a calm and peaceable mind, and endeavour to despatch them in order, one after another – for if you make an effort to do them all at once or in disorder, your spirit will be so overcharged and depressed that it will probably sink under the burden without effecting anything.[1]

The application of such advice was seriously tested during Murray's conflict with fellow prelates over the national education system. Now, from 1842–45, it was to be put under severe pressure once again, as Murray tried to stand aloof from the public emotion surrounding Repeal and to respond, in the face of public abuse and criticism from bishops and his own clergy, to the benefits offered by the government's Charitable Bequests Act.

THE QUEST FOR REPEAL

By the end of the 1830s, Daniel O'Connell had become disillusioned with the Whig alliance and disappointed with the amount of reform achieved through parliament. In addition, he was conscious that his own popularity had waned, judging by the drop in the O'Connell Tribute. This latter referred to the voluntary collection at all chapels throughout the country, which had been paid to O'Connell since 1829 on two fixed Sundays of the year, to enable him to devote himself entirely to a political career.

O'Connell was convinced that justice could only be obtained for Ireland by means of a native parliament. To that end, a Precursor Society was established in Dublin in 1838. It became the National Association of Ireland in April 1840, and was renamed the Loyal National Repeal Association in July that year. Organised on the model of the Catholic Association, its object was the establishment of an Irish parliament. It committed itself to loyalty to the crown, the disavowal of physical force, the use of constitutional means of organising public opinion, the assertion of equality before the law for all classes, the exclusion of sectarianism and freedom of conscience.

In the general election of 1841, the Tories succeeded to government with Robert Peel as prime minister. O'Connell's party was reduced from approximately thirty to sixteen members of parliament. He decided to concentrate on extra-parliamentary agitation, and to a greater extent than anything he had previously achieved. His campaign received considerable impetus in 1842, when the *Nation* newspaper was published by a group of young men who became known as the Young Irelanders. The weekly paper was estimated by its editor, Charles Gavan Duffy, to have a readership of some 250,000 people. O'Connell set out to enrol the support of as many clergy as possible. Archbishop John MacHale led the way by openly supporting Repeal as early as 1840. Later, many bishops and clergy followed. The campaign was financed by a repeal rent – like the previous Catholic rent – based on a shilling a year for associate members. The movement was highly organised, and O'Connell availed of the temperance movement, launched by Fr Mathew in 1838, to the advantage of Repeal. 'Ireland sober would mean Ireland free', he told a mass meeting at Kilkenny.[2]

The campaign for Repeal attracted little attention at first in Britain. The agitation in Ireland only began to gather momentum in the winter of 1842–43. It was only when a tenfold leap in membership and in the repeal rent was reported, in the early summer of 1843, that the government took alarm. O'Connell planned carefully. After Easter, he began his great tour of Ireland, with monster meetings held on Sundays or holy days throughout the country, often at locations having strong historical associations. The first of the forty massive outdoor rallies took place at Trim in March 1848. Thereafter the meetings, with their heightened public feeling, moved on inexorably towards what was planned to be the final monster meeting at historic Clontarf in October. The tour demonstrated the peaceful character of the movement, and the gravity and numerical strength of its demand. Concurrently, a campaign of enrolment was under way, with the object of recruiting three million members by the end of July. In addition, each of the districts, into which the association had divided the country, was to send individuals to meet 'spontaneously' in Dublin, as the 'Council of Three Hundred', to plan a bill for Repeal. The programme aimed at putting protracted pressure on the government, increasing it steadily stage by stage over a period of five months until it culminated in a full-blown challenge to British authority that would be difficult to resist by legal counter-measures.[3]

As the weeks and months passed, the mounting enthusiasm created problems for people trying to stand aloof from the agitation surrounding Repeal. Archbishop Murray counselled his clergy not to attend Repeal meetings and not be involved. This led to public criticism. Other bishops faced similar reaction. Dr Kinsella of Ossory wrote to Murray, on 4 June 1843, that he had not attended O'Connell's meeting and banquet, as he was determined to keep clear of politics. His stance gave great offence to the younger clergy in Ossory, he added. He had asked Dr Healy to write a letter in support of Murray's position, he explained, but after writing it Healy did not have the courage to publish it.[4] Earlier, unfair pressure had been imposed on individual bishops by the typically exaggerated claim by Dr O'Higgins of Ardagh, following the mass meeting at Mullingar in May 1843. He announced formally that all the bishops had declared themselves repealers, and he defied the government to put down Repeal in his diocese. 'If they bring us to the scaffold', he declared, 'in dying for the cause of our country we shall bequeath our wrongs to our successors.'[5] Faced with this sweeping and embarrassing declaration, for which O'Higgins had no evidence, Murray was faced with the dilemma of saying nothing and leaving his views open to misrepresentation, or challenging the statement and being accused of indifference to the struggles of his own people. He decided to brave the wrath of the repealers in order to reveal his true position. In a public letter to his priests in the *Dublin Evening Post* of 23 May 1843, he referred to the surprise they must have felt on seeing the statement that all the bishops were repealers. He pointed out that he had taken no part whatever in the movement and explained that he had always acted in accordance with the resolution of the hierarchy in January 1834, which excluded clerical participation from proceedings of a purely temporal character. He was determined to continue adhering to that policy.

Such emotive, defiant language as that of O'Higgins was part of the frenzy O'Connell created as the movement grew in numbers and intensity. At Kilkenny, O'Connell announced that he stood at the head of a body of men who, if organised with military discipline, would be sufficient for the conquest of Europe. At Mallow, his militant defiance declared that the time for speeches was over, it was time for action. He defied the government and its troops to suppress them. In Cromwell's time, he reminded them, they were a paltry remnant, but now they were nine million strong. In Cork, he declared that if they were attacked, fathers and mothers would be cut down and sisters become the victims of the ruffian soldiery. If this happened, he continued menacingly, 'I would ask Mr Peel how many fires would blaze out in the manufactories of Britain?' And yet, behind all this, he personally claimed that nothing was worth the loss of one human life or the spilling of blood.[6] His weapons were words, and the powers to incite and to organise.

For its part, the government was moving towards repression from May to October. Thousands of soldiers were brought into the country, the decision was taken to proclaim the Council of Three Hundred illegal should it attempt to meet, and a search for a case against O'Connell was begun.[7]

What was Murray's inner state as he tried to stand apart from politics? He admired what O'Connell had done for Catholics. His feelings were with the objective of Repeal, but he believed that the public drive for an Irish parliament would inflame public opinion, leading to violence, to strong government repression and to inevitable defeat and bloodshed, with the people left worse off than ever in the end. His personal feeling of support for O'Connell was manifested in practical ways before the movement reached fever pitch. Already, in September 1840, he talked with Fr Hamilton about subscribing to the repeal rent. He had doubts about the movement succeeding, he said, though he knew that Dr York, in the Pro-Cathedral, thought otherwise.[8] In July 1842, he gave his approval for Hamilton to start the penny-a-week collection for the repeal fund. On 28 October, he told Hamilton that, since he could not be in Dublin on the Sunday, to send £10 on Murray's behalf to the O'Connell fund.[9] On 18 May, as indicated, he was dismayed to read of Bishop O'Higgins's speech at Mullingar, which he considered to be 'an outrageous breach of courtesy towards his brother bishops. I thought at first that it had been misrepresented, but no…'[10]

Soon afterwards, as the intensity of feeling mounted and people appeared visibly excited, Murray became more concerned. He feared the movement was moving towards violence, which could only lead to government intervention and reprisals. He issued a public letter to his clergy, formally instructing them to avoid the public meetings and involvement in the movement.[11] This evoked much criticism on platforms and in the press. By August, the public excitement was too much for at least two of Murray's curates. They attended the massive demonstration at the historic Hill of Tara, where hundreds of thousands of repealers assembled to hear and to cheer as O'Connell hailed the heroes of the past – from Gaelic chieftains to the Protestant revolutionaries of 1798 – and proclaimed that the Hill of Tara was 'stained with murderous blood and the bones are not mouldered yet of the individuals who were massacred in hundreds upon it'.[12]

Fr Peter Cooper, who subsequently showed himself to be a voluble nationalist, was one of the curates who attended the meeting. He wrote to Archbishop Murray on 28 October to say that Dr Hamilton had told him that Murray 'was mortified to read in the newspapers that he and a fellow curate in the cathedral figured among "the list of agitators at the dinner in Tara" (after the monster meeting)'. He and his companion, Cooper explained, were not at the dinner. They were at the meeting and went there simply out of curiosity and stood on the edge of the crowd. Later, Cooper explained, he approached the editor of the paper and asked that their names not be given. Due to some error, however, they were named as being present at the dinner, though they were then far away from Tara. He then apologised, saying that he deeply regretted the mortification caused Murray by his action, which he would, if he could, now recall.[13]

This weak story met with no serious reprimand. Murray, in the spirit of de Sales, operated on the principle that a gentle reproof was likely to be more effective than a severe penalty.

Despite his clergy's respect for Murray, the spread of national feeling became such that 'twenty-four parish priests and curates' in the Fingal area were in agreement about the propriety of convening the final Repeal meeting at Clontarf. Their document was said to be 'the original requisition' for the monster meeting at the location where the Irish forces of Brian Boru had their celebrated victory over the Danes in 1014. The meeting was scheduled for 8 October 1843.[14]

The meeting was suppressed by public proclamation of the Lord Lieutenant on Saturday, 7 October. A large body of troops was sent in to enforce the banning order. O'Connell's old rival, Sir Robert Peel, who had given way before the organised force of Catholic protest in 1829, was determined not to yield this time. He had said 'deprecating as I do all war, and especially civil war, there is no alternative which I do not think preferable to the dismemberment of the Empire'.[15] Faced with a potential massacre, O'Connell cancelled the meeting. A charge of conspiracy to incite disaffection was brought against him and some other leaders, and they were sentenced to imprisonment. After four months in prison, the sentences were quashed, but Repeal was dead, and O'Connell's power greatly diminished.

THE AFTERMATH

In the wake of Clontarf, Daniel Murray wrote a letter which significantly revealed his outlook on the Repeal movement and explained his stance on political situations. He wrote to Dr Hamilton from Whiteleas, Ballymore Eustace, Co. Kildare, where he stayed from time to time. Written on 13 October 1843, the letter was something of an *apologia*.[16] He wrote:

> I long foresaw, and it required no spirit of prophecy to do so, that if the agitation were persisted in, the whole power of England would, as far as necessary, be employed to crush it. But I was ridiculed, as over timorous (or something worse) and the dream of moral influence, as able to accomplish everything, was clung to, in opposition to the plainest dictates of common sense. I was quite as much alive as any of the agitators to the benefits which a domestic legislature would be capable, if peaceably obtained, of conferring on the country; but I trembled to think of the effects of a struggle to obtain it by the means of physical force. All doubt on the subject has now vanished. England has announced its determination to encounter all the calamities of civil war, rather than submit to the monster evil of a repeal of the union, and but for the prudence evinced by our poor people, the sanguinary conflict would, ere now, have commenced and the shores of Clontarf would be again steeped in torrents of blood.
>
> God grant that this prudence may continue, but such is the intensity to which the feelings of the people have been wound up, and such are the exaggerated notions which they have been taught to form of their ability to defeat any force that could be brought against them, that there is no counting upon what might be the consequence if any accidental collision should unfortunately take place. And if this unhappy country in addition to its other sufferings should be doomed to experience the miseries of civil commotion, how bitter ought to be the regrets of those ministers of the Religion of peace who had lent the influence of their sacred character to prepare the way for such a catastrophe.

The harsh, aggressive action of the government was followed by a more welcome and beneficial approach, a practice that was to become policy into the future. For many it was too late, however. To O'Connell, MacHale and many others, including many bishops and large numbers of clergy, benefits coming from the government were viewed more than ever as something to be distrusted and rejected.

Murray was slow to make major decisions. Reflection and prayer went into his discernment, but once clear on a course of action he was resolute in the face of all opposition. Where the government was concerned, he viewed legislation in terms of its benefit to the Catholic Church and to the people. In the wake of the forced collapse of Repeal and the unfair trial accorded O'Connell, however, such a detached, objective attitude was deemed unacceptable, and it resulted in Murray experiencing fierce opposition from press, public opinion and even from fellow prelates and many of his own priests. The occasion was an attempt by government to provide improved conditions for the Catholic population by means of a Charitable Bequests Bill.

THE BEQUESTS ACT

The Repeal agitation had the effect of impressing on Sir Robert Peel the danger of the alliance between the Catholic clergy and O'Connell. The detailed reports of magistrates and police in June 1843 had convinced him that the priests were the mainstay of Repeal, and that they could not be overcome either by banning meetings or ineffective prosecutions.[17] He was determined to break up this formidable combination. Hence, when briefing Lord Heytesbury as lord lieutenant in July 1844, Peel stressed 'the absolute necessity … of disuniting, by the fair legitimate means of a just, kind and conciliatory policy, the Roman Catholic body and thus breaking up a sullen and formidable confederacy against the British connexion.'[18]

The carrying out of this policy rested to a large extent with Viscount Edward Granville Eliot, chief secretary, and Sir James Graham, the home secretary. In August 1843, Peel felt it necessary to insist with the then Lord lieutenant, Thomas Philip, Earl de Grey, that the law had changed and that 'considerations of policy and also of justice demand a *liberal* and indulgent estimate of the claims … of such Roman Catholics as abstain from political agitation.'[19]

The impulse towards reform envisaged benefits for Catholics in terms of a fairer franchise, greater educational opportunities, openings to promotion, improvements for tenants and religious equality. The Devon Commission was set up to investigate the land situation, but this was a long-term process. In practice, all that Peel felt able to get through parliament was an increased grant for Maynooth College and the reform of the law governing charitable bequests. Even then, the increased grant to Maynooth was strongly contested, and Peel was depicted as undermining the Established Church. The friendly and apparently innocuous measure governing charitable bequests offered the opportunity of a relatively easy passage. In Ireland, however, as mentioned, it met with dark suspicion and a storm of protest. It provoked divisions within the Catholic community, and provided a further testing of Archbishop Murray's courage and endurance as he found himself widely criticised and almost isolated among his fellow bishops and clergy.

Before its dissolution in 1801, the Irish Parliament had established a board to administer bequests left for charity. The board's procedure proved costly and slow. The vast majority of bequests were from Catholics, but fifteen years after the Emancipation Act there was only one Catholic on the board's fifty members. Catholics became chary about making bequests. Efforts to reform the situation failed in 1830, 1834 and 1838.

Nevertheless, the bishops kept pressing for change. The hierarchy needed money urgently to meet the needs of the expanding number of poor, as well as for educational needs and building programmes. Bequests could play an important part, but not so long as Catholics feared that the administering board might divert bequests to non-Catholic purposes. In 1840 the bishops directly petitioned the chief secretary at the time, Viscount George W. Morpeth, to include Catholic churchmen on the board. Nothing came of their proposal. In 1844 O'Connell, with the approval of the hierarchy, brought in a bill which sought to simplify matters. He proposed that every Catholic bishop be constituted 'a body politic and corporate' with perpetual succession. While this seemed a most equitable way of dealing with Catholic and Protestant charities, it would have meant placing Catholic bishops on the same level as the prelates of the Established Church, and this was unacceptable to the government.[20] When O'Connell was imprisoned, his bill was dropped.

The government brought in a bill aimed at satisfying the Catholics while avoiding recognition of their hierarchy. On 18 June 1844, the Charitable Donations and Bequests for Roman Catholic Ministers (Ireland) Bill was introduced. A new board was to be set up consisting of three *ex officio* members and ten nominated members, of whom five would be Catholic. The bill permitted donors to vest property in the new commissioners to hold in perpetual succession 'in trust for building … any place of worship of persons professing the Roman Catholic Religion, or in trust for any person in Holy Orders of the Church of Rome officiating in a district … or for building a residence for his and their use'. A proviso stated that the bill could not be construed as repealing the sections in the 1829 Relief Act which made bequests to religious orders illegal.

Despite this negative constraint, and blunders in presenting the bill, the measure was a considerable advance on existing legislation. In addition, efforts were made to respond to a number of Catholic criticisms made by Archbishop Murray and others. Thus, the word 'Ministers' in the title to the bill was changed to 'Clergy' because the original word was viewed as having Calvinist overtones; and, of greater import, in the description of the measure, the words 'for any person in Holy Orders in the Church of Rome' were replaced by 'for any archbishop or bishop or other person in Holy Orders of the Church of Rome'. This change marked a recognition of the Catholic bishops' spiritual functions, and was probably as far as Peel and Graham could go while insisting on the position of the Established Church.

CONTROVERSY AND DIVISIONS

The bill met with little opposition in both houses of parliament, and Peel set about implementing the act. He met with almost immediate hostility in Ireland, however, where the in-built suspicion of government intentions had been stirred further into anger by the arrest of O'Connell. To make his bill effective, Peel planned to have Catholic bishops on the board of commissioners, and a key figure in this regard was the Archbishop of Dublin. He was the most respected figure among the bishops and also had a history of cooperating with the government on matters beneficial to the Catholic majority.

Murray was conscious of the government's insensitivity in bringing in a measure involving the Catholic bishops without consulting them beforehand. Nevertheless, when copies of the bill were sent to him he saw it as a distinct improvement on the unhappy prevailing situation, and felt that he could support it subject to certain amendments. On receiving the bill as amended by committee, however, he challenged certain clauses,[21] and felt disinclined to support the measure.[22] Then, in August, he changed his mind, presumably following certain modifications by the government.

On 24 August, Daniel O'Connell gave direction to the wider Catholic reaction to the measure, when he asserted that the act would injure the doctrines, discipline and constitution of the Church, and bring all bequests, current and future, into the 'greedy grasp' of the commissioners.[23] Murray's support for the Bequests Act was fortified by the behaviour of his old antagonist, Archbishop John MacHale. Confirmed in his deep suspicion of government policies by O'Connell's sweeping statement, MacHale, on 26 August, took the discourteously defiant step of meeting bishops John Cantwell of Meath and Patrick McGettigan of Raphoe in Murray's diocese, without making any effort to inform him of their presence. The purpose of the meeting was to warn fellow bishops against cooperating with the government's scheme. At Coffey's Hotel in Dominick Street they drew up a protest, cautioning bishops who might contemplate becoming commissioners that they would be interfering with the spiritual jurisdiction of other bishops and fomenting disunion.[24] They circulated their document to the bishops for their signatures and those of their clergy, and encouraged them to make their opposition public. The manifesto reached Murray by post. Angered at being treated in this cavalier and impersonal manner in his own diocese, he nevertheless decided to ignore the document.[25] MacHale's behaviour and Murray's reaction were clearly influenced by their previous intense disagreement on the issues of national education and Repeal.

A week later, on 6 September, the government's plans received a further setback. The Law Lords reversed O'Connell's sentence, and celebrations were held throughout the country, with O'Connell holding a triumphal parade through the streets of Dublin. Murray presided at a solemn pontifical Mass with *Te Deum* in the Pro-Cathedral, and the sermon was preached by a priest of the archdiocese, Fr John Miley, a well-known friend of O'Connell. Sir James Graham, responsible in England for Irish policy, was furious, regarding Murray's presence as an act of 'culpable weakness, if not of duplicity'.[26] Nevertheless, he commented revealingly to Lord Lieutenant Heytesbury that, while he feared Murray would 'not have the courage to beard the Lion (O'Connell) who is now at large and roaring fearfully … still we must endeavour to bring him to terms and to bend him to our purpose'.[27]

As mentioned in a previous chapter, a source of advice and assistance to Murray over a number of years was the lawyer, Anthony Blake. Blake was a man of great charm whose political influence was so many-sided that to some he was a Machiavellian figure. Committed to national education, he was one of the most active commissioners. He worked well with both Archbishops Whately and Murray. At Murray's request, he was to become a Catholic commissioner on the bequests board.[28] By the third week of September, Murray, at Heytesbury's entreaty, had provided the names of acceptable Catholic commissioners.

Then, on 21 September, the *Freeman's Journal* published the manifesto of protest that MacHale had circulated a month previously, together with the signatures collected in the interval. These last included an archbishop, twelve bishops, seven hundred diocesan clergy, and many members of religious congregations. It was known, moreover, that such important names as Paul Cullen and Tobias Kirby, rector and vice-rector respectively of the Irish College in Rome, supported the protest. The manifesto had found fault with certain provisions of the act, including the exclusion of any donation in favour of a religious order, and then declared that the real intention of the government was to select 'ministerial favourites' from the hierarchy, thereby creating divisions among the bishops and destroying the confidence of the people in their spiritual leaders. The people, it claimed, distrusted the government and would view with alarm and hostility bishops accepting 'place and patronage under the crown'.[29]

A POLARISED HIERARCHY

The publication of the protest, its hostile tone and the opposition of O'Connell transformed the history of the bequests. Attitudes were polarised within the hierarchy. Public pressure against the act was palpable. Blake, speaking to the Lord Lieutenant, described Murray as 'exceedingly nervous'.[30] The Archbishop's nervousness and frustration were increased on 23 and 24 September when two prelates, whom he expected to be fellow commissioners, bowed to public pressure and declined to act in that role. Francis Haly of Kildare and Leighlin, who owed much to Murray, hesitated, then declined, and thereafter was absent in Rome at critical junctures. The other prelate, the primate, William Crolly of Armagh, who had been very supportive of the new act, now told Murray that it was not prudent for either of them to place themselves in opposition to 'Mr O'Connell, a majority of bishops and clergy'. The protesters, he said, had plausible reasons, including the exclusion of the regular clergy and the possibility of Protestant interference with the bishops' authority. It was possible that the measure 'may eventually prepare the way for a pension to the Catholic clergy', which would tie the clergy to the state.[31]

Further pressure was piled on Murray by the fact that several of his own diocesan priests had signed the protest, and some, like Frs Peter Cooper and Mathew Flanagan, had publicly condemned the act. Cooper believed that the nefarious Blake was responsible for misleading Murray.[32] To Murray it must have seemed like an encroaching victory for his old antagonist, MacHale. What could be done? If he continued his support for the government's programme, the prospect outlined by Crolly seemed likely to follow. If he withdrew his support, the government reform measure seemed certain to fail. It would be frustrated by the lack of cooperation from the bishops and clergy. Moreover, further reforms benefitting Catholics – in such areas as Maynooth and academic education – would be jeopardised.

Having received assurances from the government on its offending aspects, Murray believed that the act had good possibilities for his people. Now that he had committed himself to the general principle, he was reluctant to withdraw his support. Although his health had been poor for many years and he was now seventy-six years of age, he was not accustomed to giving way on matters of importance, least of all to someone as aggressive as John MacHale. He summoned his inner resources and met with Heyetesbury. He explained how the protest had been contrived, his own indignation with MacHale, and his hope of winning over Crolly and Haly. Moreover, he assured the Lord Lieutenant that many bishops were favourable and that the laity were favourable 'almost to a man'.[33] The wish was father to the thought, however, for it was a remarkably over-sanguine assessment. Crolly refused to budge, Haly was unreliable, and no lay person came out in favour of the government's act. Prelates and laity seemed cowed by the combination of O'Connell and MacHale and the plausibility of their presentation.

Blake at this stage made an effective intervention. He wrote a letter addressing the objections raised in the protest. He pointed out that the position of the religious orders remained as it had been prior to the act, and he claimed that there would be no interference in Church affairs as the duties of the board were to be purely administrative.[34] He revealed to the chief secretary, Eliot, that the bishops' memorial in 1840 had asked for far less than was now being offered them. Equipped with all this information, Eliot wrote to Archbishop Crolly, with whom he was friendly. Crolly declared himself impressed, but requested that appointments to the board be deferred until after the bishops' meeting in November. This was granted by the government.[35]

Meanwhile, on 1 October, Murray had canvassed Dr Michael Slattery, Archbishop of Cashel, but his arguments failed to convince him.[36] Another influential prelate, William Kinsella of Ossory, acknowledged the cogency of Murray's argument, but he awaited the decision of a large majority of bishops, and meantime refused to commit himself.[37] All seemed likely to hinge on the meeting of the hierarchy in November. Meanwhile, Daniel Murray appeared increasingly isolated as the nationalist and Catholic press published articles and numerous letters in support of Archbishop MacHale, and week after week there appeared supplemental lists of clergy in support of the protest.

ROMAN INVOLVEMENT

Shaken by the volume of criticism, Murray wrote to Cullen to counter its possible effects in Rome. All the protest had achieved, he declared, was to proclaim to the world the disunity of the Irish bishops. He made his feelings clear on the disreputable manner in which the protest had been enacted. Union and general cooperation were undermined, he said, when two or three bishops could go into the diocese of another bishop and ignore him, although he was residing almost next door. Union was further undermined by posting a circular to the local bishop and to other absent bishops, calling on them, separately and without the opportunity of consulting together, to send answers, not to a bishop or bishop's secretary, but to a newspaper office for immediate publication. Murray also exposed the discrepancy between the opening words of the protest – 'Having studied with attention the provisions of the act' – and the well-known fact that many of the signatories had not had the opportunity to read the text.

Giving little consideration to the usual criticisms of the provisions of the act, Murray reminded Cullen of the 1840 memorial, and added that 'the government thought they were doing great things for us when they granted our request; but they did it in a bungling and unsatisfactory way, because they did not take the trouble of consulting us'. Even that defect he excused on the grounds that it might have involved difficult consultations with many religious bodies. He was prepared, despite the government's bungling, to accept its good intentions. In any event, the act was now the law of the land.[38]

Writing to Murray on 12, 15, 24 and 28 October 1844,[39] Cullen accepted that the new board was an improvement on its predecessor. He believed, nevertheless, that the government had deliberately omitted consulting the bishops, and now sought their support to save the act, knowing that in so doing the bishops would 'put public opinion at defiance', and undermine their standing with their people. He appealed to Murray to preserve the unity of the bishops and not scandalise the faithful. Knowing Murray's respect for Pope Gregory, he urged him and the bishops to submit their case to the pope. He had presented his version of the situation to His Holiness, who observed that he would not have approved of such a bill. Cullen was expecting a similar response if the bishops brought their case to Rome.

Murray was unconvinced by Cullen's letters. At this stage, he did not expect an objective view from him. His only scruples, he responded, were whether bishops could with a good conscience refuse office and thereby leave 'the treasury of the poor' in less trustworthy hands.[40]

For some time the government had been concerned lest MacHale appeal to Rome and the act be condemned by the pope. It was decided to send an envoy to Rome to present the government's case. Its representative, William Petrie, an English Catholic, arrived there on 16 October. He came with a full dossier, which included a copy of the act and of the 1840 memorial and an account of MacHale's role in starting and promoting the protest. It also contained certain items of information supplied by Murray and Blake: that Cullen was a on MacHale's side, that the Congregation of Propaganda was largely in favour of MacHale, but that a likely supporter of the government was the influential English Cardinal, Charles Acton.[41]

Thereafter, the whole matter involved numerous letters and reports between all concerned: between English officials and Rome; between English government ministers and Murray; between Irish bishops and Rome; and among Irish bishops themselves. There were public meetings and newspaper comments opposing the Bequest Act, attacking Murray and his supporting prelates for their endorsement of the act.

Concerned about the divisions among Irish bishops, Pope Gregory instructed Cardinal Acton to examine the entire issue and provide a report. Acton's report was presented on 8 November 1844. After a full examination of the situation and its context, he recommended that, despite failings in the act and in the government's manner of proceeding, the measure opened the way for the Church to acquire property. The protesters, he judged, were unrealistic in thinking that the government would alter the new law or would be unable to find substitute commissioners if the bishops refused a place on the board. He appreciated the strength of feeling among the protesters, but he felt they were wrong to stir up the people. Given the strength of public feeling, however, it would be unwise to censure the conduct of the clerical and episcopal protesters.

Acton saw a similarity between the compromise reached in the case of the national schools and what was advisable now. In the former situation, Murray had been criticised, but his policy had proved right. Now, Acton recommended that Murray's moderate line be again followed, with the bishops taking the places offered them on the board. The new law was an improvement on the existing situation and, as in the case of the national schools, there was nothing to stop the bishops further improving it.[42]

Four days later, on 12 November, a meeting of the Irish Catholic hierarchy took place, largely unaware of these developments.[43] At this meeting, eight bishops, led by Crolly of Armagh and Murray of Dublin, supported the presence of prelates on the Bequests board. A majority supported MacHale in opposition.

MURRAY'S PASTORAL LETTER

Within a few days, Archbishop Murray determined to go on the offensive. On 16 November 1844, he issued a pastoral letter on the Bequests Act. It ran to some fifteen quarto pages. The time had come, he said, to address the people of his archdiocese on the Bequests Act, which had given rise to so much angry discussion. The machinery for carrying the act into operation was now formed. It was his duty to place it in its true light before them. It was a source of 'inexpressible pain' to him that 'the deep convictions of his mind' compelled him to adopt a course of proceeding on this subject that was at variance with what some of his most respected and beloved brethren would commend. He continued firmly:

> Conscience is a stern monitor. It is unsafe to despise its admonitions. And it warns me, with a voice which penetrates my inmost soul that it would be in me a gross dereliction of pastoral duty to fling away, through any human respect, the opportunity which this Act, imperfect as it is, places within my reach of preserving in safety the treasure of the poor, and of securing for the service of the Church whatever property benevolent individuals may choose to vest in the new Board to be permanently dedicated to that purpose.

This was the sole and whole duty, he continued, which would devolve on those whose office it was to carry this act into effect. 'It is a duty worthy of Religion and dear to God; a duty in the faithful discharge of which this Minister should think it well worth his while to encounter any share of unjust obloquy, which the mistaken zeal of his opponents might move them to cast upon him'.

There were defects in the act, Murray conceded, which might perhaps be removed or lessened when parliament assembled, but meantime the act was due to come into operation after the first day of January 1845. By then the commissioners of the board of management would be named. 'The commissioners', he explained, 'will have five persons professing the Roman Catholic Religion. It will be their peculiar duty to watch over the due application of Catholic charities whether intended for the poor or for the Church.' If Her Majesty were forced to appoint professing Catholics at random, due to the want of accurate information from the heads of the Catholic religion, 'how could we ever afterwards complain, how could we render with confidence an account of our stewardship to God, if, through our fault … those important interests were confided to unworthy or incompetent hands?' Then he added, 'Blessed be God, appointments have been made, which, as far as human vigilance can avail, will render those interests secure'.

He then went on to pose two key questions. The first of these – 'Were not our charities safe hitherto?' – gave Murray an opportunity to dwell on the history of charity bequests and the long discrimination against Catholics, and hence the need for change. The second question – 'Who called for any new act on the subject?' – led him to introduce the memorial presented by the Catholic bishops in February 1840 to the Lord Lieutenant, which sought changes which the current Bequests Act more than met. He also dealt with misconceptions about the act. It was not true that it discriminated against members of religious orders. The act in no way changed their situation, despite what protesters said. Furthermore, the suggestion that bishops, as commissioners, would be obliged to enforce a penal law against religious, was without foundation. 'Their office does not even invest them with any such odious power.'

Finally, Murray emphasised the benefits of the new act, including the fact that Catholics now had their own countrymen and bishops administering it, and he remarked that the benefits were such as to render the defects of the act 'of little moment'. In this situation, it was surprising that 'denunciations of the most awful nature have been poured out unsparingly against those, who, without any hope of earthly remuneration but the consciousness of doing good', had undertaken the meritorious task of bringing into effect the beneficent objects which the act contemplated. [44]

APPOINTMENT BY ECCLESIASTICAL TITLES

The Archbishop's letter was received with much praise, and he was further consoled by news from Rome. The secretary of state, Lambruschini, had called together a selected group of cardinals to consider Acton's report. On 29 November, a letter, approved by Pope Gregory, thanked the British government for the consideration shown to Catholics in the Bequests Act. It found, nevertheless, that some of the act's provisions were not in keeping with canon law. The letter expressed the hope that the government would reassure the Irish bishops that the religious congregations would not suffer as a result of the new law, and that the Protestant commissioners would not interfere with Catholic trusts. In short, there would be no Roman condemnation of the Bequests Act; instead, a cautious endorsement of the act had been obtained. On receiving the news, Murray was greatly relieved.

Unimpressed, John MacHale remained determined to force Murray and his episcopal minority to abandon their support of the act. He protested to Cardinal Franzoni and Pope Gregory that the will of the majority was being ignored, and he encouraged O'Connell to wage a public campaign against the act. O'Connell held a series of major public meetings across the country, stirring the people to fever pitch. In his campaign, he re-enkindled the familiar objections to the act: that it brought all bequests into 'the greedy hands' of the board; that it robbed religious congregations of their property; and that it violated Church law. The act also raised the question, he said, of 'loyal' and 'disloyal' bishops, and he reminded his audiences that thirty years previously there had been a similar hesitation by some bishops with respect to the veto until the people cried out, 'We will have no bishops made by an English pope'. Now, he proclaimed, to roars of approval, 'People of Ireland, you have the same remedy now'.[45]

The public agitation in O'Connell's electoral county of Clare resulted in the Bishop of Killaloe, Patrick Kennedy, withdrawing his name as commissioner. A strong supporter of Murray, he had agreed to join Crolly and Murray as the third episcopal commissioner on the board, but could no longer continue.[46] O'Connell triumphantly announced his withdrawal at a public meeting. The next day, 4 December, Murray moved swiftly and decisively. Foreseeing the defection of Kennedy, and supported by Archbishop Crolly, he asked Cornelius Denvir, bishop of Down and Connor, to take Kennedy's place.

The pressures on Murray and, to a lesser extent on Crolly, were many-sided and intense. Their meetings with the Lord Lieutenant in Dublin Castle, where the board of bequests met, evoked public protests. Heytesbury, the lord lieutenant, reported on 16 December, 'Dr Murray fears, and not without reason, that in going to the Castle he will be exposed to hisses and insults most desirable to be avoided. "Subserviency to the Castle" is the watchword now raised against the prelates'.[47]

Sir Patrick Bellew and Anthony Blake were the two remaining Catholic commissioners named by Murray for membership of the Bequests Board.[48] Murray, on 10 December 1844, gave Crolly an insight into a factor stiffening his resolve:

> Dr Slattery trembles at the contemplation of the disunion which our acceptance of the office of Commissioner will create. But this disunion is not our work, it began elsewhere, and the same means, which have produced it and are daily widening it more and more, will, if not checked, be had recourse to, whenever it may serve the purpose of agitation so to do.[49]

On 16 December, Lord Lieutenant Heytesbury, fearful of the impact of O'Connell's campaign, urged London to have the names of the commissioners on the bequests board gazetted as soon as possible.[50] The request received immediate attention, and the *Gazette* appeared in Dublin and London the following day. The names of the three Catholic bishops were presented with their full ecclesiastical titles, and were accorded precedence over members of the peerage on the board. This recognition was of constitutional importance and occasioned much comment. The *Morning Chronicle* of 20 December 1844 remarked, 'This is the first time since the enactment of the penal laws that the Roman Catholic prelates have been recognised by their titles in an official document emanating from the Queen in Council and published by authority'.

At his final public meeting in Dublin, O'Connell acknowledged defeat, but reminded his audience that no prelate from Munster, and only one from

Leinster, supported the act. He then created grounds for a further and even more intense campaign of public anger, by stating that an English agent 'Mr William Peter' [*sic*] was in Rome and, aided by the Austrian envoy, was 'negotiating a concordat with England'.[51] He knew that nothing was more calculated to rouse Irish Catholics than suspicions of collusion between the English government and the Papacy in Irish affairs.

THE PROSPECT OF A CONCORDAT

The outcry over a possible concordat between Britain and the Holy See exposed Archbishop Murray to new outbursts of obloquy. The occasion of a rumour about a concordat appears to have been a visit to the Irish College in Rome by William Petre. He is said to have announced himself grandly as the representative of the British Crown in Rome, and to have stated that he was 'engaged in most important negotiations, which would soon terminate in a regular treaty from which the Catholic Church would derive great benefit in all British dominions'. Cullen informed Fr John Miley of this on 5 December.[52] He also informed MacHale and Fr Cooper.[53] The word spread. O'Connell heard it, but got Petre's name wrong. The Repeal newspaper, *The Pilot*, on 30 December 1844, published an editorial on 'The Crisis in the Catholic Church'.

At the same time, MacHale was reprimanded by Cardinal Franzoni because of his attacks on fellow bishops who were following their conscience, and the Pope and Propaganda appealed to him to refrain from creating dissension among the bishops.[54] This, nevertheless, did not deter MacHale from actively challenging the idea of a concordat and of availing of the hostility to it to attack the Bequests Act again. Murray and Crolly, because of their public support of the Bequests Act, were labelled 'government men'. A letter in the *Freeman's Journal* was so 'grossly offensive' to Murray that the editor, John Gray, wrote to the archbishop the same day apologising sincerely.[55] Feeling against Murray was so intense that early in January 1845, his secretary, Dr John Hamilton, chaired a public meeting aimed at refuting 'the calumnies propagated against Dr Murray';[56] and Revd Thomas O'Carroll, a priest at Westland Row church, spoke openly of a threat against the life of the archbishop.[57] Public attendance at the Archbishop's Pro-Cathedral greatly diminished, as also at Westland Row and the Church of St Nicholas, Francis Street, where the priests openly supported Murray. Some fifty-eight Dublin priests expressed their affection for and confidence in the Archbishop, but almost three times that number signed a memorial condemning the Bequests Act and a concordat.[58] Moreover, a considerable body of the laity of the diocese expressed their concern by sending a joint petition to each member of the hierarchy, and preparing an appeal to Rome. [59]

By the second week of January 1845, the old cry 'Religion from Rome, Politics from Home' had become the theme of speeches, articles and letters. Concerned at the tumult the issue of a concordat was causing, the government decided that Murray and Crolly be informed that reports of a concordat were without foundation. The Lord Lieutenant wrote to Murray to that effect on 15 January,[60] stating the he could use his letter as he thought best. Two days later, in the *Dublin Evening Post,* Murray explained that he had received an official note from the Lord Lieutenant, which stated that he had been instructed to give to the archbishops of Dublin and Armagh the government's strongest assurance that it never had the slightest intention of entering into any negotiations with the Holy See on the subject of a concordat. In the atmosphere of the time, however, the government's assertion was not trusted. 'It was generally believed and publicly asserted', according to a Dublin priest, James Corr, 'that our metropolitan (Murray) in his seventy seventh year is cajoled by them.'[61]

Meantime, the controversy over the Bequests Act and now the concordat had roused interest abroad. On 25 January, the Pope saw Cullen and made it clear that there was no question of a concordat. It appears that he rebuked Cullen for spreading unfounded rumours about a concordat and for his part in the controversy. A chastened Cullen wrote to Murray on 25 and 28 January. In the first of these letters, he wrote:

> I was extremely sorry to hear the reports that have been spread of threats against your Grace. God grant that there is no truth in them … I am happy to state that the reports about a projected concordat are quite unfounded. I have it today from the pope himself. The reports were put in circulation by an English agent to give himself a diplomatic … consequence – at least that is the explanation now given.[62]

In the second letter he was more openly contrite: 'God grant that I may do penance for any evil I have occasioned. I have come to the firm resolution of *never,* never interfering in political reports or discussions. I speak to your Grace with the greatest sincerity and confidence in this matter … Oh that peace could be restored to the Irish Church.'[63]

Cullen also wrote to his friends MacHale, Dr Blake of Dromore, and Fr John Miley, pleading for moderation. His fall from papal favour was sending him into depression. He could not sleep at night and became so ill that his friends were worried. In his concern, he asked Bishop Walsh of Halifax, Nova Scotia, a mutual friend of his and of Murray who was then in Ireland, to smooth matters with Crolly and Murray. Walsh reported to him on 10 March 1845, 'If you knew all the two archbishops have suffered you would really pity them and would not be surprised at all they feel. I softened everything as well as I could'. [64]

There remained the prospect of a direct lay appeal to Rome. There was no way that Cullen could now be of assistance to such a deputation. He appealed to John Cantwell, bishop of Meath, who with MacHale was a leading figure among the protesters, 'for God's sake' to oppose 'the intended lay deputation to Rome'.[65] Cantwell, impressed by Cullen's alarm and state of mind, ensured that the preparations for a delegation were put aside.[66] With that, the fierce controversy died away; but Daniel O'Connell continued to rumble to friends and supporters about the inadequacies of the Bequests Act, and to assure them that 'the Bishops have the ball at their feet. If they hold out firmly on the truest Catholic principles, believe me, everything will be conceded.'[67] It was the sort of judgement and perception that Murray considered misleading and unreal.

That so much division arose among the Irish hierarchy on a relatively minor act of parliament points, once again, to the *cultural* change that became increasingly apparent in the decade after the Emancipation Act.[68] It first came into public view on the national education issue. The voluble Peter Cooper, one of Murray's curates who had attended the Repeal meeting at Tara, observed in the course of a letter to Cullen on 2 October 1844[69]:

> Charity and unity of purpose and sentiment is gone from among ourprelates since the unfortunate controversy on the Education Board.

He attributed most of the blame to Anthony Blake who, as mentioned earlier, was believed to have had an unfortunate influence over the over-trusting and venerable Archbishop Murray. Significantly, Cooper viewed Murray's and Blake's policy as the 'timid, crouching policy of the last century'. O'Connell was the pivotal figure in the change. How he viewed Murray was suggested in a private letter O'Connell wrote to his friend P. V. Fitzpatrick on 25 March 1844:

> What, for example, could we expect from that most excellent man and exemplary clergyman, our archbishop? The numbing effect of any kind of connection with the Government operates upon the best minds without their perceiving it.[70]

In short, the cultural change in attitude towards the government – an attitude marked by suspicion and hostility, and a desire for a form of political home rule – had resulted in people like Murray, principled supporters of aspects of government policy, appearing out-of-date and even unpatriotic. Nevertheless, as Cooper observed to Cullen, even the clerics who disagreed with Murray still retained affection and esteem for him.[71]

The extent of the change in outlook was to be found, not only in the Catholic population, but also among some youthful Protestants. It was reflected in the foundation and functioning of the *Nation* newspaper (1842–48) which, according to its editor, Charles Gavan Duffy, took its name out of a desire to make Ireland a *nation.*[72]

NOTES

1 Francis de Sales, *The Devout Life*, ch.7.
2 Donal McCartney, *The Dawning of Democracy: Ireland 1800–1870* (Dublin: Helicon History of Ireland, 1987), pp.151–3.
3 Oliver MacDonagh, 'Politics 1830–1845', in W. E. Vaughan (ed.) *A New History of Ireland*, vol.v, *Ireland under the Union I. 1801–70* (Oxford: Clarendon Press, 1989), p.184.
4 Kinsella – Murray, 4 June 1843, DDA. Murray Papers, f.32/1/33.
5 Cit. McCartney, op. cit., p.153.
6 Idem, p.155.
7 MacDonagh, loc. cit. in op. cit., p.185.
8 Murray – Hamilton, Sept. 1840, DDA. Hamilton Papers (1), no.109.
9 Murray – Hamilton, 15 July 1842; Hamilton Papers (1), no. 131; Murray – Hamilton, 28 Oct, 1842; idem. No.134.
10 Idem, 18 May 1843, no.141.
11 Ref. in J. de Courcy Laffan – Murray, 2 June 1843, no.54.
12 Cit. McCartney, op. cit., p.156.
13 R.P. Cooper – Murray, 28 August 1843. Murray Papers, no.59.
14 Copy of the statement signed by 24 parish priests and curates, Murray Papers, no. 25.
15 Cit. McCartney, op. cit. p.157.
16 Murray – Hamilton, 13 Oct. 1843; Hamilton Papers (1), f.35/1/145.
17 Donal A. Kerr, *Peel, Priests and Politics* (Oxford: Oxford University Press, 1982), p.120. This work provides valuable information on the Bequests Controversy based on the Papers of Sir James Graham (1792–1861), and Sir Robert Peel (1768–1850).
18 Peel – Heytesbury, 8 Aug. 1844. Additional Manuscripts, British Library, 40479, 23-30; cit. Kerr idem.
19 Peel – De Grey, 22 Aug. 1843. Add. Mss 40478, ff.160–61, cit Kerr p.112.
20 Graham – Peel, 7 April 1844. Add. MSS 40449, cit. Kerr p.123.
21 Murray – Lord Eliot, 9 Aug. 1844. Murray Papers, f. 32/1/162A.
22 Murray – Hamilton, 11 Aug. 1844. Hamilton Papers (1), 35/1/158.
23 The *Pilot* newspaper, 26 Aug. 1844.
24 Charitable Bequests folder, 26 Aug. 1844. Murray Papers; and *The Pilot,* 23 Sept. 1844.
25 Murray – Slattery, Abp. Cashel, 30 Aug. 1844. CDA. Slattery Papers.
26 Graham – Heytesbury, 13 Sept. 1844, Graham Papers (G.P.).
27 Idem, 11 Sept. 1844.
28 Heytesbury – Graham, 17 Sept. 1844, G.P., cit Kerr pp.139–40.
29 *Freeman's Journal*, 21 Sept. 1844.
30 Heytesbury – Graham, 22 Sept. 1844, G.P.
31 Crolly – Murray, 23 Sept. 1844. Murray Papers.
32 Cooper – Cullen, 22 Sept. 1844, Cullen Papers.
33 Heytesbury – Graham, 25 Sept. 1844. G.P., cit. Kerr p.145.
34 Blake – Heytesbury, 27 Sept. 1844. Add. Mss. 40450, cit. Kerr p.146.
35 Eliot – Crolly, 12 Oct. 1844. G.P. cit. Kerr p.147.

36 Murray – Slattery, 1 Oct. 1844. Slattery Papers.
37 Murray communicated the letter to Eliot, who informed Graham, 16 Oct. 1844, cit. Kerr p.148.
38 Murray – Cullen, 1 Oct. 1844. C.P.
39 Cullen – Murray, 12, 15, 24, 28 Oct. 1844. Murray Papers.
40 Murray – Cullen, 31 Oct. 1844. C.P.
41 Eliot – Graham, 7 Oct. 1844. G.P.
42 Acton – Lambruschini, 8 Nov. 1844. Kerr pp.159–160.
43 Meeting of Irish Bishops, 16 Nov. 1844. DDA.
44 Bequests Act. Abp's Pastoral, 16 Nov. 1844. Murray Papers, f. 32/1/165.
45 The *Tablet*, 7 Dec. 1844.
46 Kennedy – Murray, 7 Dec. 1844. Murray Papers, No.169.
47 Heytesbury – Graham, 16 Dec. 1844. G.P.
48 Heytesbury – Murray, 26 Nov. 1844. Murray Papers, f.32/1/167.
49 Murray – Crolly, 10 Dec. 1844. DCDA.
50 Heytesbury – Graham, 16 Dec. 1844; G.P. : *Gazette* is an official journal issuing government appointments and bankrupts.
51 The *Pilot*, 20 Dec. 1844.
52 Cullen – Miley, 5 Dec. 1844. C.P.
53 Kerr, op. cit. p.195.
54 Franzoni – Mac Hale, 30 Dec. 1844. Murray Papers, No.176.
55 J.Gray – Murray, Murray Papers, f. 33/1. No.8. Undated but evidently at this time.
56 Mr Dwyer – Hamilton, 7 Jan. 1845. Hamilton Papers, f.36/7/58.
57 *The Tablet*, 11 Jan. 1845.
58 *Dublin Evening Post,* 14 Jan.1845; *Tablet*, 8 Feb. 1845.
59 Battersby, *Catholic Directory 1846* (for 1845), pp.409–18.
60 Heytesbury – Murray, 15 Jan. 1845. Murray Papers, f.32/2/45.
61 Corr – Cullen, 17 Jan. 1845. C.P.
62 Cullen – Murray, 25 Jan. 1845. Murray Papers, f.32/1/180.
63 Cullen – Murray, 28 January 1845.
64 Walsh – Cullen, 10 March 1845. C.P.
65 Cullen – Cantwell, 8 Feb. 1845. Mac Suibhne. *Paul Cullen and his Contemporaries with their letters*, vol. 1, 258.
66 Cantwell – Cullen, 12 March 1845. C.P.
67 O'Connell – P.V. Fitzpatrick, 21 June 1845; O'Connell – Mac Hale, 21 June 1845; M. R. O'Connell (ed.) *The Correspondence of Daniel O'Connell*, vol.vii, 3147, 3148.
68 Italics mine.
69 Cooper – Cullen, 2 Oct. 1844. C.P.
70 O'Connell – Fitzpatrick, 25 March 1844. *Correspondence of D. O'Connell,* vii, 3063.
71 Cooper – Cullen, 22, 25 Sept. 1844. C.P.
72 Italics mine.

CHAPTER 12

Years of Famine and Turmoil (1846–50)

In the second half of the 1840s there occurred the Great Famine, the major divide in nineteenth century Ireland. It happened mainly in what has been termed the 'subsistence' part of the country, where the Catholic population was mainly Irish-speaking: the south, west, north-west, and parts of the east and the midlands. The Catholic population in the maritime cities – Dublin, Cork, Limerick, Waterford, even Galway – was largely spared the ravages of the famine, as well as nearby towns. Their language was English, except amongst the poorer people. Nevertheless, as archbishop of the capital city and as one of the best-known Irishmen of the time, much aid was sent to Murray for the famine victims.

At the end of June 1845, potato blight caused extensive damage in Belgium, the Netherlands, north-east France and Switzerland. It also affected parts of England. Ireland, however, was the major sufferer. Out of a population of eight million, 3.3 million people lived exclusively on the potato, while for 4.7 million it was the predominant item of diet.[1]

POTATO BLIGHT IN IRELAND

By September 1845 the blight had reached Ireland. Alarmed by reports of a major failure of the potato crop, Archbishop Murray turned to his priests in outlying parts of his diocese for information. Reports came during November. Fr John Smyth, parish priest at Balbriggan, Co. Dublin, explained that 'three-quarters of the crop is blighted, and since livestock, pigs, cattle and horses are all fed on potatoes, there is going to be great distress'. He added that 'the people sell potatoes to the starch mills, two of which are in Balbriggan'. Already the mills had bought 8,000 barrels full. 'This means that the poor cottiers and labourers will not have nought *(sic)* to last them to the end of the year, and what then is to become of them, or where will they get money to buy meal for their famishing families? Their only resource will be the poor houses.'He further reported that the blight had affected all Co. Dublin north of the city, and also County Meath.[2]

Two days later, somewhat similar reports came from Arklow and Wicklow. Fr James Redmond, parish priest of Arklow, announced that one-third of the potato crop had been lost in the mountainy districts, a half in the midlands, and two-thirds in coastal areas. Fr John Grant, parish priest of Wicklow town, had a similar story about this 'mysterious malady'. He anticipated great distress among the poor.[3]

During the winter of 1845–46 the loss to the potato crop was about forty per cent. This meant that a catastrophe was avoided. A further saving factor was the decisive action taken by the prime minister, Robert Peel, who established public works to provide employment and imported Indian corn for sale at cost price. Private enterprise and Peel's government programme helped to divert disaster; but when Peel's government was replaced by that of Sir John Russell, the situation deteriorated disastrously. Russell relied on private enterprise and withdrew government aid, adhering entirely to the classical economic doctrine that the government must not interfere with the economy, and that market forces must be allowed free rein.

The blight struck once more in August 1846 and five-sixths of the potato crop failed. Angry men, whose wives and children were dying of hunger, marched in protest as they could find no work. They saw grain leaving the country while thousands starved, and witnessed penniless peasants being evicted and their homes levelled. Again and again, violence was averted by the local priests, who believed that Sir John Russell was a friend of Ireland and would come to their aid.[4] Meantime, the hunger, suffering and dying continued and, in the midst of so much pain, merchants exploited the situation. Without government intervention and control of prices, the outlook was grim.

Fr William Flannelly, from Clifden, Co. Galway, complained in December 1846 that the relief committees were forbidden to sell at less than market prices, thereby protecting the exorbitant prices charged by merchants.[5] Two weeks later, as Christmas approached, Archbishop Murray put forward a motion at a meeting in the Music Hall in Dublin criticising the government 'who allowed the poor to perish sooner than interfere with the interests of the general trader'. His motion was seconded by a Protestant clergyman, the Revd David Creighton.[6]

The extent of the disaster led to a diverse groups of people – Catholic and Protestant clergy, bishops and caring landlords – working together in relief committees across the country. In the religious culture of the time, a famine was seen by some as a visitation from God, a punishment for sin, a humbling of pride and a call to repentance. Such interpretations, however, did not in any way hinder the clergy and great sections of the laity from rallying to the aid of their neighbour in distress. The *Times* newspaper, for its part, did not hesitate to express the view, held widely in England, that the Irish famine was the result of the 'innate indolence' of the people.[7] Despite that, there was a generous financial response from the English public to the Irish famine relief effort, once the extent of the tragedy became known.

In the long and bitter winter of 1846–47, hundreds and thousands of the peasantry died. The appalling scale of deaths through starvation and fever in Skibbereen, Co. Cork, was highlighted in the *Illustrated London News*, but similar horrific scenes occurred throughout Munster and across the west of Ireland in particular. Soup kitchens, belatedly set up by Russell's government, were overwhelmed by the demand. Murray and his secretary were snowed under with cries for help. The Archbishop appointed a special assistant, Thomas Synnott, to deal exclusively with famine requests. Increasingly, hard-pressed clergy wrote to him. Among them was John Madden, parish priest of Roscommon, who wrote to Synnott on 5 February 1847, 'My house is surrounded by the starving poor … calling for work or food … We are doing what we can to distribute soup. What can we do? The applicants are so numerous; our means so limited.'[8] The historian, T. P. O'Neill, observed that the Catholic clergy 'worked like tigers' in the relief work, writing begging letters, attending sessions and meetings, and travelling long journeys on delegations. All this was in addition to their main work of bringing the sick and dying the consolation of the rites of the Church.[9]

The world as people knew it was disappearing around them. What was once one of the most densely populated areas in Europe saw farms, hamlets and villages abandoned. In addition, there was the demoralising effect on the people. Archbishop Slattery, horrified by this development, wrote from Cashel to his friend, Laurence Renehan, president of Maynooth College, in June 1847:[10]

> We are still struggling with famine and fever, and, what is more than both, the demoralisation of our people consequent on the system of relief that this incapable Government has inflicted on the country. Every feeling of decent spirit and of truth has vanished, and instead there is created for us a cringing lying population, a nation of beggars.

As news of the disaster spread abroad during 1847, relief committees were set up in various parts of Europe, and in Britain, America, Mexico and Australia, as well as in Ireland itself. Aid came from India and Africa, and from Irish people scattered across the world. The bishops and clergy of the Catholic Church provided one major source of relief, especially following an appeal to them by Pope Pius IX. Having sent money to Ireland for the relief of the famine, the pope then issued an encyclical letter, *Praedecessores Nostros*, appealing to

Catholic bishops across the world to exhort their varied flocks to contribute to the aid of the Irish people.[11] A considerable amount of this aid, as well as some contributions from Protestants and from Irish laity in exile, was directed to the best-known Irish churchman of the time, one who could be trusted to convey the aid to those most in need: Archbishop Daniel Murray.

RESPONSE OF THE IRISH HIERARCHY

On the home front, the disunity among the bishops prevented a strong combined approach to the government, until the horrors of 'Black '47' brought about a joint memorial of more than usual vigour in October of that year. At the outset, the bishops rejected the view propounded by the *Times* attributing the famine to the 'innate indolence' of the Irish people. The real causes, the bishops asserted, were penal laws which deprived the mass of the people of the right to property and denied them the fruits of their labour. 'Hallowed as are the rights of property,' they declared, 'those of life are still more sacred, and rank as such in every well regulated scale.' Had this been honoured in Ireland 'we would not have so often witnessed … those heart-rending scenes of eviction of tenantry.' The government's relief measures, their lordships continued, were wholly inadequate. The workhouses were overcrowded, fever-ridden and capriciously managed. The grim choice of the people was either to starve if they did not enter them, or die of contagious diseases if they did. Conscious that gratuitous relief was viewed as demoralising, they called for productive employment. The bishops further appealed to the Lord Lieutenant, George William Frederick, Earl Clarendon, asking that 'in such an awful crisis' he would use 'his influence with Her Majesty's government to procure measures of relief commensurate with the magnitude of the calamity'.

Finally, the bishops spoke of 'prospective measures calculated to check the recurrence of famine and promote the prosperity of the country', suggesting that what was required was an equitable arrangement of the relations between landlords and tenants, founded on commutative justice, which was so necessary, that without it they despair of seeing the poor sufficiently employed and protected, and the land sufficiently cultivated, or the peace and prosperity of the country placed on a secure foundation.

They added: 'Large tracts of land capable of cultivation are now lying waste; the coasts abound in fish which would give a large supply of food; encouragement to work these and other mines of wealth with which the country is teeming, would be well worth the solicitude of Her Majesty's government.'[12]

On 18 October 1847, in Dublin, the bishops began their meeting, and three days later they drew up the above memorial. Archbishop MacHale and some others wished to send it directly to Her Majesty through the prime minister, but Murray advised that they follow the protocol of operating as usual through the lord lieutenant. He was conscious that Lord Clarendon was very concerned about the famine and its effects. This was the course followed. With Dr Kennedy of Killaloe standing in for Archbishop Slattery, the archbishops presented their address on 25 October 'to his Excellency the Earl of Clarendon Lord Lieutenant General Governor of Ireland'. They were received graciously, and Clarendon replied at length to their memorial. In the course of his reply, he promised that in the many districts where 'dreadful misery' could not be relieved by any amount of local exertion, 'there *the* sacred and paramount duty of government – the preservation of human life – *will be* performed'.[13]

The bishops responded in turn, on 26 October. They thanked His Excellency for the 'great courtesy' with which he received them and for his enlightened response, but they deplored his silence about 'the wicked attempts at proselytism' to which they had directed his Excellency's attention. They then issued a resolution of protest. In order to strengthen His Excellency in his efforts to secure effective measures of relief commensurate with the magnitude of the calamity, 'and in order to avert the destruction of human life, and the disorganisation of society, which otherwise may be apprehended with fearful certainty,' some members of the hierarchy, 'accompanied by clergymen from the various districts of Ireland, and supported by some of our most efficient representatives … {will] be deputed to wait on Her Majesty about the middle of November to lay at the foot of the throne the starving and awful condition of this portion of Her Majesty's dominions'.[14]

This memorial, in its criticism of the social order, its condemnation of government policy and its expression of principles of social justice, went beyond the usual bounds of 'religion'. It reveals how hostility to and dissatisfaction with the government had greatly increased among the Irish bishops, in the face of the suffering of their people and the inadequate government response. This was further reflected at the bishops' lengthy meeting, which was chaired by Archbishop MacHale, by the following resolution, which was passed: 'That not withstanding the explanation so kindly given by His Grace, the Archbishop of Dublin, we are still of opinion that the changes introduced into the National System of Education are most serious and dangerous … We, therefore, petition parliament for the amendment of such portions of the system as we deem incompatible with the discipline of the Church.'[15] That such a petition would be passed by a majority – a petition which they knew had no chance of succeeding, and which indicated a spirit of protest and defiance rather an a serious attempt to deal with an educational problem – indicates an increased number of bishops at variance with Murray.

RECEIVING AND DISTRIBUTING AID

Knowing that parish priests were likely to know who among their flocks most needed help, Murray sent cheques or money drafts to priests in seriously afflicted areas. His papers for 1847 and 1848 have numerous examples of the aid he sent, and of the replies he received from clergy in the midst of poverty, hunger and helplessness.[16] Most of the correspondence is concerned with famine areas in Munster and the west of Ireland. There are also many letters from bishops across the world, especially following the pope's encyclical. With respect to aid sent to Murray, he usually wrote in acknowledgement. Thus, on 6 May 1847, he wrote to Pope Pius IX to thank him for issuing the papal encyclical, saying that he would have it published in Ireland as soon as possible.

On 26 June 1847, £150 was sent to him from the diocese of Münster in Germany, and this was followed by a further £1,050, with an acknowledgement of Murray's previous response. Among other German contributors were William Arnoldi, Archbishop of Trier, who sent 8,579 francs on 23 November 1847; Francis Dreppe, Bishop of Padderborn, who sent 5,640 imperial *borrussicos* on the same date; and the Vicar Van Wahner of Bonn, who contributed $1,144. From Italy, John Anthony Oddoni, Bishop of Susa, contributed 1,200 francs on 28 June 1847; Cardinal Placidus Tadini, Archbishop of Genoa, in a letter dated 26 May 1847, noted that £5,633 had been sent by the St Vincent de Paul Society, and that a further collection after the pope's encyclical had yielded another £5,000; and on 20 July 1847, Count Revel, Sardinian chargé d'affaires in London, sent two bills for £450 and £150 on behalf of Mgr Franzoni, Archbishop of Turin. Meantime, on 13 February, prior to the papal encyclical, Fr Paul Cullen, who was very active in collecting aid, wrote from Rome to Dean Meyler of St Andrew's parish in Dublin, 'The famine collection is going well and should realise £14,000 or £15,000, that before any public appeal has yet been made. People come to the Irish College with subscriptions or leaving money and gifts of jewellery, painting etc at the church of Saint Andrea … The English have organised a ball for famine relief in Ireland and Scotland. They have collected £1,000.' Dean Meyler, while relating all this to Murray, gave him 'the enclosed £50 from Cardinal Franzoni, a further contribution to the relief fund'.

Given the major diocesan matters he had to address, including a controversial bill relating to university education for Catholics, Murray was obliged, as we have seen, to appoint a substitute, Thomas Lambert Synnott,[17] to deal directly with famine appeals and aid distribution within Ireland. Synnott did so very effectively, making it clear always that the funding came through Murray. The latter was now eighty years of age, but his activity was still remarkable.[18]

Gifts from two Protestant lawyers in Lichfield were among the earliest of those recorded that Murray received.[19] His extensive network of friends and contacts rallied to support the victims of the famine. Lady Lucy Foley, widowed aunt of the Duke of Leinster, sent him £100 from Marseilles; Mary Leonara Sheil of Grosvenor Square in London sent a similar amount; and later Philip Howard of Corby Castle in Carlisle sent a contribution.[20] Relief funds came to Murray, as noted, not only from Europe, but from America, Canada, Australia, Turkey, Africa and India.

The appeals for relief came from parish priests across the west and south of Ireland. Many of their letters were harrowing. Fr John McCullagh, parish priest of Spiddal, on 22 April 1848 thanked Murray for £15 received. He used to have 5,000 people in his parish, but 1,000 of them had died from famine or its effects. More would have perished but for £43 sent by Dr MacHale and small supplies of meal given by the Society of Friends. Now, with those funds exhausted, the £15 had arrived. He went on to say that the landlords – all absentees – exacted thirty to forty shillings an acre for what was worth three shillings. The fever hospital holds only fifty, but there are two hundred cases. The priests are daily attending the dying, and he condemned the cruelty of the Blakes of Tully and Gurtamara who destroyed fifty cabins and left the people to die in the ditches.[21] Fr James Dwyer of Lackagh, Claregalway, reported that he had attended nine persons in one hour on an unspecified day in 1848, all suffering from typhus. Others were dying, thrown together in ditches or in shacks. He, their only visitor, had to crawl on hands and knees to get into these abodes of death.[22] Fr John Noone of Menloe, Castleblakeney, informed Synnott on 25 June 1848 that the Outdoor Relief Act was working so badly that his parish would be ruined were it not for the £15 Synnott had sent. 'The poor are treated in a most inhumane manner; economy is the order of the day and the misnamed "guardians" look on with indifference while deaths multiply daily. The next six weeks are critical; all sources of charity have now been drained and the poor are falling and dying on the roads.'[23]

The impact of the suffering and helplessness of the people on their priests is reflected in a letter to Murray from Fr Thomas Timlin of Ballinaskeary, Ballina, on 19 December 1848. Christmas was approaching but his 'faithful people' were unable to buy even a pound of Indian meal. He was torn with distress, 'finding myself between the dying and the dead and unable to help them in their need'.[24]

The final absence of Christmas spirit was graphically related by Fr Edward Waldron of Kilmaine, Ballinrobe, on 31 December 1848. He thanked Synnott in the name of his parishioners for the £10 he had received. He regretted to tell him that things were worse than ever in his parish. 'On Christmas Eve, the sheriff, with horse and foot soldiers, police and a posse of well-paid men, came to evict forty-eight poor tenants and levelled their houses. These people are now wandering about the roads. There is no room for them in the workhouses and they sleep in places not fit for pigs. It is terrible to see how men are treated by their fellow-men.'[25]

PROSPECT OF REVOLUTION

That same year, 1848, witnessed revolution across Europe. In Milan, Cardinal Archbishop Romilli took his place at the barricades. In Rome, the patriotic Pius IX's cry, 'God bless Italy', appeared to Italians to be a blessing on those seeking to unite Italy and expel the Austrians. In Ireland, a number of priests responded to the spirit of rebellion. On 3 April 1848, Revd Dr Michael O'Brien declared in Limerick that the priests would 'brave any danger to wrest their (countrymen's) souls and bodies from the debasement, destitution, and destruction of foreign rule'. The following day, in Waterford, Fr Nicholas Coughlan asserted:

> England's treatment of us for the past two years would abundantly prove that there is *practically* no government in this kingdom, and, therefore, in conscience, no allegiance is further due ... The unworthy deaths of some 800,000 honest men attest it.

Other priests, too, insisted that the existing social contract between government and people had been broken. A Limerick clergyman protested that it was 'far better to die as men died in Berlin, Vienna and Paris than that another million should die the death of Skibbereen'. And Bishop Edward Maginn, the administrator in Derry, denounced the government saying:

> Sooner than allow the misery of my people to continue, like the Archbishop of Milan, I would rather grasp the cross and the green flag of Ireland and rescue my country, or perish with the people.[26]

In Dublin, Archbishop Murray felt it necessary to tell 'Mr Cooper not to preach again until further notice'.[27]

Most bishops followed Murray's example and endeavoured, with success, to keep their priests from involvement in rebellion. Murray went further. He issued a statement to the press appealing to people to have no part in revolution. He recounted his own fearful experience in 1798, when he barely escaped from the Orange yeomanry who had brought a canon up to the doors of the Catholic church in Arklow. Should anyone be surprised, he asked, that he felt a thrill of horror at the thought of the recurrence of such a calamity?

Because of their stance, the bishops were criticised by the Young Ireland leaders, who instigated a rebellion in July 1848. The ill-prepared nature of the insurgency gave clergy good reason to persuade the poorly equipped and half-starved peasantry to return home. In England, an effect of the Irish revolt was the alienation of public opinion, and a decline in subscriptions to aid Irish distress.

Following the rebellion, the government seemed to think that the clergy had lost the trust of the people for not supporting the rebellion and, knowing that many of the priests were in a poverty-stricken state, decided that the time was right to offer the clergy a state salary. Some priests, but especially the bishops, rejected the offer. Archbishop Murray, however, and the independent Archdeacon O'Sullivan, from Kerry, made a reasoned case for accepting the offer, observing that it was all very well for the bishops to refuse payment, but that many of the curates were starving. O'Sullivan was also concerned that the people were poorly instructed because of a shortage of priests, the reasons for which was the lack of money to support them. Young men had been refused ordination at Maynooth because their bishops could not afford to employ them.

In November 1848, the hierarchy took a unanimous decision against government payment which, they argued, would sever the people from their pastors and reduce the influence of the priests.[28] Sir John Russell expressed his sense of frustration with the Irish situation in a letter to Sir George Grey on 3 September 1848: 'The great problem remains ... How are the Roman Catholic masses to be attached to Imperial Rule? All the franchises we have granted, all the relief we have bestowed have failed to do so. The middle and lower classes are against us – the higher afraid of what may happen and unwilling to act.'[29]

CONTINUING GOVERNMENT VACILLATION

In 1849, Charles Trevelyan, a guiding figure in the government's attitude towards the Irish famine, announced mistakenly that the famine was over, with the result that such government aid as existed was withdrawn. The Society of Friends also wound down their relief work. As other sources of support dried up, the aid provided by the Church took on greater prominence. The year 1849 was, in fact, nearly as bad as 1847. According to Fr Noone of Castleblakeney, the years 1847 and 1848 were 'years of plenty compared to this year ... The hard-hearted poor-law guardians are all for economy, and this condemns many to coffinless graves;

there is no sympathy from government or relief societies.' Murray, Fr Noone asserts, was their only help, and he offers Mass for him.[30]

As the year commenced, Fr Peter Ward wrote from Partry to thank Synnott and Murray, 'the best of bishops', for the money he had received. He would use it to buy Indian meal and turnips to make soup for the hungry. 'All means are now exhausted', he commented. More than 700 houses in his parish were levelled to the ground. 'The sufferings of the people in the cold of winter are terrible.'[31] From Drumcollogher in Co. Limerick, Fr Patrick Quaide reported, 'In one week I attended between two hundred and three hundred sick calls ... by the ditches, in quarries, in ruined buildings ... in every shape that misery can present itself'.[32]

Not only did the deaths in 1849 approach the record level of 1847, but evictions soared to 90,000, and were to reach 104,000 in 1850. Emigration had reached its highest point yet. Faced with the catastrophe, Prime Minister Russell had no plan. In his diary of 9 February 1849, Charles Greville, secretary to the cabinet, noted, 'All call on the government for a plan and a remedy, but the government have no plan and no remedy; there is nothing but disagreement among them; and while they are discussing and disputing, the masses are dying.'[33] Graham and Clarendon petitioned for aid without success. Russell agreed with Graham that for a solution it was necessary to employ 'large remedies', but a great plan for Ireland would require borrowing and lending which the cabinet was not prepared to accept.[34]

A VISIT FROM QUEEN VICTORIA

In 1849, Lord Lieutenant Clarendon and Prime Minister Russell hoped that a visit from Queen Victoria might be a boost to morale and a symbol of unity among the subjects of the United Kingdom. The Queen had given £2,000 in famine relief in 1847, and had led a national day of prayer and atonement. Archbishop Murray, who normally wrote the hierarchy's addresses, circulated a draft address of welcome to the monarch. Archbishop MacHale, who had immediate experience of the horrors of the famine, rejected it because there was no allusion whatever to the sufferings of the people. When Murray inserted a reference to 'the many woes of our suffering poor' in his address, this was considered quite inadequate. Archbishop Slattery, also closer to the ravages of the famine, was dissatisfied as well, describing Murray's text as 'a milk and water address'. In the event, Murray could persuade only twelve bishops to sign his document. The relevant section of the address, mildly modified, eventually read:

> On an occasion so truly cheering as the present we will not place before

> your Majesty a detail of the many woes of our suffering poor, the thought of which has, we know, pressed already so severely on your Majesty's paternal heart. We wish this to be a visit of unmixed joy to your Majesty, and we hope it may be the forerunner of happier days for Ireland...[35]

The wording was typical of Murray's style in its use of a subtle, gentle approach rather than direct confrontation, even at this time of crisis for so many.

EPISCOPAL ANGER AT THE GOVERNMENT

Meantime, it was clear that, as the famine continued, disillusionment with the government and anger at its neglect had increased amongst the hierarchy. It found frank expression at the national synod in Thurles in 1850. In an 'Address to the Catholic Clergy and Laity' the bishops spoke of their people as frequently 'the victims of the most ruthless oppression that ever disgraced the annals of humanity'. They spoke of the desolating track of the 'Exterminator', as displayed in levelled cottages and roofless abodes, where numerous families had been flung upon the highway to perish in the extremity of want 'without distinction of age or sex, sickness or health'. Turning to the prevailing economic philosophy at work, the bishops asserted:

> One of the worst fruits of the false teaching of the age has been to generate a spirit of contempt, hard heartedness, and hostility to the poor. The Mammon of iniquity, not the Spirit of Christianity, and ... avarice ... not the charity of Jesus Christ, have furnished the principles and maxims by which they have been estimated and ranked in the social scale.[36]

The bishops' forthright criticism infuriated Clarendon and Russell. A few months later, the parliament passed the Ecclesiastical Titles Bill, which condemned as 'papal aggression' Cardinal Wiseman's pastoral letter announcing the setting up of a Catholic hierarchy. On that occasion, the Prime Minister, introducing the bill, shifted the blame from Wiseman's pastoral letter to the Irish bishops' address that excited 'the feelings of the peasant class against those who were owners of the land'. The bill caused consternation and deep upset in Ireland.

MURRAY AND THE ECCLESIASTICAL TITLES BILL

The Ecclesiastical Titles Bill proposed that every deed or writing by a Catholic bishop was void if the name of the see appeared in the document, and that any property devised for a bishop or a dean by the title of his see or deanery was declared forfeit to the crown. Murray wrote to Sir James Graham, the home secretary, that the measure made it extremely difficult for an episcopal Church such as the Catholic Church to function. Graham read Murray's letter in parliament.

Taking the matter a further step, Murray, in a public letter to his clergy, expressed his disappointment at this penal legislation. 'The hand of persecution is about to be once more extended over us', he wrote. He asked for prayers to the Lord of Mercy that he might inspire our rulers to 'execute justice … not for the benefit of a faction, but for the peace and happiness and social welfare of the entire people.' He pointed out that the law worked against the poor, for 'aid was sent to him under the title of bishop' and this could now be confiscated and 'employed by Protestant hands to corrupt the faith'. He ended with a bitter complaint against the government's hypocrisy and ingratitude. 'And this, too,' he wrote, 'is for us called religious freedom, and this is the return which the Catholic clergy are to receive for their efforts in the hour of trial for the preservation of public order.'[37]

As Murray was respected in parliament and was known to many in England for his moderation, his pastoral letter caused a stir. Yet, despite his criticism of the government, Murray remained in friendly contact with Lord Clarendon, to the annoyance of Paul Cullen, who was now archbishop of Armagh.[38] The Archbishop of Dublin was noted for loyalty to his friends. Besides, he knew that Clarendon had strongly argued for effective state intervention during the famine, only to be faced with a cabinet largely dominated by non-interventionists such as Trevelyan and Sir Charles Wood, the chancellor of the exchequer, supported by members reflecting the landlords' interests. He also believed that Clarendon, and to a large degree Russell, sought to improve the situation of Irish Catholics in so far as they could within the political constraints of England and Ireland. The enlargement of the Maynooth grant and the provision of a university plan for Catholics were, in Murray's view, an earnest of this; and he understood their frustration and sense of ingratitude when faced at every turn by the suspicion and hostility of MacHale and Cullen.

THE ACTIVITY OF PROSELYTISERS

One area, however, where all the bishops found common cause was Clarendon's failure to respond to their concern about the activity of Protestant proselytisers. It is in the nature of Christian Churches to wish to expand, but problems arise when unacceptable means are used to promote their message.

The activity of the proselytisers added considerably to the pressure on a clergy already overwhelmed by work and their inability to provide materially for their starving people.

Fr Flannelly, of Ballinakill in Clifden, Co. Galway, complained to Murray on 6 April 1849 about proselytisers, who had plenty of money and were accompanied 'by apostate priests and laics'. 'They go from cabin to cabin,' he charged, 'offering food and money and clothing to the naked and starving on condition of their becoming members of their conventicles.' They 'scatter scurrilous tracts by the thousand and post the same to Roman Catholic clergy … This is far worse than the years of persecution.' Meanwhile, he came face to face with 'fever and dysentery, the sure precursors of cholera … in every hut and cabin', and no medical aid existed in his 'wild and extensive district'. The homeless poor, if they showed any sign of sickness, were thrown out of the workhouses. Half a pound of Indian meal per household per day was the sole food of the poor in his district. 'Men offer to work a whole day for two pints of meal, but cannot get work.' [39]

The famine continued through 1850 before fading the following year. Improved harvests brought essential relief.

THE AFTERMATH

Reviewing those terrible years from 1846 to 1850, and leaving aside the government's failure, the heritage of bitterness it created and the psychological effects of the famine on survivors, certain aspects stand out. Among them are the generosity of people across the world to the Irish people in their time of hunger and helplessness, and the courage and commitment of the Catholic clergy, risking fever and death in support of their people. A few of the clergy seem to have fled the scene, and a handful became 'apostate priests' and worked with the proselytisers, but they were very few. Again, the suffering of vast numbers brought people together from different social and religious backgrounds in order to provide assistance. Bishops, as we have seen, were joined on relief committees by Protestant clergy and laity, and by landlords. Some landlords worked actively for their tenants and, indeed, a small number became bankrupt because of their efforts.

On the negative side, however, many landlords and their agents acted harshly and without humanity, raising rents exorbitantly, evicting tenants and levelling their houses without concern for the suffering and likely deaths of entire families. As often at a time of upheaval, there were also others ready to take advantage of the weak and defenceless, with the greed of merchants being mentioned frequently during those years. There were instances, too, of local politics and avarice leading at times to unfairness in the distribution of aid and of work. Writing to Fr Hamilton on 3 January 1847, Mrs Laura Moore of Moore Hall in Co. Mayo, herself a concerned landlord, complained of clergy in good parishes not contributing generously to the relief funds, and of clergy placing obstacles in the way of her son, who was head of the committee administering three workhouses endeavouring to provide for 10,000 people. Almost a fortnight later, she observed, 'There is frightful jobbery going on; work is given to people who are selling meal and making money, while starving wretches are without work'.[40]

Above all, there was the great loss to Ireland of the hundreds of thousands of its people who were obliged to emigrate. That, in turn, brought long-term benefits to Britain and North America, not only in terms of the Catholic population but also in the social and political contribution the immigrants made to their new homelands.

CONTEMPORARY HAPPENINGS AT HOME AND ABROAD

While the famine raged in Ireland, members of the Young Ireland movement embarked on a short-lived revolution that resulted in exile and long prison sentences for the leaders. Meanwhile, a further bitter contest was taking place over the government plan to provide openings to university colleges for Irish Catholics at Cork and Galway. Once again, the bishops were divided, and Murray found himself under heavy fire.

Of more international concern for the hierarchy was Pope Pius IX's flight from Rome in November 1848. Pio Nono, as he was widely known, found shelter at Gaeta, a papal enclave in Neapolitan territory. The Catholic world rallied with material aid and with strong support for the pope's spiritual authority. Archbishop Murray wrote to the secretary of state, Cardinal Antonelli, on 6 April 1849, expressing sorrow and sympathy with the pope. He explained that the Irish bishops had ordered a collection for His Holiness in every diocese in Ireland. So far, the Dublin collection had realised £2,700. Enclosing a draft for £1,500, he explained that he would forward the remainder when he heard of its safe receipt in Rome.[41]

TOWARDS A DOGMATIC DEFINITION

From Gaeta, on 2 February 1849, the Pope issued an encyclical letter to the whole Church concerning the question of defining the immaculate conception of Mary as an article of faith. It was the age of special devotion to Mary, and a number of Marian apparitions had been recorded. The doctrine of the immaculate conception of Mary – that Mary, because of her role as Mother of God, had been conceived without original sin – was widely accepted by Catholics, and Pope Gregory XVI had actively promoted the doctrine. Pio Nono himself had a deep devotion to Mary, attributing to her his recovery from epilepsy. In May 1849, Murray confirmed that he had received copies of the encyclical and had forwarded duplicates to the other bishops in Ireland.[42] In response to the encyclical and its instruction, Fr Hamilton, on 3 July 1849, sent a circular letter to the parish priests of the archdiocese and to superiors of religious communities in Dublin, asking them to respond to two questions: (a) If they and the members of the faithful believe in the doctrine of the Immaculate Conception; and (b) If they think the Pope should define it as an article of faith.[43]

Sometime later, in a long letter to Cardinal Franzoni, Murray reported that all of the clergy, and many of the laity, had responded to the questions. Devotion to the Blessed Virgin Mary was widespread and sincere. All believed the doctrine of the Immaculate Conception, as did Murray himself. As regards the defining of it as a doctrine of faith, some who were deeply devoted to Our Lady did not consider that it should be defined. Murray outlined four reasons for this point of view:

1. Dogmatic definitions have arisen when there is controversy about a doctrine. There is no controversy in this case. Again, definitions of articles of faith, in the Church's tradition, have been preceded by much theological reflection and discussion. This has not occurred in this case.
2. The doctrine is believed peacefully, and no one attacks it. To disturb a peaceful situation, when there is no necessity to do so, is unwise; especially in the present crisis when people's minds are confused and, in foreign parts and in Italy itself, there is little reverence for the Church and a tendency to limit its powers.
3. It is doubtful that devotion to Mary, already very strong, would be greatly increased by a definition of faith. On the other hand, such a declaration is likely to stir up vigilant critics who may accuse the Church of thinking up a novel doctrine not approved by the Council of Trent.

4. The many Protestants who have been moving towards the Church, seeking refuge there from constantly changing errors, might be pushed away from the Church by this article of faith 'being viewed as something thought up by us'.

'These are some of the reasons', Murray observed, 'which move those who do not think it appropriate to define the doctrine as an article of faith. All the professors of Maynooth College, and the Jesuits in Dublin, are of this opinion.' Murray goes on to say that he knows these men so well, and their fervent devotion to Our Lady, that he 'cannot make light of their opinions and, therefore, cannot add his own voice to those pressing for the declaration'. Nonetheless, he concluded his letter by stating, that the Holy See's decision will be accepted by Murray and those about him with the greatest docility as having been divinely guided.[44]

Meantime, Pope Pius IX had appealed to the Catholic powers to restore the Papal States to him. In July 1849, French troops restored Rome and the territories to the Pope, and in April 1850 he re-entered. Thereafter, he ruled for some twenty years protected by French forces. His exile, and the public criticism of him within Italy and from liberal and anti-Catholic organisations and governments, served but to strengthen the reverence of many Catholics for the Pope's spiritual eminence and their wish that he express it in definitive pronouncements. This support for papal authority and assertiveness within the Church acquired the name 'ultramontanism'. Partly responding to this, perhaps, as well as to his own strong belief, Pope Pius IX, in 1854, proclaimed the Immaculate Conception as an article of faith, solely on his own authority. Four year later, heaven seemed to approve, when the apparition at Lourdes proclaimed herself the Immaculate Conception.[45]

Pio Nono's experiences – his flight from Rome to escape from people who had previously cheered him, his time in exile, and his return to papal territories with the help of a foreign power – all had the effect of changing him. From being a supporter of political and social reform he became abidingly hostile to liberalism and revolution, suspicious of governments supporting such, and especially of governments with an anti-Catholic history. This was to have an impact on Murray's backing of the British government's plan for university education in Ireland. Adding to Murray's problems, moreover, was the fact that the major opponent of the plan was the recently appointed archbishop of Armagh, who had spent most of his life in Rome, who was trusted there, and who was openly ultramontane in his views.

NOTES

1 A. Bourke. '*The Visitation of God'? The Potato and the Great Irish Famine,* ed. J. Hill and C. Ó Gráda (1993), pp.140-9, cit D. A. Kerr. *'A Nation of Beggars'? Priest, People and Politics in Famine Ireland 1846-1852* (Oxford 1994), p.30.
2 Smyth-Murray, 28 Nov. 1845. DDA. Murray Papers, f. 32/2/23.
3 Fr Redmond - Murray, 30 Nov. 1845, idem, f. 32/2/24; Grant - Murray, 30. Nov. 1845, f. 32/2/25.
4 See Kerr, op. cit. pp.34-5, for examples of clergy intervening to halt violence.
5 *The Nation*, 5 Dec. 1846.
6 Idem, 23 Dec. 1846.
7 The *Times*, 22 Sept. 1847; cit. Kerr. op. cit. p.81 note.
8 Madden-Fr Synnott, 5 Feb. 1847, Murray Papers. The Synnott appointed by Dr Murray is presumed by the recipients of aid to be a priest. He is identified by D.A. Kerr, op. cit. p.38 n.13, as Thomas Lambert Synnott (1810-97), high constable for city of Dublin (1842-48), secretary of the Mansion House Committee (for aid), 1845 and for the Indian Relief Fund, 1846, subsequently governor of a female prison. Kerr refer to an unpublished work by B. Cullen. 'Thomas L. Synnott, Famine Relief Secretary and Dublin Prison Governor'.
9 T.P. O'Neill. 'The Catholic Clergy and the Great Famine' in *Reportorium Novum* (1956), pp.461-9.
10 Slattery-Renehan, June 1847. Maynooth College Archives (MCA), Renehan Papers; cit. Kerr. p.41.
11 *Catholic Directory 1848*, p.206. It reproduces the encyclical.
12 21 Oct. 1847, cit idem, pp.238-241.
13 Idem, pp.241-45. *Italics* in text.
14 Idem, p.246.
15 Idem, 23 Oct. 1847, p.245.
16 Murray Papers, 1847-48, references under 'Great Famine' and elsewhere.
17 For Synnott see note 8 above. John/Thomas seem to be the same person.
18 J. Madden-Murray, 5 Feb. 1847; P. Sheehy-Murray 27 March 1847.
19 J. Kirke, Lichfield – Murray, 11 Jan. 1847, f. 32/3/4.
20 Mary Leonora Sheil -Murray, 30 May 1849, f. 32/5/124. Philip Howard, Corby Castle, Carlisle – Murray, 2 Jan. 1849.
21 Fr McCullagh (?) – Murray, 22 April 1848, f. 32/4/104.
22 J. Dwyer-Murray, 1848 (no other date), f. 32/4/105.
23 J. Noone – Synnott, 25 June 1848. Murray Papers, f. 32/4/112.
24 T. Timlin – Murray, 19 Dec. 1848. Idem, f. 32/4/ 124.
25 Ed. Waldron – Murray, 31 Dec.1848; f. 32/4/ 133.
26 D.A.Kerr. *The Catholic Church and the Famine* (Dublin 1996), pp.64-5.
27 DDA. Hamilton Papers (1), 1848, no. 219.
28 Kerr. *Catholic Church and the Famine*, pp.66-7.
29 Cit. J. Prest. *Lord John Russell* (London 1972), p.291.
30 J. Noone – Murray, 1849 (no other date), f. 32/5/ 131.
31 Peter Ward – Synnott, 17 Jan.1849; f. 32/5/ 119.
32 Kerr. op cit. p.71.
33 Idem, p.79.
34 J. Prest. op. cit., pp.293-4.
35 *Catholic Directory, 1850*, p.135.
36 Cit. Kerr. op. cit. pp.77-79.

37 *The Nation*, 22 Feb. 1851.
38 Cullen – B. Smith, vice-rector Irish College, 29-30 July 1851, Smith Papers, Archives of –St. Paul – Outside –the Walls, Rome, cit. Kerr. *A Nation of Beggars*, p.267.
39 Fr Flannelly – Murray, 6 April 1849, f. 32/5/121.
40 Laura Moore – Synnott, 3 Jan. 1847. Hamilton Papers (11), no. 89; and 16 Jan. 1847, no. 93.
41 Murray – Card. Antonelli, 6 April 1849. Murray Papers, f. 32/5/151.
42 Abp. Nice – Murray, 28 May 1849. Murray Papers, f.32/5/ 86.
43 Murray Papers. Circular letter from Hamilton, 3 July 1849, f.32/5/86.
44 Murray Papers. Murray – Card. Franzoni, concerning response to questions re. Immaculate Conception, 1849, no other date and end of letter is missing; f. 32/5/ 161.
45 Eamon Duffy. *Saints and Sinners. A History of the Popes* (Yale U.P. 2014 ed.), pp.292-4.

CHAPTER 13

University Education for Catholics (1845–52)

After the failure of the Repeal movement, the government attempted to placate and win over the Catholic population not only by increasing the grant to Maynooth and passing the Bequests Act, but also by providing university education by means of provincial colleges. As in the case of the Bequests Act, the university measure involved Murray in a principled stand that brought controversy and obloquy.

THE GOVERNMENT'S PLAN

The idea of using provincial colleges to provide third-level education for Irish Catholics is associated with Thomas Wyse, chairman of a Select Committee on Foundation Schools and Education in Ireland, and a member of the Catholic Association. In 1841 he summarised his recommendation in a letter to the chief secretary, Lord Morpeth. Later, Sir Robert Peel offered a plan for tertiary education on not dissimilar lines. He envisaged three university colleges, two for Catholics and one for Presbyterians. A college for Catholics in Dublin University was mooted, but was quickly put aside. Any such development was likely to be strongly opposed by Irish Protestants, while the Irish Catholic bishops, including Murray, viewed any links with Trinity College, the sole college in Dublin University, as a potential danger to Irish Catholic students.[1]

Unlike Wyse's projected colleges, the new government establishments were to be non-denominational, along the lines of the national primary school system. No theology or religion was to be taught in the colleges. At Peel's suggestion, however, lecture rooms were to be made available to enable students to receive religious instruction from clergymen, but with such developments being funded from private endowments. There would be no subsidy from the colleges for such activity.

The bill, as noted earlier, received its first reading on 9 May 1845. The exclusion of theology and religion as part of the measure soon evoked criticism. The Anglican high churchman, Sir Robert Ingles, described it as 'a gigantic scheme of Godless education',[2] a criticism later annexed by Daniel O'Connell in his dismissal of the 'Godless colleges'. As with the bequest issue, the government made the mistake of not discussing a measure designed to benefit Irish Catholics with their spiritual leaders.

The new bill met with an immediate and lively response in Ireland. It was attacked by the *Freeman's Journal* and the O'Connellite *Pilot,* while the *Nation*, the influential organ of the Young Irelanders, gave the principle of the bill an enthusiastic welcome. On the moving of the bill, Dr William Crolly, the Catholic primate, acted quickly. He called a special meeting of the bishops with a view, as Murray informed the new Lord Lieutenant, William Heytesbury, to 'softening asperities and reconciling, if possible, conflicting opinions'.[3] That there would be 'conflicting opinions' was virtually inevitable in a bill which Crolly himself described as 'pregnant with danger to the faith and morals of the youth of the country'.[4]

Despite the short notice, twenty-one prelates attended the meeting. On 23 May, they announced that they could not give their support to the measure as it stood. They were prepared to cooperate, however, on the basis of certain 'fair and reasonable terms'. These terms were presented in a memorial to the Lord Lieutenant by archbishops Crolly, Murray and MacHale, with Bishop Edmund Ffrench of Kilmacduagh and Kilfenora standing in for Dr Slattery. The memorial required that a fair proportion of professors and other office-bearers should be Catholics, that they be appointed by a board of trustees, which included bishops, and that Catholic chaplains should be appointed, paid by the state but removable by the bishops. Catholic professors should be appointed in particular areas which the bishops judged to be occasions of serious danger to the faith of Catholic students: history, logic, metaphysics, moral philosophy, geology and anatomy.[5]

Such demands virtually nullified the policy of non-denominational mixed education. Murray, writing to John Hamilton on 8 June 1845, explained that the memorial 'contains some demands, the concession of which could hardly be hoped for. It was thought by some that we had only to ask, and we would receive. I never thought so'.[6] At the bishops' meeting with Lord Lieutenant Heytesbury, the latter was of the opinion that Crolly, Murray and Ffrench were open to negotiation but not MacHale, who emphasised that the requirements of the memorial were the minimum, and that there could be no cooperation without them.

To Murray's horror, MacHale leaked the text of the memorial to the press, where it was presented as an ultimatum by the corpus of bishops.[7] Murray can scarcely have been surprised by this development. After all, MacHale had earlier challenged Murray for the leadership of the Irish Church over the national education system. In that case, when defeated by a majority, he had appealed to Rome over the heads of his colleagues, before finally bringing the appeal to the country by publishing the differences between the bishops. In the 1840s, MacHale appealed to Rome and to the country again and again. He had little respect for the corporate sense of the hierarchy that Archbishop Troy and Murray had helped to develop. MacHale's action on this occasion, in May 1845, placed the government in a difficult situation. Sir James Graham, the minister concerned, urged Heytesbury, nevertheless, to maintain contact with Murray to see what was 'the real minimum which would satisfy the better portion of his brethren'.[8]

At the second reading of the bill, on 30 May, Graham promised that a fair share of the professors would be Catholics and that proselytism would be guarded against. But he rejected the other three points in the memorial: episcopal involvement in appointments, Catholic chaplains paid by the state, and Catholic lecturers in certain subjects. This was viewed by many as a flat rejection of the prelates' memorial. During the debate in the House of Commons, however, Lord John Russell insisted that the bishops should be recognised as part of the government's plan, especially 'such men as Archbishop Murray – a man no less distinguished for his moderation of opinion than he is by an unswerving fidelity to his own Church'.[9] Despite the varied criticisms of the bill, it passed the second reading by a majority of 311 to 46.

O'CONNELL'S REACTION

A critical factor in Irish attitudes to the bill was O'Connell's decision to come out against it. The government's readiness to make amendments to the measure seemed to him a definite indication that they would yield to the bishops' demands if the bishops only stood firm. To his friend and supporter, P. V. Fitzpatrick, he wrote on 21 June 1845, 'As to the bishops, they have the ball at their foot, literally at their foot. If they hold out firmly on the truest Catholic principles, believe me everything will be conceded … How I wish I could venture to write to Dr Murray. I wish he knew of what pliable materials the present government are made'.[10] That same day, O'Connell wrote to MacHale, one of his closest political allies, in a manner that contributed to the hardening of attitudes. He criticised Graham's amendments as making matters worse, and he assured the archbishop that 'if the prelates take and continued in a high firm and unanimous tone the ministry will yield. Believe me that they are ready to yield … to all the Church's sanctions relative to Catholic education'.[11]

This uncompromising advice, based on a mistaken political calculation, did not make for unity at the subsequent bishops' meeting at Maynooth, where they were gathered on college business. Archbishop MacHale, who was chairman at this time, proposed that they take advantage of the meeting to draw up an address to parliament, along the lines of their May meeting, to be presented as the final decision of the Catholic bishops. According to Paul Cullen, in a letter to Tobias Kirby at the Irish College, Dr Crolly, feeling railroaded by MacHale, protested against such a step, since they were not assembled to discuss politics, and the meeting adjourned in great confusion.[12] According to an account Murray wrote to Heytesbury, when MacHale made his proposal, Murray moved successfully that the discussion about Maynooth affairs should continue. MacHale, much annoyed, then left the chair, and had to be persuaded to return to it. The next day, MacHale's close supporter, Dr John Cantwell, Bishop of Meath, proposed that an early date be fixed for a meeting of the bishops to draw up an address to parliament. Murray then moved that 'there appeared to be no sort of occasion for any meeting of the prelates before the usual time in November, and that that time should be appointed accordingly'. Murray's motion was carried by a 'considerable majority'.[13]

Murray and Crolly were pleased at having foiled MacHale, whose aggressive temperament and the leaking of the May memorial added further to their memory of previous treatment at his hands. Their success, however, prevented any possibility of a united episcopal stand concerning the bill, which would be well passed before their November meeting.

The bill was passed in the Commons by a large majority on 10 July. The government set about establishing sites for the colleges in Cork, Galway and Belfast, and also arranging the employment of staff. At the Belfast college, Dr Shuldham Henry (1801–81) was appointed president, catering for the Presbyterian population. Two Catholics, Professor Robert Kane (1809–90) and Revd Joseph Kirwan (1796– 1849), were appointed presidents of the Cork and Galway colleges respectively.[14]

THE BEQUESTS ACT AGAIN

While the government was working out the administrative details of the colleges, Sir James Graham made a statement in the House of Commons that added to the divisions among Irish prelates and Irish nationalists. It was in connection with the Bequests Act. The Catholic commissioners, he commented, had made representation to him that their duty of determining which ecclesiastics were entitled to the benefits of the bequests was at variance with the canons of their Church.[15] O'Connell seized on this to justify his argument that the bill was uncanonical. At a Repeal meeting, he declared that he had been abused for his humble opinion, but that now it was 'confirmed by those venerable characters themselves, the Most Reverend and always-esteemed Doctor Murray, the Most Reverend Doctor Crolly and the Right Reverend Doctor Denvir'.[16] He hoped that the three prelates would not commit themselves any longer to the exercise of an uncanonical power. Murray expressed annoyance with Graham, who, he observed to Hamilton, 'has completely bungled the Bequests affair'.[17]

To salvage the situation, Murray wrote a public letter to O'Connell. He proposed that 'the minister (Graham) must have alluded to objections which had been urged by opponents of the act – objections which, in the opinion of the commissioner prelates had no solid foundation … but which they thought right to bring under the notice of the government, in the hope that every pretext … would be … taken away'. Murray assured O'Connell, in a gentle remonstrance, of his determination 'to persevere as a member of the board with the sole view of serving the poor and of protecting the interests of the Church'.[18]

The fact that Murray stood up to the mighty O'Connell drew congratulations from his colleagues of the minority party, who had previously experienced rough treatment from O'Connell and MacHale. Dr Crolly, on 3 August, trusted that O'Connell would now realise 'that we are not disposed to submit to his insolent dictation'.[19] Dr Kennedy, of Killaloe, praised the gentleness of the well-deserved rebuke, and wondered if the archbishop of Tuam would now come forth 'with some bold and reckless declamation'.[20] On the other hand, the strongly nationalist Fr Peter Cooper, of the Dublin archdiocese, urged O'Connell to take on the archbishop and not to allow the vigour of his reply to be checked 'by any sense of respect for the person'.[21] O'Connell did not take Cooper's advice.

CONFLICTING VOICES

In Rome, meantime, Tobias Kirby was rallying support against the 'Godless colleges'. Among those he contacted was Cardinal Franzoni, prefect of Propaganda and the person in charge of the affairs of the Irish Church. In Ireland, Kirby's rector, Paul Cullen, was busy endeavouring to win over the more moderate prelates to oppose the government's bill and to appeal to Rome for judgement on it. He found a key figure to oppose the measure in Dr Michael Slattery, archbishop of Cashel. Slattery had been a student at Trinity College, and his fears about the danger to Catholic belief in the government's colleges owed much, it appears, to his experience at Trinity.

The Irish bishops met for their annual meeting on 18 November. They were to consider, among other matters, the question of the Queen's Colleges. Many of the bishops, as mentioned, were fearful that the colleges would propagate infidelity and O'Connell played on this fear. While the bishops were meeting in Dublin, O'Connell, at a public meeting in the city, called on the people of Ireland 'from the Giant's Causeway to Cape Clear' to 'rally round the majority of their prelates'.[22] Crolly, Murray and the other bishops on the minority side complained to Rome of this unfair pressure on the freedom of the members of the conference; because of O'Connell 'our consultations could scarcely be called free'.[23]

On 23 November, as the bishops were still meeting, Cardinal Franzoni sent a letter to Murray, in which he enquired of him if the government's changes were of such a nature that young Catholics could take part in such a system without risk to their faith and morals.[24] Murray replied on 11 December 1845. The government's amendments were good for Catholics who would be attending the colleges. As to the danger to faith and morals, 'time will tell and the bishops will be vigilant'. He assured Franzoni that the government did not intend to oppose Catholicism through the colleges. Religious instruction would be left to the clergy of each denomination. Professors would be from all religions, since the students came from all religions. Some professors would be Catholics. There would be precautions against proselytism and irreligious teaching. 'Three colleges are being built', Murray continued. 'They will be ready by about 1848. When they are ready and the professors are appointed, and statutes published and the halls of residence completed for Roman Catholic students, and regulations for them made known, then we'll see whether the amendments to the act are sufficient to render the system safe. If not, we can then take measures to warn our flocks against them. Meanwhile, I think it wise to wait until the principles of the new system are more developed.'[25]

THE DUBLIN MEETING

What took place at the bishops' Dublin conference in November 1845 was largely kept secret. Eighteen out of twenty-seven bishops attended. It appears that the voting on the colleges resulted in twelve opposing the government's plan and six supporting it. The minority prelates were Crolly, Murray and Denvir, together with Ryan of Limerick, McGettigan of Raphoe, and Browne of Kilmore. All agreed, however, on making a submission to Rome. The British government concurred with the appeal to Rome, feeling that the Pope would regard the British government with more favour than he would MacHale.[26]

The case for the majority of bishops seems to have been drafted largely by Dr Slattery of Cashel. It made the criticism that although the government's measure was said to be for the benefit of Catholics, the government had not consulted the Catholics' spiritual leaders beforehand, nor had their reasoned pleas been listened to after the bill had been introduced in parliament. Furthermore, the Catholics were not being offered equal treatment with their Protestant contemporaries, even though they constituted the vast bulk of the population. As regards the government's motives behind their academic colleges, they were part of their on-going attempt to destroy the Catholic religion, and an encroachment on the rights of the Catholic Church.

The minority bishops' statement singled out O'Connell and MacHale for criticism, the former for bringing public pressure to bear on the bishops' meeting, and MacHale for causing dissension within the episcopate. The minority report questioned how those opposing the government could reconcile their actions with Propaganda's rescript enjoining obedience to the civil power. The report then focused on its main argument, the parallel between the present system and that of the national system of education. The latter had been denounced by Dr MacHale as dangerous to faith and morals, but it had not proved so and was an acknowledged success. The new colleges were founded on similar principles. The government, besides, had demonstrated its good faith by its recent generous grant to Maynooth, and by its appointments of Catholics as presidents of Cork and Galway. The government, indeed, was anxious 'to remove completely all our doubts concerning dangers to faith and morals'.

Trust in Peel's government was the pivotal difference between the two sides. A majority did not have that trust, and the clamorous outcry in the press and among a large part of the population, due to the efforts of the revered O'Connell, made trust more difficult. There was also the fact that many bishops saw little need for university education. The great mass of their populations were poor and with, at most, some primary education. Those likely to avail of higher education – the well-to-do middle class – were, as Bishop Cantwell of Meath observed to O'Connell, 'not always the most amenable to the salutary influence of the clergy. They are more selfish and less religious than the poor'.[27]

THE FIRST VERDICT FROM PROPAGANDA

Slattery and MacHale bombarded Rome with letters, and they promptly forwarded the result of a petition against the colleges that was published by the *Freeman's Journal*, 12 February 1846. The petition was signed by 1,626 priests from nineteen dioceses. At the same time, Cullen and his fervid assistant director, Tobias Kirby, used all their relevant contacts to build up opposition to the government's scheme. Cullen, in the process, appears to have used misleading, if not deliberately false, information to undermine prominent supporters of the colleges.[28]

A congregation of cardinals was appointed to examine the scheme. As usual, they appointed two consultors to study the submissions, provide summaries and offer their opinions. The two men appointed were Monsignor Giovanni Carboli-Bussi, secretary of the College of Cardinals, and Paul Cullen – surely a strange appointment because of his partisan views. During their deliberations, Pope Gregory, who had such a high regard for Murray and who had occasion to censure Cullen, died suddenly on 1 June 1846. Carboli-Bussi favoured a solution similar to that arrived at in the case of the national schools, while Cullen, showing greater acquaintance with the Irish scene, argued strongly about the dangers to faith presented by the university colleges and the fact that people and clergy and a majority of bishops were opposed to them.[29]

Some six weeks later, 13 July 1846, the congregation issued their verdict. They considered it their duty, they declared, to warn the venerable Irish prelates not to take any part in implementing such a scheme of education. They also expressed regret that some bishops had entered into negotiations with the government; and they urged the bishops generally to set up their own colleges and – following, it seems, a suggestion from Cullen – they pointed to the example of the bishops of Belgium in founding the University of Louvain.[30] The new pope, Pius IX, however, decided to make no decision for a year.

THE DEATH OF O'CONNELL

Meantime, in August 1846, the British government, through the lord lieutenant, offered Murray a position on the Privy Council of Ireland. On 30 August, Murray expressed his gratitude for the honour but felt that 'after serious consideration' he must decline, as he could serve Church and state better in his present condition than if he were to accept this new responsibility. He assured his Excellency that he would always cooperate with whatever was for the good of the country.[31]

During the pope's year of deferred decision, Murray and Crolly continued their appeal to Rome. Murray wrote to Cardinal Franzoni, through Cullen. The latter replied to Murray on 12 October 1846 saying that he had passed on his letter to the cardinal. Cullen thought that the modifications suggested by Murray seemed important, and that some control over the appointment of professors seemed necessary. He instanced a situation in France where pantheism was taught, and the Church was powerless to interfere. There was not a word from Cullen about his own strong views and his campaign against the government colleges.[32]

While the Irish bishops made their case and waited for the papal decision, Daniel O'Connell's health declined. A sick man, he determined to visit Rome, but didn't succeed. On the way, he died at Genoa, on 15 May 1847. The most renowned Irishman of his time, his death was mourned not only in Ireland but in Rome and across Europe. His massive funeral took place in Dublin on 5 August 1847. Archbishop Murray presided at the obsequies, office and high Mass, all of which were conducted with great solemnity. His passing added a final penumbra to the cruel famine year of 'Black '47'.

ROME'S RESPONSE

On the question of the colleges in Ireland, Cardinal Franzoni, on 9 October 1847, confirmed Propaganda's former verdict against the colleges. They were declared 'harmful to religion', and the archbishops and bishops were admonished 'to take no part in them'. The document, approved by the pope, went on to say, however, that the congregation was ready to hear further representation so that the matter might be fairly judged.[33]

Murray, in the meantime, had negotiated with the lord lieutenant for further amendments regarding the operation of the colleges and changes in their statutes, and he and Crolly also had won over a number of bishops to their side. A draft letter in Murray's hand, dated 3 November 1847, has 'the Archbishops and Bishops of Ireland' responding to Cardinal Franzoni's letter of 9 October, and informing the cardinal that Propaganda was not correctly or fully informed about the new colleges. The letter referred Franzoni to Murray's letter of 11 December 1845, and then went on to explain the current position on the colleges.[34]

Crolly, in conjunction with Murray, wrote to Franzoni on 5 November. He promised obedience to the rescript, but indicated that he did not consider it a final and irrevocable judgement. He went on to point to the weakness in Rome's position. The cardinals were much concerned with the way education had been secularised in France, the German States and Prussia, and they tended to see the situation in Britain and Ireland in the same light. They viewed the way forward as lying with the extension of Catholic colleges and the erection of a Catholic university on the Belgian model.

As regards the Irish scene, Propoganda were confused about the nature of the educational system and of the government's university colleges, and about the virtual impossibility of finding resources among the Catholics of Ireland to build, support and staff a Catholic University. There was no doubt in the government's mind that the colleges were in fact, if not in name, universities. The Roman authorities, however, did not perceive the clear distinction in the British system between tertiary and secondary education, between university and secondary colleges, and between seminaries and universities. The Irish bishops had secondary schools or colleges which were primarily geared towards preparing students for seminaries. In the seminaries, the rules and disciplines obtaining were not accommodated to a university–style education.[35]

In the minds of most Irish bishops, there had to be a sad irony and sense of unreality about Rome issuing a rescript calling for a Catholic university in 1847. It was a time when the struggle for survival against famine and disease took priority over everything else. Indeed, on 25 October, a fortnight after Franzoni's letter, Crolly, Murray, MacHale and Bishop Kennedy of Killaloe led a deputation from the hierarchy to the lord lieutenant seeking relief measures.

SUPPORT FOR AND OPPOSITION TO THE COLLEGES

On 12 November, again presumably in conjunction with Murray, Crolly and several other bishops – Limerick, Kilmore, Raphoe, Kildare and Leighlin, Killaloe, Down and Connor, Cork, and Kerry – wrote to Franzoni and Propaganda. They were most ready to obey His Holiness's rescript on the provincial colleges being built by the British government in Ireland, but they considered that the character of those colleges had not been fully explained to Propaganda. They then set out the rules composed for the safeguarding of the students' faith and morals, rules which the bishops considered satisfactory. The writers warned that 'if the colleges are forbidden to the Catholic students, these will return to the former practise of attending Protestant and Presbyterian colleges, with none of the aforementioned safeguards'. Again, if the colleges were banned, the bishops feared that the students would just ignore the ban. Finally, they explained that as they, the bishops, were unable to pay for the education of the poor, they accepted the help of the British government for that purpose. Rome would understand that they, the bishops, were unable to build and endow colleges.[36]

Meanwhile, the new colleges continued to face huge opposition at home. On the reception of the Roman rescript, an exultant MacHale assured Franzoni that it had been received with euphoria in Ireland, and that already a few pious Catholics had contributed a not insignificant sum towards a Catholic university. The *Freeman's Journal*, on 23 October 1847, echoed these views with hyperbole as it welcomed the rescript: 'Rejoice Catholic Ireland,' it read, 'your dearest treasure … your glorious ancient faith is safe.' The steep hill that Murray, Crolly and their episcopal supporters had to climb was further indicated by the *Freeman's Journal*, as it summed up the Catholic and national consensus by announcing that a scheme that afforded no adequate guarantee against the corruption of faith and morals, that secured no religious instruction for any class, that took away the Catholic youth from the control of their divinely appointed guardians, that transferred the parent's natural right to a stranger, that tended to denationalize by leaving the professors dependent on the caprice of the minister of the day, and that was modelled on systems which filled France and Prussia with infidelity, was deservedly condemned by the people, priests and bishops of the Irish Catholic Church and by the supreme head – the Sovereign Pontiff.

Murray, nevertheless, assuming that there was still scope for change on the part of the Holy See and, anxious to remove some of the above grounds for criticism, continued to press the government for revisions in the statutes of the colleges. On 19 April 1848, George William Frederick, 4th Earl of Clarendon and the Lord Lieutenant, apologised for the delay in achieving Murray's requests. Nevertheless, he enclosed some extracts concerning professors, students and religious matters, and added that the official visitors of the colleges would include archbishops and bishops.[37]

AN UNFAVOURABLE TIME

Two days previously, on 17 April, Murray had written to Pius IX recommending Dr John Ennis to him. Ennis, who had previously been sent to represent Murray's views regarding national education, was being sent once again to convey Murray's position on the colleges and to counter the strong propaganda coming from the opponents of the government. Unfortunately, it was not a propitious time to make representations to the pope. It was the year of revolutions, and the Papal States were affected. Within a fortnight, on 1 May 1848, the Catholic clergy and faithful of Dublin were urged to pray for His Holiness; and in a pastoral letter, on 24 May, Murray asked prayers for the Pope, who was 'now virtually a prisoner in his palace'.[38] On 24 November, Pope Pius was to be obliged to flee to Gaeta in the Kingdom of Naples, following the assassination of his chief minister, Pellegrino Rossi.

A FINAL DECISION FROM ROME?

The efforts to win recognition for the colleges proved of little avail. On 11 October 1848, Cardinal Franzoni wrote to Murray that Propaganda had considered the extracts from the statutes of the new colleges, but remained doubtful as regards the force they might have in the future. Hence, they were obliged to repeat the Pope's decision of 9 October 1847. They did not despair of the possibility of erecting a Catholic university, however, and they urged that every effort be made to achieve this end. Their document was to be circulated to all the Irish prelates, and everything possible was to be done to maintain unity among the bishops.

In a further letter on the same date, Franzoni assured Murray that Fr Ennis had conveyed Murray's views concerning the colleges to the Pope and to Propaganda. He also brought letters from Irish bishops, and other relevant documents. Murray was urged – whatever his previous opinions may have been – to take every care to implement the decision and to foster unity.[39] Franzoni's letters were a body blow to Murray. Sir Thomas Redington, the undersecretary at Dublin Castle, who was a Catholic, met Murray on 5 November, and reported that he found him in very low spirits, much afflicted by the Roman decision.[40]

It was 30 December 1848 before Murray responded, at some length, to Franzoni. He completely accepted, he said, Propaganda's letter of 11 October expressing the Pope's wishes and he would take no part in implementing the government's law erecting the new colleges in Cork, Galway and Belfast, despite his belief that they would be useful and suitable in the prevailing circumstances in Ireland. He then went on to clarify this. None of the new colleges were in Dublin. There, Trinity College, the only university, was Protestant, and Catholics who had flocked there to obtain qualifications in law, medicine etc. had frequently lost their faith. He, Murray, had hoped that the new colleges would in great measure obviate the necessity of Catholic boys going to Trinity College. He then outlined the precautions he, and those of his opinion, had succeeded in obtaining. On the issue of a Catholic University, he saw 'absolutely no hope of erecting a Catholic University in the foreseeable future'. Murray concluded his letter by explaining that his actions in this whole matter were what he, in conscience, believed were for the best; and that was why he had set out all the circumstances clearly for consideration by the pope and Propaganda. Now, however, 'having fulfilled his duty, he acquiesced with all his heart to the decree of 11 October 1848'.[41]

On the same date, in a letter to Cullen, Murray emphasised for his benefit some of the effects of the Papal decision. Referring to the colleges and the letter he had received from Rome, he expressed his regret that the Holy See had seen fit to repudiate the whole system. 'The result of that repudiation is that' – as he had feared – 'a Protestant professor of history has been appointed; also Catholic youths are flocking to Trinity, even O'Connell's grandchildren.'[42]

The government, meanwhile, had opened the Queen's Colleges. Catholic presidents, as noted, were appointed for Cork and Galway, and several Catholic clergymen and a considerable number of Catholic laity took up positions in the new establishments. The bishops who had supported the colleges accepted the papal decision as applying to themselves but not to the clergy and laity who proposed to take office in or attend the colleges. Matters stood thus until 1850.

CULLEN AS ARCHBISHOP OF ARMAGH

In April 1849, Archbishop Crolly died suddenly. He and Murray were of one mind on many things, and they were similar in character and style of government. As Bishop James Browne of Kilmore, a close friend of Crolly's, commented, 'poor Dr Murray's heart will be scarcely able to bear the shock'.[43] Meantime, Church procedures for a replacement were set in train, and three names were forwarded to Rome, as was customary. On 20 December 1849, Giacomo Filippo Franzoni, the prefect of Propaganda, reported to the secretary of Propaganda, Alessandro Barnabo, that he had had a long session with the Pope the previous day, the appointment to Armagh being the one that outweighed all others. He explained that the Pope and he had discussed the candidates who had been formally proposed but that the Pope 'in his wisdom has chosen instead Dr Cullen, who he hopes will be acceptable to all parties and reunite the Irish Church'.[44]

Cullen had been in Rome for some thirty years, from the age of seventeen. He had absorbed the Vatican vision of the Church and had made a favourable impression as a lecturer and then as rector of the Irish College. Ultramontane in outlook, capable and single-minded, if limited in vision, he had little first-hand experience of Church life in Ireland. He came to Armagh determined to carry out the Pope's wishes to reform and reunite the Irish Catholic Church. To that end, he decided on an Irish national synod, the first since the seventeenth century. Rome appointed him apostolic delegate to the synod, which greatly enhanced his status. The synod was held in Thurles, Co. Tipperary, from August to September 1850.

THE SYNOD OF THURLES

In its first week, as the Irish Church attempted to conform to the Counter-Reformation model, the synod dealt with religious reform. The duties of bishops, parish priests and curates were carefully set out. Much time and attention was given to faith, its preservation and the danger from proselytisers. The most contentious issue was the Queen's Colleges and the effort to arrive at an agreed policy, which was Cullen's very reason for the synod. He tried to pre-empt discussion and disagreement by declaring that the bishops' task was merely to accept the Roman rescripts, since they could not change what the pope had ratified. He was quickly disabused, however. The bishops supporting the provincial colleges had gathered in Dublin prior to the synod. There was a full discussion.[45]

To Dr Cullen's argument of the dangers to youth inherent in the colleges, Bishop Browne of Kilmore replied that every college had certain dangers. Dr O'Donnell of Galway claimed that those in charge of the new colleges were honourable men on whom they could rely. Others pointed out that the colleges would provide the Catholic community with the opportunity of higher education, which the bishops could not provide. One prelate expressed the fear that the condemnation of the colleges might lead to a schism. Murray, even though his own diocese of more than 400,000 Catholics would not directly benefit from the new colleges, spearheaded the support for the new establishments. He suggested that Rome did not understand the current situation in Ireland, and that the bishops should adopt the same attitude as they had done in 1816, when they successfully challenged the letter of Cardinal Litta, purporting to be from the Pope, recommending the veto.[46]

Cullen was taken aback by the strength of the opposition, but he argued his case vigorously, reminding his fellow bishops that they were opposing the decisions of the Holy Father. He managed to get all to agree to a general condemnation of the colleges. The debate came to a collision point, however, on two further motions put forward by Cullen. The first forbade clerics, under pain of *ipso facto* suspension, from accepting office in the colleges. The bishops were evenly divided on this, and it was the Abbot of the Cistercian abbey of Mount Melleray who broke the stalemate when he voted for the motion. The second motion required that parents should reject and avoid the colleges, because of the grave and intrinsic dangers to the faith and morals of the Catholic students. This was carried by sixteen votes to twelve.

The increase in the number of those supporting the colleges, despite the government's neglect and failure during the famine, and the vigour with which they presented their case, surprised and upset Cullen. In 1845 only eight bishops voted for the colleges; now there were thirteen. These included one new prelate, and four who had had a change of heart. A factor in bringing about this change was the government's willingness to adapt the statutes of the colleges; but perhaps the most persuasive of all factors was the person, the commitment and reputation of Murray. A year later, Bishop Timothy Murphy of Cloyne, a strong supporter of Cullen, commented to Cullen that 'there is a prestige and act about the name of Dr Murray in this country, that will for a while counteract and even neutralise the beneficent recommendation of Pio Nono!'[47] The disparaging implication that Murray was disloyal to the pope could not conceal the acknowledgement of Murray's special standing in Ireland. It was a standing that Cullen felt it necessary to undermine.

Although opposed on the colleges by the other three archbishops, Murray retained the support of almost half the total number of bishops. Many influential priests in Maynooth and elsewhere took the same line, and many middle-class Catholics welcomed the inexpensive university education offered by the Queen's Colleges. This was true of Dublin, but also of Galway and especially Cork, with its estimated population of over 100,000. Cork Catholics had been among the first to press for university education, and they were pleased with the offer of a college for their city. Their bishop, William Delaney, sided with Murray, as did Laurence O'Donnell of Galway. That city's leading citizens welcomed the college, and its bishop was the first to break ranks within the Connaught hierarchy, despite continuous pressure from MacHale.[48]

Cullen was very conscious of how narrow his victory had been at Thurles. Writing some months later, on 7 December 1850, to Bernard Smith, the vice-rector of the Irish College in Rome, he commented:

> When the colleges question was first broached, Dr Murray spoke with as much confidence as if he were sure of putting all opposition down. *Era un vero miracolo* [it was a real miracle] that he did not succeed. If he had a majority of one, the authority of the Holy See would have been exploded.

Apart from his exaggerated view of the fragility of the Holy See, Cullen's picture of the confrontation at Thurles suggests that the venerable and experienced archbishop of Dublin had tried to impose his personality and standing on the new and inexperienced archbishop of Armagh. If this were so, he found that Cullen was made of sturdy material and unflinching purpose.[49]

In his address at the close of the synod, Cullen sought to copper-fasten his case regarding the Queen's Colleges by calling on the authority of the 'Successor of Peter':

> All controversy is now at an end – the judge has spoken, the question is decided. Recognising, with reverence and awe, in that decision the voice of him who said, 'He who hears you me' … this synod has received not only with profound respect but unanimous acclamation the decisions which were asked for in the name of the Irish Church.

The address came out strongly against proselytism, in defence of the poor and in criticism of landlords evicting tenants, and was assented to by all the hierarchy. Cullen soon found, nevertheless, that the colleges' question was still not fully decided. At the end of the synod, the bishops of the minority view appealed the contentious part of the proposed synodical legislation to Rome, pointing out the damage this legislation would effect.[50]

AN APPEAL TO ROME AGAINST ROME?

This formal appeal of the bishops reflects a notable aspect of the Irish Catholic Church before the Romanisation and ultramontanism brought in by Pope Pius IX and Archbishop Cullen. Professor Emmet Larkin put it succinctly if strongly: 'Because of the special nature of the episcopal office, a bishop derived, through God's grace, his spiritual authority and teaching responsibility by virtue of his apostolic succession, directly from Jesus Christ and not from his brother bishops, or even from the pope.' Professor Larkin explained further:

> The minority, and even the majority, among the Irish bishops did not consider themselves bound by a majority vote of their colleagues in their differences over both the educational question and other issues raised by British legislation affecting the Irish Church. They refused either to remain silent while the matter was being considered by Rome, or to accept loyally and without reservation the Roman decision when it finally came.[51]

One might add, however, that such was true until the bishops were sure that the Roman decision emanated from the pope fully informed and not just from officials, and that the matter was one of doctrinal import.

Archbishop Murray greatly respected the papacy all through his life, and he would never dream of challenging the pope on a matter of doctrine. The issue of the colleges, however, whether or not they would endanger the faith of Catholic youth, was not a matter of doctrine, but of practical judgement. As a young bishop he had negotiated in Rome on the question of the veto, and had seen the Holy See change its position. He had also seen the decision against the national education system reversed. He hoped for something similar with respect to the Queen's Colleges. It was far from being a vain hope. The British government was endeavouring to use its influence in Rome also, and quite apart from that there was the view held by many and expressed by the redoubtable John O'Sullivan, Archdeacon of Kerry, who assured Corry Connellen, the private secretary of Lord Lieutenant Clarendon, that the Pope 'will never over-rule the opinion of so large and respected minority' of bishops.[52]

UNFORTUNATE PUBLICITY

To strengthen their case, it seems, someone connected with the minority contacted the *Dublin Evening Post.* An anonymous 'memorandum' appeared in that paper on 21 September 1850, claiming that many bishops 'were averse to any publication from the synod regarding the Queen's Colleges, apart from the rescripts, until certain points … should have been submitted to the final judgement of His Holiness.' It further revealed that on some points the views of the bishops were so finely balanced that there was but a majority of one vote between them. As regards the synodical address, the memorandum stated that it contained statements of which many bishops disapproved.

Further publicity occurred in the form of a public letter to Archbishop Murray. On 30 September 1850, John R. Corballis, a Dublin solicitor, commissioner on the Board of National Education and an old friend of Murray, issued a public letter addressed to the archbishop, asking if Catholic parents were now forbidden to send their sons to the Queen's Colleges, even though for over fifty years they had been permitted to send their children to Trinity College. Murray replied that a petition signed by thirteen bishops had been sent to the Pope asking him to refuse his sanction 'to certain proposals on points yet undecided relative to the subject of academic education'.[53]

The anti-college majority were infuriated at what had occurred. MacHale, Slattery, Cantwell, Murphy of Cloyne, and Kelly (coadjutor in Derry), as well as Cullen, wrote separate complaints to Kirby, now head of the Irish College, who duly forwarded their grievance to the Congregation of Propaganda.[54] Cullen placed the blame for this setback, as he saw it, squarely on Murray. In a letter to Propaganda on 8 October, he overstated his case, writing as if Murray and his supporting prelates were mere minions of the government. 'The real question to be decided', he declared, 'is whether one ought or ought not obey the decisions of the Holy See; whether the pope ought to rule the Church in Ireland through the majority of the bishops, or, whether, on the other hand, the

English government ought to rule it by means of the archbishop of Dublin.'[55]

Murray's prospects were greatly weakened not only by the activity of Kirby and Smith in Rome and Cullen's contacts there, but also by the publicity in the press and the very personality and outlook of Pius IX.

THE PAPACY OF PIUS IX

Following the revolution in the Vatican States and his having to flee Rome, Pope Pius IX became increasingly concerned about his control as supreme pontiff. On his re-instatement in the Papal States, centralisation of authority in Rome and uniformity in Church affairs became marks of his rule. In the process, the authority and independence of local hierarchies were eroded and, as one author expressed it, 'bishops were increasingly thought of as junior officers in the pope's army, links in the line of command which bound every Catholic in obedience to the one real bishop, the Bishop of Rome.'[56] Murray was to experience the early marks of this development, which would become largely effective in Ireland under Cullen as his successor.

It appears, however, had Murray known it, that the Pope already had a pre-disposition against colleges under lay control, let alone dependent on a non-Catholic government. According to R. B. Lyons, the able unofficial representative of the British government in Rome, who informed his superiors in 1856, Pius IX had always been disapproving of all systems 'in which religious and general education are separated', and he 'invariably claimed for the clergy, the right of superintending all instruction whatever'. He often expressed these views in respect of the educational systems of foreign countries. 'Even in the early liberal days of his reign, he never admitted the right of the laity in his own dominions to a voice in questions of education … To the Church and its Apostles, its Divine Founder has committed the great right and duty of teaching.'[57]

Adding further to the weight of opposition to Murray were the facts that Cardinal Franzoni, prefect of Propaganda, was a mentor and protector of Cullen, as also, in turn, was Cardinal Barnabo. The Pope, moreover, felt indebted to Cullen for staying on in Rome in 1848, assuming rectorship of the College of Propaganda, which was in danger of being closed by the republican government, and providing asylum in the Irish College for cardinals and priests proscribed by the government.

OPPOSITION IN PROPAGANDA

Against that background, there was not much sympathy in Rome for Murray's reputation or for his appeal against the decisions of the Thurles synod. At the beginning of 1850, Murray wrote to His Holiness and to Cardinal Franzoni complaining about pamphlets defamatory of him that had been printed in Rome and circulated there, in Paris and in Ireland. Franzoni replied on 14 February from Naples, where the Pope and curia had sought refuge. He had presented Murray's letter to the Pope. Franzoni deplored the writings mentioned by Murray and insisted that they were published without his knowledge, and were more likely to cause dissension than to serve the truth. This, too, was the opinion of His Holiness.[58] Following this unsatisfactory reply, Murray wrote on the same matter to Cardinal Barnabo, secretary of Propaganda, on 23 March.[59] There is no record of Barnabo's reply. There is no doubt, however, about his reply to the September letter of Murray and the bishops on the Queen's Colleges.

Cardinal Barnabo replied on 7 October 1850. In his letter he declared that he had read the letter of the bishops, which included the mention of the rescripts being read at the synod and placed among its acts. He was also aware of the published but anonymous memorandum dealing with events during the synod, which Fr Kirby had translated into Italian. Barnabo then commented pointedly that he was sure the rescripts 'were read with the respect due documents from the Holy See'. He continued:

> It is intolerable that some act as though it were necessary to await the Holy See's decision and behave as if the question of the Queen's Colleges were not yet decided. It is displeasing that certain newspapers publish articles on differences of opinion during the synod's deliberations. The actions of bishops not in accordance with the wishes of the Holy See should be covered with complete silence.[60]

Murray, very conscious of the concern about the colleges in his own diocese as well as in Cork and Galway, responded quietly that he hoped His Holiness would not endanger religion and cause schism among Catholics by confirming the synod's decrees.[61]

THE POPE'S ANGER

Pope Pius IX, however, appears to have been deeply angered by Murray's behaviour. In the presence of Kirby and Fr Miles Gaffney – one of Murray's priests and dean of students at Maynooth – the Pope launched into an extraordinary outburst against a venerable and greatly respected archbishop, who had for so long been helpful to Propaganda. Kirby, a hostile critic of Murray, gave his account of the astonishing interview to Archbishop MacHale, on 2 November 1850:[62]

> His Holiness asked Gaffney whether he was in Ireland at the celebration of the synod, and then quickly passed on to speak of the late disedification given in the newspapers. He reprobated in the strongest and most indignant terms the conduct of a certain archbishop, whose name he did not even suppress; and after many more severe remarks, characterised his conduct as truly scandalous: *c'etait un vrai scandale* … the tone and language of the Holy Father awed me in the extreme. I can never forget it.

Confirmation of the Pope's attitude was provided by John Talbot, Earl of Shrewsbury, who was taken aback by the Pope's reaction after he himself had praised Murray. 'Yes,' said the Holy Father, 'he professes to submit but yet ever tries to divert the Holy See from its decisions.' Pius did not want the Church's differences made public, and expected Murray to accept Rome's decisions without question.[63]

MURRAY AND THE CATHOLIC UNIVERSITY

Murray's response to the project of a Catholic university provided his opponents with further grounds for complaint to Rome. He considered the project unrealistic, yet he allowed himself to be persuaded by Cullen, during the synod, to join the university committee.

A major problem for the university project was funding, which was planned to be independent of the government. The university committee had set aside Sunday 16 March for a nationwide St Patrick's Day collection at the church doors. Murray, in reply to a query from one of his priests, declared that 'he would have nothing to do with such a collection'. When his curate in Marlborough Street, Canon Peter Cooper, a secretary to the university committee and a frequent critic of the archbishop, announced that a collection would be made, Murray, quite annoyed, took the unusual step of writing to the *Freeman's Journal,* denying that he gave any order for a collection. He added, characteristically leaving an opening for differences of opinion, that 'each parish priest, however, keeping in view the state of his parish, will act in this case as his own judgement will direct'.[64] In a letter to his administrator and secretary, John Hamilton, he applauded those who voluntarily subscribed to the establishment of so useful an institution as a Catholic university, but 'in the present impoverished state of our city, while our charitable institutions of prime necessity are … languishing for want of adequate support … I could not bring myself to call on the poor labourer and the struggling shopkeeper for a collection at the entrance of their place of worship for the establishment of an institution, which many think of doubtful possibility, and which, if attainable, ought, they think, to be procured by other means'.[65]

The following day, 13 March 1851, Hamilton placed an advertisement in the *Freeman's Journal* stating that 'there is no authority for any other Door-collection of the Metropolitan Church on Sunday … than the usual Door-collection devoted to Church purposes'. On 14 March, an angry Cooper replied in the same newspaper, blaming the archbishop and Fr Ennis. He was wrong in doing so, but Murray, in departing from the public line taken by his colleagues and allowing the dispute to get into print, gave his opponents another occasion to criticise him. Cullen denounced him to Kirby, knowing that the criticism would be passed on to a higher authority.[66] Cullen was deeply embarrassed, however, when three of the bishops in his own province – Browne of Kilmore, Denvir of Down and Connor, and Blake of Dromore – refused to take up a collection for the university on the grounds that they had other heavy demands.[67]

Murray's lack of support for the Catholic university was also linked to Cullen's critical attitude to Maynooth. Murray feared that a Catholic university would be detrimental to Maynooth. The Catholic University at Louvain catered for Catholic clerical students, as Murray knew. Would the Irish model try to do the same? If it did, it would be in open defiance of the government, possibly leading to the withdrawal of the Maynooth grant. Such a move would, in turn, undermine the vital priority of training 500 priests for the Irish mission.

Murray exchanged letters with Cullen during November 1851. On 22 November, in a forthright response, he thanked Cullen for his letter of the twentieth, but stated that it had not allayed his fears for the national seminary; neither had it proved that 'the proposed university should be considered as a necessary link to bind our Episcopal Body to the Holy See.' Murray continued:

> The Pope has expressed the satisfaction he would feel at finding a Catholic University established in Ireland, if such a blessing could be procured. So would we all. But His Holiness has wisely issued no order on the subject; and he would be still more disinclined to do so, were he aware of the heavy calamity which the fruitless attempt at such a measure would be likely to draw down on our Church.

As to Cullen's use of a text from St John on unity, Murray viewed it 'inapplicable to the present case. We are *One* in everything that requires oneness; and we differ as ever has been the case in the Church on matters of mere prudence. St Peter and St Paul seem to have done so.' Murray goes on to say that he was not aware of the 'violations of charity' to which Cullen alluded. 'I have not opposed your Grace in any manner with respect to the proposed measure to which you and some other Bishops cling: I merely protest against being dragged into a proceeding which I consider highly dangerous to the Church.' If charity had been violated, he was 'assuredly the victim, not the aggressor'. He utterly protested 'against the justice of being charged with disobedience to the Holy See'. He concluded by asking about 'the best means of carrying the Thurles Decrees into effect'.[68]

THE PRIME MINISTER'S INTOLERANT LANGUAGE

A further setback for Murray and those prelates who supported him had already occurred at this stage, following the papal brief of 29 September 1850, which restored the English Catholic hierarchy. Archbishop Wiseman's flamboyant pastoral letter, 'Out of the Flaminian Gate', had aroused fears and anger in the Protestant population against 'papal aggression', and *Punch* magazine, on Guy Fawkes Day that year, depicted Pius IX as proposing to blow up all England. All this made little impact in Ireland, until Prime Minister Russell issued a public letter in reply to his friend Dr Maltby, Bishop of Durham.

Maltby had asked what Russell or the government thought about 'the late aggression of the Pope upon our Protestantism', which he deemed 'insolent and insidious'. Russell's public reply from Downing Street, on 4 November 1850, was greeted with applause in the British press and with widespread Protestant acclaim, but it gave great offence in Ireland. In it, Russell spoke of the glorious principles of the immortal martyrs of the Reformation, which were held in reverence 'by the great mass of the nation, which looks with contempt on the mummeries and superstitions, and with scorn at the laborious endeavours which they are now making to confine the intellect and enslave the soul'.[69] It seems that this comment was aimed primarily at the Tractarians,[70] but it was evident that it also reflected his views on Catholic Church practices and teaching.

This insulting language came from the government leader whom Murray and his supporting bishops had asked the people – and Rome – to trust! Cullen latched on to Russell's words. The Prime Minister, he stated, was being honest about his hostility to Catholicism, and so 'our indignation should be reserved for those who think it wise to put the education of Catholic youth in the hands of men who draw so frightful a picture of our doctrine'.[71] Murray, dismayed at the attack on his Church and the undermining of his position on the colleges, called his clergy together on 19 November 1850. He came out in support of the English Catholics – the first Irish bishop to do so – and, as noted previously, was very critical of the Ecclesiastical Titles Bill and its likely impact on the Irish Church.

Praising once again the basic good sense of the English people, Murray characteristically endeavoured to take a positive approach – indirectly in responding to Russell's reply to the Bishop of Durham, and more directly in regard to the public criticism of the Catholic Church in the British press. He explained that the Pope's brief affected only the members of the Catholic Church. There was no hostility intended to Protestant believers. 'We can readily make allowances for the unconsiderate expressions of unkindness towards us,' he observed, 'which the advocates of intolerance were enabled to evoke from many an upright and generous heart, while the real state of the case was studiously kept out of view; but the delusion cannot continue; the good sense of England will check that spirit of intolerance, so hostile to religious freedom and to social improvement.'[72]

Murray's measured language and his readiness to make allowances for people's background and their reactions in the heat of public feeling were typical of him, and were reminiscent of the appeal he had made to the English people's sense of fair play during the earlier 'no popery' scare of 1838.

CULLEN'S IMPACT

Papal approval of the decrees of the Synod of Thurles came in April 1851. Cullen was now able to devote his energies to the Catholic university project. Seeing Murray as the major obstacle, he increased his personal campaign against him. He referred to Murray as the *vecchio* – the old man – and complained continually that he was standing in the way of progress, and was under the influence of Lord Lieutenant Clarendon and the government. The continuous harassment he endured during his struggle for what he considered best for his Church and people took its toll on the outwardly serene archbishop of Dublin. It did not pass unnoticed that Cullen had overstepped the mark in his treatment of Murray. The distinguished Maynooth theologian, Dr Patrick Murray, would later complain that Cullen had worried the archbishop to his death.[73]

That statement was made in 1855, a few years after Cullen himself had become archbishop of Dublin. In that role, Cullen pursued his own plans single-mindedly, with full backing from Rome, creating a form of ecclesiastical imperialism that greatly disturbed a number of bishops and theologians. Revd Patrick Leahy, a friend and theological adviser to Archbishop Slattery at the Synod of Thurles, himself destined to succeed Slattery, wrote feelingly to Slattery in 1854, of 'the deep dissatisfaction of the prelates, caused by their seeing one person but lately coming among them, and having but little experience of things here, set at nought the feelings and the opinions, and the authority of his brethren in the episcopacy.'[74] That same year, Cullen's unfavourable report to Rome on the province of Cashel evoked an even harsher criticism from Revd John O'Sullivan, archdeacon of Kerry and parish priest of Kenmare. He wrote in his diary that Cullen's method, by which he hoped to advance the cause in Ireland, is 'to alienate not only every bishop individually but the whole bishops of a province collectively … Bravo, brave Cullen … snub them all in the round. Take it for granted there is not a pious, nor a zealous, nor an active bishop in the Church but yourself or some of your choosing.'[75]

Archbishop Murray, with his more gentle, benign manner, his play of mind and his broad sympathies and ecumenical friendships, found the focused authoritative zeal of Cullen difficult to take. Adding to his discomfort was the knowledge of how Romanised Cullen was, having been removed from the Irish scene for so long, and his memory of how Cullen had abused his position in Rome to thwart Murray's case for the primary schools and the Bequests Act.

FINAL CORRESPONDENCE WITH THE POPE

On 28 September 1851, Murray's admirer, the revered Passionist priest Fr Ignatius Spencer, wrote to him from Rome to warn him that there was 'a widely held opinion' there that he was opposing the Holy See on the controversial question of the Queen's Colleges. The Pope had for the third time condemned the said colleges, and was annoyed and embarrassed that not all the Irish prelates – and more especially Murray – were accepting his decision.[76]

Stirred by Fr Ignatius's letter, Murray responded at some length on 13 October 1851. This letter, in which Murray expressed his devotion to the Papacy and its principles, was brought by Spencer, it seems, to the Pope's attention, and subsequently, on 21 November, Pius IX wrote to the archbishop of Dublin. Unfortunately, due to a badly addressed destination, the letter went to Lublin in Poland, and traversed much of Europe before it eventually reached Dublin in January 1852.

In his letter, the Pope commented that Murray's letter to Fr Ignatius Spencer gave further proof of his fidelity to the Holy See. He praised Murray's sentiments, his piety and his defence of the cause of religion. He was pleased that as archbishop he had warned the clergy against being embroiled in politics. Then, turning to the decision about the Queen's Colleges, the pope expressed his gratification to learn of Murray's 'unhesitating submission'. He was sure that Murray would not only execute the decree with eagerness himself, but would strive to encourage the other prelates, who had joined him in signing the letter of 11 September the previous year, to execute the decree 'with alacrity and zeal'. It was a matter of regret, the Pope continued, to hear of the occurrences after the termination of the Synod of Thurles, and of its transactions being publicly divulged despite his recommendation 'that silence on these matters be carefully observed'. His Holiness concluded by saying that so exalted was his opinion of Murray's piety that he had no doubt that he would devote all his wisdom and efforts 'to the greater welfare of the Catholic Church'.[77]

On 31 January 1852, Daniel Murray, interpreting the Pope's letter in the most positive way, thanked His Holiness for his 'delightful letter' which had just arrived and which had filled him with 'unspeakable consolation'. He then returned briefly to the colleges and made a final effort to explain his stance, and that of the other like-minded bishops, to the Pope. With all the judgement he possessed, he wrote, he had weighed the situation 'in the peculiar circumstances of this country', and had conferred with 'those other ecclesiastics' whom he 'deemed most evident for piety and wisdom'. In that context he had arrived 'at the full persuasion, that, for the protection and preservation of our holy religion, it were safer far to tolerate these colleges, though not unattended with danger, and allow our priests, aided with proper precautions, to watch over their progress, than to repudiate them utterly'. Murray then added, 'The moment, however, that the Holy See gave utterance to a different opinion forbidding our bishops to mix themselves up in any manner' with the concerns of the colleges, he had at once announced it as their duty to conform themselves 'with all possible submission to this judgement', and he had shown himself to be an example of the obedience which he preached.

At this point, Pius IX might well have asked why it took three condemnations from Rome before the bishops desisted from their defence of the colleges. To which Murray, had he dared, might have replied that he had had experience of officials presenting biased evidence to popes which resulted in erroneous decisions.

In his letter, Murray came to the defence of the bishops who had signed with him the letter of 11 September 1850. He assured His Holiness that these men stood 'in need of no incitement … to accept and venerate every decree that may emanate at any time from the Holy See'. Indeed,

> they added their signature to the document in question … influenced

> only by their zeal for the welfare of religion, deeming it their duty, in a business of such grave importance to the interests of the Church in this Kingdom, to pour out into the bosom of our most Holy Father, without reserve, whatever, in the presence of God, they considered most useful to be done.

Murray then added, 'It was possible for them to err, even in the management of matters under their immediate observation, but to decline obedience to the Chair of St Peter was what never once entered their thoughts.' He concluded this dutiful letter by saying that 'animated by the salutary admonitions' of His Holiness and 'inflamed with a more ardent zeal than ever for the welfare of religion', he ventured to hope that all of his thoughts and efforts 'shall be combined to promote, more and more, the interests of the Catholic Church, and its all saving doctrines'.[78]

It was a carefully drafted letter, compliantly ritualised, yet dignified in its presentation. It had as its most striking feature Murray's defence of the bishops who had supported him. It marked the closure of his voluminous correspondence with the Holy See. He had little more than three weeks to live.

Some weeks prior to his letter to Pope Pius IX, Murray had reached an entente with Cullen. His letter of 22 November received a response from Cullen indicating 'the mode of making known the Thurles Decrees'. On 25 November, Murray wrote back thanking him and stating that he would accept the mode outlined by Cullen. The entente occurred sometime shortly after this. At the start of December it was greeted with pleasure and relief by a number of bishops, notably Cullen's supporters, Cantwell of Meath, McNally of Clogher, and Murphy of Cloyne.[79]

OUTCOME OF THE UNIVERSITY QUESTION

The failure to gain papal support and the controversy surrounding the Queen's Colleges marked a diminuendo in Murray's venerable and greatly respected career. In previous contests – over the national schools and even the bequests issue – he had succeeded in the face of intense opposition. His personal standing and the regard in which he was held by Pope Gregory XVI were important factors at these times. Regarding the Queen's Colleges, other issues came into play: a greater intensity of national feeling, partly orchestrated by O'Connell and fuelled by the government's inactivity during the famine; Roman concerns about educational trends in France and Prussia; and, most important of all, the change of pope.

The new pope trusted Cullen, who personally had reason to resent Murray for his previous setbacks at Murray's hands. Centralisation and regulation from Rome, joined to distrust of lay control in education and of the government's intentions, were indicators of the new order under Pius IX, and of the Irish Church under Cullen. The latter was held in high esteem by the pope, as he was by the key cardinals in Propaganda. For his part Murray, quietly determined not to be deflected from what was best for Church and country, found himself outmanoeuvred and treated as an old man, a venerable relic of the past.

Cullen learned from the struggle the need to have a controlling voice in the appointment of bishops, something he largely achieved. He also brought about the Romanisation of the Irish church, though not without criticism from priests and prelates, as indicated above. Ironically, Murray's opponent for many years, Archbishop John MacHale, himself became Cullen's chief antagonist. Assured of Rome's backing, Cullen dealt with MacHale more ruthlessly and more effectively than Murray's gentler and more accommodating personality could condone. In the course of a letter to Propaganda, Cullen astutely singled out MacHale's inability 'to resign himself to thinking like his colleagues', and even changing 'his own opinions when they come to be adopted by others, so as to remain always in opposition'.[80]

What of Cullen's dream of a Catholic university? He brought it about, and creatively invited John Henry Newman to be its rector. The latter's *The Idea of a University* gave Ireland's Catholic University a degree of immortality. But the university failed for the reasons foreseen by Murray: the lack of adequate finance and the absence of recognition and support from the government. In effect, the Irish bishops failed to provide sufficient financial support, and student attendance was inadequate for the provision of substantial fees. Student attendance was influenced by two factors: the absence of a network of secondary schools in the country, and the fact that the university did not have a charter, leaving it with only pontifical degrees, which were relevant mainly to students of theology. In addition, there was tension between Cullen and Newman, but that was incidental to the failure of the enterprise.

At its highest enrolment point, in 1862, there were no more than thirty-six new students, while the entry of new students plummeted to just three in the 1870s. Cullen strove to rescue the enterprise into the 1870s but, despite much endeavour, the ambitious venture of a Catholic university proved unsustainable.[81] Meantime, censured by the bishops, the Queen's colleges in Cork and Galway limped along, far from the well-attended, successful and effectively Catholic colleges that Murray had envisaged.

NOTES

1 An unsigned list in the Dublin Diocesan Archives (DDA), drawn up around this time, names seventy-four students, who, from 1801–31, had abandoned the Catholic faith while staying at Trinity College. Cit.
2 9 May 1845. *Hansard*, lxxx, 377080.
3 Heytesbury – Graham, 17 May 1845; Graham Papers, cit. Kerr. op. cit. p.303.
4 Crolly – Bishops, 14 May 1845. *Catholic Directory 1846,* p.239.
5 Memorial of Bishops to Ld. Lieutenant, 23 May 1845. *Catholic Directory 1847*, pp.373–5.
6 Murray – Hamilton, 8 June 1845. DDA. Hamilton Papers, file 35/1/167.
7 *Freeman's Journal,* 26 May 1845.
8 Graham – Heytesbury, 28 May 1845. Graham Papers, cit. Kerr. op. cit. p.305.
9 2 June 1845. *Hansard,* lxxx, 1247–8.
10 O'Connell – P. V. Fitzpatrick, 21 June 1845. *O'Connell Correspondence,* ii, 354.
11 O'Connell – MacHale, 21 June 1845, in Cusack. *The Liberator*, p.743, cit. Kerr. p.315.
12 Cullen – Kirby, 6 July 1845, Kirby Papers, Archives Irish College Rome (AICR), cit Kerr, p.315.
13 Heytesbury – Graham, 27 June 1845. Graham Papers, Kerr, p.316.
14 Dr S. Henry had been the Presbyterian commissioner on the Board of National Education, 1838–81, and commissioner for Charitable Bequests, 1844–67. Robert Kane, a Dublin-born chemist, who published *Elements of Chemistry*, 1841–43, and *Industrial Resources of Ireland*, 1844. In 1846 he was to form the Museum of Industry in Ireland, and was knighted. He was a nephew of the late Archbishop Troy. Joseph Kirwan (d. 1849) was a distinguished Galway priest and preacher, whose candidature for the see of Galway was blocked by MacHale. See Kerr, op. cit. notes pp.313, 316.
15 18 July 1845. *Hansard*, lxxxii, 673.
16 The *Pilot*, 23 July 1845.
17 Murray – Hamilton, 24 July 1845, DDA. Hamilton Papers.
18 Murray – O'Connell, 1 August 1845; the *Pilot*, 4 Aug. 1845.
19 Crolly – Murray, 3 Aug. 1845. DDA. Murray Papers.
20 Kennedy – Murray, 4 Aug. 1845, idem.
21 Cooper – O'Connell, 3 Aug. 1845. O'Connell Papers, N.L.I., 13649.
22 The *Nation*, 22 Nov. 1845.
23 *Lettera degli Arcievescovi de Armagh e de Dublino e de altri cinque Vescovi d'Irlanda,* 24 Nov. 1845. *PFA. Acta,* vol. 209, ff.293–5. cit. Kerr, p.327.
24 Idem. Acta 1846, vol. 209, f. 288, cit. Kerr p.325.
25 Murray – Franzoni, 11 Dec. 1845 (draft). Murray Papers, f.32/2/56.
26 Graham – Heytesbury, 25 Nov. 1845. Graham Papers, cit. Kerr 329.
27 Cantwell – O'Connell, 2 Feb. 1845. O'Connell Papers, NLI, Ms.13649.
28 Abp Crolly – Franzoni, 28 Oct. 1847. Murray Papers, f.32/3/154. Crolly complained to Franzoni to refute a report made by Cullen to Propaganda that he, when Bishop of Down and Connor, had encouraged students intended for Maynooth to attend non-Catholic colleges in Belfast. He also denied a report by Cullen that Dr Denvir, Down and Connor, on the day of his Consecration, allowed a blasphemous statement by Dr Montgomery, a Presbyterian minister. Crolly and his suffragan bishops deny that Dr Montgomery made the statement reported by Cullen.
29 See A. Macauley. *William Crolly, Archbishop of Armagh, 1835–49* (Dublin: Four Courts Press, 1994), pp.384–88.
30 PFA, Acta, vol. 209, ff.260–2, 13 July 1846.

31 Murray – Ld. Lieutenant, 30 Aug. 1846 (draft), Murray Papers, f.32/2/121.
32 Cullen – Murray, 12 Oct. 1846. Idem, f.32/2/141.
33 Fergal McGrath, 'The University Question' in P. J. Corish, *A History of Irish Catholicism* (Dublin 1971), p.89.
34 Abps and Bps of Ireland – Franzoni & Propaganda, 3 Nov. 1847. Murray Papers f.32/3/152
35 Macauley, op. cit. pp.403–4.
36 Crolly & Bps – Franzoni & Prop. 12 Nov. 1847. Idem, f.32/3/158.
37 Clarendon – Murray, 19 April 1848. Murray Papers, f. 32/4/138.
38 Pastoral letter, 24 May 1848. Idem, f.32/4.
39 Franzoni – Murray, 11 Oct. 1848, f. 32/4/ 161 and 162.
40 Thomas Redington – Clarendon, 5 Nov.1848, Clarendon Papers,cit. Macauley, op. cit. p.434.
41 Murray – Franzoni, 30 Dec. 1848, idem, f. 32/4/145.
42 Murray – Cullen, 30 Dec. 1848, idem, no.50
43 Browne (Kilmore) – Denvir, 9 April, 1849. Down & Connor.
44 *Scritture referite nei congressi, Irlanda(S.R.C),* vol.30, fol. 286, PFA, Rome; cit. E. Larkin. *The Making of the Roman Catholic Church in Ireland, 1850–1860* (Univ.North Carolina Press, 1980), p.4.
45 Larkin, idem, p.26.
46 DDA. Thurles 1850, file iv, notes in Cullen's writing, cit. Kerr in *A Nation of Beggars? Priests, People and Politics in Famine Ireland, 1846–1852* (Oxford: Oxford University Press, 1994), p.226.
47 Murphy – Cullen, March 1851, DDA. Cullen Papers AB4.
48 Kerr, *A Nation of Beggars ?...,* p.283.
49 Cullen – Smith, 7 Dec.1850,f.n. Kirby Papers, ICA, Rome, cit. E. Larkin, 'Paul Cullen the Great Ultramontane' in Keogh & McDonnell, *Cardinal Paul Cullen and His World* (Dublin 2011), p.24.
50 Murray & 12 Bps - Pope Pius IX, 11 Sept. 1850. APF. Acta (1851), vol. 213, fos.163–238, cit. Kerr. *A Nation of ...,* p.233.
51 E. Larkin. art. cit. in op. cit., p.25.
52 Connellan – Clarendon, Sept. 1850, Clarendon Papers, Box 9, cit. Kerr. op. cit. p.234.
53 *Dublin Evening Post,* 2 Oct. 1850. *Nation,* 5 Oct. 1850.
54 Kirby Papers. Oct. Nov. 1850, ICA Rome (ICAR).
55 Cullen – Propaganda, 8 Oct. 1850. PFA. Acta 1851, vol.213, f.207, cit. Kerr, idem, p.233.
56 E. Duffy, *Saints and Sinners. A History of the Popes* (Yale, 2002), p.305.
57 R. B. Lyons on 29 Oct. 1856, in Foreign Office Papers 170/76, Public Record Office, London, cit. Larkin. art cit. op. cit., p.22.
58 Franzoni – Murray, 14 Feb.1850, Murray Papers, f.32/6/59.
59 Barnabo – Murray, 23 March 1850, Idem, f.32/6/56.
60 Idem, 7 Oct. 1850. Idem, f.32/6/63.
61 Clarendon – Russell, 3 Nov. 1850, Clarendon papers, letter book 6, cit. Kerr. op. cit. p.287.
62 Kirby – MacHale, 2 Nov. 1850, cit. B. O'Reilly *John Mac Hale, Archbishop of Tuam...* (1890), vol.ii, pp.243–5, cit. Kerr. p.288 & f.n. At the First Vatican Council, Pius IX also scolded Cardinal Guidi for what he interpreted as disobedience – G. Martina. *Pius IX, 1846-1850* (1974), pp.555–7.
63 Ref. to John Talbot in Kerr, p.288, no ref.
64 *Freeman's Journal,* 12 March, 1851.
65 Murray – Hamilton, March 1851, DDA.
66 Cullen – Kirby, 18 March 1851. Smith Papers. St Paul-Outside-Walls Archive, Rome, cit Kerr, *A Nation of...,* p.290.

67 Denvir – Cullen, 11 Jan 1851; Blake – Cullen, and Browne – Cullen wrote on 13 Jan.1851. Cullen Papers, section 39/2, file 1, DDA.
68 Murray – Cullen, 15, 22, 25 Nov. 1851. Cullen Papers, section 39/2, File 1. DDA.
69 J. Prest, *Lord John Russell* (London 1972), pp.429–30.
70 The Tractarians (otherwise described as the Oxford Movement, beginning in 1830s) thought of Anglicanism as one of three branches of the One, Holy, Catholic and Apostolic Church. Their best-known figures included John Henry Newman and Edward Pusey.
71 Murray's address to his clergy. And see E.Larkin, *The Making of the Roman Catholic Church in Ireland*...p.88.
72 W. Meagher, *Notices on the Life and Character of His Grace, Most Reverend Daniel Murray ... (1853), pp.75–76.*
73 Patrick Murray – Gavan Duffy, 12 Feb. 1855. Letter preserved, with Murray's diary, in Maynooth College Library, cit. Kerr, p.314 f.n.
74 Leahy – Slattery, May 1854, Leahy Papers, Cashel Diocesan Archives, cit. Kerr, idem.
75 O'Sullivan diary, 10 March 1854, Kerry Diocesan Archive, cit. Kerr, idem.
76 Spencer – Murray, 28 Sept. 1851. Murray Papers, f.32/7/78.
77 W. Meagher. op. cit. p.199.
78 Idem, pp.201–3.
79 They write respectively on 1, 3 and 15 Dec. 1851. DDA. Cullen Papers, section 39/2, file 1.
80 Cullen – Propaganda, 26 May 1854. PFA. Acta (1854).Vol. 218. fo.336, cit. Kerr, p.22; the letter of 25 Nov.1851 is in DDA. Cullen Papers, 39/2/I/138.
81 Colin Barr, 'The Failure of Newman's Catholic University in Ireland', *Archiv. Hib* . LV., 2001' pp.126–139.

CHAPTER 14

The Final Years (1851–52)

In Daniel Murray's final years, his extant papers indicate that his life proceeded as usual. Neither he nor his friends had any idea that he had only a short time to live. For the account of these years, the historian is largely reliant on the memoir of William Meagher, mentioned previously in this biography.

ACTIVE IN MIND AND BODY

According to Meagher, Murray, while at the Synod of Thurles, showed himself active in mind and body, 'joining with his accustomed rigid punctuality in all the public duties and devotions of the occasion, and entering with spirit and ability into all the important disquisitions … for the entire fortnight through which the sessions continued'.[1]

After the synod, Murray returned to his diocese with renewed energy.[2] He took an active part in his diocesan duties, met with his lay friends, and ministered to them in times of spiritual need. The Corballis family recalled his kindness during this time, when he attended a member of the family who was dying. John Richard Corballis, in a letter to Anthony Blake, recounted the scene as his father died at the family house at Roebuck, outside Dublin.

> Myself and my sisters at his bedside and my two sisters on our knees at his bedside and his attached and steady friend … of fifty years standing, the Archbishop … who gave his parting Benediction to him the night before, slept here that night; immediately after his decease on Monday morning said Mass for the repose of his soul – and with what fervour and sincerity he prayed by my poor father's bed after! To see this venerated and venerable old archbishop … in his cassock, on his knees at the bedside where his deceased friend of near 80 years of age lay – and in the same house where for near fifty years they had so often met together, was truly a touching, an interesting scene to the greatest stranger ... For two successive mornings after, did this good man rise out

> at seven o'clock to celebrate Mass in the house for him – professing all these duties with more humility and less parade, than the youngest and rawest curate in the Archdiocese.[3]

That phrase, 'less parade', catches something characteristic of Murray and the kindness he communicated. 'Parade' he avoided. His many personal donations to charity were given on the clear understanding that they remained private.

FIRST SIGNS OF DECLINE

Up to May 1851, Murray's constitution appeared unimpaired. Then, on 7 May, as he laid the foundation stone of the Church of Our Lady Star of the Sea at Sandymount, the weather broke and he was caught in a storm of wind and rain. He received a wetting from which he contracted a severe cold, which lasted for weeks. Most seriously affected was his sight. A total loss of sight was feared by his friends.[4] It gradually improved, but on 16 June, writing to John Hamilton from Naas, Murray mentioned that his health was good except for his sight.[5] He spent a while at Whiteleas, Ballymore Eustace, where his sister lived, but returned to Dublin for confirmations on 3 July.[6] On 23 July he retired to Rahan Lodge, where he stayed until 3 August.[7] Gradually, as Meagher recalled, his health 'returned to its wonted vigour, while his clearness of intellect and memory, and gentle gaiety never forsook him'. He celebrated Mass each morning as usual, and conducted the visitation of his rural parishes – preaching, confirming and regulating matters in his customary way. At Christmas he led ordinations at Maynooth with all his usual composure, and exactness. The New Year, 1852, settled in with the promise of others to come.

His friends were heartened by the despatch with which the archbishop arranged his pastoral functions from the Epiphany to Lent. As was his custom at this time of year, he set about the laborious task of administering the Sacrament of Confirmation in the city parishes 'as cheerfully and untiring as ever', confirming more than 1,400 children and adults. At each location he followed the ceremony with a brief exhortation, demonstrating the special ease he had in speaking to children. He next met with the heads of his clergy assembled together, to deliberate upon the fasts and devotions for the approaching Lent. The meetings were held with ease, good spirits and cheerfulness. A few days later, however, the first signs of serious decline appeared.[8]

The occasion was a solemn office for the repose of the soul of the celebrated orator and politician, Richard Lalor Sheil, who had died suddenly in Florence. Sheil's family arranged for a solemn office for him at the Jesuit church in Gardiner

Street, Dublin, before moving on to the family burial ground at New Orchard, Co. Tipperary. Sheil, a past student of the Jesuit college at Stonyhurst and a staunch Catholic and admirer of Archbishop Murray, had spoken eloquently at the opening of the Pro-Cathedral. In remembrance of this remarkable man, Murray presided at the ceremony, and did so, as usual, with calm presence and dignity. When the time came for him to minister around the coffin, however, he surprised the master of ceremonies by asking, 'Where am I to proceed now?' This was a surprising question from someone who was known for his familiarity with the rite. That evening, nevertheless, the Archbishop dined with the Revd Mr Pope in Marlborough street, in company with several lay and clerical friends, and gave every sign of enjoying himself and the company.[9]

A SUDDEN AFFLICTION

The following day, Shrove Tuesday, 24 February, he rose early as usual and, before celebrating Mass in his domestic oratory, he went down to the drawing room for the altar wine. There, according to the author of the first biography of Mary Aikenhead, who took a particular interest in Murray's life, he met Anna Maria O'Brien, his friend of more than forty years, who often attended Mass in the oratory. As he came in, she noticed him rubbing his hand in a peculiar manner, and asked if he was in pain. She received the answer that he felt a stinging sensation, adding, 'I hope it is not rheumatism that I am getting'. These were the last words uttered by Archbishop Murray. Soon after, as he went to vest for Mass, Anna Maria O'Brien saw his countenance change, and she had just time to place a chair behind him as he sank into it in a state of apoplexy.[10] When asked about his condition, there was no reply. He had lost his speech and his right arm was paralysed.[11]

His medical adviser, Dr O'Farrell, was called, and he diagnosed a stroke. Although he could not speak, Murray, at least for a while, could understand what was said to him, and when the physician asked about the location of the pain he could point to it with his left hand. The surgeon general was also called. As the archbishop was unable to swallow, it seemed clear that his death was just a matter of time. Dean Meyler, his vicar general and an old and devoted friend,[12] and John Hamilton, his secretary and friend, hurried to the archbishop's bedside. The Sacrament of Extreme Unction was administered without delay.

By the evening of the following day, Ash Wednesday, 25 February 1852, all Dublin knew that Tom Moore, the much-loved poet and songster, had died that morning in London. But it was rather for the dying archbishop that the bells of the city tolled that day, with people crowding the churches, at the invitation of the clergy, to pray for his happy death. From eight o'clock on Tuesday morning till five o'clock on the following Thursday morning, Murray lingered. Numerous clergy and close friends came to pray at his bedside. A member of the Sisters of Charity, the congregation founded by the archbishop, described the scene. 'Everyone who wished to do so was allowed to go up and pass through the front drawing room to the back room – the folding doors standing open between the apartments … On each side of the dying prelate's bed knelt one of his vicars, alternately repeating the Church prayers for the dying, and every quarter of an hour giving the last absolution … Mrs O'Brien knelt like a statue at the side of the bed, and two of the Sisters of Charity knelt at the front. The most intimate friends passed one another without a sign of recognition, and when they had offered a heartfelt prayer, retired in perfect silence'.[13] As the end drew near, one of the priests read aloud an account of the passion of Christ from the gospel. When he came to Jesus' parting exclamation, 'Into thy hands I commit my spirit', it was observed that the archbishop had died. His body was laid out in his apartment, and a flow of people came to visit and to pray.[14] On the following Sunday, the funeral commenced.

FUNERAL CEREMONIES

The *Freeman's Journal* of Monday, 1 March 1852, reported that 'willing shoulders of our Dublin citizens were anxious to contest' to carry the coffin. Six of them carried it on their shoulders. The presence of 300 clergy and many distinguished laity resulted in the short route to the church being extended to allow for a procession that proceeded through Gardiner Place, and included on its route various streets before entering Marlborough Street and proceeding to the Pro-Cathedral. From an early hour, the newspaper commented, 'every street and avenue leading to the church was thronged with crowds of people of all classes'. They occupied 'the entire length of Marlborough Street, and from Great Britain Street to the quay … The usual sound of children's play and merriment, usually so rife in crowded neighbourhoods after prayer hour on Sundays, all were hushed'. The writer continued, 'Not in our remembrance has there been anything to exceed the vastness and density of the crowds that blocked up every foot of the streetway on this occasion, saving the well kept and orderly passage made for the line of procession … The coffin carried aloft on the shoulders of the people, and surmounted by the archiepiscopal mitre, seemed to act as a spelling reminding all of their loss and chastening down every feeling save that of subdued grief and respectful regret.'

The procession was led by Bishop George Browne of Elphin and Right Revd Dr Patrick Griffith, vicar apostolic of the Cape of Good Hope. They were followed, two by two, by hundreds of clergy, and by countless laity. Amongst the laity taking part in their private equipages was the Lord Mayor, the Duke of Leinster and Lord Fingal. As the front rank reached the Pro-Cathedral, the procession continued into the church, which had its pillars and parts of its walls draped in black. After the office for the dead and further prayers, the lid of the coffin was removed and the body lay in state, where the people of Dublin could view it and pray for the one who had served them as priest and bishop for more than fifty years. The previous night, at St Michan's Church, the well-known preacher, Dr D. W. Cahill, delivered a panegyric. He spoke eloquently of the late archbishop's mildness, benignity, charity and presence, which were inseparably 'interwoven with the daily acts of social intercourse'. Cahill went on, 'Full of sound learned knowledge, he lived by deep reflection in the presence of God ... He ordained most of the priests of Ireland ... He was the father, the patriarch of the Irish church. He was a true servant of God, a faithful follower of Christ – in our narrow span of life we shall never look upon his like again.'

A REMARKABLE SHOW OF AFFECTION

On the Tuesday, the solemn obsequies and interment took place. At eleven-thirty the office of the dead commenced, chanted by a choir of between three and four hundred priests. Fourteen prelates attended, including the archbishop of Cashel, and headed by the Primate of All Ireland, the Archbishop of Armagh, Dr Cullen. The Bishop of Kildare and Leighlin, Francis Haly, was celebrant at the Mass. Immediately afterwards, the obsequies were performed by Dr Cullen, assisted by the Archbishop of Cashel and the three suffragan bishops of Leinster. As these ended, a truly remarkable thing happened. Fr Meagher described how, as the coffin was lowered from the catafalque to the bier, there was

> a rush of priests ... from every quarter of the choir. They removed the lid of the coffin and in a tumult of anxiety sought to catch a parting glimpse of their beloved chief ... bending over him with streaming eyes, kissing his hands most reverently; or when too far off for that, touching whatever part they could of his person, and applying their hands as they withdrew them to their lips.[15]

It was the ultimate testimony to the life and person of their archbishop.

INDIVIDUAL AND PUBLIC COMMENT

Many tributes in words and letters were paid to the dead prelate. A number of bishops wrote to John Hamilton, mourning the loss to the Church and to themselves personally. Bishop Myles Murphy of Ferns added that the late archbishop 'has left us a splendid and noble example for imitation'. One of Murray's most unremitting critics, the contradictory bishop of Ardagh, William O'Higgins, excused himself from the funeral because of personal ailments, but wrote, 'He was a prelate of many, very many, most admirable qualities and, though latterly we differed on some points, I say with truth that I never for one moment ceased to esteem him'. The final episcopal tribute was not sent until 29 April 1852. Uncertain mail from Europe delayed William Walsh, bishop of Halifax, receiving word of the death. On 29 April he paid his 'tribute of respect to the sacred memory of our sainted archbishop. Under his even, kindly and paternal rule, I had the happiness to spend all the years of my missionary life in Ireland, and I need not tell you what warm admiration I always felt for the angelic character, and what gratitude for his unvarying goodness … Whilst I was his spiritual child, I never did anything that would give the least pain, inconvenience or dissatisfaction to that gentlest of Fathers.'[16] That last comment, about avoiding any cause of pain or dissatisfaction to the archbishop, was echoed in different ways by a number of priests.

Various Irish newspapers carried tributes to Murray and commented on his career. Frequently it was mentioned that, when he became coadjutor archbishop in 1809, there was but one well-built church in Dublin. A friendly commentator noted that 'by the time of his death, ninety-seven churches had been erected in the diocese, at an expense of less than £700,000'. Again, it was noted that, where previously there had been few Catholic schools for poor children in Dublin – only one good school for girls (that of the Presentation nuns) and two or three for boys under Fr Betagh's inspiration – now education was becoming widely available. The schools of the Christian Brothers had been established, and three new congregations of women, supported by Murray, had resulted in twenty-nine communities devoted principally to the care of the poor and the education of youth. The men's Society of St Vincent de Paul and the Ladies' Association of Charity 'were in active work relieving the sick and destitute, while the Vincentian Fathers, the Society of Jesus and the Loreto nuns had undertaken the education'[17] of the better-off middle class. Moreover, the archbishop's support and vision had contributed to the foundation of the Missionary College of All Hallows, with a view to preparing men for missionary work across the English-speaking world, and he had encouraged the establishment of a branch of the Association for the Propagation of the Faith to aid, with its prayers and contributions, the Church's missionary outreach worldwide.

TOWARDS AN ESTIMATION

Daniel Murray entered on the episcopacy at a time of uncertainty and change. Following the disorder of the penal years, there was need for Church reorganisation and spiritual renewal. He joined with Archbishop Troy in bringing about restructuring not only in the Dublin diocese but across the country, by promoting episcopal meetings, workshops for priests, and a climate of pastoral unity among bishops. For anyone fostering spiritual renewal, Murray offered zeal, wisdom and encouragement. These qualities were combined with a discipline that preserved freedom from social or political entanglements. As a bishop, he was available to his priests and people – in so far as his health permitted in later years – and he was revered by both.

The *Catholic Registry* of 1853 mentioned the energy of the archbishop. This is an aspect often overlooked, perhaps because of his bouts of illness, but it is a characteristic that is underlined by the frequent references to his capacity for work right to the end of his life. The *Registry* also devoted much attention to Murray's oratory. 'Oratory may be defined', the writer suggested, 'as the power of enlisting the hearts of men in the cause we advocate ... That power he possessed to an eminent degree.' His preaching involved the 'language of the heart'. The same writer added a supreme compliment to Murray by applying scriptural language to him: 'The spirit of wisdom, and understanding, and counsel, and fortitude, and piety, and the fear of the Lord seem to have descended upon this great bishop.'[18]

Finally, a comment from a neutral and non-Irish source, the *Illustrated London News*, of Saturday, 6 May 1852, should be noted. 'Archbishop Murray was one of those ministers of God whose virtuous character, amiable disposition and dignified bearing bring peace and goodwill to all Christian men.' The paper went on to give an account of Murray's life, reaching the pinnacle of praise, in its own estimation, with the observation that he was one of the chosen guests who dined with Her Majesty the Queen at Dublin Castle. On that occasion, it was reported, 'Her Majesty expressed at the time how much she was struck by the venerable and saintly appearance of the archbishop'. Needless to say, this was an encomium that would have been viewed in a most negative light by Murray's notable fellow prelates from Tuam and Ardagh.

THE ARCHBISHOP AND CULTURAL CHANGE

Leaving aside possible motives of personal rivalry and desire for power, Tuam and Ardagh in their opposition to Murray reflected the cultural change that had taken place in the Catholic population. Following its experience of collective power in the final years of the struggle for emancipation, and in its actual achievement, the Catholic population was more ready to express its dissatisfaction and resort to the power of public pressure. The issue of the tithes and the government's slowness in enacting the benefits of the Emancipation Act provided grounds for dissatisfaction with the government, and fed distrust of its policies and initiatives. Even when government initiatives took a positive turn, following the shock generated by the Repeal movement, awareness of the power of the people and suspicion of the government continued. This suspicion was inflamed by the ineptitude of the government and by the avarice of landlords during the famine. This process of cultural change resulted in the challenge to the government's scheme for national schools, opposition to the Bequests Act, over-reaction to rumours of a concordat, and hostility to the university colleges – not to mention the nation-wide drive for Repeal, and even the minority's outbreak in rebellion.

In this intertwining of religion and national identity with hostility to government policies, Daniel Murray's readiness to avail of government laws and initiatives to promote the education for the poor, including higher education, ran counter to the prevailing tide, and earned him public hostility and abuse. He was accused of being a government man and being, somehow, unpatriotic. That he persevered through it all, because he believed that he was right, indicated remarkable independence and courage. More remarkable still, despite the public obloquy, he retained the respect of almost all his critics. The fact that he was able to rally the support of so many bishops for the 'Godless colleges', in the face of opposition from Rome and Rome's representative, Paul Cullen, indicated both the regard in which he was held by his fellow prelates and the confidence he had in his own judgement. Happily for himself, he had the ability to accept defeat without recrimination and with peace of mind.

Looking at the wider pastoral picture, the scene changed greatly after the famine years. The population was much reduced, but there was a growth in vocations to the diocesan priesthood and to the religious congregations. These factors combined to make possible the 'devotional revolution' and educational advances so often attributed to the efforts of Archbishop Cullen. In fairness, it must be kept in mind that at a time when there were too few priests for a rapidly expanding population, Murray had made a big impact in these areas. He helped to coordinate the work and to stimulate the zeal of his clergy; he established confraternities and sodalities for the laity; he encouraged spiritual and literary reading; he founded religious congregations and guided their spiritual formation; he welcomed other religious bodies to his archdiocese. He availed of the combined services of these groups to benefit the poor and to promote, very often in conjunction with the national education system, literacy and self-confidence that enabled people to advance themselves materially and spiritually.

Despite divisions among bishops and clergy, despite political turmoil and famine, much had been achieved. Parish missions had been inaugurated, a hospital was in operation, schools had been established for the poor as well as for the wealthier Catholic population, the temperance movement and the Society of St Vincent de Paul had been welcomed, numerous churches had been built, and the clergy of Dublin had experienced an ease with and warmth for their archbishop that has not been surpassed. Already, at the time of his death, the Sisters of Mercy, the Sisters of Charity and the Christian Brothers were responding to needs outside Ireland with the Archbishop's blessing.

MURRAY'S WILL AND LIBRARY

The archbishop paid little attention to the question of a will. His sole will was made twenty years before he died, on 10 July 1832. In it, he appointed Revd Walter Meyler and Revd John Hamilton, both of the Church of the Immaculate Conception, Marlborough Street, as executors. He arranged for £5 to be given to each priest in that church to say Mass for the repose of his soul. To each servant who happened to be in his service at the time of his death, he bequeathed 'one year's wages over and above what should be due to them'. Any pontifical books and ornaments were to be passed to his successor. The rest of his books were to be reserved by his executors and to be applied by them, as they saw fit, towards the formation of a clerical library. All the rest of his estate he bequeathed to his executors for the following purposes. They were to procure a suitable number of Masses for the repose of his soul as soon as possible after his death. The remainder was to be divided, in such proportions as to them seemed meet, between the Sisters of Charity, for distribution amongst the poor they would visit, and the following charitable institutions: the Female Orphan House in North William Street, the Orphan Establishment attached to Townsend Street Chapel, the House of Refuge in Stanhope Street, and the Penitent Asylum in Townsend Street.[19]

The books Murray left behind amounted to 747 volumes. The catalogue of his library, contained in a soft-covered notebook, lists works in theology and spirituality, occupying some thirty-two pages. There are one-and-a-half pages of bibles, breviaries and missals; four-and-a-half pages of Irish history and antiquities, and ten pages of miscellaneous matters – literature, biographies, history etc. A number of the books were in French, some in Latin, a few in Italian, but most were in English. The overall emphasis was on pastoral issues, but included also were books on spirituality, the history of the Catholic Church, and the writings of Protestants, including Archbishop Whately. There were many books on sermons, a few poetry books, works on philosophical themes and material relating to the Bible. There were also some volumes of the Fathers of the Church – all publications from the eighteenth or seventeenth century, suggesting that they may have come from Archbishop Troy.

The amount that eventually Murray had to leave seems to have been negligible. During his life he gave generously to charity, and he did not accumulate. The very house he lived in had been purchased for him by a few friends, who also looked after its maintenance.[20] The Residuary Account from the Inland Revenue Office indicates that Murray's personal estate – including cash in the house, furniture, wine and other liquors, books and various debts – amounted to £617. 7s. 8d. However, the total payments – probate and administration, funeral expenses, debts on rent, taxes, wages, Masses, money to servants etc. – came to £716. 15. 10d.[21]

This man, who was often described as a prince of the Church because of his elegance, his presence and his courtesy, and who was accused by his critics of being too friendly with and unduly influenced by government ministers, was also viewed by many as a model bishop because of his humanity, his humility, and his care for others, especially the poor. Fittingly, he died without material possessions.

NOTES

1 William Meagher. *Notices of the Life and Character of His Grace Most Rev. Daniel Murray*, p.132.
2 The *Catholic Registry 1853*, p.358.
3 D. Kerr. cit in 'Dublin's Forgotten Archbishop: Daniel Murray, 1768–1852' in Kelly & Keogh. *History of the Catholic Diocese of Dublin*, p.263.
4 Idem, p.133.
5 Murray – Hamilton, 16 June, 1851, Hamilton Papers (1), no.281.
6 Hamilton Papers, no.284.
7 Idem, nos.288–90.
8 Meagher, op. cit. p.133.
9 Idem, p.134.
10 S.A. *Mary Aikenhead, Her life, Her Work, Her Friends*, p.385.

11 Meagher, p.136.
12 Walter Dean Meyler, D. D, P.P., 1764–1864, was ordained 1807, curate at St Mary's, Liffey Street chapel, the church that preceded the Pro-Cathedral. The parish was changed to Marlborough Street in 1825. In 1831, he was made administrator of the Pro-Cathedral; in 1833 he became P.P. of St Andrews, Westland Row, then being built to supersede Townsend Street chapel. For many years he was a Commissioner of National Education. He was vicar-general until Murray's death in 1852. He received nine votes in the election for archbishop.
13 S.A. op. cit. p.386.
14 Mary Purcell. 'Death Comes for the Archbishop' in *Irish Press*, 26 Feb. 1952.
15 Meagher, op. cit. p.139. Italics mine.
16 Walsh – Hamilton, 29 April 1852; see Hamilton Papers (11), file 37/2.
17 S.A., op. cit. p.384.
18 *Catholic Registry 1853*, pp.358–60.
19 Abp Murray Personal File, 33/8/9–22. DDA.
20 S.A. op. cit. p.387.
21 Murray Personal File, as above.

INDEX

PLAN OF THE

Rumsey, 1883